W9-BIH-677

Property of
FAMILY OF FAITH
LIBRARY

FAMILY OF FAITH
Christian School
30 Kin-ville
Shawnee, OK 74801

Principal

Date

PUBLIC ADMINISTRATION: A SYNTHESIS

21.95/11

M. D. Plotnick

PUBLIC ADMINISTRATION: A SYNTHESIS

Property of
FAMILY OF FAITH
LIBRARY

Howard E. McCurdy

The American University

Benjamin/Cummings

Menlo Park, California
Reading, Massachusetts
London—Amsterdam
Don Mills, Ontario
Sydney

Copyright © 1977 by Cummings Publishing Company, Inc.

Philippines copyright 1977 by Cummings Publishing Company, Inc.

All rights reserved. No part of this publication may be reproduced, stored in a retrieval system, or transmitted, in any form or by any means, electronic, mechanical, photocopying, recording, or otherwise, without the prior written permission of the publisher. Printed in the United States of America. Published simultaneously in Canada. Library of Congress Catalog Card Number 76–21541

ISBN 0-8465-4600-0
EFGHIJKLMN-MA-89876543210

ABBREVIATED
TABLE OF CONTENTS

Family of Faith Library

CONTENTS

CONTENTS

CONTENTS

*To my wife Peggy, who now knows
more about public administration
than she ever wanted to*

PREFACE

Public Administration: A Synthesis presents the essential lessons contained in the books, articles, and management strategies that have had the greatest impact upon the development of public administration. The book is a synthesis in the sense that it brings together the divergent theories and methods that make up this shifting field of study. It presents the various approaches that public administrators must master in order to manage government programs, whereas most textbooks in the field have concentrated on the functions of administration.

The book is written for all those who will have to wrestle with the administrative side of government tomorrow and who today are struggling to understand the field of public administration as students in undergraduate political science courses, schools of public affairs and administration, and government training programs. This is an impressive audience, both in size and in diversity of interest. In the United States, for example, government employees comprise 20 percent of the work force. They are supervised by a tidal wave of public administrators, people who increasingly are expected to possess formal training in the administrative profession as well as in their primary field of specialization.

BACKGROUND

The first textbook on public administration was published fifty years ago, during the administration of Calvin Coolidge. Back then, a public administrator had to know something about personnel, budgeting, and departmental organization—and learn it without much formal training. Since that time, the field of public administration has changed dramatically. To be effective, the modern public administrator must be familiar with concepts, techniques, and theories drawn from political science, social psychology, economics, management science, and business management, as well as from the traditional administrative sciences. The scholars who assemble this knowledge are obliged to relate their theories of management to the solution of practical administrative problems. The practitioners who face the problems are expected to keep up with new developments in administrative theory and technique and to possess special training, degrees, and credentials. These trends point up the increasing professionalization of the field of public administration.

Unfortunately, the teaching of public administration has not always kept up with these trends. Most introductory textbooks still treat public administration the same way it was treated fifty years ago—in terms of planning, organizing, staffing, and budgeting. As an alternative, public administration is occasionally taught as a political science course dealing with the fourth branch of government (in conjunction, one imagines, with courses on the legislature, the judiciary, and the chief executive).

These approaches, while valid, simply do not relate the whole story. Granted, public administration is budgeting; it is politics. But it is also bureaucracy, policy analysis, collective bargaining, program evaluation, bureaucratic risk taking, systems analysis, employee motivation, linear programming, project management, contingency theory, and the ecology of public administration, to list only a few of the more important developments in the field. These developments simply cannot be contained within traditional views of administration. The field has grown too complex, its sources of knowledge too diverse.

Such developments have created a need for a new type of textbook, one which embraces the profusion of approaches that make up public administration. Fundamentally, this textbook attempts to do that by synthesizing the knowledge and practice that have made public administration grow. The book does not synthesize by forcing knowledge and practice to conform to one point of view, treating public administration as wholly a problem in human relations or wholly a problem of politics, for example. So numerous are the approaches, the methods, the problems, the theories, the concepts, and the ultimate purposes of public administration that it would be foolish to suggest that one single point of view could act as an effective synthesizer. Rather, this textbook presents and compares all of the divergent approaches to public administration in the belief that each contributes something special to the growth of the whole. It attempts to assemble the sources of our knowledge and weave them into a pattern reflecting the richness and diversity of the field.[1]

PLAN OF THE BOOK

The various approaches to public administration are presented in the following manner. The fundamentals from the administrative science movement and the behavioral revolution are summarized in Part 1 as the principal characteristics governing the operation of public (and private) organizations. Part 2 examines the most pervasive problems facing public administrators today: the difficulties of government by bureaucracy and the politics of administration. Part 3 explains the analytic, political, scientific, and behavioral strategies that public administrators have used to solve these problems. Finally, Part 4 reviews the state of professional public administration under two special conditions—the context of the non-Western world, with its lessons on the connection between administrative strategies and local conditions, and the context of the future, with an assessment of recent developments in the field. Traditional topics, such as governmental budgeting and personnel administration, are discussed throughout the book where they are relevant. They are presented in less detail than has traditionally been the case, not because these details are unimportant, but because they must be trimmed back to make room for the developments in theory and practice that have enlarged the field.

xiii

The textbook is abundantly illustrated with case studies. Some are factual; some are fictional. The use of factual case studies has a long and noble history in public administration. The relevance of fiction to public administration is not so firmly established. In theory, the novelist can enlarge the perspective of the scholar by dramatizing administrative issues and giving insight into the causes and motivations underlying certain administrative phenomenon.[2] In practice, the use of fiction tempers the profession's curse of dullness.

Some professors prefer to begin their courses in public administration by reviewing the paradigmatic problems plaguing the profession. If this is the case, the professor is advised to turn to the conclusion of Chapter 10, where these problems are summarized. I believe, however, that before students can appreciate the complexity of the whole, they must become familiar with the parts. This book is organized so that students can progress from the simple to the complex, in much the same way as the field of public administration has progressed from the administrative science movement through the political awakening and the behavioral revolution down through the administrative strategies of the last decade. So we begin, as did the field of study, some ninety years ago, with the first systematic probes into the world of administration.

ACKNOWLEDGMENTS

If you peel away the facade of government, you will find that most of its accomplishments are built upon the labor of young people who, in the words of one famous public administrator, are expected to retain a "passion for anonymity." So it is with this textbook. Over two hundred students—both novices and career public servants—contributed to its development. Most of them wrote research papers on special topics. An aide to the chief of naval operations gave me insights that found their way into Chapter 8; the research of a political science undergraduate on the administrative methods of Count Dracula was the inspiration for a paragraph in Chapter 6. Other students witnessed the development of the book and criticized its content. When I say that this textbook is written for the people who will be public administrators tomorrow, I mean exactly that. They were my critics as I wrote the book.

I am also indebted to my professional colleagues—other professors teaching public administration—for their assistance in constructing and revising this introduction to public administration: Alan P. Balutis, Robert P. Boynton, A. Lee Fritschler, Lowell H. Hattery, Laura L. Irwin, Herbert Kaufman, Lawrence F. Keller, Allyn Morrow, Fred W. Riggs, Bernard H. Ross, Emil J. Sady, George Satterthwaite, Morley Segal, Allen Schick, William J. Siffin, Carl W. Stenberg, Frederick C. Thayer, Dwight Waldo, and Paul P. Van Riper. In addition, I want to thank Richard Heimendinger, who helped me locate many of the photographs that appear throughout the book.

PRINCIPLES

Certain fundamental characteristics govern the operation of all large organizations. Some of these characteristics are created by administrators straining to improve the structure of their organization or to control the work of their employees. Other characteristics arise because the behavior of the employees tends to follow patterns of its own, often without regard to the wishes of management. The realization that these phenomena could be described systematically awakened the search for a "science" of administration some ninety years ago. The first discoveries were called "principles of administration"; in general, all of these characteristics can be treated as principles since they are the fundamentals upon which the study of public administration is based.

ORGANIZATION

1

Experts in administration began to study management in a systematic way during the last two decades of the nineteenth century. In Philadelphia and Princeton, Florida and France, specialists in different fields searched for the ideal administrative system. In the coal fields of France, two men uncovered what appeared to be the source of administrative power. One was an industrial engineer, the other a novelist.

The industrial engineer, Henri Fayol, managed a group of miners working in coal pits that were part of a large economic combine. He felt that management of the mines was essentially a technical problem requiring a proper system of administration. While Fayol was writing a technical paper titled "The Spontaneous Combustion of Coal Exposed to Air," the miners were battling the owners over the worker's right to organize and strike for higher pay.[1] Fayol thought that a skilled manager should be able to pierce through the confusion of contemporary events and perceive the necessary administrative functions that had to be performed. Knowledge of those functions would give the manager the power to organize any operation—to create a union, command an army, or manage a coal mine. Fayol believed that the functions could be written down and taught as principles of administration.

The French novelist Émile Zola was concerned with the social implications of the power struggle taking place in the mines. Like many novelists, he tended to treat effective management as a study in tyranny. Effective management does contain the potential for tyranny, since administrative skills give the manager exceptional power—power to organize people's loyalties and direct them toward a special purpose. That is what careful observers—managers, scholars, and novelists—discovered. The first discoveries in the science of administration were prescriptions for teaching managers to teach us how to behave.

THE ADMINISTRATIVE PROCESS

During the winter of 1884 a great strike began at a group of coal mines in France as workers left their jobs to protest reductions in pay. Émile Zola wrote a novel, *Germinal,* which explored the implications of the strike on the organization of the French society. He set the story at the pits near the town of Montsou.

In the novel, the strike begins as the result of the introduction of a wage incentive system. To pay for the incentives, the directors declare a flat 20 percent cut in pay. The miners decide to strike.

The workers believe that they are fighting the capitalists who own the mines. The mine owners, however, never enter Montsou. In all labor relations, the owners are represented by paid employees, managers skilled at mine engineering.

The strikers are represented in the negotiations by Étienne Lantier, a socialist laborer. The manager of the mines meets with Lantier and promises to pass the demands of the miners onto the board of directors in Paris. When nothing happens the miners join a mob, which, among other things, destroys company property, threatens the director's home, and castrates the grocer who runs the company store.

Lantier goes into hiding and the director calls in foreign strikebreakers. When the strikers and their families storm the mine and charge the soldiers guarding the pit, the soldiers shoot into the mob; fourteen die and twenty-nine are wounded.

The mines are idle; the workers are hungry. When the managers remove the foreign strikebreakers, a few of the miners reenter the pits, where they are trapped in a subterranean flood of water released by faulty timbering in a mine wrecked by a saboteur.

Paul Négrel, the chief mining engineer, organizes a rescue. It is a great honor to be chosen to work on the face of the excavation. All of the workers participate; the strike is forgotten. On the fifteenth day the rescue party cuts through to the trapped miners. There is only one survivor. It is Étienne Lantier.

The entire incident can be viewed as a test of organization skill. The workers are poorly organized. Some lose their lives; the rest go back to work without ever settling their grievances. All of the owners of the mines lose money during the strike; some are ruined and lose their mines. Only the mining engineers emerge with appreciably more power. They take over the management of the mines and eventually gain control over both the workers and the general economy.

Henri Fayol exhibited many of the same characteristics as Paul Négrel. During the strikes of 1883–1884, Fayol was managing a group of pits at Commentry. He was forty-three years old, very ambitious, and an excellent manager. He was skilled at drawing up plans of action, making accurate economic and technical forecasts, and evaluating the performance of the workers that he supervised. He was willing to spend an enormous amount of time coordinating different units within the organization. And he knew how to set up a

3

control system to verify whether operations worked according to plan. These are all skills that Négrel displays in the novel.

Fayol's skills allowed him to survive the struggles for power in the coal fields. The more that economic misfortunes wracked the ownership of the mines, the more that Fayol prospered. Economic misfortunes forced the coal companies to merge their operations, which tended to bureaucratize the industry. The more bureaucratic the industry became, the higher Fayol rose, until he controlled the entire combine, managing the coal fields, the blast furnaces, and the steel mills. When France entered World War I, Fayol organized the industry to serve the needs of the French fighting bureaus. At that time, at the age of seventy-five, Fayol began to write down what he knew about administration.

Fayol treated administration as a process, whereas the prevailing practice was to place administration under the control of specialists. To manage a mine, one studied mine engineering. To manage an army, one specialized in military strategy. Fayol was dissatisfied with this approach to training managers in business and government. In his opinion, good administration was a process consisting of "a certain number of conditions" which were common to all organizations. It did not matter whether the manager administered a mine or a regiment, whether the manager worked in an industry or a government bureau.

> The meaning that I have given to the word *administration* embraces enterprises of every size and description, of every form and purpose. All undertakings require planning, organization, command, coordination, and control, and in order to function properly, all must observe the same general principles. We are no longer confronted with several administrative sciences but with one alone, which can be applied equally well to public and private affairs.[2]

The scholar most responsible for incorporating Fayol's theory into American administration, Luther Gulick, condensed the duties of an administrator into an acronym—POSDCORB. Each letter stands for one of the critical functions performed by administrators: planning, organizing, staffing, directing, coordinating, reporting, and budgeting. Today POSDCORB is symbolic of all the early errors and insights produced by those who first ventured into the science of administration.

The insight that Fayol and Gulick gave to managers everywhere was the idea that good administration is a process distinct from the particular management task at hand. In organizing the operation, all managers have to accomplish certain common functions. They all have to establish some system of hierarchy and authority, and some system of specialization. They have to institutionalize the power to control and coordinate operations, usually in a general staff. A system of rules, personnel administration, and some system of budgeting and financial management must be established. Managers have to set forth objectives and improve employee motivation through

Luther Gulick was a well-known administrative reformer and a professor at Columbia University when he coauthored Papers on the Science of Administration, *which summarized the principles of administration and proclaimed that public administration, guided by efficiency, could be made into a great science.* COURTESY OF THE INSTITUTE OF PUBLIC ADMINISTRATION.

human relations techniques. These elements of administration are still taught with confidence ninety years after Fayol first wrote them down.

Most important, Fayol and Gulick believed that these processes could be deciphered by experts and taught to novices. This belief is the germ of the science of administration. Gulick certainly believed that the study of administration could be made into a science equal to other scholarly disciplines. Like physics or chemistry, Gulick said, administration was governed by principles or laws. The job of the administrative scientist was to discover the principles. The object of the principles was the accomplishment of the work at hand with the least expenditure of people and materials. Not surprisingly, the principles Gulick and Fayol discovered through their gospel of efficiency favored the power of managers bent upon rationalizing the operations of government and industry by institutionalizing these operations in large bureaus.

Fayol's principles of administration were adopted by the Belgian Ministry of National Defense and the French Ministry of Posts, Telegraphs, and Telephones. Fayol pressed very hard for the adoption of his theory by the French military. But, in reality, Fayol was not all that essential. War and the expansion of the state created the necessity for other managers to discover the power of administration on their own. The principles emerged spontaneously, given conditions at the time. To understand how this happened, it is instructive to return to a situation in the French army.

HIERARCHY AND AUTHORITY: THE ORGANIZATIONAL ANATOMY

During the Great Depression the *New York Times* published a news dispatch concerning five French soldiers who had been shot for mutiny after the battles at St. Mihiel in 1915. The officers had selected

5

the five by lot from an infantry company that had refused an order to crawl out of its trenches and attack an impregnable German position. The story in the *Times* was occasioned by a ruling from a French military tribunal, meeting twenty years after the event, which cleared the names of the soldiers and granted to each of the two surviving widows awards of seven cents. The news report inspired Humphrey Cobb to write a novel about the incident.

Paths of Glory is set in front of a German fortification known as the Pimple, a low hill into which the Germans have sunk machine gun nests and light artillery. Only a corps of infantry soldiers, in close combat, could possibly take the hill. The corps commander asks his most ambitious division commander, General Assolant, to take the hill. Assolant argues that the division cannot take the Pimple by itself until the commander hints that Assolant will be promoted to corps commander if he succeeds. Assolant steps into the trap. He personally inspects the front lines and orders his regimental commanders to prepare for a dawn offensive. German machine gun fire cuts down the lead regiment before all of its soldiers can climb out of the trenches. The rest of the regiment falls back.

Assolant orders the entire regiment shot for mutiny. The corps commander agrees that some example must be set for the good of the army. The regimental commander argues them down to four men. He calls in his company commanders and orders each of them to select one man to face a military court-martial.

Each company commander approaches the problem differently. The captain commanding the First Company is a civilian volunteer. He refuses to execute the order, saying that no one in his unit could possibly be arrested since no one showed cowardice. Assolant would arrest the captain himself, but his name is the same as that of a senator on the Army Committee.

The commanding officer of the Fourth Company is a scientist. He decides to eliminate the man of least use to society. He personally reviews the civilian records of the men in his unit, and selects for the trial a thief and syphilitic who has served two prison terms for selling cocaine. The individual is an excellent soldier.

The acting commander of the Second Company is an alcoholic. Before the battle he loses an entire reconnaissance patrol due to his own incompetence. His corporal, the only survivor of the expedition, prepares a report on the incident to be sent up the line. The lieutenant chooses the corporal.

The sergeant major commanding the Third Company decides to make the selection according to the principles of equity. The survivors in his unit each draw a number out of an army helmet filled with 113 marked slips of paper. The sergeant major orders his sergeant to draw one number from a second helmet filled with duplicate slips of paper. The sergeant reluctantly draws number 68. No one has 68. Two soldiers have number 89. After much argument, the sergeant major calls upon his sergeant to make a second draw.

ORGANIZATION

After a short trial, all three men are shot for cowardice in the face of the enemy.

The managers of the army at St. Mihiel—the commanders who ordered the court-martial—perceived the entire incident as a breakdown in authority. So did the French tribunal which later cleared the names of the men.

Fayol defined authority as "the right to give orders and the power to exact obedience."[3] When any organization faces adversity (for example, when an army is under fire), giving orders and exacting obedience become paramount concerns. The organization—regardless of whether its executives have read any books on the subject—is obliged to organize itself into a hierarchy for the purpose of maintaining discipline. Certain principles of administration emerge naturally. The French army, in general, had adopted five principles that enabled commanders to order men to carry out tasks which they would not perform under normal conditions. The principles are unity of command, the scalar principle, span of control, centralization, and responsibility.

1. *Unity of command* means that each employee receives orders from one superior alone: "One person, one master." Under conditions of stress, such as war, a soldier who is subject to "orders from several superiors will be confused, inefficient, and irresponsible."[4] He will also be able to evade orders by playing off one commander against another.

2. *The scalar principle.* When the principle of unity of command is doggedly upheld from the top to the bottom of the organization, the result is a scalar chain known as the organizational pyramid. The private will be linked to the general by a relatively short chain of command, passing through, on the average, seven layers of officials. The importance of the chain of command is the fact that the officers of the organization have to work through it; that is, in issuing orders and resolving disputes, all communications must "go through official channels."

3. *Span of control.* The principle of span of control proceeds from the assumption that there is a limit to the number of subordinates that a supervisor can effectively oversee, generally set at a maximum of twelve. The object of the principle is to identify the optimal number of subordinates who should be placed under any supervisor, given the nature of the work. Most armies, for example, use a number that varies between three and five. Logically extended, the principle allows a single commanding general to control the actions of seven thousand soldiers. The commanding general directs three generals, each of whom directs three colonels, and so on down through eight layers until nearly seven thousand persons are welded into a

unified chain of command—providing that one accepts the theory of effective supervision.

4. *Centralization.* The principle of centralization affirms the idea that the organization is administered from the top down. Officers at the pinnacle of the hierarchy are supposed to direct the work of the organization, just as the brain directs the rest of the body—a strained analogy, but a popular one. This does not mean that the top officials manage everything or determine the exact manner in which detailed tasks are to be performed. Indeed, one key to successful management is the ability of executives to delegate authority while at the same time exercising leadership in such a way that the delegated work meets their expectations. The principle of centralization simply requires that ultimate responsibility remain at the top rather than being lost among subordinates in the organizational mass.

5. *Responsibility.* "Whersoever authority is exercised," said Fayol, "responsibility arises. It is its natural consequence and essential counterpart."[5] Fayol believed that it was the job of the executive to establish the degree of responsibility attached to every job and then—the most important part—to give the official performing that job the sanctions (rewards and penalties) needed to finish it off. This is particularly crucial when executives delegate authority, as they must. The executives who delegate authority also delegate responsibility; they must therefore delegate the power over sanctions which goes with it. Executives cannot delegate just one: authority, responsibility, or just the power to exercise sanctions.

With these principles in mind, one can understand why the French generals and judges see the incident at St. Mihiel as involving errors in the principles of hierarchy and authority.

From the general's point of view, it is a matter of discipline. The troops have failed to execute an order passed down through the chain of command. General Assolant does not doubt his authority to order the attack, to assemble a general court martial, or to lay on the ultimate sanction. Such powers arise from the responsibility assigned to him: to break the stalemate of the war. Nor does he doubt that the men should obey his orders. Such obedience, Fayol observed, is "in accordance with the standing agreement between the firm and its employees."[6] As citizens of France, the soldiers have made a tacit agreement with the government to defend the nation, with their lives if necessary, against foreign invaders. In the same way, all organizations that provide their employees with clothing, food, shelter, and security naturally expect their employees to cooperate with the aims of the organization. At least that has been management's traditional point of view.

The French tribunal that met twenty years later apparently did not disagree with this line of reasoning. Such court-martials, after all,

ORGANIZATION

were standard practice in France during the First World War. So why did the tribunal clear the names of the soldiers?

The primary reason arose from the method of selection. Remember that Assolant, in the fictional account of the incident, delegated practically no responsibilities to his officers. There was no staff work to be done, there was no planning, and there was no POSDCORB. Assolant simply went up to the front to issue his orders and make his own estimate of the situation. Had he delegated such responsibilities, his officers would have informed him that the mission as proposed was an impossible one. At least his subordinates would have been able to order the men back into their trenches and take the responsibility for it. The only thing that Assolant delegated was the power to select the men to be shot. Understandably, the company commanders, who had no authority over the course of the battle, devised methods of selection that were totally unrelated to the performance of their men. The real situation was similar. The tribunal understood this, and ruled that those men so selected could not be held guilty of cowardice.

Assolant was the guilty party. He was the responsible official, since he had retained all of the authority. He was guilty of placing his personal ambitions for promotion above the welfare of his division. He was guilty of simple ineptitude, a fault arising from his obsession with maintaining discipline. His administrative talents stopped with the first three principles of hierarchy and authority. This led him to denigrate his subordinates to the point where they could not question his orders even if those orders were not worth obeying.

Assolant was an incomplete administrator. The principles of hierarchy and authority, by themselves, create an incomplete organization. As any organization develops, it must adopt other principles.

PRINCIPLES OF SPECIALIZATION

Hierarchy and authority constitute only one-third of the basic principles of management. Every executive also must be concerned with the division of work. The general has to decide who will make a better infantryman than cook. The Godfather has to decide whether a lieutenant's incompetence at shylocking also precludes success in the restaurant business.

Gulick claimed that "work division is the foundation of organization; indeed, it is the reason for organization."[7] Without specialization, there would be little need for coordination and, hence, little need for administrators. No wonder Fayol compared organizations to huge animals. Animals evolved by specializing their biological structure—and the brain grew bigger. Organizations, Fayol believed, develop by refining their division of work—and the central staff gets bigger.

Amateur philosophers in the age of Darwin and Spencer—the period when administrative science emerged—seized upon the principles of specialization as the gospel truths of administrative evolu-

9

Frederick Winslow Taylor is considered the father of scientific management, the science of discovering the most efficient method of performing any job. Taylor developed his system while employed at the Midvale Steel Works in Philadelphia during the 1880s. He signed this sketch with the words "A big day's work for a big day's pay."
COURTESY OF THE LIBRARY
OF CONGRESS

tion. There was nowhere a more devoted fanatic than Frederick Winslow Taylor. His philosophy of work had an enormous influence on the study of administration.

Taylor developed his system while a pattern maker and machinist at the Midvale Steel Works in Philadelphia during the 1880s. The Midvale machine shop was run on a piecework basis, which meant that the machines ran around the clock and the laborers were paid on the basis of how many pieces they produced. Taylor surveyed the situation in the shop and concluded that the workers could triple their output (and their wages) by reorganizing the flow of work. Taylor—then twenty-two years old—showed them how. The workers called him a piecework hog for working so hard. When Taylor asked for help from the management, the workers deliberately ran their lathes so fast that parts fell off. Taylor fined them and—his ultimate weapon—convinced management to cut the piecework rate in half. Taylor's battle with the workers in the machine shop lasted three years.

Taylor was possessed with the virtue of hard work. Every morning he walked two miles from his home to the Midvale Plant, arriving at 6:00 A.M. and leaving at 5:00 P. M. He often volunteered for work on Sundays. Although one might imagine Taylor a Horatio Alger type, he was, in fact, born into an upper-class Philadelphia Quaker family, which dispatched him to Exeter Prep and Harvard to become an attorney, like his father. After passing his entrance exams, however, Taylor complained that he was going blind, returned home, and signed on as a machine apprentice. He brought his fascination with clockwork schemes home to solve his personal problems. Taylor was plagued throughout his life with hideous dreams. When frightened out of his sleep by a dream, he invariably found himself lying upon his back. Thus he concluded that there must be some connection between nightmares and sleeping on one's back. To relieve his fears, he constructed a complex harness of leather straps and wooden prods, which he wore while sleeping. If he unconsciously rolled onto

ORGANIZATION

his back, a wooden prod would poke his dorsal muscle and wake him up. His sleeping habits created quite an ordeal when Taylor traveled and slept in hotels.

The key to Taylor's system was his ability to discover scientifically the shortest possible time for performing any specific job. His tool was the stopwatch. Taylor would stand behind every worker and record the time that it took him or her to perform the most elementary motions: finding a steel rod, setting it on a lathe, picking up a tool. By studying a large number of workers, he could identify the shortest possible time for performing each individual motion. By combining the best times, discarding useless motions, and adding in gaps for unavoidable delays and rest breaks, Taylor would establish a pattern of work that was invariably shorter than the workers' informal pace.

The Midvale superintendents, who had previously regarded Taylor as a lunatic, began to see that the experiments did indeed increase worker productivity. They encouraged Taylor so much that, at the age of thirty-four, he left Midvale to become general manager of a new pulp-and-paper mill.

The mill's financiers, friends of President Cleveland, promised to make Taylor a millionaire. Unfortunately, Taylor's devotion to his system alienated both the lumberjacks who handled the logs and the financiers who handled the money. The venture collapsed, and Taylor was lucky to escape with a mere twenty-five-thousand-dollar personal loss. But Taylor got a second chance. An old friend hired him as a consultant to the Bethlehem Steel Company. But Bethlehem owned the houses rented by the workers whose jobs Taylor was eliminating with his methods, so the company directors fired both Taylor and his friend, the second vice-president of the company.

Taylor's troubles with the workers greatly distressed him. He felt he was helping the workingman, since his naive economic belief was that if everyone worked harder, a surplus would be produced that would make everyone wealthy, and management and labor would no longer have to battle over the relatively small profit produced through poorer methods of supervision.

But does one help workers by telling them that they are always going to be too dumb to figure out their own jobs, as Taylor did? Nowhere is this problem more apparent than in a dialogue Taylor himself wrote on the supervision and training of employees. The dialogue takes place with a workman named Schmidt, whom Taylor describes as the ideal worker because Schmidt has the physique and the brain of an ox.

"Schmidt, are you a high-priced man?"

"Vell, I don't know what you mean. . . ."

"What I want to find out is whether you want to earn $1.85 a day or whether you are satisfied with $1.15, just the same as all those cheap fellows are getting."

"Did I vant $1.85 a day? Vas dot a high-priced man? Vell, yes, I vas a high-priced man. . . ."

"Well, if you are a high-priced man, you will load that pig iron on that car tomorrow for $1.85. . . . You will do exactly as this man tells you tomorrow, from morning to night. When he tells you to pick up a pig and walk, you pick it up and you walk, and when he tells you to sit down and rest, you sit down."[8]

Taylor attempted to introduce this system into public administration beginning in 1906, first in government arsenals and then in navy yards. The most famous incident took place at Watertown Arsenal, eight miles west of Boston. The arsenal was run by rule of thumb. The workers would receive an order for a set of gun carriages and fill it by milling assorted parts found in the yard according to designs sometimes sketched in chalk on the factory floor. Each new order was a new challenge.

By now Taylor's system had progressed considerably beyond his simple time-and-motion studies. Those studies had invariably proved that workers were using improper tools or defective equipment. (Before leaving Midvale, Taylor had astonished the engineering world by conducting no less than fifty thousand experiments on this problem, which he published as a book, *On the Art of Cutting Metals*.) Taylor's system inevitably led to a complete reorganization of the firm—the centralization of planning and engineering, the centralization of purchasing and inventory control, the centralization of maintenance, the introduction of centralized cost accounting, and the development of assembly-line techniques on the job.

When the workers at the Watertown Arsenal heard that Taylor was coming, they went out on strike, the army set a guard at the arsenal gates with fixed bayonets, and a special congressional committee was formed to summon Frederick Taylor before his government. The giants of the time took sides. Taylor was supported by men such as Louis Brandeis, Walter Lippmann, Georges Clemenceau, and V.I. Lenin. The Congress, however, responded by banning stopwatches in government-run factories, a law that remained on the books for forty years.

Despite his failures, Taylor is still considered to be the father of modern scientific management. The principles of specialization, popularized by scholars such as Gulick and Fayol, were his main contribution and are as follows:

1. *The Division of Work,* or the principle that work ought to be divided up so as to take maximum advantage of the skills of the employees. The assembly line is the most obvious application of this principle.

2. *The Principle of Homogeneity,* also called unity of direction, which asserts that similar activities ought to be grouped together in the same unit under a single supervisor and a single plan. Gulick suggested that work could be organized according to *purpose* (policies such as health, criminal justice, or environmental affairs), *process* (the professional approach, such as found in accounting, engineering, or law), the *persons* or

things dealt with (what public administrators call clientele), or *place* (geographic regions and districts).

Of course, Taylor went far beyond these two basic principles of specialization. By creating a world of work which was scientific rather than spontaneous, he ventured into the philosophy of human control. Taylor's view of the effective administrative state was one in which experts determined the one best way of working and standardized this method. The experts would then control the worker through incentives and threats so as to maintain the central work standard. This made the study of work a science. It made the selection and training of workers a science. And it took away from the workers their ability to control the flow of work by elevating it to a science of administration run out of a central office. The worker became just another machine in the technology of progress. For his part, Taylor thought his system was as all-American as a first-class baseball team:

> Every single element of the game of baseball has been the subject of the most intimate, the closest study of many men, and, finally, the best way of doing each act that takes place on the baseball field has been fairly well agreed upon and established as a standard throughout the country. The players have not only been told the best way of making each important motion or play, but they have been taught, coached, and trained to it through months of drilling. And I think that every man who has watched first-class play, or who knows anything of the management of the modern baseball team, realizes fully the utter impossibility of winning with the best team of individual players that was ever gotten together unless every man on the team obeys the signals or orders of the coach and obeys them at once when the coach gives those orders.[9]

THE STAFF PRINCIPLE

When any executive crosses the principles of hierarchy with the principles of specialization, he or she creates a primitive but effective organization. Employees are gathered into units according to the kind of work they do, and a structure of command is created. On paper, the organizational skeleton is complete. Frederick Taylor thought that this was sufficient to make the organization work—providing that employees took orders from two bosses: their shop foremen and the people in the planning department.

Taylor proposed that the planning department and other supporting services be located within the regular organizational hierarchy. Taylor's advice reflected the prevailing practice of his time. It was this system of organization that the U.S. military employed in 1898 in the Spanish-American War. One colonel commanding a volunteer regiment that was bogged down in Florida complained that this "red-tape bureaucracy . . . prevented any good organization or the preparation of any good plan of operation for using our men and supplies." One old officer tried to supply the colonel with black-powder muskets. Another proposed issuing the regiment winter clothing for the invasion of the tropics, because it was July and winter clothing was always issued in July. The assembly point at Tampa was "a scene of the wildest confusion. There were miles of tracks loaded with cars of the contents of which nobody seemed to have any definite knowledge." Each man had to find his own food and provender for his horses. In exasperation, the officers of the regiment commandeered a transport and forced the captain to take them to Santiago.

> Here we disembarked, higgledy-piggledy. . . . One transport had guns, and another the locks for the guns. . . . Soldiers landed here, provisions there; and who got ashore first largely depended upon individual activity.

One old army bureaucrat had told the colonel before he left Washington, "Oh, dear! I had this office running in such good shape —and then along came the war and upset everything."[10]

Unfortunately for the old army bureaucrats, the colonel was Theodore Roosevelt. After he became president four years later, Roosevelt commissioned Elihu Root, his secretary of war, to iron out the logistical problems which had plagued the Spanish-American War. Root was determined that every commanding officer should have the capability to coordinate his own operations. The army brass running the support services, understandably, did not want to be coordinated by anybody. Root persisted, with Roosevelt's backing, to institute the general staff system into the American military.

The primary function of the general staff is to *control and coordinate* operations. Staff officers are those persons with access to the executive who help draw up plans of action, supervise operations, make decisions, and so on. Formally, the staff officers are nothing but extensions of the executive personality. They act wholly within the authority of the executive, who is accountable for their actions—in theory at least. That is why H. R. Haldeman, as chief of staff of the White House, could issue orders to department secretaries in the name of the president, just as a major on an army general staff may issue orders (in the name of the commanding general) to a colonel on the front lines. The principle of hierarchy is not violated because both understand that the staff officer is acting through the authority of the commanding officer. In principle, the general staff officers merely help the commander to perform his or her duties. They supplement the chain of command.

The general staff officers may also give *advice*, although this function is secondary to the control and coordination function. Staff officers can interpret information, make estimates of the situation, or give technical advice which the executive may not have the time nor the ability to collect. The stories of executives who failed because they did not listen to staff advice are legion—such as the cavalry officer in World War I whose knowledge of gas was based on observations of hot-air balloons from the back of his horse. When told to disperse poison gas before a battle, he ordered a single man to move the

14

cannisters full of liquid chlorine because he assumed that gas was lighter than air.

The organization of the army general staff illustrates these functions. Each commanding officer in the field has a supporting general staff that assists the commander in five areas: personnel, intelligence, operations, logistics, and civil affairs. The personnel officer is responsible for maintaining the manpower of the unit. The intelligence officer gathers information on the deployment of the opposing force and conducts counterintelligence operations to neutralize enemy surveillance. As the principle staff assistant to the commander for the organization of the primary mission, the operations officer organizes and mobilizes the units, trains them, and plans and coordinates each mission. The logistics officer gets supplies to the units, maintains the equipment, and plans the movement of men and material. The civil affairs officer maintains military relations with local civilians. There is also a chief of staff to oversee the work of the staff on behalf of the commander and to resolve potential areas of conflict between different staff sections.

The organization and size of the general staff vary by unit and service. The five-officer organization cited above is used in tactical army field commands. The particular organization of general staff units in other government programs also varies considerably. Defense Secretary Robert McNamara relied upon the whiz kids in the Office of Systems Analysis. The White House uses a system of councils and special assistants. Each executive tends to create a general staff to fit his or her own personality and needs. Nevertheless, the primary function of the general staff does not vary: to assist the executive in controlling and coordinating operations.

The general staff function has been incorporated into most modern public organizations. Combined with the principles of specialization and hierarchy, it completes the triangle of organizational effectiveness.

RULES: THE SUBORDINATION OF ADMINISTRATION TO LAW

The manager who welds the principles of hierarchy, specialization, and staff creates a prodigious machine. Experts often call it a paramilitary organization. The term gives deference to the military origins of the model; its tone correctly implies great power. Despite that power, some experts shun these principles of administration as passé, irrelevant, or even dangerous in a truly modern organization. The headiest dissent against the principles of administration comes from the far left, from organizational revolutionaries who fear that agencies so organized will stultify change. Chairman Mao insisted that only through a constant organizational revolution can the new state avoid the evils of a permanent, entrenched bureaucracy.

In practice, of course, the doctrine submits to reality. To achieve revolutionary change, radical groups must create organizations more powerful than those of their enemies, especially the governments

15

they seek to destroy. Che Guevera, a doctrinaire revolutionary, announced that guerilla management was subject "to a definite set of scientific laws."[11] His prescriptions for seizing power admonished the rebel to create a chain of command, homogeneous combat teams, and a centralized staff for overall command and coordination. Organizations that lacked managerial skill and technical expertise, he warned, would fail.

The principles of administration as described by Gulick and Fayol, although incomplete in many respects, form the nucleus around which most revolutionary movements have been organized. An example of this is the struggle for Algerian independence, portrayed in the movie "Battle of Algiers," which many take to be a revolutionary manual couched in the language of cinema.

In the film, one of the few survivors of the early movement for Algerian independence advises the new recruits not to act "until we are organized." Since many of the rebels were officials in the French colonial government, it is only natural that they should adopt the administrative principles which the French used to control Algeria. The rebels create a general staff to direct the resistance organization. The staff plans operations, raises funds, supplies the soldiers, gathers intelligence, transmits communications, and directs action in the streets. It creates an underground hierarchy that reaches down to every Muslim home and storefront. Section chiefs supervise operations in four districts. Each section chief commands two subordinates, each of whom directs the work of two other subordinates, and so on down the line. The basic work unit is the cell, composed of one chief, one tax collector, and one or more propaganda agents. Each cell has a specific mission which corresponds to the division of work on the general staff. There are special sections for propaganda and bomb manufacturing, a trade union, and a corps of women volunteers.

Terror is the organization's most potent weapon. When a French right-wing bombing kills Algerian women and children, the general staff orders the bombing of French restaurants.

The resident-minister of Algeria calls in General Jacques Massau and the Tenth French Parachute Regiment and gives them total police powers over the city of Algiers. Massau instructs his subordinates to neutralize the rebel organization. Destroy the general staff, he says. The officers seal off the Casba and require all Algerians to show identification papers upon entering or leaving. Suspected revolutionaries are arrested, tortured, interrogated, and forced to reveal the names of their superiors.

The Algerian general staff orders each rebel to resist torture and remain silent for twenty-four hours. After that, he can talk. In the interim, the staff will remove the persons the rebel can identify and replace them with new soldiers. There are four hundred thousand Arabs in Algiers to hide the rebel organization.

Massau retaliates with mass arrests and interrogations, methodically trying to trace the identity of the rebel hierarchy. The rebels, who have called an eight-day general strike as a symbol of solidarity, are confined to their homes and cannot repair their secret organization. A section chief, after being captured and tortured, leads Massau to the house where the general staff is hiding. The French soldiers blow up the house and then establish their own system of hierarchy—the Algerian Blue Caps, informers on every block who are responsible for reporting any new subversive activity. Two years pass before rebel flags again fly over Algiers.

The Algerian revolutionaries are obliged to adopt certain principles of administration in order to survive—not only hierarchy, specialization, and staff, but a system of rules that binds each soldier to the objectives of the revolution. Although formal rules and regulations are associated primarily with highly developed, permanent bureaucracies, the Algerian rebels accept the need for fixed rules in an organization devoted to flexibility and change.

The leaders of the rebellion, as one illustration of this principle, issue the rule of silence for captured rebels. The leaders expect the rebels to obey this rule impersonally, without fear, with no ulterior motive, but out of strict loyalty to the organization. They expect other rebels to obey orders issued in pursuance of this rule—to leave Algiers, for example, should their superiors be captured. They establish procedures for enforcing the rule. Finally, the organization wears a veil of secrecy. Established procedures, the subordination of individual interest to one's official duty, sanctions, and secrecy—these are the elements which underly the basic *principle of rules.*

The resistance leaders expect the members of the resistance organization to refrain from impulsive actions, such as mob violence. The French generals have to restrain the Algerian rebels in order to protect French colonial rule. General Charles de Gaulle, as president of France, had to restrain the power of the French generals lest they overthrow the Fifth Republic.

Throughout the history of public administration, strong emphasis has been placed upon the restraint of executive power. This emphasis stems from the recognition that the paramilitary organization gives the bureaucrat enormous power, and that bureaucratic power in the raw is far superior to the weaker varieties of administrative oversight which legislators, judges, and solitary chiefs of state possess. The consequences of vast bureaucratic power are most serious in a democratic state where the bureaucrats are neither elected nor directly responsible to the public for their actions.

How does a state restrain bureaucratic power? The solution can be found in the rules. As the existence of rules gives the bureaucrat power, so it may also take power away—by requiring that all official activities be traceable to a specific grant of power, expressed or implied. This solution is sometimes called the *principle of administrative discretion,* which is to say that the power of officials to exercise their own judgment is strictly delineated by rules and law. In practice this is done in a number of ways: through authorization (a specific grant of power), direction (mandatory courses of action under certain circumstances), prohibitions (proscribed actions), and clearance (a process that allows an official to take a certain action after consulting specific superiors). Authorization, direction, prohibition, and clearance procedures are usually promulgated through a published organizational manual.

In carrying out any official duty, the administrator must also follow a specific set of procedures. There are requirements that the agency give notice before making decisions, that it hold hearings, that it set up a formal process by which the aggrieved can appeal decisions. These procedures are set out in legal statutes, court decisions, executive orders, and the rules which the agency must establish itself. They can be grouped under the general heading of the *principle of due process,* since the cumulative impact of these procedures is to insure that administrative powers are exercised in a fair and equitable manner.

Together these last two principles constitute what is commonly studied under the heading of *administrative law.* Until a few years ago, administrative law was out of fashion. No one wanted to memorize the procedures for granting audiences to aggrieved clients, or the special rules of evidence applicable in administrative hearings, especially when the really big issues were settled through informal bargains between the administrators and the special interests. Few students wanted to study administrative law until public-interest groups learned that the best way to restrain bureaucratic power was to hold the bureaucrats accountable to their own rules. The controversy over the Alaska pipeline reveals the reason for the renaissance in administrative law.

The top executives in the Nixon administration were anxious to grant a right-of-way to an oil company combine that would build an eight-hundred-mile-long pipeline across government-owned lands and bring oil from Prudhoe Bay to empty tankers at Valdez on the southern coast of Alaska. Environmental groups brought a suit against the government, arguing that the pipeline would be an ecological disaster in America's last wilderness. They submitted a 1,300-page report. The Interior Department submitted 3,700 pages. At issue was the relationship of the pipeline to the National Environmental Policy Act of 1969, which required the government to consider alternatives to projects on federal lands that might produce irreparable ecological damage. The law was vague, the issues complex, the judges impatient. The government won.

On appeal, the environmental groups radically changed their strategy. Instead of arguing the wisdom of government policy, they decided to hold the Interior Department responsible to its own laws. A lawyer discovered that the secretary of the interior was bound by the Mineral Leasing Act of 1920, which allowed him to grant a 54-foot right-of-way over public lands for the transportation of oil. The Alyeska Pipeline Service Company had to have at least 146 feet, and had convinced the secretary of the interior to grant it a "special land-use permit" for the difference. The U.S. Court of Appeals ignored the environmental issues and told the secretary of the interior to obey his own law: 54 feet, that's the limit. The government appealed to the U.S. Supreme Court. The law, the bureaucrats said, should be interpreted liberally. Nonsense, said the high court, and let the appeals court ruling stand. If the government wanted to build the pipeline, Congress would have to change the law. So it did, shortly before it became apparent that Americans were faced with a winter of long lines at the gas station. Congress widened the permissible right-of-way and, in an attempt to forestall future suits, made an official pronouncement which said that the Alaska pipeline as proposed met all the standards of the National Environmental Policy Act.

All of these appeals would have been moot had Interior officials been empowered to change their own laws. It does no good to restrain bureaucratic officials with rules if they themselves write those rules. This was the ultimate solution offered by administrative pioneers for the problem of bureaucratic power in the democratic state—the doctrine that those who have the organizational power to administer the law must be separated from those who create it. This was known as the *politics/administration dichotomy*. In the beginning, it was the holy writ of American public administration.

PERSONNEL AND BUDGETARY REFORM

Four months after his inauguration, President James Garfield was shot and killed by a member of his own political party. The man was angry because he had been refused an appointment in the new administration. Reformers blamed Garfield's death on the spoils system—the practice of choosing public officials on the basis of their partisan loyalties.

The reformers, motivated by a sense of outrage against the corruption of the spoils system, set out to strip politics from the administrative process. They sought to abolish the power of the spoilsman and replace him with a politically neutral civil servant. There was also a second motivation, more subtle, but more profound in light of the emerging science of public administration. The advocates of good government believed that they could never bring "efficiency and economy" to public administration so long as the vagaries of party politics interfered with governmental management. Public administration could be made "scientific" only if the administrators were free to concentrate on the execution of policy after the legislature and chief executive defined what that policy was. In sum, both politics and policy making were to be taken out of public administration.

The mess in the American personnel system provided the justification for applying scientific principles of administration to the business of government. One of the first persons to sense the implications of this development was a young political science professor named Woodrow Wilson. In 1887, while Fayol was being considered for promotion to the directorship of the Commentry-Fourchambault combine and Taylor was conducting experiments at the Midvale Steel Works, Wilson published an essay titled "The Study of Administra-

19

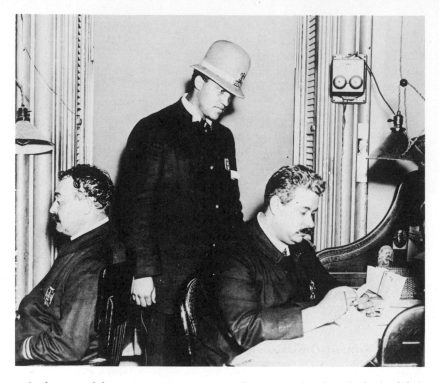

At the turn of the century, government employees were hired on the basis of their political loyalties, and departmental budgets were prepared by each agency without any central control. Public administration and the principles of good management grew out of the movement that sought to reform this situation with a merit civil service and a consolidated executive budget. COURTESY OF THE LIBRARY OF CONGRESS.

tion," which is generally held to be the founder's stone of American public administration.

"It is getting harder to run a constitution," Wilson wrote, "than to frame one."[12] Wilson's colleagues in the field of jurisprudence and politics were concerned with "great" constitutional issues, such as the separation of powers. Such legal debate, Wilson held, was largely irrelevant to the reforms needed in public administration. Effective administration, he professed, had little to do with local constitutional arrangements. "If I see a monarchist dyed in the wool managing a public bureau well, I can learn his business methods without changing any of my republican spots."[13] The French and the Prussians, Wilson continued, had developed the most advanced administrative systems in the world, and Americans should study them to learn how to manage public programs "with enlightenment, with equity, with speed, and without friction."[14]

Wilson's call for a new public administration was answered by a proliferation of citizen associations organized to reform the management of American government. Few were as famous as New York's Bureau of Municipal Research.

At that time, Tammany Hall administered New York City

through the patronage system. One-fifth of the city employees were classified at Grade Five, for which the base salary was a handsome $3,260 a year. Depending upon how many votes he controlled, a man at Grade Five could have his salary raised as high as $7,500. Two city clerks doing the same work might have a 130-percent differential in pay simply because one was a better campaign worker. It had nothing to do with merit.

The Bureau of Municipal Research decided to give New York City a reformed civil service. Its directors called in twenty-four-year old Robert Moses, later to become the most powerful public administrator in America, and told him to draw up a plan. Moses had just finished writing his Ph.D. thesis at Columbia University on the civil service of Great Britain. With his assistants, Moses set out to classify the functions and responsibilities of every employee in the New York City government, a type of analysis based on the scientific management techniques perfected by Frederick Taylor. When the city workers found out that Moses was planning to reduce all Grade Five employees to $3,260 a year and make all promotions dependent upon competitive examinations, they protested to their Tammany bosses and defeated the Moses plan.

Civil service reform was only one of three major programs which the bureau attempted to sell to the government of New York. The second was departmental consolidation. The Bureau studied the state government and discovered the existence of "no fewer than 169 separate departments, bureaus, boards, committees and commissions, many with overlapping functions. Some were responsible to the Governor, some to the Legislature and some to officials who were themselves elected by the people."[15] This was obviously a violation of the principles of span of control and unity of command. The bureau recommended that all 169 agencies be combined into twelve departments responsible directly to the chief executive. Governor Alfred E. Smith, the canny old Irishman, sniffed out the possibilities for increasing his own power and pushed the plan through the state legislature.

To round out the reforms, the bureau proposed that the state adopt an "executive budget." Under the old system of budgeting, no state official—neither legislative nor executive—added up appropriation requests or compared them to revenues. Under the new system, "department heads would submit financial requests to the Governor, who would weigh the requests against the resources and needs of the state and propose an over-all budget. Only then would the budget be submitted to the legislature."[16]

By 1926, the reformers were confident enough about their methods for someone to write the first textbook on public administration. Someone was Leonard D. White, a political scientist and historian at the University of Chicago who later served on the U.S. Civil Service Commission. White agreed with Fayol that public administration was "a single process, substantially uniform in its essential characteristics wherever observed."[17] White, however, was so smitten by developments in the reform movement that he passed by the mechanistic principles of administration. He wrote chapters on classification and salary standardization, promotion and efficiency records, discipline and removal, retirement systems, and morale—all big administrative issues associated with civil service reform. In all, there were nine chapters on the personnel problem and six chapters on departmental consolidation.

Textbooks on public administration following the White tradition have kept his emphasis upon personnel administration and added chapters on budgetary reform. They commonly dedicate half of their chapters to these two functions; business management texts do not. This is a phenomenon which has resulted from the unique path that the reform movement cleared for professional public administrators. Clearly, there are other administrative functions of similar magnitude—planning, control, and headquarters-field relations immediately come to mind. Nevertheless, the books devoted to these other functions are lost beneath the shelves of attention lavished on personnel and budgeting.

Personnel Administration

The advocates of reform sought to create a career civil service based on the merit principle, one in which all government employees would be hired and fired solely on the basis of their technical qualifications for the job. A personnel system based on merit came to be synonymous with sound public administration. It consisted of four basic elements:

1. A central personnel agency. The reformers began by proposing the creation of a central agency that would oversee personnel administration for the government as a whole. The favored form was the three-person commission, bipartisan in character. The commission would be charged with promoting the merit principle, issuing directives to agencies on personnel matters, overseeing the use of competitive exams, acting as an appellate board for employee grievances, and conducting long-range planning on the government's manpower needs.

2. Offices of personnel administration. Under a merit system, all personnel actions, from recruitment to retirement, are controlled by written regulations. Each department and agency establishes an office of personnel administration that oversees the enforcement of these regulations. The office is staffed by specialists in personnel administration.

3. Position classification and salary standardization. It is patently impossible to measure the qualifications of a candidate for a job unless the personnel officers can define the requirements of that job. So the personnel officers analyze each job, which is what Robert Moses tried to do in New York. When complete, the detailed job analysis forms the basis of the position clas-

sification plan, under which jobs with similar requirements are grouped into classes for which standard specifications are written. The position classification plan then becomes the instrument for executing a salary standardization plan, the primary objectives of which are to give "equal pay for equal work" and unequal pay for jobs that vary in importance or difficulty.

4. Selection by merit. The basic instrument for testing merit is the open, competitive examination. Ostensibly, the examination provides a reliable test of how well the candidate will perform at the specific job, not just of his or her general intelligence. At the same time, the personnel officers must establish a rating system for judging the performance of employees already on the job. The rating system becomes the basis for judging the merit of a promotion or transfer within the agency. In order to encourage employees to improve their merit, the agency must also develop in-house training programs and finance the return to school.

In spite of the holiness of the merit principle in personnel administration, merit has come under attack by persons who feel that it does not assure all persons equal opportunity to apply and compete for government jobs. Their argument goes like this. Most government employees do not work under true merit systems. Some are covered by collective-bargaining agreements; others work in agencies that are the exclusive domain of a single profession. Beyond this, many agencies use nonmerit criteria to restrict employment to persons who fit the agency mold. The mold is generally white, male, and middle class. Employers, the reformers argue, should be required to develop affirmative action programs to prove that their hiring criteria are truly performance oriented and that those criteria will have the effect of producing a public service that is more representative of the population as a whole. All of these developments have tended to cloud the future of the merit principle in public administration.

Governmental Budgeting

In theory, the executive budget is designed to give the top decision makers a fighting chance to plan and control the use of governmental revenues. Nowhere is the gap between budgetary theory and budgetary reality more apparent than in New York City, the home of the Bureau of Municipal Research. Almost everything that could go wrong with financial affairs in New York City has gone wrong. Twice the city perched on the edge of bankruptcy—first in 1933, when the banking community agreed to refinance $100 million in short-term revenue notes after the city agreed to double its interest payments and cut its budget, and again in 1975, when the city's accumulated debt surpassed the size of its annual budget.

The reformers thought that they could bring New York City and other governments sound financial management through the reforms contained in the executive budget process. In theory, the executive budget consists of the following elements:

1. A centralized bureau of the budget, reporting directly to the chief executive, supplemented by offices of budgetary administration within each department and agency. Each budget office is divided into sections corresponding to its major responsibilities: budget review, financial reporting, accounting, and management improvement. Some budget officers also set up special divisions for legislative review and, less frequently, property management.

2. A budget review cycle that allows the chief executive to review proposed expenditures before they are actually committed. The chief financial officer establishes a schedule wherein agency heads submit expenditure proposals to the chief executive, who in turn reviews these proposals and fuses the revised figures into a unified executive budget for submission to the lawmakers.

3. Accounting standards that accurately reflect financial transactions. Without accurate accounting, financial officers cannot keep track of unexpended appropriations, calculate performance, or write the financial summaries that are used in future budgetary planning.

4. An allotment system that allows the top executives to maintain control over expenditures after the budget has been approved. Generally, this is done by dividing the activities of each agency into financial accounts and subaccounts. Administrators then receive monthly or quarterly allotments—specific dollar amounts assigned to each account. In theory, administrators cannot continue an activity unless they show an unexpended balance in the proper account, nor can they transfer funds between accounts to make up shortages.

5. The audit. After the money has been spent, auditors check the accuracy of the accounts. They determine whether financial transactions were made within the law and whether the money spent produced the anticipated results. Except for the postaudit, this is usually the final step in the budgetary process and can be a real nightmare in a place like New York City.

In order to make all of this work, the chief executive has to be given a strong measure of control over the collection of revenues. This is very difficult, since most of the tendencies are in the opposite direction. Agency chiefs are fond of establishing their own revenue accounts based on user fees or commercial activities which they apply directly to their own expenditures without going through the Treasury or the bureau of the budget. Many governments segregate their income-generating activities, such as toll bridges, into public enterprises, which are run along commercial lines—selling bonds, collecting fees, and generally controlling their own financial transactions. Then there are the trust funds, such as social security, financed through special taxes that are earmarked for specified beneficiaries whose rights to the benefits are locked into law.

All of this happened in New York City. With so many sources of funds cut off from executive control—and an inadequate residue of money flowing in from general taxes—the mayor of New York was forced to sell bonds to finance city operations. Selling bonds is permissible for capital expenditures, which are segregated in a special capital budget. State and local governments generally finance improvements for schools, buildings, roads, parks, and sewers through the sale of bonds to be paid back through user fees or from future taxes generated over the life of the facility. New York, however, had to go beyond this. It sold short-term notes to finance noncapital operating expenditures, backed by the promise of state and federal funds-to-come, which the city fathers deliberately overestimated in order to peddle more bonds.

Simultaneously, the mayor lost control of the budget review process. Salaries and pensions, amounting to two-thirds of the municipal budget, were determined through collective-bargaining agreements to which the mayor was often not a major party. The mayor had relatively little control over the hundreds of millions of dollars spent on social service programs, where the level of spending was set by law. Out of what was left, he had to pay the interest on the city debt—another uncontrollable cost.

Now deeper in trouble, the city of New York began to revise its accounting procedures. In order to "balance" the budget, it charged the salaries obligated at the end of one fiscal year against the costs of the following fiscal year, an accounting trick that produced the illusion of a "savings" worth several hundred million dollars.

One day, the bankers and investors refused to swallow any more city debt. Appropriately, the man to lead New York City into default was Abraham Beame, the mayor who had worked his way up to the top after serving as the city's chief financial officer.

Even if all of these problems are put away, there is still the perplexing question of how to put the massive budget document (the federal budget runs to fifteen hundred pages) into a form that the chief executive can comprehend. There are three forms and one method.

Traditionally, budgets have listed each employee and each piece of equipment in each agency as a separate "line-item." The line-item budget allows the executive to focus on the minutiae of administration, comparing next year's budget requests against last year's expenditures. This provides a fairly effective check on excess spending at the agency level.

The performance budget is somewhat different. It lists expenditures in line with the specific accomplishments of each operating agency. The performance budget calculates the total number of people and material required, for example, to process so many gallons of sewage. It is a useful approach for improving productivity and holding down total costs.

These two forms have been challenged by advocates of program budgeting. The program budget shows the chief executive the amount of resources necessary to achieve the general goals of government, such as reducing drug addiction. The program budget allows the chief executive to judge the importance of one set of expenditures relative to other programs and priorities.

Zero-base budgeting requires agency chiefs to justify their requests for funding without reference to last year's appropriation, as if they were proposing a brand-new program. Some executives like the zero-base budget because it allows them to challenge outdated programs and encourage new initiatives.

Since all of these budget forms and methods serve useful purposes, all of them tend to show up in the budgetary review process. Perhaps that is why the budget document is so long.

MANAGEMENT BY OBJECTIVES

The reforms of the administrative scientists were predicated upon the assumption that before administration could begin, the executive had to articulate his or her objectives. The politics/administration dichotomy depended upon it, executive control was impossible without it, and administrative efficiency and economy required it. It was the orthodox dogma of public administration. The idea of management by objectives is as old as the science of administration.

Management by objectives was first advanced for public administration by the Taft Commission on Economy and Efficiency in 1911. American bureaucrats resisted it, citing political factors in administration, the lack of consensus on national goals, or the difficulties of translating missions (such as "a generation of peace") into actual operational plans.

Much of the current interest in management by objectives stems from the writings of Peter Drucker, an Austrian educated in England, who first learned how to write as a newspaper correspondent and first learned how to manage as a consultant to British and American corporations. In 1964 Drucker set out the philosophic assumptions underlying management by objectives in a book titled *Managing for Results*. "Neither results nor resources exist inside the business. Both exist outside. There are no profit centers within the business; there are only cost centers. Results are obtained by exploiting opportunities, not by solving problems."[18] Problem solving only restores normality. Resources, therefore, should be spent on opportunities rather than on problems. This requires leadership. Just because an agency is exercising leadership today does not mean it will be in that position tomorrow. "What exists is getting old."[19]

There is a natural tendency in all organizations for executives to become preoccupied with the settlement of internal problems. Consequently, says Drucker, only a few people may be working on the work of the agency. In most organizations, 20 to 30 percent of the agency's resources may be producing 90 percent of its results. The key to organizational success, Drucker observes, is concentration—concentration on the few activities that are capable of producing significant results. This requires the public executive and the corporate manager to slaughter a few sacred cows—the staff that wants to do a little bit of everything, the agency chiefs who want to establish a program or product for every client that comes along. The smart executive realizes that the agency will have to be weak in some areas so that it can be strong in the places that count—the places that produce results.

Managers who want results must accept the responsibility for making three critical decisions. They can involve others in the decision-making process, but they must eventually make these decisions and accept the risks for their failure or success.

First, executives must decide why their agency is in business—its objectives, goals, and directions. This may be no more than an assessment of the organization and its special capabilities as an outsider might see it.

Second, executives must identify the agency's points of excellence. What does it do best? Who are its best people? What are its unique resources? Definitions of excellence "cannot be changed very often; the definition is embodied in and expressed through people, their values and their behavior. But no excellence definition will remain valid forever; it must be periodically reviewed."[20]

Finally, executives must act upon the definition of excellence by setting priorities: the ranking of organizational activities so as to maximize opportunities for attaining results in the areas of excellence. Just because a task can be accomplished efficiently does not mean that it is in the best interests of the organization to undertake it. Just because it makes money does not mean that it is wise. If it doesn't produce results, Drucker says, don't do it.

Management by objectives (MBO) finally arrived in American public administration during the regime of Richard Nixon. A formal system was established which required agency directors and their staff to complete the following exercise.

1. Clarify the *mission* of the agency and the nature of the problems it is trying to solve.

2. Define specific *objectives* within the framework of the agency mission. The Department of Agriculture, for example, set as one of its objectives the eradication of hog cholera, a major livestock disease, by 1980.

3. Prepare an *annual operating plan* for each objective. The plan should include a review of existing programs in light of the objectives; a brief analysis of alternative programs, their costs and effects; and a statement of the specific results that each program should produce.

27

4. Develop *performance reports* which measure how well program managers are meeting the desired objectives.

Is this management by objectives? As some agencies approach it, the system is little more than a pale counterpart of what is known in the business sector as "the manager's letter."

> Here a subordinate writes a letter to his superior in which he defines the objectives of his own and his supervisor's job. The subordinate also outlines the plans he will follow in achieving his objectives, the obstacles he expects to face in carrying out his plan, and the aid he will need from others in the organization to overcome the obstacles. When the letter is approved by the superior, it becomes the subordinate's planning guide.[21]

Management by objectives has enjoyed some of its greatest success in public administration when left at this level—as a tool of personnel evaluation where the worker and the boss sit down together and decide definitively what the worker shall be held accountable for.

A complete MBO program goes further, in two respects. First, it results in a genuine redefinition of government priorities. The manager's letter is only the first step. The top policy makers—political executives and legislators—use the managers' letters and mission statements drawn from them to establish new initiatives, abolish outdated programs, and redefine agency objectives. It is a process that usually cannot be shared with the career bureaucrats, who tend to define their own programs as the crucial ones. Once the new priorities are announced, however, the bureaucrats come back into the process. With the political executives, they make the strategic program decisions: which risks to take, which programs to contract out, which specializations to stress and how to coordinate them. The executive then can delegate to the bureau chiefs the responsibility for establishing the specific objectives, operating plans, and measures of performance.

Second, a complete MBO program will be integrated into the other management systems: the budget system, the personnel system, and the information system. These systems will be redesigned to support organizational objectives and the operating plans that underly them. Budget funds are redirected toward the mission, agency personnel who embody the agency's excellence are promoted and more recruited, and new information is generated to measure results. Reluctance to integrate the MBO program into the other management systems is the most common source of MBO failure. Agency personnel view MBO as a threat, the MBO staff is isolated, budget allocations do not follow objectives, the performance measures become artificial, and the MBO program collapses.

When an administrator is armed with the principles of hierarchy, specialization, staff and rules; backed up with the principle of merit and a centralized budget process; and provided with the refinements of management by objectives, there emerges the basic outline of a powerful public organization. Such power presents an irony of sorts.

28

The public administration movement in America was launched in an effort to check the discretion of political administrators—the spoilsmen and the bosses of the big city machines. It created in their place a new class of public executives, neutral in spirit but professional in technique. The science of public administration armed these executives with more raw power than their predecessors had ever thought of stealing under the old spoils system.

And where were the restraints on this new concentration of administrative power? For a while, scholars flirted with the idea that executives ought to be subjects of the law—the politics/administration dichotomy. This idea was reenforced by the emphasis upon management by objectives, which provided a moderate amount of control over bureaucratic discretion. Nevertheless, the restrictions of the politics/administration dichotomy were cast aside when scholars discovered that executives needed power to grease the administrative machine. The politics/administration dichotomy was never strictly enforced.

If the politics/administration dichotomy is unrealistic, then how does one restrain the power of the administrative executive riding atop a large public organization? Well, the administrative scientists began to discover that the organization was not as responsive to the techniques of executive control as the advocates of efficiency wanted us to believe. The first flaw in the science of administration appeared at the Hawthorne Works of the Western Electric Company.

THE HUMAN RELATIONS MOVEMENT

In 1924 The National Academy of Sciences sent a research team to the Western Electric Company's Hawthorne Works near Chicago to study the effects of illumination upon worker efficiency.

The work of Frederick Taylor had indicated that corporate productivity could be improved by redesigning each job and providing the worker with well-placed breaks. The research scientists were familiar with the studies of fatigue and monotony that had been utilized to reduce absenteeism and turnover and speed up the pace of work. It seemed likely, given these results, that improvements in the physical work conditions would also result in higher productivity. This section reviews the findings of the three critical Hawthorne experiments.

The Hawthorne Works employed twenty-nine thousand men and women for the purpose of manufacturing telephones and telecommunication equipment. After a number of inconclusive tests, the researchers decided to conduct their illumination experiments on workers who wound small induction coils onto wooden spools. The scientists improved the lighting in the experiment room. For every increase in illumination, productivity went up.

The more scientific administrative scientists were not satisfied with these results. If production was tied to illumination, then

29

The human relations movement grew out of a series of experiments conducted at the Western Electric Company's Hawthorne Works near Chicago. These women took part in the relay assembly room experiment, where administrative scientists discovered that organizational effectiveness depended more upon the cohesiveness of the work group and a democratic style of supervision than upon any formal principles of administration. COURTESY OF THE WESTERN ELECTRIC COMPANY.

wouldn't a *decrease* in lighting produce a *decrease* in worker efficiency? The scientists put back the old bulbs. Production went up. They put in smaller bulbs. Productivity increased "slowly but steadily. When the level for the test group finally reached three-foot candles, the operators protested, saying that they were hardly able to see what they were doing, and the production rate decreased."[22]

The research team checked their findings by setting up a control group in an adjacent area. The scientists never changed the level of light in the room. Worker productivity, nevertheless, steadily increased.

The administrative scientists were baffled. Thereafter, they began a second series of experiments. In 1927, the scientists recruited five women who built telephone relays and segregated them from the other employees. The women worked in a special room where the scientists could control temperature and humidity. Even the women's hours of sleep were regulated. The objective of the experiment was to test the role of fatigue and monotony on productivity.

The scientists experimented with longer rest periods and shortened the work day. In their conversations with the women, the scientists discovered that the workers frequently had no time to eat breakfast, so the scientists provided sandwiches, coffee, and soup. Productivity went up.

Productivity steadily increased until rumor spread through the plant that the Hawthorne plant executives were about to dismiss the research team because of the effects of the experiments on the other workers. At that point the women participating in the experiment began producing an astonishingly large number of telephone relays. About the same time, the scientists decided to observe the effects of increasing the women's fatigue. They restored the old forty-eight-hour work week. Productivity continued to climb. They eliminated the lunch break. Absenteeism went down. They cut out the rest breaks. Still no signs of fatigue. No matter how the research team tinkered with the rest periods or the work week, it could not get the women to slow down.

At last, after five years of experimentation, the scientists had to conclude that the employees were responding to them and not to the engineering of work. In the beginning, the women had responded to the introduction of the research team. It was novel. It meant that management was worried about productivity. Then the women began to respond to the style of supervision. The scientists felt comfortable encouraging "greater freedom, less strict supervision, and the opportunity to vary from a fixed pace without reprimand from a gang boss."[23] Said one scientist, "we could more logically attribute the increase in efficiency to a betterment of morale . . . the best way to improve morale was through improved supervision."[24]

The scientists felt that they needed to know more about sentiments toward supervision at the Hawthorne Plant. They interviewed twenty thousand employees and got as many answers, so they decided to undertake a final experiment. This time the research team would not supervise the workers being studied; they would observe them from a safe distance. Their most important experiment began in 1931 in the famous bank wiring room where workers produced telephone switchboards.

At that time the managers at the Hawthorne Plant were trying to increase worker efficiency through a combination of wage incentives and low-key supervision. By industrial standards of those times, the Hawthorne Plant was a good place to work. Anyplace was a good place to work, inasmuch as the nation was in the depths of the Great Depression. The employees were most concerned about losing their jobs; as a result, they artificially depressed their own productivity so that each man wired no more than two banks a day. Any man, on his own, could have made more money by working harder. The employees attacked those who did as speed freaks, while those who worked too slow were chided for being chiselers. Two banks a day was considered by both employees and management to be a fair day's work.

At last, the research team found the source of their confusion: the informal group. The scientists concluded that the dominant factor in employee productivity was the *group* and its attitudes. The most powerful motivators on the job were the social norms of the group and the ability of supervisors to act as leaders in modifying those norms. Workers might acquire their sentiments on the basis of individual experience, but on the job they behaved as members of groups.

Economic incentives, illumination, rest breaks, and other job-engineering schemes would never be as powerful as social controls in raising productivity. At best, the workers would manipulate the instrumental schemes. At worst, the instrumental schemes would alienate the workers from their jobs.

> Human collaboration in work has always depended upon the evolution of a nonlogical social code which regulates the relations between persons and their attitudes to one another. Insistence upon a merely economic logic of production interferes with the development of such a code and consequently gives rise in the group to a sense of human defeat.[25]

Elton Mayo, one of the fathers of the human relations movement, worried that this sense of human defeat called anomie would create a social vacuum where a person might work in a crowd yet feel no sense of identity with his or her surroundings. Like many other social reformers, Mayo cherished the social cohesion of the neighborhoods centered around towns and villages. Mayo hoped, through human relations, to recreate the communal village of rural times within the work groups of a modern factory. That required, in his view, open communication between ranks, participation in decision making by workers, job security, and a spirit of democracy wherein the administrators became concerned not just with work, but with the workers. Mayo was to the human relations movement what Frederick Taylor was to scientific management.

Mayo's philosophy, plus the research findings from the Hawthorne experiments, outlined the basic principles of human relations.

1. *Social Norms.* The level of organizational effectiveness is determined by social norms. The early experiments on illumination and fatigue demonstrated that the physiological capability of the worker was not the critical factor in productivity. Neither were the principles of administration, such as the division of work. Neither were as important as social norms.

2. *The Group.* Group standards strongly influence the behavior of individuals in organizations. The bank wiring room experiment demonstrated how the group could enforce a standard level of productivity upon all members. The group also provided a shield against executive reprisals. In both ways the group acted as a restraint on executive power.

3. *Rewards and Sanctions.* Social rewards and sanctions are the strongest motivators on the job. The workers in the Hawthorne plant responded to the respect, the affection, and the appeals to group loyalty provided by their fellow workers. Management's system of economic incentives, by contrast, was less powerful.

4. *Supervision.* The most effective system of supervision is created when the managers consult the group and its informal leaders

in order to win acceptance of organizational objectives. Human relations specialists would advise managers to be a good guy. Be human. Be a good listener. Don't be a boss. Give them the idea they're making the decision, not you. They believed that effective communication, supplemented by a willingness to allow workers to participate in decision making, was the key to effective supervision.

5. *Democratic Administration.* Workers will achieve their highest level of effectiveness when they are allowed to manage their own affairs with no gang boss in charge. A reanalysis of the Hawthorne experiments revealed that the improvements in productivity in the relay assembly room followed the decision of the researchers to allow the women to become a collegial, self-managing group. Every change in the work schedule was preceded by close consultation with the workers, because the researchers did not want to alienate the women. Only six women participated in this experiment, which was an ideal group size for the development of a collegial atmosphere. (Ironically, the administrative scientists seemed to recognize this with their span-of-control principle. Physically, a manager might be able to supervise more than the prescribed maximum of twelve subordinates, but any more than that, from the point of view of the worker, would reduce the opportunity for effective group development.)

Many see the human relations movement as the great counterbalance to the more orthodox principles of administration. This is true to the extent that the Hawthorne experiments occupy a hallowed spot as the Mount Sinai of modern behavioral science. At the time, however, the distinction between the administrative sciences and the human relations movement was more academic than practical. Managers grafted the principles of human relations onto the principles of administration producing, for example, the advantages of specialization within a humane system of supervision. The researchers at Hawthorne were no less interested in improving worker efficiency than people like Taylor, Fayol, or Gulick. All were looking for principles to help managers run a better organization.

CRITICISMS OF THE PRINCIPLES

Those early administrative pioneers thought that they were laying out the fundamental principles by which any operation would be organized. The principles of hierarchy, specialization, staff, and rules, the functions of personnel and budgeting, management by objectives and human relations—these were the things an administrator had to know to set up a program and get it running.

The best experts, from Fayol to Gulick, thought that they were laying the foundation for a science of administration that could take its place among the ancient academic disciplines. The experts incorporated the scientific method into their studies and tried to imitate the ideal of scientific impartiality in their prescriptions. Taylor thought himself to be a scientist. The researchers at the Hawthorne plant certainly considered themselves scientists.

Of course, the scientific yield was rather thin—a few principles and prescriptions. Gulick admitted that the practice of administration was more art than science. Still, he had hope for the future. The same factors that "played their part in the conquest of the natural world by science may be counted upon again to advance scientific knowledge and control in the world of human affairs."[26] Where better to begin that conquest than with the principles of administration? The principles stated cause and effect; they could be tested scientifically. The principle of span of control, for example, would cause efficiency, while ignorance of it would breed confusion. Executives could take their pick. Some might prefer confusion.

Not everyone agreed with Gulick. In the 1930s, critics began to question the principles of administration and their supposedly scientific basis. Ten years later, the final assault was led by two students studying for their doctorates: Herbert Simon and Dwight Waldo.

The principles of administration, Simon argued, were nothing but proverbs in disguise. A proverb is a popular saying, embodying some familiar truth based on common sense or practical experience. "Like proverbs, they [the principles of administration] appear in pairs. For almost every principle one can find an equally plausible and acceptable contradictory principle. Look before you leap!—but he who hesitates is lost."[27] Unity of command!—specialization.

Consider the principle of unity of command as an example. It seems reasonable to assume that supervision by one boss leads to less confusion than supervision by two. Unfortunately, the principle of unity of command is incompatible with the principles of specialization. The principles of specialization assert that confusion is reduced when tasks are accomplished by specialists. This leads automatically to a situation in which the specialists at the headquarters consult with the specialists in the field on matters of common concern without going through the official hierarchy. The result is a dual chain of command which promotes the advantages of the principles of specialization. It also violates the advantages of the principle of unity of command.

Simon revealed similar difficulties with the other principles of administration—they were ambiguous and contradictory. Every organization has to specialize, that is obvious. The principles of specialization, however, fail to inform the executive exactly how to specialize, how to do it so as to promote efficiency, and how to resolve one type of specialization with another. Was this a science, Simon asked? Hardly. "Even an *art* cannot be founded on proverbs."[28]

While Simon attacked the principles of administration, Waldo opened an assault on the criterion that guided them: the gospel of efficiency. Gulick had announced that "efficiency is axiom number one in the value scale of administration . . . the fundamental value upon which the science of administration may be erected."[29]

Not so, replied Waldo. Efficiency is a very slippery concept. It has been used by some reformers as a code word for less government and lower taxes—economizing without regard to the consequences. An important public executive once announced that it was "more efficient" for his agency to hire skilled women because they would do the same work as men but at lower pay. The drive for efficiency, Waldo said, has "occasionally served the ends of those whose purposes might be regarded as more or less reprehensible if stated in another idiom."[30]

The administrative scientists, who tried to be neutral in their quest for efficiency, simply could not escape their ideological heritage. In the American public administration movement, the quest for efficiency came to be associated with a philosophy of government that would best be described as utilitarian. In the eyes of the reformers, the gospel of efficiency became an expression of other fundamental values—their belief that progress and change were inherently good, their belief that science and technology were the engine of progress, their desire for a government run by experts who could use technical knowledge to bring about social and political control, and the brand of spiritual imperialism that drove the reformers to try to export their system of professional administration to "less developed" countries. Efficiency was hardly the "impartial" or "scientific" value that Gulick made it out to be.

Waldo concluded that efficiency was too amorphous to be treated as an ultimate value. "Things are not simply 'efficient' or 'inefficient'. They are efficient or inefficient for given purposes, and efficiency for one purpose may mean inefficiency for another."[31] The span of control needed to promote efficiency in a police department might prove totally inefficient if applied to a government research laboratory. It all depends upon the objectives being sought. To use Waldo's analogy, "for the purpose of killing a bear, a large-bore rifle is more efficient than a bag of meal, but for keeping the bear alive, the reverse is true. . . . Gulick's proposal to make efficiency 'the fundamental value upon which the science of administration may be erected,'" Waldo concluded, "must be rejected."[32]

The advocates of the human relations approach suffered similar criticism. They were accused of being as preoccupied with efficiency as the administrative scientists. Both wanted to increase our material bounty through greater productivity. The human relations specialists simply emphasized different principles. They were concerned with informal groups and improved communications and thought that executives should be benevolent toward employees because it would raise productivity as well as make the workers happy.

The critics of the human relations movement found this emphasis superficial and irrelevant to the real needs of the worker. As Henry Lansberger wrote in *Hawthorne Revisited*, "The charge has been

CRITICISMS OF THE PRINCIPLES

leveled again and again that the Mayo group stands on the side of management and regards the (organization) on the basis of an unquestioning acceptance of the goals of management."[33] Nowhere is this more apparent than on the issue of collective bargaining. The Mayo group thought that labor unions, by bargaining on behalf of employees, were driving management and worker apart, preventing effective communication, and increasing the sort of conflict which bred anomie. Nonsense, said the critics. The conflicts between employer and employees were real, based on real class differences. Unions protected the employees. Anomie was a natural by-product of the situation at hand. According to Lansberger, "Mr. Mayo assumes what he has yet to prove: that there is a natural community between worker and manager."[34]

These were devastating criticisms—thirty years ago. They pretty well removed the idea that the principles of administration were the key to a new science of administration. So the experts, dissatisfied with the principles, opened up new paths. Some wandered off through sociology and psychology in an attempt to create a science of organization based on an understanding of human behavior. Others traveled through political science to gauge the effect that politics had on the administrative process. Both groups sought a more "realistic" public administration. What they accomplished was the destruction of the hopes for a science of administration based upon a single theory of management, foreshadowing the fragmentation which would still plague public administration thirty years later.

And what about the principles of administration? Why are they still alive? Why do governments publish organization charts, why do managers still practice human relations, and why does a textbook on modern public administration open with a chapter on the principles of administration?

The answer is simple. So long as governments are run through bureaus, the principles will remain as the fundamental characteristics underlying the organization of public operations. They work as facts—simple descriptions of how most modern executives perceive their work and go about setting up their programs. Ask any executive for a recitation on authority, specialization, or staff work, and you will receive an informed response. Why? Because the principles of administration outline many of the central issues that executives feel they face. And sometimes, when modern scholarship becomes frustratingly vague, executives retreat to the principles of administration as prescriptions because they are firm and easy to apply.

FOR FURTHER READING

Many of the "classics" of management written during the first fifty years of the study of administration are still relevant. The basic principles of administration can be found in Henri Fayol, *General and Industrial Management* (New York: Pitman Publishing Corporation, 1916), and Luther Gulick and L. Urwick, eds., *Papers on the Science of Admin-*

istration (New York: Augustus M. Kelley Publishers, 1937), especially the first paper by Gulick titled "Notes on the Theory of Organization." Frederick Taylor explains his "complete mental revolution" underlying the division of work in *Principles of Scientific Management* (New York: W. W. Norton & Co., 1911). The classic statements of the human relations approach are contained in Elton Mayo, *The Human Problems of an Industrial Civilization* (New York: The Viking Press, 1933) and Mary Parker Follett, *Dynamic Administration: The Collected Papers of Mary Parker Follett*, edited by Henry C. Metcalf and L. Urwick (New York: Harper & Brothers, 1940).

It is hard to find a comprehensive treatment of the structure of modern organizations from the orthodox point of view, although one might settle for the text by Harold Koontz and Cyril O'Donnell, *Principles of Management: An Analysis of Managerial Functions*, 5th ed. (New York: McGraw-Hill Book Co., 1972), or the more public-oriented text by John M. Pfiffner and Frank P. Sherwood, *Administrative Organization* (Englewood Cliffs, N.J.: Prentice-Hall, 1960). For the "nuts and bolts" approach to administration at the local level, see James M. Banovetz, *Managing the Modern City* (Washington, D.C.: International City Management Association, 1971). The literature on special management problems is more extensive. See Ernest Dale and L. Urwick, *Staff in Organization* (New York: McGraw-Hill Book Co., 1960); . Kenneth C. Davis, *Administrative Law and Government* (St. Paul, Minn: West Publishing Co., 1975); O. Glenn Stahl, *Public Personnel Administration*, 6th ed., (New York: Harper & Row, 1971); Jesse Burkhead, *Government Budgeting* (New York: John Wiley & Sons, 1956); and Peter Drucker, *Managing for Results* (New York: Harper & Row, 1964) for the philosophy underlying management by objectives. Drucker's book and the text by Koontz and O'Donnell are used more in schools of business than in schools of public administration. Of course, the orthodox approach presented in this chapter has never really favored the distinction between business management and public principles of administration.

The criticisms of the orthodox approach can be found in Dwight Waldo, *The Administrative State* (New York: Ronald Press, 1948) and Herbert Simon, *Administrative Behavior* (New York: Macmillan Co., 1947), especially Chapter 2.

HUMAN BEHAVIOR IN ORGANIZATIONS

The belated recognition of social behavior in organizations merely confirmed the insights of storytellers and amateur philosophers. Three centuries before administrative scientists conducted the Hawthorne experiments, Shakespeare's King Henry disguised himself as a soldier so he could walk among his men at night and learn what they were thinking before the battle to be fought on St. Crispin's Day. Playwrights and novelists have always shown a predilection for explaining the sociological and psychological aspects of organizational life, a tendency refined by administrative scientists only after the study of organizational phenomenon had been underway for six decades.

From the 1880s to the 1940s, public administration was dominated by the issues explored in Chapter 1. Classical administrative theory assumed that people in organizations were instruments to be controlled, like machines, by setting up the right kind of organizational system. Even today, most organizations are established according to such principles of managerial control, a fact that foments universal trepidation among young persons contemplating their future service in a large bureaucracy, public, corporate, or military.

What the fiction writers knew (and the social scientists confirmed) was the fact that organizations are really made up of stubborn and—from management's point of view—unpredictable employees. Employees establish their own behavior patterns, set their own goals, and create their own perceptions of the organization. That knowledge revolutionized the scientific approach to administration—a behavioral revolution, they called it, which sought to replace the first principles of administration with a more realistic description of how people really behaved. The behavioral scientists believed that a full understanding of administration could be achieved only by seeing the organization as a social system. The formal structure of the organization was nothing more than the skeleton upon which the social system hung. It provided a structure, often a sense of security, but it did not explain the behavior of the people within it.

Why did the behavioral perspective suddenly emerge in public administration? Why did young professors cease to stress the principles of Fayol and Taylor and instead present the criticisms offered by Simon and Waldo?

Perhaps the best explanation for the rise of the behavioral approach to public administration was the fact that the scholars went to war. The Second World War emptied the campuses, and administrative experts found themselves in gunboats, tanks, and supply depots. To be sure, scholars had advised public officials before the war. But that was at the top. The war gave experts, old and new, a chance to study administration from deep inside the organization. The next section describes how it looked.

THE SOCIAL FOUNDATIONS OF ORGANIZATION

The Jewish prisoners in the extermination camp at Treblinka revolted so that witnesses would live to tell why this thing had happened. The ones who escaped explained how it was possible for the Nazis to condition their captives and how some had found the means to fight back. This version, taken from the novel *Treblinka* by Jean-Francois Steiner, is the story of a people's descent into submissiveness and the emergence of a spirit of resistance. It has important lessons for those who are interested in administrative behavior.

The uprisings in the ghettos of Vilna and Warsaw demonstrated to the Nazis that the Jews were capable of organizing an armed uprising. To eradicate that germ of resistance, the technicians who administered the "final solution" instituted behavioral techniques that removed the opportunity for social cohesion and thereby destroyed the group spirit around which any resistance movement had to form.

The technicians created an illusion: *arbeit macht frei*. Work and your lives will be spared. They enforced the illusion by exhorting the Jewish hope to live, and then crushed it through pogroms and forced removals, creating so much anguish within the ghetto that the Jews ceased to see themselves as members of a community. In this way the Jews were reduced to a serial existence, without groups, wherein each sought his or her individual survival alone and was incapable of reacting to the general threat or, in the end, to the inevitability of his or her own death. At the extermination camps, the technicians selected Jews whose will to live was still strong and put them through ordeals of torture. It was not difficult to convince the survivors of these ordeals to labor in the death camps, where the horrible nature of the work completed their moral disarmament.

At Treblinka one thousand prisoners performed the work that kept the camp running. They were supervised by the technicians, most of whom were members of the Secret Police, and guarded by two hundred Ukrainians. The technicians organized the prisoners into a hierarchy, divided the hierarchy into sections, divided the sections

39

into commandos, and divided the commandos into as many cadres as there were jobs to be done in the camp. The technicians even consulted experts, in one case a cremation specialist, who used time-and-motion studies to arrive at a scientific solution to the primary bottleneck in the productivity of the camp.

Still, the camp did not run efficiently. The prisoners behaved like automatons, incapable of doing anything except precisely what they were told. This infuriated the technicians, who were obsessed with the idea that everything in the camp should run like a well-tuned factory. Clearly, what was lacking was a method of motivating the prisoners to be better workers.

To solve this problem, the adjutant who ran the camp abolished the rule of rotation, under which most of the laborers were regularly replaced by new arrivals, and substituted a more subtle method to maintain the illusion that hard work brought a normal life. He created a town in the camp, which he christened Obermäiden, complete with gardens, a zoo, a symphony orchestra, weddings, a cabaret, boxing clubs, medieval gates, a main street decorated with wood carvings, and a ghetto, all maintained by prisoners recruited from the trains. Obermäiden was built in order to make the prisoners feel more subhuman by reminding them that they were still Jews.

Before the reforms, there were only three methods of resistance at Treblinka. All three were individual acts that required little social cooperation: suicide, escape, and revenge. The cultural norms upon which the reforms were modeled revived among the Jews the sense of social cohesion which encouraged them to hope that they could overcome their slavery by organizing an armed revolt.

There were three turning points in the regeneration of the Jewish society. While the revolt was being planned, eight Jews were discovered stealing the gold that was to be used to buy weapons from the guards. The Jews were taken to the "hospital" and told: the ditch or a name. They died without revealing anything. They were the first men since the conditioning began to choose group loyalty over personal survival.

In January a typhus epidemic broke out in the camp. The prisoners organized themselves to fight the disease. They bribed the guards to bring them food and manipulated the price of foodstuffs by lowering demand. They set up a secret infirmary in the latrines. "Barely eating, sleeping little more, ill clad, beaten constantly, the sick went to work with fevers of 105 degrees." The epidemic gave them something to fight against. "The machine was running. The killers were becoming prisoners of their victims."[1]

The third event was the burning of the dead, who heretofore had been buried in ditches. No longer slaves to an illusion, the prisoners accepted the fact that the technicians intended to close Treblinka and erase all traces of its horror. Acceptance of the truth was accompanied by a strange sense of identification with the camp. "The early days had been hard, God knew, but they had lived through them to-

CHAPTER 2: HUMAN BEHAVIOR IN ORGANIZATIONS

gether, they had suffered together, and now they were going to part."[2]

The resistance committee had planned the uprising, rehearsed the method for securing weapons, and organized four combat teams to cover the retreat. The committee communicated the plans to the other prisoners in the camp, who were now as anxious to start the revolt, despite its inevitable dangers, as they had once been to secure their own lives. All that remained was to select the date.

On the second of August in 1943, a Monday, the Jews of Treblinka took guns and grenades from the armory, seized an armored car, set fire to the camp, and forced their way out. Six hundred out of a thousand escaped across the fields and into the forests. Most of the prisoners in the combat teams died in the uprising. The last combat team lay down a protective line of gunfire across the open fields which forced the pursuing German soldiers to retreat.

What Treblinka revealed was the powerful effect of social behavior in creating an organization and shielding its individual members from formal authority. At Treblinka the Jews were prevented from constructing a *formal* resistance organization. They had no organization charts, no budgets, no chief administrators. Their resistance was purely a social phenomenon, yet it possessed all the characteristics of a real organization. The resistance committee organized the prisoners on the basis of their skill and courage. Discipline was maintained through social incentives: the Jewish culture and a devotion to the objective that some should escape to tell others about Treblinka before the Germans leveled the camp. There were rules. One of the most important was the rule that no prisoners try to escape, issued so that the technicians would be lulled into thinking that their system was working. None of the rules were ever published, but were maintained solely by the behavior of the Jews.

The Jews at Treblinka created a social organization, which existed inside the formal organization. The formal organization, managed by the technicians, was devoted to the work of the camp and to keeping the Jews in a subhuman condition. Within its boundaries there arose a social organization made up of like-minded people who encouraged conformity to their own goals. Powerful, cohesive social behavior is inevitable and ubiquitous in any functioning organization, even under the extreme conditions imposed at Treblinka. The fact that the technicians treated the Jews as subhuman, even while attempting to motivate them through human relations techniques, blinded the technicians to the fact that the Jews were capable of creating their own social organization—one case in which managerial ignorance promoted human dignity.

Treblinka was only one of a number of social phenomena of which administrative scientists were aware. Alexander Leighton told a similar story about a less sinister Japanese relocation camp at Posdon, Arizona. Philip Selznick described administrative behavior in the Tennessee Valley Authority. Scores of case studies were written,

*Here a group of Polish Jews are forced to perform manual labor by the occupation
government in Poland during World War II. Cohesive work groups develop
under even the most severe organizational conditions; not far away, at Treblinka,
groups of Jewish prisoners organized a revolt and overthrew the formal organization.*
COURTESY OF THE U.S. ARMY.

and public administrators were encouraged to return to the classic
studies of group dynamics completed between 1928 and 1940—the
Hawthorne studies, Kurt Lewin's study of children in an Iowa research laboratory, William F. Whyte's study of a street-corner gang in
Boston, and Raymond Firth's enviable research project that took him
to the Polynesian island of Tikopia. The studies confirmed what the
Hawthorne experiments had first revealed—that groups are more
important than formal structure in determining the behavior of
employees.

Small groups fulfill essential functions for the individual in the
modern organization. At the least, they act as a shield to protect the
employee from administrative reprisals. By banding together,
employees increase their sense of security and power and thereby
offset the advantages that management possesses through its formal
prerogatives, which work best when they are directed individually
against employees. When formal prerogatives lose their effectiveness, one can almost always trace the cause to a shift in group senti-
ment.

Groups also provide a frame of reference for the individual
employee, who uses the group to confirm or deny his or her beliefs,
values, perceptions, and norms of behavior. Groups furnish the
employee with the most important rewards of organizational life:
friendship, support, esteem, and one's own sense of identity.

CHAPTER 2: HUMAN BEHAVIOR IN ORGANIZATIONS

Groups are often in a better position to reward or punish individual employees than management, with its formal powers over pay and prestige. As a result, groups resolve many important organizational issues, from the correct pace of work to the determination, if the groups are powerful enough, of the mission of the organization. Finally, each group contributes its task: the work it performs. The central task of the group may be surreptitious, as in the case of the Jews at Treblinka, or it may be more or less congruent with the formal goals of the organization, as was the case with the Ukrainian guards. Or the group may act like a zealous patriot and exaggerate the goals of the organization, as in the case of the technicians. This typically occurs when the members of the group have a predisposed sense of obligation to some cause and an "enemy" to oppose them.

It is only natural that administrative sociologists should want to view the organization as a collage of groups—those bands of employees who, because they work together, form bonds which are more powerful than the lines of formal authority. George Homans suggests that administrators who want to know more about their employees' behavior study the recurring patterns of activity within the organization, the sentiments of the members toward the organization, and the interaction between different groups within the organization.

Most professional public administrators find Homans's scheme confusing. If you give a public manager solid lines of authority on a chart and a lot of verbiage about activity-sentiment-interaction, the manager will choose formal authority and endure the necessary sacrifice in accuracy. So what is the behavioral organization? Can it be reduced to a set of principles? The best place to start is with the concept of authority.

AUTHORITY AND COMMUNICATIONS

If the organization is not altogether a structure of formal authority, then what is it? One of the fathers of the behavioral revolution in administration, Chester Barnard, suggested that formal authority is little more than the willingness to communicate.

Barnard was not a professional social scientist. He went to Harvard University but left in 1909 without finishing his bachelor's degree to take a job with the telephone company. He was put in the statistical department, where he became an expert on rates, and in 1927 was made president of New Jersey Bell. He sought out scholars at Harvard, including Elton Mayo, for their ideas on administrative theory, and in 1938 he published a book titled *The Functions of the Executive.* It was the first widely read study to treat the organization as a social system, that is, as a collage of physical, psychological, and social forces.

Barnard began with the idea that *coordination* was the chief function of the executive. At that time, discussions of administrative coordination led most managers to talk about issuing orders, prepar-

Chester Barnard was a practicing administrator—the president of New Jersey Bell—whose ideas on authority and communications in organizations helped launch the behavioral revolution in public administration. Here he is flanked by former President Herbert Hoover, a famous administrative expert in his own right, and former boxing champion Gene Tunney. COURTESY OF W. B. WOLF, I.L.R. SCHOOL, CORNELL UNIVERSITY

ing budgets, and staffing the organization. Barnard took a different approach; he emphasized the idea of organizational purpose. Every organization possessed some unifying purpose, he said, just as New Jersey Bell's purpose was to provide telephone service. The individual employees, by themselves, without an organization, could not accomplish that purpose. The organization came into being, Barnard wrote in a nice piece of fiction, when individuals who were in a position to communicate with one another decided to contribute their actions to a common purpose. With a stroke of the pen, Barnard did for organizations what John Locke had done for constitutions: he set the source of their power in the people who made them up. Having achieved a triumph of logic, Barnard now had to face a problem of fact. Most employees join organizations to satisfy personal needs. They do not join to contribute to any organizational purpose, but to work, to eat, to buy a house, or to make new friends.

So Barnard made the executive the trustee of the organizational purpose. The *persistence of cooperation*, he said, depended upon the ability of the executive to preserve the purpose of the organization. Persistence of cooperation, a fancy term for the survival of the organization, was Barnard's number-one administrative value. A good executive promoted it by fusing the organizational purpose to the personal needs of the employees. The executive made certain that the organizational bag of rewards contained noneconomic incentives, such as affection and a sense of belonging and, most important, he or she maintained among the members of the organization a *willingness to communicate*. Only by keeping communication channels open could the executive transmit the purpose of the organization and learn the needs of the employees. So when Barnard placed coordination at the center of his famous definition of organization—"a system of consciously coordinated activities or forces of two or more persons"[3]—it did not lead him into a discussion of POSDCORB. It led him, quite naturally for someone in the telephone business, into a discourse on communications.

It was some discourse. It was controversial when he wrote it in 1937 and it still is today. One leading scholar exclaimed how remarkable it was "that the Bell System tolerated such deviant behavior on the part of one of its chief executives."[4] In essence, what Barnard did was stand Fayol on his head. Barnard simply observed that all organizational authority flowed from the bottom up—from the worker to the foreman, from the client to the bureaucrat, from the child to the parent. All authority depended upon the willingness of subordinates to accept orders from their superior. This was in stark contrast to the orthodox belief that executives acquired official authority from a specific grant of power from a higher office, relevant to their responsibilities, to which obedience was assured through the forces of command and discipline. Barnard insisted that formal authority of this sort existed only in the abstract. In real organizations, he said, authority was always attached to a communiqué to do this or not do that. If the communication channels were snarled, and the meaning of the order never received, then authority did not exist. If the communiqué was heard, but ignored, then authority did not exist. Subordinates ignored communiqués for a number of reasons: because they were physically unable to carry them out, because the orders conflicted with their personal interests, or because they believed that the orders were inconsistent with their own perception of the true purposes of the organization. In an organization where the purpose is legitimized through the cooperation of its members, authority depends entirely upon an effective system of communications.

There is a famous scene in *Cool Hand Luke* where a state prison farm administrator tells Luke, who is resisting just about every order the prison boss gives, that "what we've got here is a failure to communicate." After Luke escapes from the prison farm for the third time, and is captured for the third time, he hands the line back to the boss and is shot through the neck by a prison guard for insubordination. Barnard did not say it any better. What both Lucas Jackson and the prison administrator recognize is that the breakdown in formal authority resides in Luke's reluctance to accept the communiqués as legitimate. Luke is too much of an individualist and possesses an unusual ability to communicate his own spirit of resistance to the other prisoners. He weakens the formal authority of the prison administrators, so they want to kill him.

Until Luke arrives, the other prisoners are willing to accept orders from the boss and the guards without question. Barnard was enough of a realist to recognize the prevalence of this phenomenon. He invented a term to describe it: the *zone of indifference*. Every member of an organization creates in his or her own mind a zone of indifference within which certain communiqués are accepted automatically as being legitimate and worth obeying and respects the fiction that the person issuing the order has some sort of formal authority. Some people, such as Lucas Jackson have a very narrow zone of indifference which may clash with a manager's expectation that employees will be indifferent toward most of the controls exercised over them. As any convict or soldier will tell you, the state is not without advantages in shaping each employee's zone of indifference.

Of course, not every public servant is treated like a convict. In complex organizations, the system of authority is determined by the kind of work being done and the possibilities it creates for effective communication. Amitai Etzioni, the sociologist, showed how executives in complex organizations mold their authority systems through three forms of compliance. One is coercive, as in a prison, and is based upon physical threats. Another is utilitarian, which means that the executive attempts to enlist the participation of the employees by offering them economic incentives, as a city manager might bargain with sanitation workers over pay and productivity. The third basis is normative and includes a broad class of situations wherein employees already agree with the purposes of the organization and are anxious to please. At the height of its power, the executives in the American space program typically recruited and socialized their employees through the use of subtle normative controls, appealing to each employee's need for prestige, esteem, and affection. Of course, the challenge of the work in the space program clearly presented different opportunities for organizational cooperation than a group of prisoners stamping out license plates does.

We know that the type of work being done has an enormous impact upon the creation of the authority system and the possibilities of communicating that authority to employees at different levels of the organization. So do the attitudes that the employees hold about their role in the organization—particularly their indifference or predisposition toward authority. But how are those attitudes formed? Obviously, there is more at work than just group pressure. The genesis of such attitudes is bound up in the decision each employee makes (consciously or unconsciously) to participate in the affairs of the organization—and the largely unwritten conditions attached to that decision.

ENLISTING PARTICIPATION IN ORGANIZATIONS

Why do employees participate in an organization? Why are some employees gung-ho and others stubborn as hell? Before the behavioral movement, there were two prevailing explanations, both based largely on experience from labor and industrial relations. One dealt with economic rewards, the other with social incentives.

The first explanation, which reflected the instrumental view of the scientific management movement, claimed that individual workers were motivated by cash rewards, providing the work was arranged scientifically and the workers properly trained. Taylor promoted this view when he identified Schmidt as the ideal worker because a nickel looked as big as a cartwheel to him.

Informal work groups and labor unions pretty well destroyed this explanation of reality, so scholars such as Morris Viteles and William Whyte constructed an alternative theory of incentives. They explained why cash was not the primary motivator of workers and why workers were able to manipulate all of the piece-rate economic incentives that management dreamed up. These scholars concluded that group pressures and social incentives were as important as money in satisfying workers and keeping them on the job.

Neither explanation really satisfied the new behavioral scientists. Neither, for example, could explain the enormous variations in self-motivation among employees doing the same job. So the behavioral scholars broke with these two traditional explanations and invented one of their own.

In 1958, two behavioral theorists closely associated with public administration wrote a book titled, simply, *Organizations*. The theorists, James March and Herbert Simon, attempted to summarize the knowledge about organization theory gained from the behavioral period, which Simon had helped launch twelve years earlier in a book with similar findings. *Organizations* was as important to the behavioral movement in public administration as Gulick's *Papers on the Science of Administration* was to the previous era. Unfortunately, *Organizations* was not as easy to read, due to the tedious behavioral style, and its lessons were not as easily passed on to new students of administration.

March and Simon approached the issue of participation in this way. They knew that pay and prestige were important, but not as crucial as the nature of work and the attitude of each employee toward it. They sensed that each individual created a "psychological contract" with the organization—a balance between the expectations which each person placed on the organization and the expectations which the organization placed upon that person. Individual participation in the affairs of the organization, they thought, depended upon four factors.

First, employees will be encouraged to participate to the degree that their actual job conforms to their own characterization of themselves. Apparently E. Howard Hunt was encouraged to participate in various undercover capers, including the Watergate affair, because they closely conformed to his personal fantasies, as reflected in the various spy novels he wrote. The organization expands such opportunities when it allows employees to choose between a number of challenging jobs.

Second, employees will be encouraged to participate to the degree that they are able to predict the consequences of taking certain actions on the job. All this means is that a city manager, for example, who allocates public funds for police uniforms, knows that the funds

47

will be spent for clothes and not to pay off police informants. Public agencies employ auditors just as insurance.

Third, employees will be encouraged to participate to the extent that their work requirements are compatible with the other roles they play outside the job. Employees play lots of other roles: in the family, in politics, clubs, and sports, or at the tavern. To the extent that the organization intrudes upon these other roles, like forcing an employee with a family to work the graveyard shift, it reduces willingness to participate.

An employee's satisfaction with his or her job will depend largely upon these three factors. Dissatisfaction triggers a desire to get out. That introduces a fourth factor: the employee's perception of the possibilities for moving from his or her current situation to something better. What about the employee who perceives few alternatives, who feels trapped in the organization? In the long run, such employees will lower their aspirations and their participation. As their job dissatisfaction increases, the quality of their work declines. Clients complain and outsiders become less willing to support the organization, which in turn leads to a situation wherein the organization suffers a loss of resources—for example, through cuts in its budget. This means that the organization has fewer incentives on hand to reward performance, which further depresses the willingness of its employees to participate. Out of such cycles of dissatisfaction the most rigid bureaucracies arise.

If dissatisfied employees are in a position to "renegotiate" their psychological contracts, then the possibility of increased participation reappears. Employees who perceive few opportunities for leaving the organization may relieve their discontent by improving the inducements they receive. It is even possible for prisoners to come to support their captors' mission, a process vividly illustrated in the novel *Bridge over the River Kwai*.

Colonel Nicholson, a British officer captured at the Battle of Singapore, is ordered by the Japanese to go with his men and build a bridge over the River Kwai, a bridge that will link the capitals of Thailand and Burma and allow the Japanese to invade India. Colonel Saito, the commandant of the prisoner-of-war camp to which the men are taken, places the British soldiers under the supervision of Japanese engineers and orders Nicholson to carry hod alongside his men.

Nicholson refuses. He will not compromise the authority of the British officers by allowing them to perform manual labor. So the Japanese torture Nicholson. The men retaliate with a work slowdown. Those who are forced to work place the bridge pilings in a swamp so that the high span will sink into the River Kwai when the first Japanese train crosses over it.

Colonel Saito fears that he will face a firing squad if he fails to construct a workable bridge on schedule. So he frees Colonel Nicholson and gives him command of his men. Nicholson is infuriated by the deliberate inefficiency of the men—it may be impairing construction of the bridge, but it is also destroying military discipline in the camp. The rickety style of Japanese bridge design is especially maddening to Nicholson and his chief engineer, an army major with considerable construction experience.

Nicholson confronts Saito and demands that the bridge be moved one mile downstream. He insists that the POW camp be relocated and that the Japanese engineers and workers be placed under the command of the British officers who will complete the railroad bridge over the River Kwai.

Neither punishment nor permissiveness motivates the British officers to build the bridge. Only when the British officers are left alone, to define their own responsibilities, to tackle a really big job without being badgered by bureaucratic details or Japanese confusion, does a surge of professional pride arise in officers who are trained in the ideology that hard, disciplined work always brings success. The British officers cannot endure being responsible for a bridge whose performance is so totally unpredictable. Building a faulty bridge is totally incompatible with the image they have of themselves as the world's most skilled managers of men and machines. Nicholson's role as a military disciplinarian erases any misgivings he has about building the bridge and defending it against a British special forces team sent in to sabotage the project. Nicholson becomes a perfect participant—from his captors' point of view.

A BEHAVIORAL ORGANIZATION CHART

The behavioral scholar promises the administrator a better set of concepts for understanding the operation of the organization. So far this set has consisted of concepts like the social organization, the group, authority as communications, the zone of indifference, the psychological contract and the decision to participate. Can the vitality of these concepts keep the administrator from reaching back for the old organization chart?

Suppose that you were asked to analyze the administration of a fire department. Where would you start? Would you ask to look at the organization chart, or would you want to observe the behavior of the fire fighters at work? The formal organization chart is simpler; however, from the behavioral point of view, it is also misleading. Those short and long lines on the organization chart, after all, represent little more than the willingness to communicate, and that willingness largely depends upon the extent to which the employees have decided to participate in the organization. The organization chart misleads the analyst by suggesting that the way the administrator wants employees to behave is in fact an accurate description of their activity. So instead of starting a priori with the formal organization chart, the behavioral scientist could begin by analyzing the patterns of behavior which recur frequently within the organization. There are many ways

Most organizational activity is based upon familiar patterns of behavior that are reenforced through experience and training. A casual observer might see only confusion at the scene of a fire, while a fire fighter will see cues that call for certain behavior patterns and will respond to the cues without having to be commanded to do so. COURTESY OF THE HUNTINGTON, WEST VIRGINIA PUBLISHING CO. JACK BURNETT, PHOTOGRAPHER.

to conceptualize the behavioral side of administration, but none seems to work as an analytical wedge so well as the concept of *patterned behavior.*

When a bell rings in a fire house, a fairly predictable series of events occurs. Fire fighters pull on their pants and boots, slide down a pole, wake the dalmatian, and speed to a fire. Often they speed to a heart attack, to an automobile accident, even to a youngster who is dying of an overdose of drugs. Says one fireman, "A man once told me that he was told by an immigration officer in Puerto Rico to call the Fire Department if he ever needed emergency help in New York City. The only real sure thing in this town is that firemen come when you pull the handle on that red box."[5]

The social scientists call this patterned behavior—the unfailing fact that fire fighters are motivated to risk their lives responding rapidly to an alarm even if it is called by a prankster. Fire departments have models of how their fire fighters should act in response to various calls for help: the models are inculcated through training and repetitious practice. Many of the models, usually called standing operating procedures, are described in manuals of operation.

Social scientists think that repetitive patterns of routine behavior provide the best characterization of how people in organizations really behave. When the alarm rings, and the nature of the emergency is communicated, the fire fighters initiate the routine behavior pattern that best fits the situation and meets department standards. They do not have to be ordered by an ēxecutive officer. They do not treat each situation as if it was novel. They apply familiar patterns of behavior, which are part of the social consciousness of the organization. The executive reenforces them by training and by hiring people who fit the mold. The employees reenforce it by embracing sentiments that support the behavior patterns they already know. The organization becomes a little culture, familiar to insiders. Where cultural norms reenforce familiar behavior, the organization becomes a social system whose fabric is as strong as an iron suit.

Complex organizations contain thousands of behavior patterns. Single employees, highly trained, may be capable of performing hundreds. Social scientists like to call these *repertories:* the list of pieces that the company is prepared to perform. The tendency in all organizations is for members to escape uncertainty by constructing repertories for recurring situations. Few persons possess the stamina to climb through each new day with the attitude that all of its events are novel. To avoid organizational exhaustion, they subject uncertainty to norms of rationality.

Administrators equip their employees with the ability to define new problems in terms that fit old patterns of behavior. A bystander might see in a fire a scene of novel confusion. Fire fighters, however, are trained to perceive within the chaos of events the important *cues*, a term borrowed from the theater. Cues may come in the form of commands; often they are more subtle. Fire fighters do not need a direct command to give oxygen to a smoke victim. In effect, they have already been commanded, through training and by observing the actions of their peers.

The perception of a cue sets off a search for the appropriate pattern of behavior. This is called, appropriately, *search behavior,* in the sense that the person searches through his or her repertory of behavior patterns for the action that seems to fit the situation. Executives do this on a grand scale when they define each new problem before them and assign it to the appropriate part of the organization. ("What we have here is a public relations problem.") Employees do it when they execute an action in response to a cue.

Search behavior is more difficult than it sounds. In principle, executives have a frame of reference which allows them to compare all possible alternatives in order to locate the behavior pattern that is preferred above all others. That behavior pattern is called the *optimal* choice. In fact, such textbook solutions rarely work. In the process of matching repertories to cues, there is always some element of surprise; moreover, there is rarely enough time to search through all of the repertories that might be relevant. In searching for appropriate behavior patterns, real executives usually choose the first course of action to come along that is satisfactory for the situation at hand.

ORGANIZATIONAL DECISION MAKING

There is an old bromide among public servants that when a particular product—whether a weather report, a housing project, or a new army rifle—fails to meet standards of excellence, it be issued anyway because "it is good enough for government work." The decisions of administrators and employees to accept less than optimal performance is a prime concern of administrative theorists, as are the consequences of this behavior when the suboptimal fails to solve the problem.

Social scientists call this *satisficing* behavior. By this they mean that the organization has developed standard criteria that outline minimal performance, and that when any problem arises, managers search through existing behavior patterns and apply the one that meets these standards.

This is not to stay that organizational executives fail to push their employees to perform at their peak. They do. But the result is rarely optimal performance. Optimal performance requires managers to review all courses of action, estimate their consequences, and choose the alternative that is best. In the real world, there are very substantial limits on the ability of any manager to walk the optimal path.

The first limitation stems from the common preference for operating on the basis of familiar behavior patterns. It is far easier to improve organizational performance by perfecting routine than by encouraging employees to adapt to each situation as if it were novel. A fire chief will train fire fighters by having them perform the same routine over and over again until they perfect it. Of course there will always be some element of surprise in each situation—even in something as routine as a fire drill. Nevertheless, it is easier to perfect the routine than to treat each problem as if it were unique, with the result that a performance gap will always arise because the routine behavior pattern will never quite fit the actual situation.

This is only one of the limitations that lead to satisficing behavior in government operations. The most important limitations are cognitive; that is, they concern the way in which managers think about administrative problems and arrive at their choices. Choice underlies everything that has been discussed so far—the choice of which behavior patterns to apply, the choice between different types of social control, the decision to participate in the organization, and the choice of which groups to join. The behavioral revolution in public administration began with a book which opened with the recommendation that social scientists make choice the focus of administrative research. The book was Herbert Simon's *Administrative Behavior*, published in 1947.

In the chapter titled, "The Psychology of Administrative Decisions," Simon outlined the cognitive limits on optimal performance. "My view of administrative decision-making," Simon said, "can be stated very simply. It is impossible for the behavior of a single, isolated individual to reach any high degree of rationality. The number

In his book Administrative Behavior, *Herbert Simon dismisses the formal principles of administration as nothing but proverbs and calls upon public administrators to focus on behavioral issues, such as the decison to participate and the limits of administrative rationality. Simon is currently a professor of computer sciences and psychology at Carnegie-Mellon University in Pittsburgh.* COURTESY OF CARNEGIE-MELLON UNIVERSITY.

of alternatives he must explore is so great, the information he would need to evaluate them so vast, that even an approximation to objective rationality is hard to conceive."[6]

To behave rationally, an administrator must know and anticipate the consequences of each alternative course of action. In fact, knowledge about consequences is usually incomplete. Even if such knowledge were attainable, the pressures of time and money would probably preclude an exhaustive exploration of it.

An administrator who wishes to behave rationally must also understand the values held by people in the agency and clients outside of it in order to predict how they will respond emotionally to certain alternatives. This is terribly important in any situation that involves risk, whether it is a fire company fighting a petroleum refinery blaze or a federal agency trying to improve automobile safety. It is usually impossible to predict response with any degree of accuracy.

Rationality requires imagination and ingenuity in designing alternative courses of action, sometimes in the absence of any real experience. Besieged administrators operating agencies with scarce resources rarely have the time to sit and dream up ideal solutions.

To execute a rational decision, all members of the organization in crucial positions must be ready to carry out the optimal choice. In fact, one person's optimal solution is often another person's stupidity. It depends upon one's perception of the organizational mission, one's prior commitments, one's inhibitions, and the fact that one must often depend upon persons who are inadequately trained.

Finally, rationality implies that the organization is set up rationally. Anyone who has studied the history of departmental reorganization knows that structural problems are too often a handicap to administrative improvement.

Twelve years later, Simon again concluded:

Organizational behavior calls for simplified models that capture the main features of a problem without capturing all its complexities. Optimizing is replaced by satisficing. Alternatives and consequences are discovered sequentially through search processes. Repertories are developed and these serve as the alternatives of choice in recurrent situations. Each specific action deals with a restricted range of situations and a restricted range of consequences. Each action is capable of being executed in semi-independence of the others.[7]

THE HEURISTIC PROCESS

What happens when the suboptimal fails to solve the problem? Granted, this does not happen frequently. Most organizational problems have precedents and are susceptible to solution through familiar patterns of behavior. Satisficing behavior usually works—or at least it satisfies minimum standards.

Occasionally an agency faces a really unique situation. It may be a new agency with a new program. It may be an old agency that wants to improve its performance. Or perhaps the agency is gripped by the forces of change—a change in technology, a change in the labor force, new competitors, or economic alterations such as scarcity. For whatever reason, the agency may find itself in a situation where it can no longer apply old patterns of behavior and still satisfy minimum standards.

The study of organizational response to unique situations is the study of *heuristic decision making. Heuristic* means inventive, encouraging further investigation, or helping to discover or learn. This is exactly what the agency does. Like pupils who are told to find out things for themselves, the agency searches through its previous behavior in the hope of finding some experience upon which to build a new behavior pattern.

The heuristic process is not wholly unstructured; there appears to be some sort of pattern to it. William Gore, an administrative scholar, suggested the existence of such a pattern after observing decision making in a Kansas fire department. Crane Brinton, the historian, was certain that he had found a pattern underlying whole societies in revolution.

In the beginning, the organizational leaders receive certain cues that times are changing. Public attitudes toward the organization change; grievances increase; the legislature might launch an investigation. In sum, leaders develop a sense of disequilibrium, a sense that their survival is threatened.

Administrators respond with a behavior pattern selected from the organizational repertory, one that matches the cues they are receiving. No new behavior pattern is created, although conditions may require some slight restructuring of the sequence of action within the old pattern. The response meets minimal organization standards—that is sufficient. It may seem to solve the problem, at least temporarily.

Since the environment of the organization has changed, the

routine response will in the long run fail to allay the sense of disequilibrium. New grievances and loss of confidence in the organization will lead to general frustration or to a feeling of drifting. Conflict within the organization over the appropriate response will become open and more widespread and new leaders will come forward.

The following stage might be described as a maneuver for position. It is likely that the moderates will fail, either in their definition of the problem or in their ability to estimate the consequences of it. Persons of consequence who nevertheless are not current members of the top organizational regime will struggle with the moderates and among themselves for control of the organization. This is the heart of the heuristic process. It is not so much a process of creative decision making as it is a battle over whose definition of the problem shall prevail. In theory, the faction to emerge on top will be the one whose past history best prepares it to search through its experiences and come up with an appropriate solution. The result is nearly always a centralization of power, which is necessary not only in order to select the appropriate behavior patterns but, more importantly, to prepare to execute it upon the members of the organization.

This is the hardest part. New behavior patterns have to be grafted onto the old habits of the members of the organization. The members, who may have no part in the preceding power struggles, have to adjust to the definition of the problem created by the leadership. They are told to learn new roles and master new skills. The trauma of the heuristic process frequently provides the motivation necessary to encourage many members to adopt new modes of behavior. Others may resist, refusing to adjust their attitudes. They may be exiled, or, as the army likes to say, neutralized.

The turbulence of change generally is followed by a period of consolidation. The organization seems to relax, an impression created by the quiet process of reenforcing the new behavior patterns adopted during the crisis. Again new leaders come forward, this time experts at institutionalizing the reforms created during the preceding stages. Old values that appeared to be expendable during the period of rapid change reassert themselves. This often leads to an impression of reaction. In fact, the major achievements of the heuristic process are rarely undone. They are simply consolidated with the old behavior patterns that still have relevance.

To many social scientists, individual adjustment to change is the most fascinating part of the heuristic process. A whole subdiscipline has grown up around the study of individual change. It seeks an answer to this question: what is the process by which members of any organization put away old behavior patterns and learn new ones?

ADMINISTRATIVE PSYCHOLOGY

"No matter how good a plan or an idea hatched by an administration may be, it is of little value until it becomes part of the consciousness and activity of the people."[8] Leighton developed this proposition as an observer of social change at a relocation camp in Poston, Arizona, where the U.S. government interned Japanese-Americans during the Second World War. Leighton found planning and decision making in organizations simple to understand in comparison with the problem of understanding how people learn new organizational habits. The camp directors would say "I know how these people feel" and make decisions for them. Leighton suggests that real change—in this case the goal of self-government in the camp— required patience, effective communication, and a willingness to work under conditions of stress, such as the illegal strike that the Japanese-Americans staged.

These challenges are the province of administrative psychology. Public administration has not developed a theory of administrative psychology that is as sophisticated as the various theories of decision making and authority. Nevertheless, a few key concepts may be extracted from occasional scholarly excursions into this area. The elements of an elementary theory of administrative psychology are the roles people play, their perceptions of reality, and the way in which people learn to adapt to the stress that inevitably accompanies change.

Role Behavior

People are obliged to play different roles within the organization. The roles they play, when there are demands for repeat performances, become habitual, reenforced by attitudes, and often difficult to change. Role behavior, consistently performed, is the foundation of all patterns of behavior within the organization.

Organizational roles are created as a result of the tension existing between the personalities of the employees and the role expectations that the organization places upon them. In general, the organization generates two sorts of expectations—one is dramaturgical and the other protects the equilibrium of the organization as a social system.

Like actors in a play, employees are expected to *dramatize* the roles they play in the organization. The purpose of dramaturgy, in general, is "to control the information imparted to others in order to control the impressions others form about us."[9] A good example is the use of dramaturgy to reenforce the deference patterns supporting the organizational hierarchy, as in the case of breaking in the new boss. Subordinates play games to show their deference to the new executive's ability, industry, impartiality, loyalty, and wisdom—the qualities expected of a highly placed executive. Realistically, of course, the subordinates know more about the work of the bureau than the executive does. They are veterans: the executive is new. They have relevant technical skills: he or she is a generalist with a few ideas. The aim of this game is for the subordinates to tell the new boss what to do while giving the outward appearance that they are receiving orders from the executive.

Dramaturgy is not all play acting. Often it is highly compatible

CHAPTER 2: HUMAN BEHAVIOR IN ORGANIZATIONS

with the employee's own cognitive style—that is, how the employee thinks about organizational life. Professional training has a significant influence on this sort of role playing. An engineer, a lawyer, a doctor, a politician, a labor union representative—all may work for the government, but each will have a different way of thinking about and controlling reality. Some of this is simple dramaturgy. Doctors wear white smocks as a uniform of cleanliness; lawyers take notes on long yellow paper. Other actions represent real differences in cognitive style. The doctor's approach to problem solving appears to be essentially diagnostic and curative. The lawyer seems to match advocacy with a concern for precise meaning and legal detail. At least that is how they appear to other people.

An organization cannot allow all of this role playing to go on willy-nilly. To maintain its equilibrium, the organization as a social system must insure that certain critical role functions are institutionalized in the behavior of its members. If the executive does not assign them, they will emerge spontaneously—or the organization will die. Talcott Parsons, the famous American sociologist, has suggested a list of the most essential functions. All organized systems, he says, must satisfy the prerequisites of adaptation, goal attainment, integration, and latent pattern management. Roughly translated, these are the administrative functions of specialization, planning, coordination, and adjudication. Some people must play the role of specialists who convert the resources of the organization into a useful product; others must engage in the politics of goal setting and the formulation of procedures to support these goals. Still others must use their knowledge and skills to integrate the disparate parts of the organization into a single system; while others must be in a position to resolve potential sources of conflict that might tear the system apart. Sociologists say that these functions are so essential that they become the primary source of role expectations in all social systems: agencies, governments, and societies as a whole.

Administrative Perceptions

Each person's perception of reality is conditioned by the roles he or she is expected to play. Since no important organization exists in which all members play the same role, one can surmise that a number of conflicting views of reality will coexist within the same organization.

An example may be useful. In his commentary on the American presidency, Theodore Sorensen insists that the president has a unique view of reality that no one in any other position can acquire. Nothing, says Sorensen, "can give anyone else his perspective."[10] Differences in perspective stem from differences in duty. No one else experiences the particular obligations—to the office, to constituents, to one's own hope for a place in history—that converge upon the chief executive. Likewise, the president is not likely to feel obligations that converge upon a cabinet secretary with different responsibilities.

57

Things that are vivid to the secretary of agriculture may be invisible to the president. Different job responsibilities create a different world view.

Since everyone's view of reality is a creation of their own particular situation, reality in public administration becomes completely relative. What one person perceives as rational may appear suboptimal to someone else in a different situation. One person's truth becomes another person's lie. Scientists may insist that "facts" exist and reveal those facts through scientific analysis, but "facts" in public administration exist only as a result of having passed through the perceptual keyhole of an administrator who has placed an interpretation upon them.

Each person brings to the job a perceptual grid for dealing with reality. The grid contains perceptual categories through which the person interprets events. There are categories for forming impressions of others, such as the stereotypes of doctors and lawyers mentioned above. There are categories for collecting and synthesizing information. There are categories for the organization itself—and for other organizations with which the person deals. Altogether, these perceptual categories constitute the *image* each person has of organizational reality. The image is the sum total of all the subjective knowledge the person has obtained.

Each person's image of reality will correspond to the repertory of patterned behaviors which the individual has acquired in life and his or her familiarity with them. The image also corresponds to the goals of the individual, his or her needs, and the roles he or she is expected to perform. If a message cannot be forced into an existing perceptual box, the person will search for ways of creating a new category that is compatible with the rest of the perceptual grid. Each new message tends to enlarge the image of messages one has already acquired.

As a rule, individuals tend to seek out messages that conform to the way they are already behaving. An executive who has just made a difficult decision will tend to seek out information that supports his or her choice—especially if the selection was between two unwelcome alternatives. No executive, however, can screen out all conflicting information. The decision maker may seek support only to receive information that raises doubts. Another person may be obliged, for the good of the cause, to defend an official position that he or she knows is not true. Few of us can escape propaganda that conflicts with our behavior, such as the health warnings on tobacco products. The result is what behavioral scientist Leon Festinger calls "cognitive dissonance"—knowledge inconsistencies.

Festinger has studied all sorts of abnormal cases of cognitive dissonance, such as a group of believers that was warned by aliens of a great flood from which the faithful were to be rescued by flying saucers. The aliens named place and date. Festinger recounts how the believers were driven to reconcile their image of the world with the troublesome fact that neither the flood nor the spaceships arrived. The believers sought out information that reconfirmed their faith, even though it conflicted with reality. They misinterpreted the meaning of events; they denied the validity of messages. Some actually believed the flood had occurred.

The critical variable in denying reality—for the believers—was the reenforcing properties of group support. The believers who waited in cohesive groups were most successful in blocking out troublesome facts and the situations that produced them. Believers who waited by themselves for the appointed interstellar journey—alone in their own back yards—quickly became disillusioned. In the absence of group support as a point of reference for their fantasies, individuals have to be offered fantastic rewards (or fantastic punishment) before they are able to simultaneously hold two conflicting beliefs and act upon them.

Learning Theory

If each person's image of reality is so resilient, then how does it change? How do people alter their perceptions, acquire new behavior patterns, learn new roles? Learning, say the social scientists, is a function of two things: the personal needs of each employee in the organization and their reaction to stress.

Where does the stress originate? The organization can create it by interfering with the routine. A frequent source of stress is role conflict, in which individual employees receive role expectations that they perceive to be punitive or ambiguous. Bureaucrats in contact with the public typically endure role conflict. They are expected to empathize with the needs of their clientele; simultaneously, they are expected to defend the organization against unreasonable demands. The stress generated by such situations is the basis of behavioral change.

Each person's response to stress—which is to say the propensity to learn—will tend to follow those patterns of adjustment which are most relevant to the needs of the individual. These are the needs as the individual, not the organization, perceives them.

Individuals differ enormously in terms of the personal needs they expect the organization to fulfill. Some need little more than security, privacy, and a steady paycheck. Some respond to group pressures and a sense of belongingness. Others are motivated by a need for status, esteem, or fame. Some are content only if all of their abilities are utilized in a challenging job. Whatever their needs—and the short-range goals they create—no person will learn new behavior patterns unless the rewards they receive are relevant to the needs that motivate the person at that instant. The organization can motivate people to change only if it understands these personal needs. Lyndon Johnson's friends said that he could manage people because he knew what all of his colleagues wanted. He knew their motives. He understood their ambitions and he knew exactly how far they would allow themselves to be pushed in order to get them.

In the short run, humans demonstrate considerable dexterity in adjusting to stress. They learn new behavior patterns; they enlarge their image of reality. But if that change is not promptly reenforced by rewards that bring the learners closer to the goals generated by their needs, they will cease to learn and will become frustrated. They will direct their energy toward blocking out the stress, lower their aspiration level, lose sight of initial goals, and reduce performance. Their anxiety may be directed outward, toward a scapegoat—either an animate or an inanimate object, such as "big government"—or it may be directed inward and in the form of self-depreciation.

Learning to adjust to an era of rapid change requires employees to develop an enlarged capacity for enduring stress. Institutional leaders can help to expand that capacity, but only if they know the breaking point between productive anxiety and general frustration. Here psychology gives way to administrative intuition. Managerial psychologists say that each individual's capacity for enduring stress depends upon training, experience, personality, physical stamina, and upon the sort of group support the person receives. There are no administrative formulas for determining exactly where that breaking point is.

CONFLICT AND POWER

Administrative psychology illuminates the enormous differences in behavior within complex organizations. Different people naturally have different perceptions of the same situation. They have different roles to play, different needs, different reactions to stress, and it is only natural that these differences should cause people to come into conflict. Conflict is one natural outgrowth of a healthy organization.

Conflict typically occurs between labor unions and management, especially now that public unions have established their ability to strike. In part these are struggles over resources; in part they arise because of irresolvable class conflicts between different people at different levels of the government. Management, with its weapons of authority, status, and ideology, typically attempts to define such sources of conflict out of existence. Ideology is particularly important. Workers are expected to accept an ideology that results in their subordination to "properly constituted authority." The prevailing managerial ideology in the West views organized work as a social value that brings inner satisfaction and salvation to lost souls. In other countries (or at other times) organized work has been sold as a social or religious duty. In sum, the ideology of administration seeks to bind public workers to the dominant white-collar beliefs of their managers.

A few social scientists have tried to show how the organization looks to the worker. If the organization is defined in terms of formal authority and status, then the workers have little claim to power because they know that legitimate authority and the dispensation of status are prerogatives that belong exclusively to the managers. So the worker sees his or her role in terms of how essential it is. The maintenance engineers who control the air conditioning in government office buildings may have little formal authority or status, but they perform a very essential function. If the bureau chief stays home, work continues as usual; if the engineer strikes on a hot day, everyone goes home. Industrial relations specialists such as Reinhard Bendix and Robert Dubin suggest that workers define the organization in terms of who performs the essential functions, since that is the best definition for establishing the power of the worker.

In general, scholars contributing to the behavioral movement in public administration have viewed the organization from the point of view of the manager, not the worker. Conflict, as a result, has gotten a bad name—or in social science terms, is viewed as an imbalance in organizational equilibrium. Melville Dalton, writing in *Men Who Manage,* suggests that social scientists "frequently do not get close enough to situations" to understand "the covert activities and the meaning assigned to them."[11]

Organizational conflict, says Dalton, is real. It arises because too many people want more than there is to be had—resources, promotions, or control over operations. Power struggles often arise over resources when top executives attempt to economize operations. The natural reaction of the bureau chiefs is to defend their own programs as essential and fight like hell to hold on to everything they have, even if that means sabotaging the executives. Power struggles frequently intervene in the promotion process, where advancement into the upper- and middle-management classes is based as much upon one's power as it is upon the rubbery standard of ability. Power struggles also arise from line-staff conflict—from the attempts of staff to aggrandize power for their executive, from the staff's difficulties in convincing the executive to punish deviation in the line, and from the stereotypes that the line and staff form of each other.

Without conflict, these power struggles could not be resolved. A few social scientists have argued for the benefits of conflict. Mary Parker Follett proposed a theory of "creative conflict" and Georg Simmel and Lewis Coser described what they called "the functions of social conflict." Coser set forth sixteen propositions on the importance of conflict in organization. His main points may be summarized as follows.

Conflict is essential for maintaining the identity of the organization. Every public agency needs combatant pressures from opponents in order to reaffirm its mission and reenlist the support of its members. This helps the agency delineate its boundaries within a changing world. The military needs a menace; the environmentalists need polluters; the police need criminals—or their organizations would fall apart. Conflict between employees *within* such agencies serves the same function. In the absence of a visible enemy, for example, the grunts at army boot camp learn to hate their drill sergeant, a hatred that builds group solidarity and helps the soldiers to identify with the organization. Later the conflict can be transferred to a foreign menace. Conflict between employees also helps to reenforce the formal hierarchy—by creating loyalties among persons who perform similar roles at similar levels in the organization.

Conflict is an essential safety valve. Conflict between people brings sources of hostility into the open where they can be resolved. Conflict between organizations protects against absurd perceptions of reality. If conflict is suppressed, if it is driven inward upon the individual or the group, the result is often a feeling of powerlessness, which leads to withdrawal. Submerged conflict encourages groups to create fantastic beliefs that are unchecked by contact with reality. This inevitably leads to the sort of rigidity that is symptomatic of bureaucracies in the worst sense, and eventually to unrealistic conflict. Unrealistic conflict, Coser says, is the release of tensions against phantom objects without the expectation of attaining specific results. Coser suggests that the closer the relationship between two people, the greater the potential for conflict—and thus the greater the need for friends to fight. This applies to chief executives and their advisers as well as to husbands and wives and close friends.

Conflict is an essential ingredient in molding the ideology, beliefs, and goals of the agency. When individuals fight against individuals, they tend to characterize their opponents as inherently evil. They tend to lose sight of their goals. When individuals stand as members of organizations in a power struggle, they become more realistic. Like lawyers representing clients, individuals representing organizations are more objective about the nature of the conflict. They begin to believe in the worth of their position and the inevitability of a prolonged conflict with opponents whose contrary beliefs cannot be changed. They become less merciful, less compromising, less willing to sell out their aims simply in order to terminate the conflict.

Strangely enough, such conflict does not drive opponents apart. Conflict is the great unifier. In the beginning, conflict brings the antagonists together to fight. It forces them to set up new administrative procedures and new norms so that they can institutionalize their conflict. It encourages them to seek out new associations—to make alliances with previously uncommitted groups that might alter the balance of power. Conflict helps maintain the balance of power giving each antagonist a true understanding of the comparative strength of its opponents, thereby serving to restrain antagonists from fantasies about their imagined invincibility—such as an impervious belief in total victory. After a protracted conflict, if the power balance continues, the primary antagonists, who have learned to deal with each other through controversy, may learn to work together in a grand coalition.

INSTITUTIONAL LEADERSHIP

At one level the modern organization can be thought of as a collection of human beings who expect to work together toward compatible goals. The organization charts, the long-range plans, the formal rules and statutes become mere formalities; they are only structure. The essence of the organization is the behavior of its people.

Organizational behavior cannot be reduced to a single principle. It is a way of thinking about organizations that requires an understanding of the social foundations of the organization. At the least, it requires the manager to perceive the basic elements of organizational behavior discussed in this chapter:

- *The Importance of Groups,* how they create the social fabric of administration and the degree to which group behavior supports or negates the formal mission of the organization;
- *The Social Basis of Authority,* primarily a matter of communications;
- *Why People Participate,* and how they make a "psychological contract" with the organization based on their role expectations;
- *The Concept of Patterned Behavior,* the behavioralist's organization chart;
- *Organizational Decision Making,* and why managers tend to seek out solutions that are less than optimal;
- *Heuristic Decision Making,* or what happens when satisficing behavior fails to solve the problem and the leadership must create new patterns of behavior for the organization;
- *Role Behavior, Perceptions, and Learning Theory,* and their influence in determining how the members respond to pressures for change; and
- *The Functions of Conflict* in resolving power struggles that inevitably arise in a complex organization.

Complex organizations tend to become more than the sum total of all the behavior patterns within them. Modern organizations, once successfully set in motion, tend to activate so effectively the behavior of their members that they speed toward a mission even after the purpose for which they were created disappears. It is far easier to convert one heretic than to reverse the course of a large organization.

When the behavior of its members mesh together, the complex organization becomes something special. It becomes more than a system of consciously coordinated activities, an early definition that would have to include certain indoor sports. It becomes an *institution,* or as one writer called it, a "big animal."[12]

The biological analogy has always had a certain appeal to administrative scholars as a convenient way of showing that the effective institution is more than the efficient functioning of its parts. A human lung can be technically efficient: it can even show a profit by dispersing more energy than it expends. Yet what a science of parts misses —whether it attempts to improve the health of lungs or of organizations—is the view of the parts of the system functioning together. The institution, like the living animal, is an adaptive social organ-

63

ism. Its parts function together to preserve the equilibrium of the organism, so that it might resist entropy and death. Its primary function, say many behavioral scientists, is to survive.

The equilibrium of the institution is maintained by the inducements that it can offer its members in return for their participation. Every employee receives various inducements to participate in the institution. In return, each employee makes certain contributions of effort or skill to the institution. Employees are motivated to participate when the inducements they receive—which may be any combination of economic, social or psychic rewards—consistently exceed the value of the contributions they are expected to make. Of course the employees do not balance these rewards on an electronic calculator; but just because the calculations are usually performed subconsciously does not mean that they are not made.

The contributions of all employees are the source from which the institution manufactures its inducements. The institution is *solvent* "so long as the contributions are sufficient to create inducements in large enough measure to draw forth these contributions."[13] When this happens, to use a favorite behavioral term, the institution is in a state of *equilibrium*.

Participants have a huge stake in the continued equilibrium of the institution—pay and security; a sense of accomplishment; friendships in informal groups; a sense of identity with the mission of their agency; and the hope that the accomplishment of the mission will enhance their own status and self-respect. In return, the institution makes the usual demands of loyalty.

This view of institutional life is known among social scientists as the open-systems approach. Open-systems theory may be viewed in general terms as the interaction between organizations and their environment; specifically, it stresses the need for the institution (the system) to respond to the needs of its environment by converting the contributions of its employees into a service or product for which a real demand exists. Human beings are at the heart of the conversion process. If they are not activated, the institution will not be able to produce a useful product. In that case, the institution will either wither away or become bureaucratic, generating false demands for its own products.

The job of the executive is to regulate the conversion process—to preserve and protect the unique capabilities of the members of the institution and make them relevant to their environment. In 1957 Philip Selznick, a sociologist, set forth this tenet in a book titled *Leadership in Administration*. Selznick argued for effective administrative leadership based upon an appreciation of behavioral principles. Institutional leaders, he said, must perform certain key tasks.

First, institutional leaders are responsible for defining the mission of the institution. For some leaders, this means little more than ascertaining what the organization's clients are willing to buy. Effective executives, Selznick argued, will do more. They will match this external expectation against the habits, skills, and ambitions of the members of the organization and mesh them. Effective executives will select missions and methods of accomplishing them that complement the talents of their employees.

No mission will become effective until it is embedded in the social consciousness of members of the institution. This is the most creative task the leader will face—the institutional embodiment of purpose.

An effective executive understands that the institution, as a complex system, is a collage of specialized groups and individuals. Each has its own values, its own skills, its own perception of the work of the institution. Because each has a special perspective, each makes special demands. The effective executive knows that these specialized demands are more powerful than any abstract notion of organizational *esprit de corps*. The institution is really a pattern of specialized parts, and the job of the executive is to insure that all of the particular perspectives and all of the particular specialties face in the same direction—so that they point toward the institutional mission, even if they do not swear allegience to one monolithic cause.

How can the executives influence these special perspectives? What tools does the institutional leader possess to infuse a complex institution with a sense of purpose?

Traditionally, executives rely upon formal prerogatives. They establish a general staff, an institutional core that can coordinate the formal organization and spot deviance from the institutional mission. They hire a chief of personnel who can help recruit people who fit the institutional purpose while conducting training programs for those people already in the organization. Executives hire planners who set up model programs and reward employees who adapt to expected behavior patterns.

Selznick does not place all of his eggs in the basket of managerial prerogatives. He recognizes that central controllers cannot combat all the special interest perspectives within the institution. To mobilize these special interests, Selznick suggests two additional strategies of institutional leadership: selecting the social base and bargaining with the interests.

Executives enjoy unusual advantages in selecting the social base of the institution. Because executives represent the institution, they have tremendous influence in determining the kind of environment within which the institution will operate. Such influence includes the identification of clients and allies, cooperation with similar institutions, and the selection of the basic technology that the institution will utilize. The behavior of each internal interest is checked by its interaction with outside clients, allies, legislators, other institutions, and even technology. To the extent that the executive can select the outsiders with whom the employees deal, and the conditions of their interaction, he or she can modify the behavior of people inside the institution.

The selection of the social base, however, is at best only an indirect control. Eventually the executive will have to bargain with the groups within the institution that have particular interests. In exchange for support toward institutional objectives, the executive can offer the groups the advantages they seek. Sometimes this requires the executive to compromise his or her own view of the mission to fit the attitudes of the members. The more the executive knows about these attitudes, the better his or her ability to offer the right inducements. For this reason, it is advantageous to secure the representation of internal interests on formal policy-making boards.

Bargaining inevitably brings conflict. The institutional executive thus acquires another task—retaining control over the boundaries of that conflict. This means that the executive sets the rules of the game—both formal appeal procedures and the informal limits on what sorts of open conflict the institution will tolerate. In order to achieve voluntary acceptance of adverse decisions, the leadership must convince conflicting groups to abide by the rules. Again, a fair system of representation is essential, but it cannot displace the executive's responsibility to maintain a balance of power that serves the institutional mission.

Finally, the effective executive has the primary responsibility for defending the integrity of the institution: its state of being. Organizations are unique social systems that have expended great energy mobilizing people to work together. It is only natural that they should continue to exercise their capabilities after the task for which they were originally created has been accomplished. When the March of Dimes achieved its goal—the discovery of a vaccine for polio—it did not disband. It had expended too much human energy in its own creation, so it found new diseases to cure. The most essential task of administrative leadership is to maintain the values and distinctive identity of the organization, not for the sake of sheer survival, or for some temporary task, but so that its members can continue to perform useful functions for society. It is here, says Selznick, that "the intuitively knowledgeable leader and the administrative analyst often part company, because the latter has no tools to deal with it."[14] It is here that the mechanistic application of administrative formulas defer to a full understanding of the behavioral basis of administration.

FOR FURTHER READING

The literature on organization theory is overwhelming, both in its volume and in the difficulty of its language. The novice might begin with Herbert Simon, *Administrative Behavior* (New York: Macmillan Co., 1947), a pioneering study on administrative decision making; George C. Homans, *The Human Group* (New York: Harcourt, Brace & Co., 1950), an early attempt to establish a general theory of group behavior; or Harold J. Leavitt's more recent study, *Managerial Psychology: An Introduction to Individuals, Pairs and Groups in Organizations* (Chicago: University of Chicago Press, 1964). Scholars tend to see each of these as separate approaches to the field: formal organization theory, group behavior, and administrative psychology. The neglected approach—class and power—is well represented by Lewis

A. Coser, *The Functions of Social Conflict* (New York: The Free Press, 1956). The advanced student would also want to look at Chester I. Barnard, *The Functions of the Executive* (Cambridge, Mass.: Harvard University Press, 1938), the book that launched the behavioral revolution in administration.

The following books are important as treatments of special problems in organization theory: Alexander Leighton, *The Governing of Men* (Princeton, N.J.: Princeton University Press, 1945), on patterned behavior and social change in a Japanese-American relocation camp; Melville Dalton, who looks at organization theory as a problem of political power in *Men Who Manage* (New York: John Wiley & Sons, 1959); William J. Gore, *Administrative Decision-Making: A Heuristic Model* (New York: John Wiley & Sons, 1964); Amitai Etzioni, *A Comparative Analysis of Complex Organizations* (New York: The Free Press, 1961), one of the few behaviorists to create different theories for different organizations; and Leon Festinger, *A Theory of Cognitive Dissonance* (Stanford, Calif.: Stanford University Press, 1957), a psychological study of how persons select information. Philip Selznick ties the different perspectives together in his advice to executives in *Leadership in Administration: A Sociological Interpretation* (New York: Row, Peterson, 1957).

For more detailed summaries of the behavioral approach one could consult any of the following books. James G. March and Herbert Simon wrote *Organizations* (New York: John Wiley & Sons, 1958) as an inventory of the field at the height of the behavioral revolution. Their findings are brought up to date in the anthology by Albert H. Rubenstein and Chadwick J. Haberstroh, eds., *Some Theories of Organization*, rev. ed. (Homewood, Ill.: Richard D. Irwin, Inc., 1966). One of the most popular anthologies is James G. March, ed., *Handbook of Organizations* (Chicago: Rand McNally & Co., 1965); it opens with an excellent summary of the field. Bertram M. Gross translates organization theory into practical administration in his nine-hundred-page, two-volume study, *The Managing of Organizations: The Administrative Struggle* (New York: The Free Press, 1964). The text most responsible for promoting the "open systems" approach to behavioral theory is Daniel Katz and Robert L. Kahn, *The Social Psychology of Organizations* (New York: John Wiley & Sons, 1966). The rich diversity of the field is captured in the papers published by Mason Haire, ed., *Modern Organization Theory* (New York: John Wiley & Sons, 1959).

PROBLEMS

Chapter 1 described how organizations are usually set up, and Chapter 2 told how people in them are likely to behave. This is important, but it is not the heart and soul of public administration. The actual business of government revolves around two special characteristics. First, the overwhelming majority of government programs are conducted through bureaucracies. Second, despite all of the attempts to separate politics from administration, a large number of administrators find themselves involved in political affairs. In general, these characteristics create problems for public administrators. Bureaucratic organizations, despite their potential for technical efficiency, often degenerate, become overly rigid and unresponsive to change. The politics of administration creates difficulties by obligating bureaucrats to seek political support, build coalitions, and share control of the program with groups that are outside the executive branch.

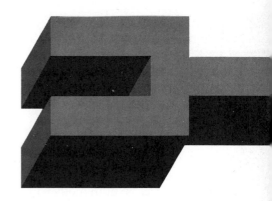

PROBLEMS OF BUREAUCRACY

3

Bureaucrats are the pariahs of modern government. No state seems to want them, yet none can get along without them. Bureaucracy gets the blame for red tape, clumsy regulation, and policy blunders. It is called the dead hand of government. Bureaucrats are accused of behaving like public tyrants instead of public servants. Bureaucracy means big, unresponsive government, a program that doesn't work, an agency that no one can control.

Nevertheless, modern public administration is practically synonymous with bureaucratic management. Nearly all government programs are executed through bureaus, and the science of administration arose ninety years ago in conjunction with efforts to improve management in bureaucracies. Most principles of "good administration" tend to make the agency more bureaucratic, not less.

Why has the bureaucratic form of organization become the dominant methodology for executing the public's business? Why does this purportedly superior form of organization become so pathological, and can it be cured? What are the costs of bureaucratic government in the democratic state? This chapter looks for the answers to these questions in the research and practice of modern administration.

BUREAUCRACY DEFINED

Public administration is as old as village government. According to the latest archaeological estimates, that gives the profession a life span of nine thousand years. Archaeologists suggest that administration arose around permanent agricultural settlements because of the need to store the surplus of food and construct fortifications strong enough to protect it. Those tasks created the need for a managerial class that could assign workers specialized tasks, plot out some system of coordination, and maintain an organizational hierarchy through appropriate methods of authority.

70

Of the thousands of societies faced with the need to establish some well-ordered system of administration, only a fraction have sought to organize a permanent civil service along bureaucratic lines. In large empires of conquest—the Hellenistic, Mongolian, and Germanic—affairs of state were conducted through personal trustees, table companions, or court servants, not bureaucrats. The Carolingians and the caliphs constructed impressive organizations, yet their systems of administration were essentially patrimonial and prebendal. The Holy Roman Empire lasted upwards of ten centuries, yet never established a large, permanent bureaucracy.

Historically, bureaucratic systems of public administration have arisen only under special conditions to satisfy special needs. Despite the preponderant overrepresentation of bureaucratic administration among modern states, not all public organizations are bureaucratic. An organization is not bureaucratic unless, by definition, it possesses special structural characteristics designed to maximize efficiency in pursuit of established goals. The most important structural characteristics are a permanent class of civil servants with clearly defined duties, whose authority is officially fixed by law, and record keeping, so that past decisions can be used as the basis for future administrative actions. The result is a system of administration that can provide routine, uninterrupted services where officials are prone to emphasize operational effectiveness and rational behavior over other organizational values.

The first Western society to adopt the bureaucratic solution, four thousand years after the appearance of village government in the fertile crescent, was ancient Egypt. The Egyptians were master builders, which made them master organizers. They organized to build a civilization that farmed by flood watching and irrigation rather than by rainfall, which was not possible without calendar making, astronomy, mathematics, and record keeping on the rise and fall of the Nile. Record keeping led to efforts to calculate the labor potential of the country in an annual census and to record the financial transactions of the government in an office of the Treasury. A permanent class of administrators, assisted by scribes, was created to write the technical regulations governing the system of hydraulic management, which were passed down through a rigid hierarchy to officials in the field. Once the top officials, backed by their scribes, learned how to organize the population to execute the irrigation plans, it was a simple matter to enlist the people to build the tombs and temples that remain the hallmark of Egyptian civilization. It was a relatively static system of organization, but it lasted three thousand years.

The Athenian Greeks created a system of democratic administration that remains the model for one alternative to bureaucratic government. The Athenians refused to establish a permanent civil service, except for a few messengers, dock inspectors, and record keepers. The vast majority of administrative posts were held by ordinary citizens. When one leather merchant criticized the handling of a military campaign, the assembly elected him general and told him to

71

finish off the job. It was altogether a government of amateurs. Generals, ministers, and financial officers were elected to their posts annually or selected by lot. Most were confined to a term of a single year and prohibited from holding the same office twice. Excessive accumulation of executive authority was checked by the assembly of all citizens, which channeled all matters of administrative policy through elected councils of five hundred, fifty, and ten. The size of the city-state (Athens had only fifty thousand citizens), the emphasis upon education, plus the intense preoccupation of the Greeks with self-government, all contributed to the success of this early model of democratic administration. Death, war, and the plague wore it down, and the Athenian ideal eventually gave way to a society of specialists and a government run by professionals.

The typical medieval system of administration was the court, another alternative to bureaucracy. Administrative functions were assigned to friends in the military following or personal household of the king. They organized the supplies, managed the finances, and kept the records, all on an ad hoc basis. They followed the King, who traveled constantly, administering the affairs of the realm, dispensing justice, and collecting revenues. For major undertakings, such as a military campaign, the court would mobilize the lords, who were generally unwilling to leave their lands for more than ninety days at a time. This modest system of public administration fit neatly into the institution of feudalism under which most of the functions of government, such as the coining of money, were decentralized to fiefs created by the King. Obligations between kings, lords, and vassals were strictly personal, based on a pledge of loyalty, binding between the people involved only so long as they lived and upheld the contract. There was no conception of official authority as distinct from personal loyalty and little motivation to divide up the duties of administration into permanent, well-delineated offices. The system sounds medieval, but in fact is still practiced in twentieth-century institutions like the White House, whose fluid style of organization is essentially courtlike rather than bureaucratic.

The development of modern bureaucracy began when the kings, responding to the forces of nationalism and their own ambitions, began to station their own assistants at permanent locations to manage affairs of state, particularly financial affairs. These officials, separated from the household, provided the king with an organization powerful enough to extend his control over the crumbling feudal institutions.

> The state was essentially a "private enterprise," a "business." At its center was military force, in many ways increasingly "bureaucratic." The emerging civil bureaucracy had essentially two tasks: to feed and arm the military and to administer the king's realm, conceived basically as his property. The military and the civil were inextricably joined in one "enterprise," the military being a means to protect and enlarge the realm, the realm a means of supporting and improving the military.[1]

CHAPTER 3: PROBLEMS OF BUREAUCRACY

Bureaucratic management advanced considerably in France under the monarchy; Napoleon improved and consolidated it. The formation of a unified Germany under Bismarck in 1871 was accomplished by consolidating administrative functions around the Prussian bureaucracy. Both of these classical bureaucratic systems survived the political turbulence that followed and remain relatively unchanged today.

The importance of the Prussian bureaucracy in the development of the modern German state encouraged one German scholar to write an essay setting forth the theory underlying this special organizational form, an essay which today still constitutes the best definition of the structure of bureaucracy. The scholar was Max Weber, who lived at the turn of the century and possessed what historians call a Renaissance mind. He avoided the prison of mental specialization by studying medieval business operations, Roman agricultural practices, Buddhism and Hinduism, industrial psychology, economic history, political parties, historical jurisprudence, the Russian Revolution, the Hebrew prophets, and ancient China. He helped to draft the constitution of the Weimar Republic; constructed the theory of sociology that underlies one wing of the modern behavioral sciences; and wrote various social, economic, and cultural interpretations of world history. And he wrote that short essay on the coming of bureaucracy, although when placed in charge of a hospital during World War I he refused to run it along bureaucratic lines.

Weber was not abstract; he lived his own theories. He had a bitter argument with his father, after which his father died. Weber felt so guilty that he refused to lecture, maintaining that his back and arms were paralyzed. He was so depressed that in four and one-half years

Max Weber was an established expert on sociology, history, law, politics, economics, and religion. In 1911 he wrote his famous essay on bureaucracy, defining its principal characteristics and predicting that these characteristics would enable bureaucracies to achieve a higher degree of efficiency than any other form of organization. COURTESY OF THE GERMAN INFORMATION CENTER.

he was able to publish only one book review. On a tour of the United States, after seeing Chicago, he suddenly recovered, and on returning to Heidelberg expurgated his guilt by writing a book on the significance of religious anxiety in creating the industrial revolution. In travel and hard work, Weber sought escape from his fits of depression. "If I don't work until one o'clock, I can't be a professor."[2] He died of pneumonia, at the age of fifty-six, during a period of intense productivity in Munich.

Weber wrote his famous "Essay on Bureaucracy" in 1911. In it, he discusses the structure of the bureaucratic form of organization as he witnessed it emerging in European governments during the last half of the nineteenth century. This is what he saw.

Fixed Authority and Official Jurisdictions

The authority of all individuals in a modern bureaucracy is based upon a specific grant of power to an official office. The powers, jurisdiction, and regular activities of each office are ordered by laws or administrative regulations that are written and published. Provision is contained in the rules for the continuous fulfillment of the duties of *offices*. Ideally, any person can walk out of a bureaucracy and not be missed. The office is permanent; the person is not, and doesn't count. Historically, the practice of vesting authority in offices instead of people has been the exception, not the dominant method of doing business in affairs of state. The older practice requires the office holder to possess some traditional virtues, such as age, or charismatic qualities, which become the basis of his or her authority. In the modern bureaucracy, traditional and charismatic authority are replaced by bureaucratic authority, in which the power of officeholders is based wholly on the "properly constituted authority" residing in the office which they happen to occupy.

Written, Formal Rules

The management of the bureau is based on rules. The job of the bureaucrat is to discern the essential element in a situation and apply the appropriate organizational rule. The rules and the history of their application are written down and preserved in the files. The expert knowledge necessary to operate the bureau requires special training in the use of the rules. "The reduction of modern office management to rules is deeply embedded in its nature."[3]

Impersonality

In medieval courts, public administrators were considered personal servants of the king. Vassals administered local government as part of their personal farming operations. Even today, in many developing countries, public officials are allowed to maintain businesses on the side. Bureaucracy was supposed to change all this. "In principle, the executive office is separated from the household, business from private correspondence, and business assets from private fortunes."[4] Bureaucrats are expected to apply the rules impersonally, without regard to their own interests, the special features of the case, the status of the clientele, bestowals of favor, or traditional values.

A Hierarchy of Offices

All forms of organization provide for some system of hierarchy. The bureaucratic organization is unique insofar as it establishes the hierarchy in the arrangement of the offices: the empty boxes on the organization chart. The power of any official to oversee another depends completely upon their relative position in the official hierarchy; it has nothing to do with their personal skills or competence. In the purely bureaucratic organization, all relationships between persons —from the delegation of authority to the appealing of decisions—are regulated by the rule of hierarchy.

Career Service

In the history of human affairs, most governments have been run by persons who are temporary in their posts. In a bureaucracy, office holding becomes a vocation, requiring professional training, special knowledge, and an eternal devotion of one's energies to the affairs of the organization. For the bureaucrat, "entrance into an office is considered an acceptance of a specific obligation of faithful management in return for a secure existence."[5] As career servants, bureaucrats are expected to be loyal to their office, its purpose and rules. They are "not considered the personal servant of a ruler," even though they are subordinate to the political executive."[6] For this the bureaucrats receive a fixed salary based on their rank, tenure for life, a pension as old-age security, and at least the promise of promotion to higher office, generally on the basis of seniority.

Permanence

The bureaucratic system sets up a web of power that is almost impossible to destroy. Its institutions become permanent because the bureaucracy provides a continuous service deemed essential to the proper functioning of the state. The masses depend upon the continuity of the bureaucracy for their material fate; if its services are interrupted, chaos results. The individual bureaucrat cannot change the purpose of the bureaucracy because he "is chained to his activity by his entire material and ideal existence."[7] Neither can the political rulers, who, Weber predicted, would increasingly find themselves in the positions of dilettantes unable to change the course of government because they lacked the technical skill to challenge officialdom. Even though the bureaucracy would serve the rulers, its objective, impersonal character would assure that the rulers would not be able to alter its goals.

75

Secrecy

Every bureaucracy attempts to keep its knowledge and intentions secret. The expert knowledge generated through the work of the bureaucracy, after all, is the main source of bureaucratic power, so why should the bureaucrats be expected to share this knowledge with amateurs? Weber correctly predicted that bureaucrats would be reluctant to share knowledge acquired through bureaucratic channels with legislators and public interest groups. He foresaw the demise of the legislative branch in the administrative state and prophesied that only private economic interests would be able to amass sufficient knowledge to compete with the public bureaucracy.

Weber's definition of bureaucracy closely resembles the principles of administration advocated by Fayol and Gulick. Weber often gets the credit (and the blame) for promoting bureaucratic methods of management. In fact, Weber was not an advocate of bureaucratic administration. He simply offered what scholars call an ideal-type model, an analytical tool to help experts classify organizational types and analyze the emergence of this dominant form of organization. Practitioners, of course, took the "ideal" characteristics of bureaucracy to mean "the best," and strengthened the formal side of administration in the hope of making it more bureaucratic.

Indirectly, at least, Weber encouraged the view that bureaucracies are best. A fully developed bureaucracy, he advised, would be technically superior to any other type of organization. The elements of efficiency—"precision, speed, unambiguity, knowledge of the files, continuity, discretion, unity, strict subordination, reduction of friction and of material and personal costs—these are raised to the optimum point in the strictly bureaucratic administration."[8] Nevertheless, Weber stressed that the superiority of bureaucracies was strictly technical. Bureaucracies were objectionable on other grounds —they tended to dehumanize personal relations and had the power to close the era of representative government.

So why have so many modern governments done what so many ancient governments refused to do—make the bureaucratic form the dominant method of public administration? Weber suspected that something more than their technical superiority was involved, that the answer to the question "why bureaucracies?" depended more upon the economic and social climate underlying the modern state.

THE ORIGINS OF MODERN BUREAUCRATIC ADMINISTRATION

To probe the causes behind the ascendency of bureaucratic government in the modern state, Weber reached back into his knowledge of ancient history. The Romans, he remembered, had inherited an avocational system of administration from the Greeks. Even at the height of the early empire, there was no colonial office in Rome. Provincial governors were sent out from Rome to serve for a single year, and the size of their administrative staffs was severely restricted. Julius Caesar tried to create a permanent civil service and failed.

Augustus and Hadrian succeeded, and by the reign of Diocletian, the civil service had developed into a full-scale bureaucracy that contributed as much to the fall of Rome as did the corruption of its rulers. The Roman bureaucracy suppressed civil liberties, dominated weak rulers, and forced the enactment of special taxes to finance its burgeoning machinery. In this last fact Weber found the clue he was looking for. The Romans, he concluded, simply could not afford a permanent civil service. Rome and her provinces were not far enough removed from a subsistence economy to support a large, expanding bureaucracy. A developed money economy, capable of sustained economic growth, seemed essential to the survival of bureaucratic administration.

A developing economy carries with it the supposition that citizens can raise themselves well above the subsistence level by producing a surplus of food and commodities. This surplus, in the form of money, provides the constant source of income necessary to pay the salaries of career officials. The need for revenue, moreover, creates pressures upon the state to develop a rational system of public finance, which in turn encourages executives to organize their financial experts into a bureaucracy. In the absence of a developed money economy, the organization of public affairs will generally be overcome by tendencies favoring collegial administration, except in the military, where the nature of the task favors bureaucratization.

Citizens in a postsubsistence economy find their material state substantially improved through economic development. Rulers in newly emerging states, however, may continue to use privilege as a policy of administration and distribute services on the basis of personal whim or traditional status. The bourgeoisie, insecure in its newly acquired wealth, rebels against unstable political rule. Unstable administration, they sense, leads to unstable economies. Bureaucracy, with its stress upon the stable, expert, impersonal enforcement of written rules, seems like a divine promise to the newly emerging middle class. Weber concluded that the demands of a large middle class for the benefits of a mass democracy were a second prerequisite of bureaucratic development. By mass democracy he meant the thrust toward social and economic equality, not the more recent democratic ideal of extended suffrage.

It is interesting that bureaucratic organizations are accused of homogenizing individual differences as if this were one of their faults. As Weber noted, bureaucratic development was closely associated with the rebellion against the practice of granting special privileges. If privileges are the sort of freedom that critics of bureaucracy languish for, then clearly bureaucracies can be criticized for ignoring individual distinctions.

Weber recognized that a developing money economy and a mass democracy could not, by themselves, account for the rapid ascendency of bureaucratic government in the modern state. He knew that these prerequisites were merely the fertile soil of bureaucratic government, not its causes. Weber traced the causes to the human motivations arising from the Protestant ethic and the spirit of capitalism.

The prevailing philosophy of capitalism defined the advance of civilization as the survival of the fittest in the marketplace of commerce, a strained analogy drawn from Darwin's theory of evolution. To conquer their competitors, army and industry generals needed the highly efficient form of organization that bureaucracy provided. Capitalism supplied the motivation—or the excuse, depending upon your point of view—to subvert human values to the necessities of production and organization. When the competitors were replaced by cartels, bureaucratic principles gave the corporation the capacity to accomplish economic planning on the scale necessary to preserve a stable market for goods and services.

Bureaucratic government, from this point of view, grew up in conjunction with bureaucratic capitalism. Capitalists demanded that corporate principles of administration be transferred to public agencies by industrial leaders brought in "to make government more businesslike." Capitalists demanded governments that were strong and stable, governments that could promote credit, coin money, and promote the domestic tranquillity that was a prerequisite to prosperity through corporate planning. Tyrants, pirates, and crusaders might be more exciting than the civil servant with the green eyeshade, but they were also far too unsettling for the economic system.

Capitalism and bureaucratic organization were in turn strengthened by the psychology of work arising from sixteenth-century religious radicalism. According to Weber, Martin Luther gave bureaucracy its starting shove when he tacked those ninety-five theses on the door of the Wittenberg church. The Reformation, guided by the religious doctrine of the Puritans, created a spiritual climate in which bureaucracy could thrive. The early Protestants believed that everyone's spiritual fate was secretly predestined. Only those born into the elect would escape the fires of hell. One could identify the elect here on earth by their devotion to good works. The anxiety of worrying about one's fate, Weber said, caused the Puritans to work too hard, to devote themselves to a worldly asceticism, and to pursue their worldly vocations *religiously*—at least so long as it took their minds off the burning question. The doctrine stood in stark contrast to the monasticism of the Catholic faith, with its stress upon a Pope and priests to act as spiritual policemen and forgive sins.

Weber saw in the Protestant ethic a revolution in human affairs—a transformation from an insular feudalism to a worldly asceticism. Protestantism provided a social rationale that became the basis for accepting rational planning, personal discipline, technology, and bureaucratic organization. In this Weber provides the great antithesis to the theories of Karl Marx, who saw the rise of capitalism as a result of the profit motive and some rather favorable economic conditions for the middle class, such as the availability of rare metals, expanding markets, population growth, technology, and new possibilities for accumulating capital. Weber insists that we would have never had the idea to create a capitalistic, materialistic society without the Protestant ethic. Weber also recognized that once people became accustomed to the joys of materialism, capitalism would be stripped of its religious significance and stand on its own merits. He predicted that this orgy of organized consumption would occur first in America.

THE INFORMAL SIDE OF BUREAUCRACY

Weber's essay on bureaucracy is an ideal theory. It focuses on the formal side of bureaucracy and sees organizational life from the point of view of a theorist standing high above the sweep of history. It must necessarily be amended by the observations of social scientists who observe the workings of fully developed bureaucracies firsthand.

Social scientists observe that there is more to bureaucracy than the rules and structure of Weber's ideal theory. Informal patterns of behavior are as important to the proper functioning of large-scale bureaucracies as are the formal, written rules. One cannot exist without the other. Informal activity, when it functions in concert with the formal bureaucracy, facilitates the search for efficiency and helps to prevent organizational rigor mortis.

One social scientist, Alvin Gouldner, immersed himself in the informal structure of a factory owned and operated by the General Gypsum Company near the village of Oscar Center in the Great Lakes region of midwestern America. The community was a typical T-shirted, beer-drinking, volunteer-fire-department, amateur-league-baseball town where families that moved in twenty-five years ago were still considered newcomers.

When Gouldner and his student assistants arrived to study the gypsum plant they found what could be termed at best an "indulgency pattern" of rules. The plant manager, Old Doug, wasn't too strict. The only person he ever fired was a prizefighter who kept punching out employees who kidded him about his consistent string of losses at the local Saturday night bouts. Workers in the plant where the gypsum board was made were allowed to take out materials to do home repairs. In the mine, where men worked to bring gypsum out of narrow tunnels in the earth, the indulgency pattern was even more fixed. The miners were traditional, pragmatic, tough men who would not submit to formal authority because they had taught themselves the skills they needed to survive in their high-risk job.

Old Doug died one day. His lieutenants felt that Johnson, the board-building superintendent, was the legitimate heir to the job. The company directors at the Lakeport headquarters ignored the lieutenants and picked Vincent Peele, an outsider. The directors sent him to Oscar Center with instructions to hike up production at the plant.

Peele arrived at Oscar Center and fired a plant veteran with twenty years of seniority—for removing a case of dynamite from the plant for the annual fishing holiday. Peele replaced the personnel and safety manager, a man who had hardly finished grade school, with a

79

college student who had a passion for paperwork. When the old lieutenants shunned Peele, and worked against him, Peele and his assistant tightened up the rules. Peele told the workers he was only carrying out orders from the Lakeport office. In effect, Peele *bureaucratized* the plant. It was the only way that he could control it. The result was a stand off between Peele and the lieutenants.

Under the ground, the miners ignored Peele. Because of their informal solidarity, and because Peele knew little about mining except that it was dangerous, the miners were hardly affected by the bureaucratization of the plant.

Gouldner concluded that three distinct varieties of bureaucracy existed within the Oscar Center General Gypsum Company. Each variety was a result of the informal activity of the men and their bosses.

Gouldner calls the first variety a *mock bureaucracy*. It had all the structural characteristics of Weber's ideal model, but nobody paid any attention to them. Written rules existed but were often ignored. An example would be the rule against taking materials from the plant without paying for them. When Peele decided to enforce this rule, he created a *punishment-centered bureaucracy*. He enforced the rule, and the workers resisted—first by ignoring the rule and then by isolating Peele by not talking to him. Then the labor unions adopted the punishment-centered strategy as well by forcing the adoption of rules for hiring and promotion on the basis of seniority. Peele did not like these rules and he resisted them by using merit standards whenever he could get away with it.

When the formal rules and the informal groups work in concert, Gouldner says, a *representative bureaucracy* is produced. An example was the safety program. Peele legitimized it by tying it to production. Workers liked it because it reduced danger, prevented hernias, kept up their income, and added to the general cleanliness of the plant. Since their own lives were involved, the workers zealously enforced the safety rules on accident-prone employees through informal, social controls. Peele and the supervisors cooperated by holding periodic meetings with the workers during which modifications in the written safety rules were considered.

The obvious question—for production-minded managers and work-oriented employees—is how to create a representative bureaucracy. What are the conditions under which informal groups will work in concert with formal rules to facilitate organizational goals? Gouldner never answered this question. He left that task to Peter Blau, a sociologist who applied Weber's model to two public agencies.

Public executives always seem to be trying to improve the performance of their agencies, usually by thinking up new rules. They reorganize the offices, restructure operations, and use incentives and punishments to promote compliance with the rules. What happens?

Blau explained what happened in the two agencies. One was a law enforcement agency whose employees were investigating commercial firms suspected of violating federal law. The other was a state employment agency. In both agencies, the executives attempted to improve performance by selective alteration of the rules. They tried to be bureaucrats.

In the employment agency, the executives set up a system requiring employees to report how many applicants they placed on jobs. To make their records look better, some employees would hide job requests underneath their desk blotters until the right person came to them. It did not matter that the employee next to them might be interviewing an applicant that fit the bill. Each employee did what was necessary to raise his or her own productivity.

The situation in the law enforcement agency was more complex. All of the agents faced the same difficult decision—whether to prosecute or negotiate with a company violating the law. Naturally, the agents wished to consult with each other on the matter, but the rules prohibited this. The rules said: if you have a problem, see your superior. The superiors would refer the problem to a specialist, or give the advice themselves. Of course no agent wanted to admit that he or she had a problem.

A number of employees in each agency were distressed by these developments. These employees created an informal solution. They adopted work-facilitating behavior that deterred them from giving an irrational response to a rational rule.

In the state employment agency, the employees cooperated—at least half of them did, by deciding to share information informally. This decision increased productivity for the group as a whole.

The federal enforcement agents solved their problem by ignoring the rule. They consulted with each other, even on the routine problems they faced daily. This solution transformed the agents into a cohesive work group, raised the self-confidence of each agent, improved the quality of decisions, and contributed to efficiency. It also violated the rule.

In both cases cohesive work groups provided the support that the employees needed in order to promote the work of the bureau by making informal adjustments in the formal rules. Effective bureaucratic performance requires strong work groups, especially if the work of the bureau is complex. Executives cannot promote productivity simply by insisting that individuals closely follow the rules.

How does the executive promote cohesive work groups in the bureau? Cohesive work groups will not develop, Blau says, unless employees are reasonably secure in their jobs. "The insecurity engendered by the knowledge that his job hangs in the balance constrains the employee to adhere closely to familiar and officially sanctioned procedures and to avoid taking risks." The solution, says Blau, is to encourage workers to develop "fully internalized rigorous standards of workmanship." These will not develop unless management evaluates employees upon the basis of clearly specified results. If employees "are qualified, it is probably enough to standardize the end products of their operations and not the precise ways they arrive at them. Evaluation on the basis of clearly specified results encourages ingenuity and simultaneously assures the standardization necessary for effective bureaucratic operation."[9] To promote this sort of evaluation and to insure that it does not lead back to job insecurity, Blau suggests that managerial authority be split so that the persons who supervise and evaluate the work of employees are removed from the office that sets salaries, employment procedures, and general working conditions. The latter might be a separate civil service commission or a public labor union. The result of such reforms, Blau says, will be a reduction in personal anxiety accompanied by a willingness among employees to exercise personal initiative in the execution of difficult tasks.

Blau is concerned about a central tendency in Weber's model— the tendency to create the kind of anxiety that destroys individual initiative. Such anxiety is created by managers who fall back upon formal authority because they cannot lead their employees. The naked exercise of formal authority to enforce the rules creates a punishment-centered bureaucracy, akin to the ancient military practice of stationing a sergeant behind advancing soldiers to shoot retreaters, enforcing the belief that the worst thing that can happen to you always will be executed by your own organization. This always results in bureaucratization in the vulgar sense of the word and suggests why an ideal model of bureaucracy, ideally exercised, can produce such undesirable results.

The ability to create anxiety among employees is a powerful weapon in the managerial bag of tricks. In the eyes of employees, it encourages them to enforce the rules without any regard for the reason that the rules were written. The consequences of such behavior are explored in the following sections on bureaucratic pathology.

BUREAUCRATIC ANXIETY AND ITS EFFECTS

People learn to behave like bureaucrats in order to avoid the anxiety attached to their jobs. Organizational anxiety motivates the employee to avoid disfavor and seek gratification. The organization reveals the desired behavior, and the individual adjusts to it. Depending upon the individual's personality and ambitions, but mainly the situation at work, he or she may adjust in ways that are detrimental to the purposes of the organization. In short, the individual may become a bureaucrat.

Bureaucratic organizations cannot function without the creation of some personal anxiety. Without the use of anxiety, they could not maintain allegiance to the system of organized authority. The problem arises because of the artificial nature of authority in bureaucratic organizations. As Max Weber observed, people are prone to defer to three types of authority: traditional authority, which is based on custom; charismatic authority of the sort that entices people to follow those who exhibit superhuman qualities; and legal-rational authority. Of the three, legal-rational authority is the most compatible with the operation of a bureaucracy. It is also the most artificial. While charismatic and traditional authority are tightly attached to the persons possessing them, the legal-rational style vests authority in formal offices through legal formulas. It is essentially a fiction, nothing more than a hollow box on the organization chart. Seen through the perspective of traditional or charismatic values, the person exercising legal-rational authority may be a nincompoop. His or her personal authority may be nonexistent.

In order to encourage respect for legal-rational authority, the bureaucracy must create certain organizational rituals. The executives could, of course, maintain that respect through naked force. Few executives, however, want to admit that they control the behavior of their employees so closely. Subtleness is the rule. To accomplish this, most bureaucracies strive to make legal-rational authority palatable through rituals. These rituals are the methods by which bureaucracies legitimize their manipulation of employees or, as the social psychologists say, motivate employees to internalize deference toward authority within their own personal norms.

What are the rituals? First, all organizations attempt to legitimize their authority by evoking allegiances, such as patriotism. One can be patriotic towards a program or an industry as well as a nation: "What's good for General Motors is good for the U.S.A."

Another psychological ritual used by big organizations is unanimity. The bureaucracy promotes the illusion that its members unanimously support agency policy—once that policy is established.

The most important rituals supporting bureaucratic authority are contained in the status system. In effect, the organization calculates what it is that its employees covet and then gives more of it to those who occupy the positions of higher authority. In America, the conventional symbols are a big house, an expense account, and an office on the top floor with a carpet and a window. In the future it might be gasoline and personal security.

All of these rituals serve a useful purpose. The status system reduces ambiguity; it clarifies the official hierarchy. If all the employees had the same status, much time would be lost discovering who was in charge. At the same time, these rituals produce personal anxiety since employees are never really quite sure whether they are making the right moves.

Unfortunately, status anxiety is a natural byproduct of the uncertainty younger employees endure as they try to move up the promotion ladder. The executives hope that employees will adjust to that anxiety in ways that fit the organizational purpose, by being ambitious, loyal, or showing initiative. Some employees, however, may find the anxiety of the promise of status so overpowering that they adopt defenses—becoming, for example, overly methodical or bureaucratic. They walk a tightrope between turning anxiety into productive ambition and yielding to the frustrations that lead to what is known in country-club circles as the nervous breakdown. When intense anxiety over one's job security becomes entwined with power-

83

ful pressures to succeed, the stage is set for the severest pathological consequences.

Perhaps the strangest story of individual adaptation to bureaucratic anxiety is "The Metamorphosis," a dreamlike tale told by the novelist Franz Kafka about a salesman named Gregor Samsa. Samsa's family expects him to work to support an incompetent father and a shy sister, whom Samsa dreams of sending to music school. Samsa has to rise daily at 4:00 A.M. to take a train and a case of samples to various cities and sell things to small stores. He hates his work, yet is consumed by an overwhelming fear that he might fail his family.

The first line of Kafka's story begins:

> As Gregor Samsa awoke one morning from uneasy dreams he found himself transformed in his bed into a gigantic insect. [10]

Three hours later the chief clerk from his office arrives to find out why Samsa has not caught the early train. His father pleads with him to open the door, admit the clerk, and "be good enough to excuse the untidiness of your room." From the hall the clerk advises Samsa that his position in the firm is "not so unassailable" and that his work "has been most unsatisfactory" and they might have to lay him off until business gets better. [11]

Samsa has spent the morning hours struggling on his armor-plated back, his domelike brown belly and wavering legs pointed toward the ceiling. His fear of the chief clerk gives Samsa the strength to fall from his bed and crawl on his numerous legs to the door.

> "I'm going to open the door this very minute. A slight illness, an attack of giddiness, has kept me from getting up. I can still catch the eight o'clock train." [12]

Samsa's words are heard by those outside the door only as hisses. Samsa opens the door, his mother faints, the chief clerk retreats, and his father beats him back into his room with a rolled up newspaper. The family hides him there until he dies.

Various literary critics have interpreted the metamorphosis of Gregor Samsa as some sort of self-inflicted punishment caused by the incredible guilt he feels about his work. Kafka provides few clues to the reason for the transformation. We know through Kafka's other stories, however, that he was possessed by a hatred of the impersonality and mediocrity he foresaw in the bureaucratic state. Kafka's story, appropriately, was written during the same years that Weber prepared his famous essay on bureaucracy.

In more academically respectable fashion, Robert Presthus has attempted to characterize the ways in which individuals adjust to the demands of bureaucratic life, particularly the anxieties generated through the authority system. Employees, Presthus says, become upwardly mobile, indifferent, or ambivalent.

Upward-mobiles have high morale and unfailing optimism. They identify their personal worth with that of the organization, and have the capacity to make quick decisions in spite of all the ambiguities around them.

The great majority of employees, however, are frozen into patterns of indifference or withdrawal. Alienated by the work they do, they have learned to expect little from it; their inner needs are gratified outside of the thirty-five to forty hours spent weekly on the job. For these individuals, this mode of accommodation is both realistic and healthy. From the point of view of executives trying to increase productivity, it creates problems.

The third pattern of accommodation is ambivalence. This response is often associated with scientists, academicians, and assorted artists of ambition. The ambivalent desires status but, unlike the upward-mobile, is incapable of responding to the organizational demands for loyalty and decisiveness in the face of ambiguity. Says Presthus, "the ambivalent can neither reject its [the organization's] promise of success and power, nor can he play the roles required to compete for them."[13] Presthus believes that the inability of ambivalents to play the organizational game makes them the source of innovation. The ambivalent provides "the insight, motivation, and the dialectic that inspire change. The upward-mobile honors the status quo and the indifferent accepts it, but the ambivalent is always sensitive to the need for change."[14]

The groups to which each person belongs reenforce the pattern of accommodation. Bowling leagues are associated with indifference; the country-club circuit creates pressures that promote the ambition of the upward-mobile; professional associations further ambivalence. The type of work being done is also a major influence. Menial jobs, such as assembly-line work, breed indifference; creative or high-risk jobs tend to encourage ambivalence.

The upward-mobile, the indifferent, and the ambivalent are all co-conspirators in the maintenance of a bureaucratic system in which things are not quite right. Indifferent employees become impersonal and unresponsive. Ambitious employees can do as much damage with their zealous insistence upon loyalty and hard work. The ambivalents, despite their role as agents of change, are shut out of the organization.

So long as executives have to use anxiety to maintain legal-rational authority, a situation made quite inevitable given the nature of authority in bureaucratic organizations, employees will tend to adopt methods of defense such as these. They will, in effect, learn to become bureaucrats.

THE PATHOLOGICAL BUREAUCRACY

"You do understand," Big Nurse tells Randle Patrick McMurphy, "*everyone* must follow the rules."[15] The mental hospital created by Ken Kesey in his novel, *One Flew over the Cuckoo's Nest* is a well-drawn example of pathological characters in a bureaucracy gone awry. Big Nurse, a representation of the overzealous upward-mobile, is an ex–army nurse who has devoted her life to helping mankind. Bringing routine and order to the indifferent inmates of the

85

Oregon mental institution, she runs the ward like a fix-it factory, a smooth, accurate, precision-made machine, taking in men all twisted up and fixing them so that they go back outside better than new.

Only not too many men go back out. Not, that is, until McMurphy, with his ambivalent attitude toward authority, excites the inmates out of their indifference: McMurphy joins the inmates, faking insanity in order to avoid work duty on the Pendleton Correction Farm, where he has been sent for disturbing the peace. His therapy for insanity consists of giving the acutes a sense of their own power. He organizes the ward. The inmates play poker and basketball. He proposes a deep-sea fishing trip and calls a woman of the night down from Portland to serve as their chaperon. The inmates laugh. They start to feel cured.

McMurphy challenges Big Nurse, her authority, and her assumption that mental therapy consists largely of a respect for routine schedules and rigid rules of behavior. McMurphy makes a bet with the inmates, five bucks apiece, that he can "put a betsy bug up that nurse's butt within a week. She ain't so unbeatable as you think."[16] McMurphy wants to watch the World Series, but the rules say that the inmates can watch television only in the evenings. The acutes vote unanimously to change the rule. Big Nurse refuses to upset the carefully worked-out schedule. McMurphy stops his afternoon chores and sits down in front of the blank screen. The inmates all join him as Big Nurse squeals at the back of their heads about discipline and order and recriminations.

The male orderlies who help Big Nurse run the ward try to restrain the rebellious inmates. A fight ensues, from which McMurphy and Chief Bromden, the Indian acute, rescue the inmates by breaking the orderlies' ribs. This provides Big Nurse with the excuse she needs to send McMurphy and Bromden to the shock shop. When McMurphy returns to the ward, he throws a big party for the inmates. His girl friends from Portland sneak in the window with vodka and port. Billy Bibbitt loses his virginity and his stutter. When Big Nurse threatens to call his mother, Billy goes into the doctor's office and cuts his throat. McMurphy crashes through Big Nurse's glass cage and peels off the front of her uniform. She decides to eliminate McMurphy's "aggressive tendencies" and sends him to surgery, where the lobotomists cut away the thinking part of his brain.

One of the first scholars to analyze such bureaucracies run amuck was Robert Merton, an American sociologist. In 1940 Merton wrote an article titled "Bureaucratic Structure and Personality," which has become a classic in the study of bureaucratic pathology—the examination of sick bureaucracies, their symptoms, the diagnosis of causes, and the prescription of cures.

In his article Merton suggests that certain organizational malignancies tend to arise spontaneously from Weber's ideal-type bureaucracy. Merton observes that bureaucratic systems exert constant pressure upon their officials—including Big Nurse—to be methodical, prudent, and disciplined in serving the objectives of the organization. Bureaucrats are taught to be more intense in their application of the rules than is technically necessary—a margin of safety, one might say.

In time, the methods of the bureaucracy, such as the rules, begin to take precedent over the objectives for which they were created. The rules set up by Big Nurse were originally designed to promote cures, but when McMurphy threatened the routine, Big Nurse beat him down with those rules without regard to the effect on the health of the inmates. For her, adherence to the rules became an end in itself. Merton characterizes this as *goal displacement*. Goal displacement, excessive rigidity, red tape, impersonal treatment of clients, and unreasonable resistance to change are all signs of a sick organization. Merton calls them *bureaucratic dysfunctions*. They are the symptoms of an ingrained incapacity to adjust in ways that will promote the purposes of the organization.

One must remember that Weber's ideal-type model is designed to operate this way. A bureaucracy, by design, *is an organization that cannot correct its behavior by listening to its errors.* [17] The "feedback loop," the method by which all organizations listen to the impact of their policies and make adjustments in them, is deliberately made weak in a bureaucracy. By training bureaucrats to be skeptical of

Bureaucracies have been defined as organizations that are too rigid to learn from their errors. The individual does not have the power to fight the impersonality, the red tape, or the rules. Administrative sociologists describe these things as bureaucratic dysfunctions—characteristics that are designed to promote efficiency but that in fact incapacitate the organization and its ability to respond to change.
COURTESY OF THE COMMUNITY SERVICES ADMINISTRATION.

complaints, the organization assures that its rules will be applied impersonally. By helping bureaucrats to be impersonal, it lends them the tenacity to exercise the full powers of the organization in promoting the predetermined goals. In time, bureaucrats come to identify the disciplined application of the rules with their own self-interest, their desire for promotion and status.

The substitution of self-interest for organizational interest is the crucial step. Now the bureaucrats will interpret any challenge to the existing rules as a threat to their own security. To protect themselves, the bureaucrats will find it necessary to apply the rules rigidly, the only procedure which they know will bring personal approval. In time, they will cease to question whether or not the rules are relevant to the objectives of the organization.

Against such a background of rigidity, the executives of the organization will find it increasingly difficult to make even minor adjustments in the rules. Positions of authority will come to be occupied by persons who lack the ability to consider adjustments to the organizational routine. Author Victor Thompson calls this "the most symptomatic characteristic of modern bureaucracy: the growing imbalance between ability and authority."[18]

Lacking the ability to alter the course of the bureaucracy, bureaucratic managers begin to use their formal authority to protect their own personal power. Managers insist upon the "rights" of their office—their right to review all proposals; their right to screen all communications before they move through channels; their right to pass all subordinate demands on to top management rather than allow the subordinates personal access to higher-ups. Such managers will "scream like an injured animal if bypassed."[19] They exaggerate the impersonality that is a necessary bureaucratic quality into aloofness, disinterest, or subtle hostility. They keep persons with whom they must deal at a distance. Such managers are likely to welcome change in the speeches they make while privately discouraging subordinates who want to make such changes possible. These managers behave like bureaucrats, Thompson insists, because they are personally insecure—and for good reason. They hear the complaints about the performance of their bureau; they sense that the behavior of subordinates is beyond control; they are pressed by demands for loyalty from above. It is little wonder that the bleeding ulcer is the badge of the well-placed executive.

Is inflexibility and unresponsiveness to change a natural consequence of bureaucratic government? A cursory examination of actual bureaucracies would seem to suggest so. In 1803 the British government created a post that required a civil servant to stand on the Cliffs of Dover with a spyglass and ring a bell if he saw Napoleon coming. The position was abolished in 1945.

C. Northcote Parkinson noted that in the year 1936 the British Colonial Office, with its empire still intact, accomplished its functions with 372 employees. As Britain began to divest herself of her colonial holdings in the era of imperial decline, the number of employees in

CHAPTER 3: PROBLEMS OF BUREAUCRACY

the Colonial Office rose. By 1954 it took 1,661 employees to supervise fewer colonies than one-fourth that number of employees administered in 1936. This inspired Parkinson to write the first law of bureaucracy, which he called the law of the rising pyramid: *work expands so as to fill the time available for its completion.* The number of officials working in public agencies, he explained, is neither directly nor inversely proportional to the quantity of work being done. Public bureaucracies grow larger without regard to whether the volume of work is increasing, decreasing, or even disappearing.

Parkinson's law of the rising pyramid may be linked to a second observation. Increases in the size of bureaucracies seem to be accompanied by reductions in their efficiency. Lawrence J. Peter tries to explain why this happens. He traces it to the increased opportunities for promotion in a growing organization. When positions are plentiful, employees tend to rise to their own level of incompetence. All competent employees will be promoted. If they perform well, they will be promoted again. Eventually, employees reach the job they cannot perform, and there they remain. They cannot be dismissed because of tenure rules and will never be promoted again because of their incompetence. "In time, every post tends to be occupied by an employee who is incompetent to carry out its duties."[20] This is known as the Peter Principle.

Victor Thompson and Alvin Gouldner blame the bureaucratic malaise on human frailty. They were led to this conclusion while studying the behavior of clients—people on the receiving end of bureaucracy. "One must not forget," said Thompson, "that clients are notoriously insensitive to the needs of bureaucrats."[21] Gouldner observed that many clients tended to act like children in their encounters with big organizations. The clients could not delay the gratification of their needs, but wanted results *now.* They tended to view the bureaucratic organization in personal terms, as a friend or enemy, motivated by love or hate. The clients had little ability to see things from the point of view of the bureaucrat; they viewed all efforts by bureaucrats to evaluate them as intrusions upon their personal life. They accepted the services provided by the bureaucracy, but viewed these as gifts or privileges without reference to the costs involved, and resented having to give up anything in return. These clients realized that they depended upon large institutions for sustenance and security, yet felt powerless in their presence. Such behavior, Thompson suggested, was nothing more than "the dysfunctional persistence of childish behavior patterns."[22] In short, the clients behaved remarkably like young children would toward their parents.

What Thompson and Gouldner stumbled upon, of course, was the rule of passion in human affairs. Bureaucracies require people to be patient, to be impersonal, to submit to self-evaluation, to place obligations above rights—in other words, to substitute self-discipline for passion. Now passion is not all bad. It was once considered the height of human feeling. Writers in the Elizabethan era (Shakespeare for one) made passion out to be the creative force in human affairs,

Michel Crozier is a sociologist with the Centre de sociologie des organisations in Paris. In his book The
✻ Bureaucratic Phenomenon, *Crozier explains the rise of a vicious circle of rules—a situation in which bureaucrats are obliged to create new rules to make poor regulations more binding.*
COURTESY OF THE CENTRE DE
SOCIOLOGIE DES ORGANISATIONS.

even while admitting that it invariably led to one's personal demise. The point is simply that passion is out of place in an era of big bureaucracies, which draw their morality from the Protestant ethic and its commitment to self-discipline.

UNDERLYING CONDITIONS AND CURES

One of the greatest challenges for scholars who study bureaucratic organizations is to discover the conditions that underlie the slide of bureaucracy toward its pathological fate. In Paris, a French sociologist named Michel Crozier decided to investigate two government bureaus thought of as overly rigid, standardized, and impersonal. One was a clerical agency that employed forty-five hundred persons, mostly women, in a single building in Paris. The other bureau was an industrial monopoly, set up by the government to produce cigarettes. The industrial monopoly had three plants in Paris and thirty others throughout France. It faced no competition; its revenues were set by the government; its products were distributed by another bureau. In brief, it was free from most of the pressures that shape the social system of most organizations. Both government agencies, in effect, were ideal types for the analysis of bureaucratic pathology—the perfect complement to Weber's ideal-type model of bureaucratic structure.

When Crozier interviewed the workers in the clerical agency, he discovered that hardly anyone was devoted to the goals of the organization, neither the workers nor their immediate supervisors. No one resisted the organization; in fact, most of the women were reasonably well adjusted to their situation. They simply wanted to be left alone. They refused to form cliques; they preferred to remain isolated from one another. When conflicts arose, settlements were proclaimed by managers who never saw the workers for whom the rule was issued. The tensions generated within the agency existed between persons who never saw each other face to face.

The top executives in the clerical agency—the managers—were removed by four organizational layers from the workers. The managers had no staff that might coordinate operations, but relied totally upon the supervisors to enforce discipline. The supervisors, however, were reluctant to bring problems to the attention of the managers. Although the managers made all the important decisions, their supervisors stood mute on the matter of organizational difficulties. The power of decision, in effect, was located in a blind spot.

Crozier suggests that the workers, supervisors, and managers in the clerical agency engaged in a silent conspiracy to maintain the bureaucratic system. The impersonal rules, which were the source of the agency's rigidity, served a very real purpose.

For the managers, the rules provided an impersonal method of defending the unpleasant decisions that always had to be made. By strengthening the system of supervision, the managers might improve the performance of the agency. This, however, would force the managers to deal with the employees on a face-to-face basis to scrutinize their work and listen to their complaints. That in turn might lead to accusations of favoritism. It was easier to hide behind the rules.

The workers preferred the system of rules and impersonal supervision because it meant that they were left alone. Closer supervision, the workers feared, would place them at the mercy of their bosses and lead to demands that they work harder and devote more energy to the organization. For them the rules had a protective value.

The clerical agency, Crozier suggests, was locked in a vicious circle of rules. The managers relied upon impersonal rules to supervise the performance of the workers. The workers, in turn, were cautious, indifferent, and acted "by the book." When a certain rule failed to extract the expected performance, the managers tried to make the unsatisfactory rule more precise. The precise rule, in turn, reenforced the determination of the workers to take less initiative and maintain a safe distance between themselves and their supervisors. This in turn accentuated the need of the managers to make the rule more binding. When outsiders complained about the performance of the agency and the stupid rules, the anxieties of the managers were reaccentuated, which resulted in firmer efforts to control the activities of the workers more closely by enforcing the rules. The managers could not do away with the rules, since such an action would require them to rethink the entire social situation in the agency.

A bureaucracy, by definition, enters a vicious circle of rules when its pathologies become self-generating and each successive failure of the rules generates new attempts to enforce them. Crozier identifies four underlying conditions that were present in the clerical agency and that made the vicious circle self-generating.

First, impersonal rules were created for nearly every situation affecting individual behavior within the organization. There were rules for resolving conflicting demands, for distributing scarce resources, for regulating the flow of work, and for all the other different situations managers encounter.

Second, the power to make decisions was centralized, as was the power to create or change the rules. This power was lodged as far as possible from the level at which the rules were carried out.

Third, the hierarchical layers in the organization became isolated from each other. The isolation was both formal and social, and was most pronounced in the lack of communication between layers.

Fourth, peer group pressure was generated, which forced acceptance of the lack of communication. The employees actually promoted their own isolation. They preferred it that way, perceiving that the lack of communications protected them from the arbitrary interference of other employees and the managers of the organization.

On the surface, it might seem that this vicious circle of rules was produced by organizational apathy—by conditioning the employees to be indifferent toward the work of the agency. It is a testimony to the depth of Crozier's study that he was able to trace these bureaucratic dysfunctions to the pattern of power relationships existing between all members of the organization—the upward-mobiles and ambivalents as well as those who felt indifferent. He did this by examining conditions in the second government agency—the industrial monopoly.

The managers of the industrial monopoly exercised their supervisory responsibilities in quasi-judicial fashion. They established and enforced rules "for the purpose of maintaining peace and order between workers whose duties were already fixed;"[23] they did not exercise close supervision over the work in the plant. The workers, who understood the limits of the managers' power, resisted close supervision. The labor unions supported the workers by appealing even minor decisions that might lead to closer supervision. The managers could not control work in the plants by promoting selected employees because all promotions were automatically decided on the basis of seniority. Since the industry was a government monopoly, the managers had no tangible financial or production goals which they might set as a means of controlling performance.

At the plant level Crozier identified three general types of employees—the production workers who operated the machines, the maintenance workers who repaired them, and the foreman who ostensibly oversaw day-to-day operations. As in the clerical agency, the pattern of bureaucratic relationships created a situation in which people were happy to be left alone. Upon further probing, however, Crozier discovered a sense of insecurity within each group. The production workers, for example, feared that they might lose their jobs because of automation. The maintenance men seemed to occupy a secure position because they alone knew how to fix the machines, but they feared that technological change might make their skills obsolete.

Despite the pervasive bureaucratic system, Crozier said, "there is clearly some kind of fight for power."[24] That fight for power focused on the question of who would control the few remaining areas of uncertainty left uncovered by the rules. Everyone feared that someone else might be called in to solve a problem, "reopen the bargain they [had] struck" for themselves,[25] and leave their future security wholly dependent upon the whims of some new authority. All that the rules could do was to fence in the area in which the struggle for power took place.

Ideally, bureaucracies are created to eliminate such fears by subjecting power struggles and personal favoritism to the rules—"to administer things instead of governing men."[26] The industrial monopoly had achieved nearly complete bureaucratization in this respect. Yet even with all of its rules, it could not eliminate the fears of uncertainty, especially the fear of possible technological change.

Paradoxically, the success of the industrial monopoly in narrowing the arena of uncertainty made the struggle for power even more intense. There were so few areas of uncertainty that control over them became absolutely essential. Anyone who acquired the expertise to manage uncertainty acquired enormous power—the power to create new methods of production and to dictate special exceptions. Says Crozier, "the position of the experts is much stronger in an organization where everything is controlled and regulated."[27]

Of course, the power of the experts would be temporary. As soon as the experts resolved the source of uncertainty, the matter would become routine and could be regulated by the rules.

In the industrial monopoly, each group attempted to define problems of uncertainty in terms of its own abilities. The director wanted to remodel the plant; the technical engineers wanted to rebuild the machines. Crozier describes an intense power struggle over control of these areas of uncertainty—not so much for personal aggrandizement, but to make sure that one's own group could define the uncertainty in terms that would allow it to maintain the bargain it had already struck for itself within the existing system of formal rules and authority.

This, then, is the fifth condition which, according to Crozier, underlies a bureaucratic vicious circle: the intense power struggles to define remaining areas of organizational uncertainty, the power struggles to write the rules by which the uncertainty would be made routine, and efforts by experts to hold onto their unique position as long as possible before the uncertainty was subjected to the rules. Joined with the lessons taken from the clerical agency, Crozier sees five conditions that together create a perfect climate for the development of a sick bureaucracy:

Impersonal rules, centralized decision making, social isolation within the organization, and struggles for power are hallmarks of the pathological bureaucracy. In this picture women load parcel post packages for one of the largest bureaucracies in the world, the U.S. postal service.
COURTESY OF THE LIBRARY OF CONGRESS.

1. The managers create impersonal rules for nearly every situation.
2. Decision making is centralized at the top of the organization.
3. Each hierarchical level is isolated from each other so that they do not encounter each other face to face.
4. Peer groups generate pressures to accept that isolation.
5. Power struggles occur over the remaining areas of uncertainty in the organization.

Crozier goes on to explain how this system of bureaucratization is affected by the culture within which the organization exists. The French, he says, are aloof and uncooperative and have a strong sense of privacy. There is a tendency to avoid face-to-face relationships, especially when something unpleasant must be considered. Albert Camus, the famous French novelist, calls the traditional Frenchman "a stranger" in the bureaucratic culture. In his novel by the same name, he describes the stranger as a clerk in Algiers named Mersault who is driven to commit a pointless murder, then is sentenced to death for his silent ignorance of the social decorum prescribed by modern society, in particular for his failure to cry at his mother's funeral, which is taken to be a sign that he feels no guilt. In one interlude before the murder, Mersault's employer offers him a promotion with a transfer to Paris. Mersault says that he doesn't care, that one never really changes one's way of life; that one life is as good as another, and that his present one suits him fine. Crozier, in his description of the industrial monopoly, senses that the managers "are delivered not only from fear, but also from hope,"[28] so that any sense of achievement in the bureau is not possible—but then the

CHAPTER 3: PROBLEMS OF BUREAUCRACY

bureaucrats are excused from the anxiety of having to face the prospect of failure.

Crozier senses that there is no escape from organizational rigidity in a bureaucratic society.

> A bureaucratic system of organization is not only a system that does not correct its behavior in view of its errors; it is also too rigid to adjust without crises to the transformations that the accelerated evolution of industrial society makes more and more imperative.[29]

Only when the need for change reaches crisis proportions can the top executives, in a sudden burst of centralization, force the bureaucracy to make the necessary change. Unfortunately, the centralization of authority during the crisis rekindles the anxieties and the desire to be left alone which created the climate leading to the old dysfunctions. When the crisis is over—and the executives can maintain a sense of crisis for only so long before everyone is exhausted—the organization will drift into a new set of rigidities. "The essential rhythm prevalent in such organizations is, therefore, an alternation of long periods of stability with very short periods of crisis and change."[30]

Centralization of power in an atmosphere of crisis—that is the standard remedy for the pathological bureaucracy. Of course, executives have experimented with a variety of alternative reforms. Some have tried to create cohesive work groups. Others have instructed their staff to "improve feedback" by opening up new channels of communication, such as the use of the ombudsman. One innovative air force commander in Europe tried to combat shoddy work by insisting that flight mechanics take a ride in the planes they repaired—an obvious incentive for first-class performance. Some executives combat rigidity by rotating personnel between posts, or recruiting new personnel, or by setting up new organizational units and programming them to perform an urgent task.

Such reforms can lead to a bureaucratic breakout. Over time, however, the units involved tend to routinize their operations so that the reforms provide, at best, only temporary relief. It is extraordinarily difficult to "institutionalize flexibility" under the conditions of bureaucratic management.

Such facts have led a number of experts to propose a new cure. Eliminate the bureaucratic disease, they say, by abolishing the bureaucratic form—the formal rules, the routine, the impersonality, and all of the other structural characteristics in Weber's "ideal" bureaucratic model. This is the radical mastectomy of public administration.

What are the chances for abolishing the bureaucratic approach to modern government and what are the costs of failing to do so? The next two sections examine the controversy surrounding these questions.

BUREAUCRATIC POWER IN THE ADMINISTRATIVE STATE

The controversy between the bureaucrats and the antibureaucrats boils down to this: are bureaucracies necessary to the functioning of

95

the modern state? There are essentially two alternatives to government by bureau. One is to replace the bureaus with flatter, more organic forms of organization. The other is to let free-enterprise organizations in the private sector supply the services currently produced by government bureaus. The conventional wisdom in public administration generally tries to deflate both of these alternatives.

In an exhaustive analysis of bureaucratic government, Anthony Downs replies to the "death of bureaucracy" advocates. Bureaucracies are not just a temporary evil, Downs says; modern governments need them.

Downs argues his case on economic grounds. One alternative to the big government bureaucracy is the free-market system, where people purchase solutions to their problems from the lowest bidder. In fact, Downs argues, government bureaucracies are created because of the shortcomings of the open market. National defense, for example, cannot be provided through the open market because the market cannot assure that everyone who benefits from the service will agree to pay for it. Governments can, through their bureaus of taxation. The free-market system is not designed to protect citizens from their own lack of knowledge. Bureaus are, as in the regulation of drugs, food, or water supplies. Pressures for economy in operations in the free-market system tend to make companies omit external costs. The auto industry, for example, tries to avoid making decisions about smog in Los Angeles. Public bureaus at least attempt to insure that all relevant costs enter into the production process. Finally, the free market cannot redistribute income. It cannot guarantee that certain classes of people, such as the elderly or the handicapped, receive benefits at the expense of others. Government bureaucracies can.

If functions such as national defense, consumer protection, pollution abatement, and social security are to be provided, they must be provided through government organizations. But why do these organizations need to be bureaucratic? Downs replies.

> The mere size of the tasks involved requires large organizations to perform them. They must be closely coordinated by a single overall policy. Their services cannot be interrupted without harmful consequences. The personnel who carry out such functions must have received adequate training and must be extremely reliable in the performance of their jobs. [31]

There are some exceptions. Bureaucratic principles are not necessary in temporary programs nor in tiny organizations staffed by dilettantes or volunteers providing simple social services. Certain public services, such as garbage collection, can be provided by free-enterprise organizations, but these are still exceptions. "These qualifications," Downs insists, "do not alter the basic conclusion that bureaus are a necessity in modern societies." [32]

Downs goes on. It is unwise, he says, to compare the operations of bureaus to the operations of profit-making enterprises, as the critics of "big government" do when they moan about the stupidity and inefficiency of government bureaucrats. A profit-making enterprise, because it is subject to the pressures of the market and consumer demand, is in an entirely different situation from a government bureau. The bureau is deliberately isolated from the pressures of the market. Government bureaus, Downs claims "are far more efficient at carrying out essential nonmarket functions than other forms of nonmarket-oriented organizations."[33]

Downs's acceptance of bureaucracies does not lead him to praise them. He admits that bureaucrats are not wholly motivated on behalf of the public interest. Bureaucrats, he says, are "significantly motivated by [their] own self-interest even when acting in a purely official capacity."[34] In pursuing their self-interest, bureaucrats are highly rational. In his book *Inside Bureaucracy*, Downs labors to dispel the image of the bumbling, irrational clerk. Bureaucrats, he declares, will act to achieve their goals rationally "in the most efficient manner possible given their limited capabilities and the cost of information."[35] If the cost of achieving their goals decreases—in terms of time, effort, or money—then bureaucrats will attempt to achieve more of their goals. The goals, Downs explains, include power, income, prestige, security, convenience, loyalty to an idea, institution, or the nation, pride in excellent work, and last, a desire to serve the public interest.

The importance of the public interest in their hierarchy of goals depends upon how well the organization structures its rewards and incentives. Given the conditions existing in most bureaucracies, Downs says, power becomes the dominant goal. In time this leads to a situation in which most public bureaucracies are dominated by conservers. As bureaus grow older, the decisions of their officials tend to grow more conservative. The incumbents learn more about the business of the agency; they write more rules. The number of administrative officials rises; they promote people who fit their own image. The bureaucrats try to promote efficiency, but become preoccupied with the survival of the organization and their place within it. They feel the need to solidify their position against the lean, hungry, young executives; the organizational partisans; or the energetic proponents of a single sacred cause. The newcomers are anxious to see the organization reorganized, to expand its personnel, to take on new tasks, or to engage in innovative programs. These things would weaken the power of the conservers. If the newcomers win, they enter the executive ranks. If they fail, they may break away and set up a new organization. Either way, in time they will become conservers, holding on to what they have.

The tendency toward conservatism in bureaus has important implications for society. In essence, it results in a situation where bureaucratic planning replaces open competition—planning prices, planning taxes, planning which services and goods to produce, planning how to create more demand for it, and planning how to educate the personnel who will accomplish the work of the bureaus of the future.

In the long run, the drive toward planning everything means that managerial control passes into the hands of professional administrators, away from entrepreneurs, away from the risktakers, and away from the all-powerful chief executive. In the business world, control of modern corporations has passed from the hands of great organizers to committees of managers in the corporate superstructure. Similar tendencies are apparent in the public sector, where the drive for program continuity creates the need for experts in organizational survival.

The drive toward planning produces a convergence of public and private interests, inasmuch as both have an intense interest in averting the sort of economic or political oscillation that can upset their ability to execute their plans. Since the private sector has little capacity for broad-scale societal planning, it must turn to the government for the power to regulate. Government bureaus, for their own reasons, show a willingness to correct corporate instability by generating public demand for goods and services, through regulation, and through policies affecting wages, prices, interest rates, and personal income. This is a thesis which has been well articulated by the economist John Kenneth Galbraith. Galbraith predicts the rise of a "new industrial state" in which government and corporate bureaucracies will *converge* into a single superconglomerate responsible for maintaining the power of organizational conservers, all apparently run by committees of managers.

All this is still heresy to free-enterprise types, but as the evidence pours in from the history of economic controls in the 1970s, the thesis becomes more persuasive.

A Frenchman, Robert Michels, characterized all of this as the iron law of oligarchy. The European socialist movements that Michels studied began with a commitment to social change through a democratic organization open to all. It was a noble idea, but hardly practical, given the fact that the socialists were opposed by entrenched public officials. To win power, the socialists needed a powerful organization. Unfortunately, the bureaucracy they created ate away at their democratic ideals by allowing a few leaders to dominate the movement and to put their own desire to remain in office ahead of the interests of the members. Most organizations begin with great enthusiasm which is due to the charisma of a founder or the power of an idea. The inescapable tendency to routinize that enthusiasm inevitably leads to a bureaucracy managed by an oligarchy.

Radicals sense a conspiracy in all this convergence of power. C. Wright Mills, the famous American sociologist, argued that the hierarchies of the state, the major corporations, and the military are the command posts of modern society. The executives who occupy these command posts are professional organizers; they move with ease between the corporate world and the apparatus of the state, especially the defense community. Mills calls them the power elite. They control the most important decisions made for society—war versus peace, prosperity versus inflation or depression.

CHAPTER 3: PROBLEMS OF BUREAUCRACY

The rest of us, Mills explains in another book, are white collar. Nixon called us the silent Americans. We are, according to Mills, the apparatus of the bureaucratic society—corporate managers, salaried bureaucrats, junior law partners, statisticians, sales representatives and marketing executives, accountants, typists, federal inspectors, police officers, investigators, and social workers. We are bureaucrats trained in the skills of loyalty, trained to fix things, to coordinate and clean up operations. The old middle-class values of entrepreneurship, of the inventor tinkering in his garage, the corner storekeeper, the independent service station, have been replaced by an ethic of "serving the powers that be, in the hope of getting [one's] cut."[36] In a planned society, there is little chance to create new wealth. The ambitious must labor within the bureaucratic system for their status and success.

Mills's thesis is very pessimistic; it has great appeal to alienated young radicals. His first observations—that all societies distribute power unevenly, that power in the bureaucratic state is not well dispersed, and that laissez-faire entrepreneurship is being replaced by bureaucratic planning—these observations are neither original nor really contestable. What is contestable in Mills's theory is the idea that somehow the power elite conspires against the poor; that is, that the five hundred most powerful financial, political, and military leaders in any society can agree upon anything of common interest, or, barring that, actually talk to each other. Mills's proof is largely rhetorical. It sounds gutsy and realistic, but there is impressive evidence that suggests the contrary—that as the bureaucratic state develops, more centers of power arise, resulting in more competition among organizational elites.

Mills raises basic questions about the costs of bureaucracy—the sacrifice of individual freedom, the difficulty of change, the type of life that mass society produces. The most significant question is contained in his suggestion that the mass of people have no power in the modern state—that democracy is a casualty in the march of bureaucracy.

THE COSTS OF BUREAUCRACY

By and large, artists and philosophers have found the age of bureaucracy to be one of human sacrifice. The casualties in human values and democratic government seem to outweigh whatever material advantages bureaucracies have brought. Many worry about a terrible future in which bureaucratic survival is assured through the technology of behavioral control. Their worst fears are realized in George Orwell's novel *Nineteen Eighty-Four*.

Nineteen Eighty-Four represents the culmination of a half-century of artistic rebellion against modern life. With Nietzsche, European writers began to assault the spiritual stagnation which seemed to paralyze human existence in the bureaucratic era. One must remember that the modern era of bureaucracy got underway during the late Renaissance—what some have called the Age of Reason—which was epitomized by the idealism of Rousseau and Jefferson, by the worship of nature, and a general nostalgia for the virtues of Roman and Greek civilization. Yet what realists like Dickens found in their towns was the triumph of mediocrity. Winston Smith, the central character in *Nineteen Eighty-Four*, leads a life that is culturally and spiritually barren. He drinks cheap Victory gin, smokes too many Victory cigarettes, and watches too much television in his seventh-floor apartment in a battered building that smells of boiled cabbage and old rags. The elevators do not work and there is not enough electricity. He wears a uniform of blue overalls, even though his job rewriting history in the Ministry of Truth would be classified as white collar. He has varicose veins.

Orwell offers a pessimistic vision of the future, both in the banality of the life people live and in the failure of social institutions, especially the government, to create the renaissance of values of which idealists dreamed. Orwell had lost what little idealism he possessed fighting in the trenches in the Spanish Civil War, the radical cause célèbre of his generation. He learned that revolutionary governments were too anarchical to achieve their ideals and that by organizing they would inevitably become oligarchical and corrupt, a theme that Orwell developed in *Animal Farm*.

The only social revolution Orwell found imminent was one forecast by the Englishman James Burnham. In *The Managerial Revolution*, published four years before Orwell wrote *Nineteen Eighty-Four*, Burnham explained the emergence of Hitler and Stalin and totalitarian government as the rise of a new kind of planned, centralized society in which the power to rule would be lodged with managers—business executives, government bureaucrats, technicians, and soldiers. These societies would be organized hierarchically, with the managers drawing all power and economic privilege to themselves. The working class would disappear, to be replaced by a docile class of clerks. Orwell found Burnham's thesis "extraordinarily plausible," although perhaps a bit too politic. In *Nineteen Eighty-Four* Orwell warns mankind of a future in which Burnham's thesis has come true.

In the novel, Winston Smith enters into an affair with a bold, dark-haired woman named Julia. They meet in an upstairs bedroom above a charming old English bookstore, secretly, since sex for the sake of love has been prohibited. Winston and Julia subsequently enroll in a conspiracy against the government and receive a revolutionary treatise on "oligarchical collectivism," which explains the theory of modern government—and how to change it. When they return to the bedroom above the bookstore they are arrested by the Thought Police and Winston is taken to the Ministry of Love, where he is tortured and subjected to behavioral conditioning. He emerges as a new man—hairless, toothless, yet with a pure soul, for at last he loves Big Brother.

The book is a catalogue of sins associated with bureaucratic gov-

Commentators on organizational life fear that bureaucracies are subject to the iron law of oligarchy—that over time the bureaucratic state will become dominated by persons who will use organizational weapons to conserve their own power. George Orwell's Nineteen Eighty-Four *provides a good description of life in the totally managed bureaucratic state.* PIERRETTE COUNTRYMAN, ARTIST, AND CHARLES DOVE, PHOTOGRAPHER.

ernment. There is, first of all, the iron law of oligarchy—rule by a single, self-perpetuating elite. Loyalty to the state is maintained by the Big Lie and mass hysteria which the party creates during "hate sessions." Truth is a servant to the goals of the party; the bureaucratic principle of secrecy cloaks those goals. The nation is fighting with or against two other great world powers for possession of the uncaptured portions of the earth—allies and enemies change from day to day. Orwell calls this *double think,* or the ability to render inoperative previous statements thought to be true. The only violation of bureaucratic principles is the strange fact that Oceania has no laws, no constitution, no rules. The totalitarian government can apparently maintain routine so effectively through their technology of control that the publication and dissemination of formal rules becomes unnecessary.

Ludwig Von Mises, a conservative economist and leading bureaucratic critic, points out that the methods of control associated with Big Brother bureaucracies are very old. They arise whenever any government attempts to extend its control—over land, as in an empire; over the economy, as in socialism; or over the behavior of its people, as within a totalitarian system. Bureaucracy, Von Mises insists, removes the embryo of innovation from society and replaces it with a duty to comply with rules and regulations, even if the rules are absurd. Devotion to duty establishes an oligarchy based on rank, rather than on talent.

Von Mises argues that innovation is possible only in a free-market system. In a free-market system, he says, entrepreneurs are rewarded for their skills and punished for their errors at the hands of their clients. Bureaucracy, he continues, breeds a form of government far more conservative than the monarchical-constitutional regimes of the nineteenth century. He blasts progressives for adopting bureaucratic methods under the pretext of advancing individual freedom, when in fact bureaucracies do away with freedom. In his view, "the principles according to which a police department is operated differ

101

essentially and radically from the principles applied in the conduct of a profit-seeking enterprise."[37]

The liberals reply with their own set of facts. Anthony Downs argues that bureaucracies create freedom—in particular, economic freedom. "In spite of absolute increases in bureaucratic regulation, the average citizen in modern democratic societies has a far wider range of alternatives from which to choose than his counterpart in the days when bureaus were of trivial importance."[38] The growth of bureaucracy has been accompanied by rising real income, new medicines, longer vacations and better pensions, instant communications, and a mobility achieved through the technology of transportation that has finally given people the ability to move more than fifty miles from the place where they were born. The ethics of bureaucracy, particularly its stress upon technical efficiency, support scientific development. Bureaucracy has flourished in societies that trust science, worship progress, and embrace the achievement ethic. Moreover, the pressures that create bureaucratic states are the broad demands for general equality. Bureaucracy, in its ideal operation, dispenses no privileges; it treats blue bloods and serfs alike before the rules. And if that is not enough, bureaucracy can become the vehicle for conferring benevolence—by its rules insuring that minorities, veterans, the poor, and the powerless are compensated with privileges that their actual situation denies them.

The critics reply that the association of bureaucracy with individual freedom is largely a myth. Reality, they say, is the bureaucratic double standard. Those persons who are loyal to the bureaucratic state, who wear a coat and tie and speak softly, are given what freedom their subservience allows them. Bureaucrats treat them as adults, allow them flexibility within the rules, even allow them to influence the making of the rules. Clients who appear shiftless and irresponsible are forced to conform to the rules, to submit to investigation, and to defer their demands for greater participation in rulemaking. Bureaucrats treat them like children. Enough evidence exists to suggest that bureaucrats enforce rules differently with regard to the client's social position vis-à-vis the bureaucrat.

Bureaucratic organizations, the critics say, actually reenforce social differences. At last count, seventeen U.S. corporations paid their top executives an annual income in excess of $500,000—not so much because these executives are ninety times more talented than the janitors who clean their offices, but because it is necessary to pay large salaries to maintain the status anxiety that causes the junior executives to work harder in the hope of moving up the organizational ladder.

The defenders of bureaucracy point out, once again, the association between the bureaucratic state and the rise of mass democracy. Human slavery has been all but abolished, while wage slavery is weakened by a rising standard of living. Suffrage has been extended; class distinctions have broken down. There are far more democracies in the industrialized world than there were in medieval times.

And more totalitarian states, the critics reply. Orwell, in *Nineteen Eighty-Four*, is simply reiterating the fact that a nation engaged in war must achieve a level of efficiency that precludes elementary freedoms. (His own government, Great Britain, the mother of parliaments, actually suspended the call for elections until World War II was over.) Oceania, Orwell's fictional nation, is in a continual state of war. How many other organizations find that recurring crises, either domestic or international, require them to subordinate individual freedom to the good of the cause?

The contest between individual freedom and the drive for efficiency is at the center of these arguments over the bureaucratic state. Is the potential for individual choice narrowed or expanded by the quest for efficiency? Is democracy a fatality in the bureaucratic state?

As the preceding arguments reveal, there are no simple answers to these questions. Simple answers invariably produce sterile solutions. Perceptive scholars recognize that Orwell's vision of the future is but one of several possibilities.

Few single issues have preoccupied public administrators as much as the problem of reconciling democracy and efficiency. The most important contribution of American scholars to the study of public administration attempts such a reconciliation. Their solution is the subject of the next chapter.

FOR FURTHER READING

It is impossible to understand the dysfunctions of bureaucracy without first understanding the formal bureaucratic model. Max Weber's "Essay on Bureaucracy" is the classic statement. It can be found in H. H. Gerth and C. Wright Mills, eds. and trans., *From Max Weber: Essays in Sociology* (New York: Oxford University Press, 1946). The development of organizational forms through history is explained in great detail in E. N. Gladden's two-volume study, *A History of Public Administration* (London: Frank Cass, 1972). The best up-to-date summaries of the study of bureaucracy are provided by Anthony Downs, *Inside Bureaucracy* (Boston: Little, Brown & Co., 1967), an economist's point of view; and Peter M. Blau and Marshall W. Meyer, *Bureaucracy in Modern Society* (New York: Random House, 1971), a sociological perspective. Both Downs and Blau examine the formal as well as the informal side of bureaucracy. The best single study of informal activity in bureaucracies is Alvin Gouldner, *Patterns of Industrial Bureaucracy* (New York: The Free Press, 1954).

Studies of bureaucratic pathology range from the scholarly to the satirical. C. Northcote Parkinson fits the latter category with *Parkinson's Law and Other Studies in Administration* (Boston: Houghton Mifflin Co., 1957). Michel Crozier has written what is probably the best empirical study of bureaucratic behavior since the Hawthorne experiments, in *The Bureaucratic Phenomenon* (Chicago: University of Chicago Press, 1964). Victor A. Thompson inspects bureaucratic pathology from the perspective of personal deficiencies in *Modern*

Organization (New York: Alfred A. Knopf, 1961). Robert K. Merton was one of the first scholars to analyze the structural roots of bureaucratic dysfunctions in "Bureaucratic Structure and Personality," reprinted in Merton's *Reader in Bureaucracy* (New York: The Free Press, 1952). The *Reader* contains an excellent selection from the scholarship on modern political bureaucracies.

The Marxist approach, which views bureaucracies as the methodology of personal enslavement, is reflected in Robert Presthus, *The Organizational Society* (New York: Alfred A. Knopf, 1962), and in C. Wright Mills, *The Power Elite* (New York: Oxford University Press, 1956). Presthus examines how bureaucracies use anxiety to dehumanize and control their employees, a theme also explored in William H. Whyte, *The Organization Man* (New York: Doubleday Anchor, 1957), and in George Orwell, *Nineteen Eighty-Four* (New York: Harcourt Brace & World, 1949). For the antibureaucratic perspective from a conservative's point of view, see Ludwig Von Mises, *Bureaucracy* (New Haven, Conn.: Yale University Press, 1944).

Despite attacks from the left and right, the bureaucratic organization continues to dominate the political state. For an analysis of the bureaucratic state, see James Burnham, *The Managerial Revolution* (New York: John Day, 1942); John Kenneth Galbraith, *The New Industrial State* (Boston: Houghton Mifflin Co., 1967); and Anthony Downs, *Inside Bureaucracy*, cited above. Charles Perrow defends the bureaucratic society against its scholarly critics in *Complex Organizations* (Glenview, Ill.: Scott, Foresman & Co., 1972). Unfortunately, the study of bureaucratic pathology seems to be dying out just as bureaucratic dysfunctions are becoming most pronounced. Most reformers prefer to concentrate on the movement toward nonbureaucratic forms of organization, which is discussed in Chapters 8 and 10.

THE POLITICS
OF ADMINISTRATION

4

Wallace Sayre used to say that public administration and business administration were similar—in all unimportant respects. Paul Appleby put it more tersely. *Public* administration, he said, is different.[1]

This theme sits at the mainstream of American public administration—the idea that the political process creates managerial problems that are experienced only by governmental officials. Formally, the organization of government may be modeled upon universal principles of administration, but in reality their operation will always be molded by political pressures.

Paul Appleby described the shape of those pressures. While Luther Gulick was unveiling the formal principles of administration, Appleby and other New Deal executives were creating the political rules of administration. Appleby served for eleven years as a public administrator in the Department of Agriculture. Before that he had been a journalist, which gave him the twin talents of self-expression and cynicism. Like so many of the administrative experts who served under President Franklin Roosevelt, Appleby could not bring himself to believe—on the basis of his own experience—that public administration was the efficient execution of the law according to "scientific" principles that were divorced from political considerations. Appleby retired from the public service into academia to refute this dogma.

ADMINISTRATIVE PLURALISM

Appleby's message, which was remarkably simple, came at the reader in three waves. First, Appleby said, government bureaucrats make policy. That is inevitable. Moreover, in making policy, bureaucrats are subject to the same political constraints as other public officials, including legislators and judges. These external political constraints, Appleby concluded, are the public's greatest protection

106

against a public service that would otherwise become arbitrary, undemocratic, and zealously efficient.

"It is widely believed," Appleby wrote, "that Congress has an exclusive responsibility for policy-making."[2] Yet for every policy decision made by the lawmakers, there are thousands more made by administrators. Administrators make rules, they determine what the law is, they determine the rights of citizens with reference to the law, and they make specific legislative policy out of vague legislative mandates. They help make policy when the lawmakers call upon them to draft general legislation or contingency plans. No one, Appleby concluded, has identified any boundary between policy making and administration that could stand up under the test of reality.

In making policy and executing it, public administrators are plunged into the political process. They live in a goldfish bowl where "each employee hired, each one demoted, transferred, or discharged, every efficiency rating, every assignment of responsibility, each change in administrative structure, each conversation, each letter, has to be thought about in terms of possible public agitation, investigation, or judgment."[3] Their administrative power is checked by all sorts of external constraints. Public administrators are expected to be responsive to legislative intent and sensitive to shifts in legislative sympathy. They must act with knowledge of what the courts have decided or may later decide. They are expected to rationalize their decisions in terms of the public interest. They are expected to entertain inquiries from pressure groups, citizens, even their own employees—and be restrained by a sense of the impact of their decisions on these groups. They are expected to modify their agency position in order to promote intergovernmental cooperation or interagency coordination. It is such forces, Appleby believed, that make public administration in a democratic state so different from management in general.

Appleby's ultimate goal was a reconciliation of democratic values with bureaucratic necessities. He warned scholars in the field that the

As a public administrator with the Department of Agriculture, and later as dean of the graduate school of public affairs at Syracuse University, Paul Appleby worked to destroy the myth that politics could somehow be taken out of public administration. Public administrators, Appleby said, made policy; they were involved in the political process; and this political involvement acted as a check on the arbitrary exercise of bureaucratic power in a democratic state. COURTESY OF THE MAXWELL SCHOOL, SYRACUSE UNIVERSITY.

ADMINISTRATIVE PLURALISM

threat to democratic administration would come not from a politically active public service, but rather from the experts who would rationalize democracy out of administration under the guise of efficiency.

> Public administration is policy-making. But it is not autonomous, exclusive, or isolated policy-making. It is policy-making on a field where mighty forces contend, forces engendered in and by the society.[4]

Remove from the bureaucracy the obligation to contend with these forces and you will raise a bureaucracy that will destroy democratic government. Democracy and bureaucracy are compatible only when public administration is treated as one of the basic political processes. That, in Appleby's view, required an administrative corps comfortable with the political processes of negotiation, accommodation, and coalition building, preferably headed by generalists since he felt that generalists were more sensitive to the political and social consequences of their decisions.

Paul Appleby left in the field of public administration a bias on behalf of administrative pluralism, the system in which governmental administration is immersed in group competition over the shape and content of public policy. He provided a great counterweight to those who see administration as a science, governed by immutable laws, subject to the standards of rationality. Appleby thought that a humane, democratic public administration could be made compatible with both the chaos of politics and the need for bureaucratic efficiency.

SUBGOVERNMENTS AND PUBLIC ADMINISTRATION

Pluralism is a fact of life for American administrators. The term characterizes a situation in which organized groups have unusual access to the political processes, including public administration. The fact that the groups are organized—and that they are supposed to represent the special interests of their members—portends the most important feature of administrative pluralism in the twentieth century. In a wealthy, technological society, persons who have little more than an amateur's interest in the content of public policy tend not to get involved or not to get represented in the group process. In effect, narrow bands of policy specialists weave like arteries through the body politic, encased by tough, resilient walls that tend to confine participation to those willing to pay the entrance fees of time, knowledge, and organization.

Journalists prefer to characterize these swirls of power as *subgovernments:* little governments, insulated against outside interference, which internally replicate the checks and balances of the larger political system. Political scientists call them subsystems. Both terms mean the same thing. A subgovernment, simply defined, is a three-way partnership among independent groups and agencies with common interests in a specialized policy. The partnership represents

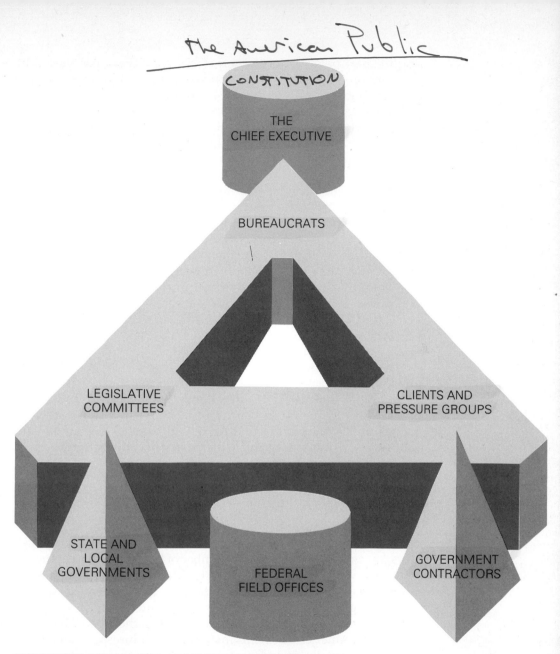

the American Public

CONSTITUTION

THE
CHIEF EXECUTIVE

BUREAUCRATS

LEGISLATIVE
COMMITTEES

CLIENTS AND
PRESSURE GROUPS

STATE AND
LOCAL
GOVERNMENTS

FEDERAL
FIELD OFFICES

GOVERNMENT
CONTRACTORS

SUBGOVERNMENTS AND ADMINISTRATION *Because the chief executive cannot provide them with all the political support they need through the official hierarchy, bureaucrats are obliged to join subgovernments. Bureaucrats build alliances with legislative committees, clients, and pressure groups, and maintain close relations with other groups that have a particular interest in the program being administered.*

the most important obligations in the life of the bureaucrat. It unites an executive agency, usually one headed by a career civil servant with considerable longevity; a pressure group representing the constituencies receiving the policy; and a congressional committee led by a powerful chairman who probably arrived in Washington about the same time that the old-line bureau chief began his career. The mediums of influence include the specialized information upon

109

which expert policy is formulated, the money that fuels the policy programs, and the professionals whose expertise allows them to pass freely from job to job in different sectors of the subsystem.

Above each subgovernment sits the politically appointed or elected chief executive, the administrator's formal superior. In most cases, the chief executive has neither the time nor the energy to get extensively involved in the work of the subgovernment. This accounts in large measure for the independence of the subgovernment, as well as for the frequent executive complaints about "bureaucratic pockets of resistance" to executive priorities.

Below each bureaucratic agency are the other agencies or industries which actually administer the programs developed at the top: federal offices in the field, state and local governments, private agencies and government contractors. These agencies also build alliances with legislative committees and pressure groups—the ones at the top as well as state legislators and local clients at the grass roots of administration. The subgovernment model is replicated at every level of the federal system in every jurisdiction in which bureaucrats have to develop political support for their programs.

The subgovernments spin through the capital city like toy tops in a closed room, each self-sustaining on the basis of its own balanced motion. Their stability is disturbed only by a sudden collision with another set of experts. As with tops, the collision causes each to change direction so as to avoid continued damage to their equilibrium. A few institutional giants—the presidency, the political parties, and the party leadership in Congress—collide even more severely with the smaller subsystems, often at random.

This organizational model of the modern administrative state is illustrated by A. Lee Fritschler's description of the tobacco subgovernment and its collision with the friends of public health. The tobacco subsystem is a three-way partnership of bureaucrats, legislators, and special interests. The number of key individuals at the top of the subsystem rarely exceeds thirty. Membership is generally assured to the tobacco specialists in the U.S. Department of Agriculture, the legislators from tobacco-growing states who sit on the agriculture committees, and the representatives of the tobacco industry, paid by the American Tobacco Institute which hires a stable of lobbyists that usually includes at least one former senator from a tobacco-growing state.

Together their job is to maintain the health of the American tobacco industry. Over time they have succeeded in enacting legislation to support the price of tobacco, influence the size of the annual tobacco yield, influence the wholesale price of tobacco, restrict foreign tobacco imports, and allow the U.S. government to prepare films for foreign distribution that depict non-Americans growing rich, young, and sexually satisfied by smoking American cigarettes. Above all, the subgovernment seeks to monopolize control over government policies that affect the tobacco economy. It generally encounters little competition from other centers of power—the House party leadership, most senators, or the president—all of whom have their own priorities to pursue.

Fritschler's book documents the rise of a competing subsystem that challenged the sanctity of the tobacco subgovernment. The challenge began when an antismoking senator persuaded President Kennedy to persuade the Public Health Service to appoint a blue-ribbon committee to advise the Surgeon General on the relationship between smoking and health. The committee issued a report placing the prestige of the nation's medical profession behind the scientific suggestion that smoking was a factor in lung cancer, heart disease, respiratory ailments and, in general, an early death. The Federal Trade Commission responded to the report by issuing an industry-wide rule—in effect, writing a law—that required the tobacco barons to disclose in all advertising and on every package "that cigarette smoking is dangerous to health and may cause death from cancer and other diseases."[5]

The tobacco lobby appealed to its friends in Congress to restrain the Federal Trade Commission. The members of Congress in turn overrode the FTC rule. They abolished the warning on advertising, prohibited the FTC from issuing similar rules in the future, and approved a warning to be placed on cigarette containers—but one which said only that smoking might be "hazardous" and did not mention cancer or death.

The friends of public health lost round one to the older, better-organized tobacco subgovernment. But as they lost, they learned. They learned that they would have to form their own subgovernment by strengthening the ties between executive agencies, congressional committees, and pressure groups. The fate of the FTC rule, Fritschler states, proves "that the bureaucracy acting alone could not be successful in its policy-making activities. Congressmen, bureaucrats, and pressure groups each have at least one political resource the other needs."[6] The key roles in the new subgovernment would be played by the bureaucrats from the Public Health Service, the Federal Trade Commission, and the Federal Communications Commission, consumer advocates on the Senate Commerce Committee, the American Cancer Society, and the American Heart Association. The health subgovernment mobilized, the warning on cigarettes was strengthened, the bureaucrats succeeded in banning all cigarette advertising from radio and television, and the Federal Trade Commission regained its power to issue rules regulating industries on behalf of consumers. Simultaneously, the consumption of tobacco products has increased. It is the nature of subgovernments that nothing is ever settled.

From the point of view of the antismoking executives, the attraction of outside support from Congress and pressure groups was a political necessity. Says Robert Rourke, the author of *Bureaucracy, Politics, and Public Policy*:

111

> A first and fundamental source of power for administrative agencies in American society is their ability to attract outside support. Strength in constituency is no less an asset for an American administrator than it is for a politician. The lack of such support severely circumscribes the ability of an agency to achieve its goals, and may even threaten its survival as an organization.[7]

Bureaucrats have to develop these special alliances, even if it compromises their loyalty to the chief executive. They are obliged to cultivate the support of legislators, pressure groups, professional associations, public officials in other governments, private contractors, labor unions representing public employees, and citizens who receive the benefits of agency policy. These groups are very proficient in the affairs of the subgovernment; consequently, they are as capable of influencing the work of the bureau as the chief executive is. This disturbs the chief executive, who clearly understands that he or she is only one of a number of forces to which the bureau must respond.

The chief executive has a number of powers that can be used to pull bureaucrats into the executive sphere of influence. Executives can publish organization charts in the *U.S. Government Manual* that preserve an illusion of hierarchy and suggest that bureaucratic autonomy is at least officially forbidden. More realistically, executives can issue executive orders, propose reorganizations, approve program and budgetary review mechanisms, establish management control, and insist upon interagency coordination. But, these are essentially *administrative* methods and do not solve the political problem, which is how to attract enough support to allow the bureau to achieve its goals. Realistically, chief executives cannot provide bureau chiefs with all of the political support they need. That support is disbursed in the American system. The only way that top executives can possibly distribute support is by first collecting it, either by winning a huge popular majority at the polls or by unifying the various branches and levels of government through a strong political party. Since these conditions are the exception in American politics, bureaucrats persist in joining subgovernments. Here is why.

First, chief executives are not in a position to protect the bureaucrats against legislative assaults on vital programs. In fact, bureaucrats may find that their legislative overseers are more sympathetic to the goals of the agency than the budget analysts and counselors who serve the chief executives. So the administrators formalize relationships with friendly legislators and the legislative committees that authorize programs and approve budgets. Both bureaucrats and legislators resist reorganization proposals that would readjust agency or committee jurisdictions. The committee members, who know that their power is ultimately based on their ability to become experts in one or two policies, assist in this arrangement by developing their powers of administrative oversight. They cultivate their natural interest in the political impact of administrative minutiae and expand their role as subnational ombudsmen by resolving problems between constituents and bureaucrats.

Second, the political system favors administrators who can formalize their ties with representatives of clientele groups. Despite mutterings about potential conflicts of interest, few executives or legislators are willing to back an agency that cannot muster outside testimony on behalf of its programs. Sometimes they positively encourage it—by approving laws such as those which require public administrators to seek out clients and place them on boards and commissions where they can officially influence policies of the agency.

Third, chief executives do not really have free choice in appointing personnel to the subgovernment. Generally, they are obliged to select agency officials from the ranks of professional groups who traditionally participate in the affairs of the subgovernment. In the long run, each subgovernment tends to come under the influence of a single profession, what is known in official circles as the "guild system." The president is obliged to look to the nation's leading hospitals for his surgeon general, to the defense subsystem for his chief military-procurement executives, and to the farming communities and the land-grant colleges of the nation for his agricultural barons. If the executive appoints persons who are loyal to him, he runs the risk that these people will not have the ability to manage the affairs of the subgovernment. If he appoints professional experts, he runs the risk that the experts will not be loyal to him. In most cases, the chief executive selects competent professionals, hoping that they will divide their loyalty between the executive and their life careers.

Finally, the president is not in a position to mobilize support for the bureau among the state and local officials with whom the bureaucrats are expected to cooperate. In part this is due to the decentralized nature of parties and elections, whereby state and local executives develop their own base of power independent of national political machinery. It is also due to the natural tendency of bureaucrats at the top to speak directly to bureaucrats at the grass roots of administration on matters of common interest—and not to bother checking with political executives. Experts on federalism, recognizing the narrowness of these channels of specialization, call it "creative feudalism." In effect, local bureaucrats become lords over their own manors, speaking only to other groups or agencies within the subgovernment. This tendency toward creative feudalism applies to private contractors as well as to state and local bureaucrats.

Bureau chiefs who ignore the necessities of subgovernment alliances peril their entire program. One administrator who committed all the sins was Sargent Shriver, the Kennedy brother-in-law whom President Johnson picked to head the Office of Economic Opportunity, better known as the War on Poverty. Shriver began by announcing that he would stay on as director of the Peace Corps while simultaneously commanding the poverty campaign. Then he proceeded to break most of the rules of political administration. He alienated congressmen, including the ones who approved his projects, and sought out no existing pressure groups to bolster and boast about

113

the program, preferring to organize the poor into tiny pressure groups through community-action agencies. The lieutenants he recruited were social scientists and settlement-house types with few ties to existing professional groups. Finally, Shriver created conflicts of organizational decentralization by bouncing local poverty control between states, counties, and multicounty jurisdictions.

So fragile was the program, and so vulnerable to outside attack, that President Johnson had to lodge it in his own Executive Office of the President. Shriver was supremely loyal to his president, from whom he drew all of his bureaucratic power, and in return anticipated presidential support for large increases in the poverty budget. But maps of Vietnam soon replaced maps of Appalachia in the White House. Deprived of an expanding budget and presidential protection, Shriver was at the mercy of the enemies of the poverty program. Every tenured bureaucrat in Washington read the lesson: form subgovernments; don't count on the president for administrative power; build bridges to Congress, clientele groups, professional associations; and formalize those ties throughout counterpart organizations at all levels of government.

The realities of administrative politics create an endless contest to decide who will influence the administrative machinery of government. Chief executives insist on administrative loyalty and grumble about autonomous bureaucrats. The charge of "bureaucratic autonomy" has little meaning to administrators, who find themselves tied into a web of alliances with many influence seekers who would restrict administrative freedom. Moreover, bureaucrats know that they must often compromise their loyalty to the official hierarchy in order to respond to these interests. In the long run, they know that favorable treatment from the top executive really depends upon the strength of their political constituency. Power breeds generosity—even if the chief executive happens to dislike the agency.

The remainder of this chapter is devoted to a more detailed examination of the impact of outside interests on the world of the administrator—the legislators, clients, professions, state and local officials, government contractors, and two new groups pressing for admission to the inner sanctum of administrative decision making. Chapter 5 renews the controversy from the point of view of chief executives and their analysts.

ADMINISTRATIVE OVERSIGHT BY CONGRESS

No business executive ever had to deal with a board of overseers like Congress. As a business executive, I would never have dreamed of spending as much as one-third of my time with my board.[8]

The American constitution vests "the executive power" in the office of the president of the United States. That proviso has never prevented the Congress from exercising its own powers of administrative oversight. In the earliest years of the Republic the congressional caucus fought to control administration by dictating the appointment of cabinet secretaries and insisting that presidents allow the cabinet to approve executive policy by majority rule. America's first case of presidential impeachment concerned an administrative issue—the Tenure of Office Act—in which the Congress asserted its power to advise on removals as well as to consent to nominations. Frustrated in their efforts to control the chief executive or frame broad social policy, legislatures from top to bottom in the American system have sought to exercise power by outflanking the chief executive and intervening in routine administration. One of the most critical constitutional questions in twentieth-century America is: who shall control the bureaucracy, the executive or the legislature?

The interplay of administrative and congressional organization is revealed by Harold Seidman, who represented President Lyndon Johnson as his management specialist in the Bureau of the Budget:

> Executive branch structure and administrative arrangements are not matters of mere academic interest to members of Congress. What may appear to be structural eccentricities and abnormalities within the executive branch are often nothing but mirror images of jurisdictional conflicts within the Congress. *Congressional organization and executive branch organization are interrelated and constitute two halves of a single system.* [9]

Administrative disputes between the dam-building Corps of Army Engineers and the reclamation-oriented Bureau of Reclamation are mirrored in the congressional conflict between the Committees on Public Works and the Committees on the Interior. The more common pattern finds cozy coexistence between executive agencies whose internal organization corresponds precisely to the specialization of interests among members on a counterpart congressional committee or subcommittee. The organization of the Department of Agriculture is matched precisely by the division of work on the House and Senate Committees on Agriculture. The same is true for defense, foreign affairs, labor, education, banking, and atomic energy, to mention only a few areas. As a rule, the more powerful an agency's clientele, the more exact its organization is duplicated in the legislature.

The power of congressmen (or women) is based upon their seniority on these committees and upon their ability to master the details of specific administrative programs. Committee appointees are carefully screened to maintain the division of labor on each subcommittee. The subcommittee on agriculture in the House Appropriations Committee, for example, always has one representative from metropolitan New York, to oversee the interests of small-crop, window-box marijuana farmers, members say. Novice committee members serve a long period of apprenticeship during which they learn the norms of committee cooperation, consensus, and specialization. Only a few committees display continued bouts of partisanship, the most notable being the old House Committee on Education and Labor, which oversaw the equally controversial War on Poverty.

The concentration on committee specialization severely reduces the opportunity for overall legislative coordination and promotes a fragmented, feudallike approach to administrative oversight. As Seidman concludes, the "growth of a congressional bureaucracy and institutionalization of committees have deepened the moats dividing the fiefdoms and accentuated the innate disposition of the Congress to concentrate on administrative details rather than basic issues of public policy."[10]

Committee members retain a formidable arsenal of power strategies by which individual members can influence the course of public administration. These powers flow from the constitutional authority of the Congress over authorizations, appropriations, and appointments. The most vulnerable agencies, from the Appalachian Program to the Federal Energy Administration, operate under authorizations that require the Congress to renew all or the major part of their operations every few years, a practice known as "sunset" legislation. Some agencies, notably in the Defense Department, are expected to solicit legislative authorization for individual projects before they spend any money. Of course, legislative approval from the authorizing committee is no guarantee that the funds for the program will be delivered by the appropriations subcommittees. As the bureaucrats in charge of the Model Cities Program painfully learned, actual appropriations can fall 50 percent short of promised authorizations. In some cases, the committee has acquired the power to authorize programs and appropriate money for them without ever putting the issue before the whole Congress, a process requiring the agency to "come into agreement" with the appropriate committee before it lets a contract, disposes of property, issues a rule, or carries out a reorganization plan. Quite often this is to the advantage of the bureau chief. The chief of the Corps of Army Engineers can plan dams, solicit local support, let contracts, and otherwise spend money from an unmarked reservoir of funds simply by acquiring committee consent—and thus commit the government to undertake the projects without prior White House or congressional review. This is known as "backdoor spending." Even after the project is completed, the committee retains administrative oversight through the General Accounting Office, which conducts audits of executive agencies to determine if the money was spent in line with congressional intent.

There are two additional techniques by which committees control administration without having to go through the legislative maze: the committee report and the congressional investigation. Nearly all committees issue written reports to accompany legislative bills. Although the reports never come to a vote before the entire Congress, their recommendations have the standing of law. For example, the Bureau of the Budget for many years sought to establish field offices in the federal regional centers so that budget reviewers could oversee governmental administration where 90 percent of it takes place. Upon learning of the plan, the House Appropriations Subcommittee reviewing the president's budget inserted in its committee report language to the effect that no money appropriated herein might be used to establish regional offices for the Budget Bureau. This was interpreted by three presidents as a bar to decentralizing the executive's chief clerks.

The committee investigation is a powerful weapon for forcing bureau chiefs to adopt a policy they oppose. Its success depends greatly upon the skill of individual committee members in breaking through the subgovernment propaganda machine and creating stereotypes that touch the public conscience. The brothers Kennedy were especially adept at affecting subgovernment behavior by the use of televised investigations. In one famous case, Senator Robert Kennedy attempted to have the Department of Agriculture force reactionary southern counties to distribute food stamps to poverty-stricken families. Kennedy picked up his subcommittee and went south, television crews trailing behind him. He began the hearings in a county courthouse whose commissioners had refused to accept federal food assistance programs. He heard the county politicians, all white and well-fed, tell the television cameras that their county had no hungry people. The television crews stored the film. Twenty-four hours later Kennedy reconvened the hearings down the road in a run-down room where haggard black and white faces pointed to their puff-bellied tots and asked why the richest nation in the world could not feed its children. The television news team combined the two—well-fed denial and hungry evidence—into a single ninety-second clip which went out to middle Americans watching the evening news at dinnertime.

Congressional control of administration is a two-way street, with advantages and strategies galore for bureau chiefs who wish to influence committee behavior. J. Leiper Freeman identifies the major strategies in a book that began as a study of the Bureau of Indian Affairs. Bureaucrats can call upon leading administration figures to testify on their behalf. The power of "executive unity," when officials from White House to field offices march together, is a powerful weapon for subduing critical committee members. The agency formalizes congressional relations through a legislative liaison office staffed with highly paid legal and political talent who can speak the language of both camps quietly and persuasively. The bureau chiefs exploit informal, personal relationships formed with committee leaders when both were young, ambitious, and invisible on the Washington scene. Bureau officials exploit committee hearings for publicity, raising the flag of good faith and public support, avoiding the morass of dull, technical issues. They wage a propaganda war orchestrated by the formidable public relations offices that all departments maintain. Finally, the bureau chiefs play one legislative committee off against another, perhaps calling upon a friendly House authorization committee to counterbalance the report of a hostile Senate investigations subcommittee.

Success in the appropriations game requires special administrative skills. Aaron Wildavsky traces agency success to the administrator's ability to cultivate a clientele, develop confidence in him- or herself, and play by the unwritten rules of budgetary politics. Richard

117

Fenno, in a study of the legislative power of the purse, reveals how different agencies use public support and legislative support to expand their budget and protect against cuts. The best lobbyists for any agency, it seems, are the congressmen themselves. Public support plus congressional support guarantees an expanding budget. In the absence of public support, the congressmen can protect the agency against a budgetary trimming. The most fortunate agencies are those whose congressmen are either members of the agency, such as the armed services, or its clients, such as farmers.

CLIENTELE RELATIONS AND BUREAUCRATIC POWER

The second major force that tends to negate executive control over public administration is the opportunity afforded clientele groups to participate in administration. Why do governmental executives solicit clientele groups, and what effect does this have upon policy making in a democratic government?

One book that reveals the extent of clientele group involvement in administration is Philip Foss's story of the Bureau of Land Management. Located within the Department of the Interior, the BLM oversees private use of 170 million acres of federal grasslands—the "open range" of Zane Grey's Wild West. During the New Deal the federal government sought to control overgrazing and cutthroat competition by ranchers. Under the authority of the Taylor Grazing Act, the BLM set out to develop new regulations for the private use of public lands. The director of grazing, sitting in Washington, needed a mass of information about local conditions in order to establish guidelines for field officials who would have to issue the grazing permits and establish the fees. He asked local grazers and landowners in each grazing district to elect a district advisory board. The boards were usually composed of leaders of the local stockmen's association, who were asked to provide advice and information. Says Foss:

> The Advisory Boards quickly assumed or were given more than an advisory role. They were most influential in drafting a code of rules and regulations; with some exceptions, they determined the allocation of permits; they supervised the expenditure of range improvement funds; they were probably the real decision-makers in setting grazing fees; they were influential in the selection and tenure of personnel; and they have played an active role in routine managerial decisions.[11]

One advisory board at Soldier Creek, Oregon, ran afoul of an intransigent district range manager devoted to strict land management. The district manager decided to reduce grazing at the expense of the cattle ranchers represented on the advisory board. The cattlemen appealed to friendly congressmen and senators and to the secretary of the interior, who happened to be the ex-governor of the state. Under local pressure, the district manager resigned and the advisory board regained its power over the allocation of grazing permits.

There is always a risk that well-organized clientele groups will overpower the agency and assume administrative responsibilities. The most vulnerable agencies are ones that provide economic benefits to special groups, such as veterans, farmers, teachers, contractors, and labor organizations.

Most bureaucrats are willing to accept this risk in exchange for the invaluable services which the clientele group can provide to the administrative agency. Strong clientele support allows the agency to oppose directives from the White House or Congress, as the groups are often in a position to protect their parent agency from reprisals by using their influence with the politicians. The clientele group can issue propaganda or take positions that the agency wants publicized but feels reluctant to issue itself. Clientele groups make program delivery more efficient by organizing the recipients of the agency's policies, or at least publicizing the availability of government funds and programs. Most important, organized clientele groups provide visual evidence that there is someone out there anxious to receive the agency's benefits—and angry if they are cut back. This is made clear through personal testimony to the legislators and executives who oversee agency programs and funds.

There are numerous managerial devices for formalizing the relationships between the clientele and the agency. The clientele's participation may be set in law, as in the case of the cattlemen's advisory board. If formal boards seem out of place, the agency may establish informal advisory committees, task forces, or call upon clientele for consulting or contracting activities. The agency may establish occupational requirements that favor members of the clientele group so that they are hired as official personnel. Field officials may be instructed to actually organize the clientele, a technique practiced from agricultural cooperatives to community action programs. Once the clientele is organized, it is typically encouraged to make demands for more services. The agency then requests additional monies or authorization to meet these "outside demands."

If a clientele group poses a potential threat to the stability or existence of the agency, it may be "co-opted" or absorbed into the policy-making structure of the agency. In exchange for participation in agency policy making, the clientele group implicitly agrees not to undermine the general goals of the agency and to defend it, when necessary, against outside attack. The term *co-optation* was introduced into the administrative vocabulary by sociologist Philip Selznick in his famous study of the Tennessee Valley Authority during its formative years in the Great Depression.

The Tennessee Valley Authority was created as part of the New Deal to bring flood control, electricity, and modern agriculture to the poor red-dirt country of the Tennessee River. It was administered by a three-person commission sitting in Knoxville—symbolically decentralized from Washington to the grass roots of Tennessee. Its protectors, President Franklin Roosevelt and Senator George Norris, made the TVA an independent agency and exempted it from many administrative regulations so as to encourage the success of this experimental New Deal program. Roosevelt appointed to the commission David Lilienthal, a young public-power advocate from Chicago; H. A. Morgan, an agriculturist with strong ties to the area's land-grant colleges; and, as chairman, A. E. Morgan (no relation), who took over responsibility for the flood control and dam-building activities.

The natural enemies of the TVA were the private electric-power companies competing to serve the Tennessee Valley; also the farmers and agricultural organizations that were suspicious of the TVA's mandate to institute self-help cooperatives, rural zoning, subsistence homesteads, broad regional planning, and fertilizer production. To the more conservative farmers, the TVA's farm mandate smacked of agricultural socialism; the fertilizer program posed a threat to local nitrate industries. To win over the farmers, H. A. Morgan entered into a "memorandum of understanding" with the seven valley land-grant colleges, setting up the states as partners in the TVA's agricultural development program and assuring that the TVA would not undertake any "radical" farm programs. Morgan also took the TVA out of the nitrate fertilizer business, converting the plant at Muscle Shoals to the production of experimental phosphate fertilizers, which the TVA widely distributed, free of charge, to "demonstration" farms. In effect, the fancy grass-roots theory of bringing the TVA close to the people became a pragmatic methodology by which the TVA effectively broadened its political base.

And the base needed broadening. In 1937, the Senate decided to investigate charges of malfeasance and corruption in the TVA—with formidable enemies ready to open wounds over the TVA's production of public electric power. The godfather of the TVA, President Roosevelt, had damaged his congressional relations in the court-packing fight and could not protect it. In his place, marching to Washington, were the farm organizations and farmers who turned out to tell how the TVA had turned on the lights in the Tennessee Valley and converted the poor red-dirt country into a productive farming community and changed the fortunes of the men and women who lived in the seven-state region.

There are a number of ways by which an agency may co-opt its clientele. The TVA practiced informal co-optation, entering into informal agreements with the farmers that allowed the farm organizations to influence TVA policy while assuring the TVA of broad-based local support. The BLM case is an illustration of administrative co-optation, where the clientele group actually becomes part of the agency's institutional structure or, as in the case of government contracting, becomes the vehicle through which the agency executes its programs. Either way, the clientele group develops a vested interest in the program which assures the agency that the clientele will always work within the system.

Co-optation provides a good illustration of what is involved in administrative pluralism. The bargain struck between the agency and its clientele may undo in part the legislative mandate that has been

Clientele groups are often allowed to influence administrative policy in exchange for their support. This is a fundamental source of power for public administrators. Officials of the Tennessee Valley Authority solidified their administrative base of power by winning the support of local farm organizations.
COURTESY OF THE TENNESSEE VALLEY AUTHORITY.

handed down to the agency. The TVA excluded progressive farm programs from the Tennessee Valley, despite the fact that these programs were part of its official policy. Says Selznick, co-optation "may result in the perversion of policy determined through representative institutions."[12] Of course, what the TVA gained was continued local support for its more controversial electric power policies and, in general, a system of administration that insured the responsiveness of the TVA to its public clientele. Nevertheless, private interests may come to dominate a program to the exclusion of other clientele, ruining the chance for both general agency responsibility and broad-scale group participation.

PROFESSIONALS IN THE PUBLIC SERVICE

The growth of the professional state is the third major source of tension in the formal administrative hierarchy. As a rule, each sub-government tends to come under the domination of a single profession. This produces a marriage of knowledge and power which rarely furthers the aims of chief executives, since one of the key features of professionalism is the drive to secure the independence of the profession from the control of executives, bureaucrats, politicians, or anyone else who has not been initiated into the inner circle of professional truth.

The power of the profession, from its own point of view, rests upon the specialized knowledge and skills that it alone possesses. There is an excessive concern for the professionally correct method of

121

performing a task—a fact that creates a natural aversion to outside control. Outsiders are seen as politically motivated amateurs who can only upset the technically correct solution to the problem that the professional has calculated. Leaders of professions are very sensitive to the possibility that a compromise in standards could damage their public prestige, and one of the central tenets of professionalism is the drive to maintain the status of the profession.

Continued resistance to outside interference in professional affairs requires a high degree of professional solidarity. As Morris Janowitz observes with regard to the military, a profession "is more than a group with special skill, acquired through intensive training. A professional group develops a sense of group identity and a system of internal administration."[13] The military has maintained this sense of identity through periods of great adversity, including times during which public-opinion polls have ranked the general status of the officer corps at the same level as that of funeral directors. Through the persistence of a stern code of behavior, the creation of a standardized pattern of career development, and a tradition of placing public service over personal gain, the military—according to Janowitz—has been able to maintain and even elevate its status.

The professional norms of autonomy, identity, and status were developed when professionals constituted less than 4 percent of the American work force, at a time when most professionals in government worked alone in relatively autonomous agencies, such as research laboratories, or were otherwise removed from the mainstream of policy making and political power. As professionals have moved into new positions of power, they have sought to incorporate their norms into the operation of the bureaucracy. And they *have* moved into positions of power. Today well over one-third of all government employees think of themselves as members of professions—teachers, lawyers, foreign service officers, social workers, civil engineers, public health doctors, foresters, architects, psychiatrists, all varieties of white-collar professionals from the natural sciences, and members of the "emerging professions," such as public administration. One of the deans of public administration, Frederick Mosher, has outlined what happens as a profession moves into a subgovernment and extends itself over the bureaucratic agency.

1. The profession stakes out its rights as the sole or dominant profession within the agency, claiming the agency as its territory, which it will defend against invaders from other professions. The military, for example, is the territory of the career officer corps, generally ones educated at the service academies. General Dwight D. Eisenhower, when he became president of Columbia University after the war, apparently forgot this lesson as he addressed the faculty as the "employees of the University." A distinguished professor stood and corrected him: "We are not employees of the University, Mr. President, we *are* the University."[14]

2. The profession sets up an elite corps of top professionals within the agency. These persons control the key administrative positions; they provide the leadership that results in policy change; and they use their prestige to extend their view of the agency to all personnel within it, professionals and non-professionals alike. This may produce substantial tension if there are members of "lesser" professions working within the agency. Generals and admirals of the elite military profession frequently must appeal to their friends in Congress to override the judgments of assorted scientists who may have more technical competence than the officers but nevertheless do not embody the specific values of military professionalism. Indeed, the greatest dissension in such agencies occurs between warring professions competing for elite status, not in traditional conflict such as that between workers and management.

3. The profession establishes control over the employment policies of the agency. First, it assumes control over the recruitment and promotion of its own kind. This is supported by the profession's insistence that their own schools and licensing boards are the only bodies qualified to approve the credentials of members of their own profession. This is usually followed by demands for a system of tenure and career development for its own members and then the demand that their people be exempt from civil service laws and the merit principle. Next, the profession attempts to extend its control to agency personnel outside of the elite profession, first by hiring its own staff, then by taking control of the general agency personnel review boards. It attempts to insure that top executives are selected from the ranks of the profession and that workers, if not fellow professionals, at least identify with their view of the agency.

Professional unity is not only a method by which the profession gains control over the organization; it is also an administrative strategy by which the executives gain control of the professionals. Consider the case of the Forest Service, whose administrative behavior is described by Herbert Kaufman. The Forest Service manages over 170 national forests and grasslands in the United States—granting timber-cutting contracts, issuing grazing permits, supervising wilderness areas, building campgrounds, maintaining roads, and fighting fires. Because conditions in different states vary so widely, no two district rangers face the same set of problems. Moreover, the Forest Service is committed to a grass-roots ideology which maintains "that resource management begins—and belongs—on the ground."[15] By decentralizing authority to district rangers, the Forest Service officials take the risk that district rangers will become captives of local interests.

In order to restrain the natural tendencies toward disunity within the organization, Forest Service officials in Washington, D.C., developed a large number of formal administrative strategies which were used to detect and discourage deviation from central policy. These included an encyclopedic manual issued to each ranger, formal procedures for settling disputes, central policies for clearing new programs, central budgetary control, extensive reporting systems, frequent inspection by headquarters teams, the practice of rotating personnel to new districts every few years, and the requirement that field officers keep diaries to remain at the post to be read by incoming replacements. Most of these strategies were viewed by rangers in the field as punishment centered, i.e., you were expected to act independently but you were punished if you made any mistakes. A zealous concern for detecting errors and punishing offenders serves to do more than discourage deviation—it also encourages officials in the field to "go underground," either by not reporting actions taken or by simply not taking any actions at all.

Recognizing that these formal administrative strategies did not serve the goal of central control, the agency chiefs developed a far more effective strategy: professionalism. They used professionalism to develop the will and the capacity to conform to Forest Service responsibilities. This was accomplished, Kaufman observes, by recruiting rangers who fit the self-image of the Forest Service, by extensive post-entry training and education programs, by building identification with the Forest Service through an environment that affected each individual's self-image, and through the use of symbols. The result, Kaufman observed, was voluntary conformity to agency policy, "not simply because the Forest Rangers have to [conform], but because they want to."[16]

Decentralization of the Forest Service ceased to be a problem for headquarters officials, because all of the forest rangers were taught to think alike. They were professionals.

ADMINISTRATIVE FEDERALISM

The fourth and fifth sources of political tension in the administrative system arise because the government must "farm out" the actual implementation of its programs. It may rely upon private firms, whose relation to the government is set by contracts and grants, or it may rely upon other governments, through what is known as intergovernmental relations. Characteristically, these relationships begin from a theoretical assumption of *separation*—in a federal system, that the states are separate from the national government; in a free-enterprise system, that the public and private sectors are autonomous. In practice, however, separation is replaced by convergence, Officials from theoretically separate levels of government or sectors of society are tightly allied within each subgovernment, an alliance that is often impenetrable to political executives pressing their own priorities.

In intergovernmental relations, the principle of separation is known as the doctrine of *dual federalism,* which sees the governments as independent layers—national, state, and local—each, with its own powers, conducting essentially autonomous functions. From this viewpoint, education and police work are seen as primarily local functions, while foreign policy and regulation of interstate commerce are preempted by the national government. Those who extol this doctrine are disturbed by what they suppose to be national encroachment into state and local affairs. Because the federal government sends so much money to state and local governments, defenders of this doctrine believe that the federal government must have a lot more power. As evidence, they point to volumes of national regulations that states and cities must satisfy before receiving federal aid, the tendency of state and local governments to gauge their budget decisions to the availability of federal money at the expense of local priorities, and the growing competition between governments for tax revenues, with the national government preempting the most powerful revenue generators, leaving localities to flounder with burdens such as the property tax. Understandably, the advocates of dual federalism want to return power to the states and cities through revenue sharing, the decentralization of federal programs, and a general reorganization of federal administration.

The doctrine of dual federalism constitutes a formidable ideology. It is difficult to challenge, yet schools of public administration, influenced by the writings of Morton Grodzins and Daniel Elazar, have come to reject this "layer cake" view of administrative federalism. In its place they have substituted the logic of cooperation, or as Grodzins calls it, the "marble cake" of American government.

> The federal system is not accurately symbolized by a neat layer cake of three distinct and separate planes. A far more realistic symbol is that of the marble cake. Wherever you slice through it . . . there are unexpected whirls and an imperceptible merging of colors, so that it is difficult to tell where one ends and the other begins. So it is with federal, state, and local responsibilities.[17]

Grodzins ridicules the notion that federalism results in a concentration of power on the Potomac. American intergovernmental relations, Grodzins insists, are highly decentralized. "This is the decentralization that exists as the result of independent centers of power and that operates through the chaos of American political processes and political institutions."[18] It is based in what Grodzins calls the "multiple crack" of American politics. Like a giant block of marble, the American system is full of fissures. At all levels there are cracks that allow organized groups to have access to policy making and administration.

Grodzins identifies the institutional centers of access that tend to decentralize the system. There are the national political parties, highly decentralized in operation, which "disperse power in favor of state and local governments."[19] There are thousands of elected officials at the state and local level who believe that they can influence the course of intergovernmental policies and force federal officials to guarantee them a share in the decision making. When the state and local officials receive no satisfaction from federal administrators, then the officials can use their congressmen to pressure the feds. The congressmen, dependent upon local parties and local support for reelection, willingly play the role of ombudsmen in promoting local demands. Then there are the interest groups that intervene in intergovernmental relations to place the views of clientele before the administrators. Add to this the inadequate enforcement of federal regulations and the natural bureaucratic tendency to fund each intergovernmental program at no less than last year's funding level, and the result will be tremendous pressures toward decentralization, a situation of shared responsibilities in which any increase of money or authority at any level of the system increases the power of all participants at all levels of the system. That is what is meant by the term *cooperative federalism*—if the groups do not cooperate, the programs will collapse.

Grodzins's theory, which he characterized as decentralization by mild chaos, was conceived during the fifties. The administrative situation ten years later revealed that the chaos was more acute than mild. The chaos arose from a new principle of separation in intergovernmental relations—not the outmoded layer-cake principle of dual federalism, but the functional separation created as each subgovernment tied its own local bureaucrats into the vertical autocracy. These vertical strips of policy specialists drew their power from the narrow, categorical grant-in-aid, from the provisions that a single state or local agency be designated to administer grant funds, from the reluctance of bureaucrats in different agencies to coordinate their work, and from the natural tendency of local bureaucrats to communicate with their functional counterparts at subgovernment headquarters rather than with the political executives elected to supervise them. The result was neither a marble cake of shared powers nor a layer cake of separate powers. As one frustrated governor wrote:

> Government is more like a picket fence. The lines of authority, the concerns and interests, the flow of money, and the direction of programs run straight down like a number of pickets stuck into the ground. There is, as in a picket fence, a connecting cross slat, but that does little to support anything. In this metaphor it stands for the governments. It holds the pickets in line; it does not bring them together. The picket-line programs are not connected at the bottom.[20]

The fragmentation of intergovernmental relations has created within the federal system tens of thousands of separate local constituencies whose instinct for survival is linked to the power and appropriations supplied by the national host bureaucracy. Any shifting of appropriations, transfer or elimination of programs, or general reorganization is strongly resisted.

To combat excessive specialization among the bureaus, federal executives created various administrative mechanisms designed to improve comprehensive planning and program coordination. They called it "creative federalism." Two of the most famous experiments were the Community Action Program and Model Cities. James Sundquist, who wrote the administrative history of creative federalism, tells the story.

The Community Action Program was conceived in 1964 as the core of President Johnson's War on Poverty. Its purpose flowed from two central assumptions: that existing programs for poor people were too specialized and complex to reach the poor, and that poverty was a result of the powerlessness of poor people to understand and gain access to those programs. Over one thousand Community Action agencies were funded as independent offices adjacent to local governments with the purpose of organizing the poor, identifying local agencies that serviced the poor, and putting the two together. The Community Action agencies also acquired a few special poverty programs, such as Operation Head Start for poor preschool children, which the agencies ran on their own. The poor were given "maximum feasible participation" in the planning and administration of all agency programs.

Model Cities was conceived three years later, in 1967, as the central instrument for coordinating the attack on the problems of urban slums. Certain designated cities set up special agencies which prepared to coordinate all federal grants to the city for housing, urban renewal, transportation, education, welfare, and economic opportunity. Model Cities agencies also received supplemental funds provided as a bloc grant, which they could spend by themselves. Neighborhood representatives were given "citizen participation" by appointment or election to local planning boards.

Five years later President Nixon called both programs monumental failures and tried to push them into the administrative dustbin. What happened? One could blame the serious lack of funding, the fuzziness of citizen participation, the tendency of many programs to fight city hall, the encouragement of advocacy and citizen confrontation, or the lack of liberal sympathies in a new Republican administration. Yet in administrative terms, what is most striking about both programs is this: Community Action and Model Cities were transformed into limited-purpose programs with their own clientele, commitments, and earmarked expenditures. Community Action programs became local agencies administering poverty programs to the poor—Head Start, manpower training, health care, and so on—often in competition with other agencies. When these programs were "spun off" to regular departments, the Community Action agencies—originally designed for coordination—found they had little left to do. The Model Cities agencies, designed for urban coordination, quickly became advocates for the concrete programs of their parent, the Department of Housing and Urban Development. When funds for public housing, parking lots, and office buildings dried up, so did Model Cities. Neither program was ever as powerful as its nearest old-line competitor. All that remained

127

of the programs after 1973 were two vertical functional autocracies—two more posts in the picket fence of federalism.

Such experience reinforces the standing rule of administrative federalism: so long as the features of the federal system that Grodzins described persist—multiple independent centers of power and open political access—then any new administrative schemes will be transformed into functional autocracies. As much coordination as exists will be a result of the "hidden hand" of decentralization by mild chaos. If the chief executive attempts to impose a more orderly system of coordination from above, then the persons with political power will veto his action from below.

The chief executives, Richard Nixon included, took a new tack. Using the rhetoric of dual federalism (they promised to "return power to the states"), the top executives tried to wrest program control from the subgovernments and vest it with political executives. They assaulted the financial keystone of the subgovernment system—the narrow, categorical grant-in-aid—with proposals for general revenue sharing, special revenue sharing, and block grants. The executives hoped to crack the political autonomy of the subgovernments by weakening their financial autonomy. This approach was called the new federalism.

The new federalism, with its pledge of decentralized government, actually sought to increase the power of political executives in the White House, the mayor's office, and the governor's mansion. When political executives like the president cry states' rights, they invariably mean decentralization by executive order. As Grodzins observed, decentralization by executive order is essentially the same as centralization by executive order. To be effective, it requires the top political executives to deprive Congress, political parties, and interest groups of the political power they currently exercise through the chaos of American federalism.

An executive must possess a power before he or she can give it away. The subgovernments naturally resist decentralization by order because they are sufficiently content with the share of the action they currently enjoy and because a rational ordering of the federal system would require them to sacrifice power to the executive chain of command. Which is preferable, asks Grodzins, decentralization by mild chaos based on real centers of independent power, or an ordered decentralization that depends eternally upon the approval of top executives? Decentralization by executive order could easily become centralization by executive order, in which case there would be no "states' rights" at all.

Seen in this context, the proposals for administrative reform in intergovernmental relations are ripe with political meaning. Proposals for "making federalism work" are usually executive or bureaucratic ideologies fought over the most ancient political question: who shall rule? (Even the holiest of liberal writs, citizen participation, tends to be used as a means of legitimizing the power of bureaucrats

CHAPTER 4: THE POLITICS OF ADMINISTRATION

or executives—whoever co-opts the small band of professional citizens who choose to participate.)

The result is conflict, tension, and mistrust in a federal system where, by administrative standards, there ought to be cooperation and coordination. Thus far the subgovernments have had the upper hand. There is a powerful tendency in intergovernmental relations toward the categorization of programs. Programs set up to further cooperation, coordination, and flexibility naturally turn into categories—because of their need to generate political support. Programs that try to remain adaptive tend to alienate their political support and wither away.

GOVERNMENT CONTRACTING

Public administrators spend as much effort working with contractors in the private sector as they do working with other governments through the federal system. In one typical year, the federal government transferred $54 billion to private contractors through government grants and contracts.[21] In return, the contractors executed public programs and provided the federal government with goods and services. The dollar volume of federal intergovernmental programs, by contrast, amounted to $52 billion that year—$2 billion less.

Despite the volume of government contracting, scholars in public administration have been far less interested in this subject than they have been in intergovernmental relations. The best studies of public–private-sector contracting relationships have come from economists concerned with military spending.

The theory of government-business relations, as written by neo-classical economists, proceeds from the doctrine of separation implicit in a free-market system, a doctrine that in turn flows from the laissez-faire principle that all economic transactions are subject to the vagaries of the market, which is to say that prices are freely determined in a contest between supply and demand. Under classical capitalism, the government has no business interfering in the free-market system. For a variety of reasons, best explored in an introductory course in economics, modern nations have moved from this classical ideology to the situation of planned or mixed economies. Governments regulate economic enterprises; they determine the amount of income left over for private consumption. Yet although governments account for better than 25 percent of all economic activities in the society, there has persisted the notion that in *purchasing* goods and services from private contractors, the government ought to pursue the principle of separation implicit in classical economic theory. The principle proclaims that governments should not produce their own goods where industry can provide them at a lower cost; that the government ought to allow open, competitive bidding for government contracts; and that the government ought not to interfere with the right of the contractor to make a reasonable profit on the transaction. Yet just as the ideology of separation has disappeared from public regulatory and economic policies, so now it is expiring in the area of government contracting.

In reality, the practice of allowing private concerns to act as the executors of public programs has produced a situation of *economic convergence*. The lines of demarcation between private contractor and public agency have become blurred and indistinguishable. Public agencies have taken over many of the prerogatives of private executives, deciding, for example, which products or services the firm will produce, how the firm will finance its operations, and which functions the firm can subcontract. The private firms, in turn, acquire the power to make public decisions affecting the direction of government policy and the distribution of public funds. They transform a temporary contractual relationship into a situation of permanent status, where the government is obliged to rescue the firm, should it encounter financial difficulties.

The way in which economic separation is replaced by economic convergence is illustrated dramatically by one case of government contracting: the C-5A cargo plane. The C-5A was conceived as a jumbo jet that would allow the American military to rapidly deploy heavy equipment into a theater of war on short notice. In 1974, the air force asked five aerospace firms to compete for the contract. Three finalists—Boeing, Douglas, and Lockheed—were given $6 million each to prepare technical proposals. In 1965, all three companies submitted bids. Lockheed made the lowest bid—$2.2 billion—and was awarded the contract.

The contract was designed to protect the government against cost overruns. Lockheed was given complete program responsibility for the C-5A, a total-package procurement policy that prevented Lockheed from escaping responsibility for any errors or cost overruns committed by its subcontractors. Lockheed's compensation for the job was based on a cost-incentive formula which rewarded the firm for delivering planes that met basic performance criteria by the deadline established in the contract. In return, the government agreed to purchase 120 planes for an estimated $3.4 billion. That was 1965.

In 1968, a cost-efficiency expert broke the conspiracy of silence and revealed to the Congress that the cost of the C-5A program had escalated to $5.4 billion. Moreover, he added, the military brass had assured Lockheed that the defense department would pick up the cost of any overruns on the first 58 planes through a renegotiated price on the next 62, an unwritten agreement known in defense circles as the golden handshake.

In 1969, the Pentagon renegotiated its contract with Lockheed and agreed to purchase 81 planes rather than 120, at the inflated price of $5.4 billion. Even under these new conditions, Lockheed stood to lose $200 million on the C-5A. Moreover, there were still technical problems with the aircraft. Its wings cracked, the wheels fell off, and the huge cargo door came unlocked in flight. Lockheed had fallen behind in its delivery schedule, it was short on operating capital, and its other government contracts for helicopters, missiles, and ships were in similar trouble, for which the Pentagon was demanding that Lockheed incur an additional $200 million loss.

Lockheed's financial house of cards collapsed when it learned that Rolls Royce, its major subcontractor for commercial jet engines, had declared bankruptcy because it could not cover its own cost overruns. Lockheed asked the Defense Department to provide it with additional working capital (called progress payments, since they are made for work in progress) and, in addition, asked the Congress to authorize the U.S. Treasury to cosign, or guarantee, $250 million in loans that Lockheed would borrow from commercial banks. The loans would not be used to finance government contracts, but to finance Lockheed's sales of aircraft to commercial airlines.

The request spurred intense controversy within the government, including a Senate filibuster. Foes of the military-industrial complex insisted that Lockheed pay the price for fiscal mismanagement in a free-enterprise system—in other words, go bankrupt. Government and labor leaders pleaded with Congress to bail out Lockheed and save the nation from an economic catastrophe. The Defense Department agreed to the stepped-up schedule of progress payments to Lockheed and, two months later, the Congress by a single vote agreed to Lockheed's loan-guarantee request.

The defense procurement subgovernment, popularly known as the military-industrial complex, came to believe that the construction of military weapons systems could not be performed without the talent and capital contained in the Lockheed corporation and was also unwilling to upset the economic stability of the market served by the subgovernment by allowing Lockheed to go under. An increasingly large number of private enterprises have acquired a status similar to Lockheed's: other aerospace firms, oil conglomerates, railroads and airlines, agricultural businesses, construction firms, think tanks, consultants, even a few private universities that are dependent upon government contracts for their financial well-being.

Critics of the system are wont to point out the advantages possessed by the contractor which, say the critics, give the contractor the upper hand in its relations with the government. Size is the main advantage. A few contractors grow large, monopolizing the technology and talent necessary to compete for government contracts. The government encourages this development by awarding contracts to fewer and fewer firms and, eventually, negotiating contracts with a single firm under the pretext that only this firm is big enough and competent enough to meet government standards. Having won a contract through negotiation rather than competition, the firm is in a better position to raise costs once the project is underway. If the government refuses to restructure the contract and pay for cost overruns, the company can strike—that is, it can threaten to stop work on its government projects.

Increasing the costs on government projects seems to have become an end in itself. The contractor is able to increase executive and professional salaries far above the government equivalent; it demands and receives enormous overhead payments and profits; and it can "goldplate"—suggest exotic new amendments to the original specifications. The contractor may demand and receive the use of government land, buildings, and equipment; it may demand progress payments to reduce the costs of financing the project. Insofar as these contribute to the contractor's private commercial activities, they constitute government subsidies—to say nothing of the straight bail-out, where the government rushes in with interim financing to save a failing firm.

Not all the advantages are with the contractor, however. In many cases, the power of the government is equal to that of the contractor. First, the government can hold to elaborate procurement regulations and product specifications as a condition for letting the contract. Some of these are substantial, some are trivial. For example, the government has required military contractors to buy all of their jewel bearings from the Turtle Mountain Bearing Company in Rolla, North Dakota. Help-wanted advertising was ruled an allowable cost on military contracts, but not if it was in color. More impressively, the government can specify the financial reporting system, planning system, engineering system, and wages the contractor can pay. Many specifications arise as a result of government cost-reduction programs and encourage producers to reduce stockpiles, standardize equipment, improve purchasing, and so forth. For grants to nonprofit enterprises, the government will insist that the group draw up elaborate plans for spending the funds, which must be approved as a condition of funding.

Second, the government has an elaborate system for combatting what is called cost optimism—the tendency of contractors to underestimate costs while negotiating an award. The government may insist upon seeing the final product before signing the contract—what the air force calls "fly now, buy later." It may encourage a number of firms to simultaneously develop prototypes of the desired system. It may insist on incentive contracting, which is designed to force contractors to make reasonable estimates of cost, product performance, and delivery deadlines, by basing the profit paid to the contractor on how well it meets or beats its targets. This contrasts sharply with the negotiated cost-plus contract, where the government in effect agrees to repay the contractor for all allowable costs it incurs plus a fixed percentage profit.

As a last resort, the government may simply toughen up. It may refuse to renew contracts, as the government has done a number of times in the area of social services. Government auditors may disallow certain expenses that were made in violation of government standards. The government may refuse to accept the product, or as in the case of the giant Litton Industries, it may refuse to settle claims for cost reimbursement, even if it means fighting the contractor in court.

In total, contracting procedures result in a balance of power between the government and the firm. The result is sort of an interference complex, where government agencies and private contractors make decisions for each other that tend to tighten up the alliances that already exist within the specialized policy arenas of modern governmental administration.

PUBLIC EMPLOYEES AND COLLECTIVE BARGAINING

The prevailing tendency in modern public administration is for the inclusion of more groups, not fewer, in the administrative process. Two groups standing at the door of the exclusive subgovernment club are government employees and citizens.

Government employees make a persuasive case for membership in the club. The standing entrance fee for admission to a subgovernment is specialization. Then why not admit government employees —who devote their life's career to a particular specialty? The primary restraint has been the administrative principle which says that workers are subordinate to the official hierarchy and that they have no business intervening in matters of administrative policy. Well, such ideals have not restrained the bureau chiefs from making end runs around their political superiors to legislative committees and clientele groups. So why should it restrain garbage collectors, postal workers, police officers, and schoolteachers from demanding that they share in administrative policy making?

Labor unions made up of public employees are not only bargaining over the traditional issues of wages and working conditions, they are asking for the right to participate in the making of administrative policy. Teachers' unions, for example, have gone to the bargaining table to settle questions of class size, the school calendar, curriculum planning, textbook purchasing, and procedures for assigning teachers to their jobs.
COURTESY OF THE
AMERICAN FEDERATION
OF TEACHERS.

133

Government employees are bargaining over policy. This should not be confused with the old practice of letting public unions, such as the postal workers, lobby with legislative committees for their annual Christmas pay raise—a practice known as collective begging. Modern collective bargaining by government employees goes beyond far this and has profound implications for the distribution of administrative power within subgovernments. A case history may help to reveal those tendencies.

In the spring of 1967, the New York City Board of Education created three demonstration school districts in which control over local schools was given to community leaders. One of the three districts was in Ocean Hill-Brownsville, a slum in Brooklyn, New York, that looks like a bombed-out city. Its population in 1968 was 70 percent black and 25 percent Puerto Rican. At the beginning of the 1967–68 school year, the community leaders who controlled the Ocean Hill-Brownsville school board hired four new elementary school principals, none of whom were listed on the New York City civil service eligibility list. The following spring, the board members fired nineteen teachers and administrators from the Ocean Hill-Brownsville district, all of whom were white. Ten of the teachers appealed their dismissal. That summer their case was heard before an arbitrator who recommended that all ten be reinstated. The school board refused to reinstate the ten teachers nor would it reinstate seventy-nine others who had been suspended for participating in a sympathy strike that spring.

On the opening day of school, 1968, the United Federation of Teachers called a city-wide strike to demand that the teachers be rehired. The board members opened Ocean Hill-Brownsville schools and staffed the classrooms with 350 nonunion teachers. The New York Supreme Court fined the union $220,000 and jailed the union president for fifteen days for violating the state law prohibiting strikes by public employees. Twice the union agreed to temporary settlements, but when the union teachers in Ocean Hill-Brownsville tried to return to their classrooms, they were barred by angry residents. The strike lasted from September 9 until November 18, when the parties agreed to a settlement that set up a complex system of supervisory committees, trusteeships, personnel transfers, and rules for "pairing" union and nonunion teachers in Ocean Hill-Brownsville. The following year the New York State Legislature upheld the demands of the teachers for protection against dismissal and shut down the three demonstration school districts.

There are many lessons in the incident, but none is as far-reaching as the fact that teachers were bargaining over decisions traditionally left to chief executives—not only the power to hire and fire, but also the question of whether or not there should be community control over local schools. Although the Ocean Hill-Brownsville case is extreme, it is not atypical. Public unions bargain over policy. Social workers in New York City went to the bargaining table expecting to negotiate how much clothing welfare families would receive.

134

The New York Patrolman's Benevolent Association demanded that their contract guarantee a minimum of two police officers in each patrol car. After U.S. postal workers went on strike and the president called out the National Guard to deliver the mail, labor-management negotiators sat down and decided to give away the post office. They also decided how the new postal authority was to be governed and how the directors of the authority would be selected. They even decided how to set the price of the postage stamp. To envision what a revolutionary change this implies, imagine for a moment that the United Auto Workers should suddenly demand that they be allowed to negotiate with General Motors "on who would own G.M., who would elect the board of directors, and on a pricing system for cars."[22]

Government officials, of course, insist that they be allowed to retain their prerogatives. Some officials will not even bargain over salaries or working conditions; the ones who will usually refuse to go further. Nevertheless, schoolteachers' unions—as one example—have settled questions of class size, the school calendar, curriculum planning, textbook purchasing, and procedures for assigning teachers to their jobs. Surely these are traditional management prerogatives. In 1972, schoolteachers in Washington, D.C., went on strike because they felt that the school administration was too rigid, bureaucratic, and out of touch with the needs of the students. The teachers insisted that they were closer to the actual execution of educational policy and thus better able to judge policy decisions.

Sometimes management wins these bouts, sometimes it loses. In the long range, of course, such conflict tends to wear out the mythical hierarchy that presumes that employees follow orders from executives who execute policy set by politicians. In fact, public collective bargaining tends to shut out the politicians—the chief executive and the legislators—who presumably set policy. Nowhere is this more apparent than over the issue of compulsory arbitration.

Compulsory arbitration is a process by which all parties agree to submit to a final and binding decision in negotiations presided over by a neutral third party. It usually follows unsuccessful efforts to resolve the dispute through direct negotiations, mediation, and non-binding arbitration. It is increasingly used to settle public disputes, especially when the union threatens a lengthy strike that will cut off essential services. Compulsory arbitration was used, for example, to settle New York City's 1968 garbage collectors' strike. While New Yorkers tripped the light fantastic around one hundred thousand tons of uncollected refuse, the garbage collectors hooted down the deal worked out between their union leaders and the city's Office of Labor Relations. Mayor John Lindsay refused to give in, so Governor Nelson Rockefeller seized the city's garbage department and gave the union a bigger raise in pay. But the New York State Legislature then killed the governor's plan. At that point, Lindsay established binding arbitration, which allowed the union to save its pay raise and the city to save its face.

135

In this case, compulsory arbitration removed policy-making power from the elected representatives—the mayor, the governor, and the legislature—and lodged it with a neutral third party meeting with union leaders and garbage bureaucrats. The arbitrator was not elected. The legislature did not ratify his nomination, and he was not constitutionally accountable to the mayor who nominated him, since he could not be fired nor could his decision be overridden except under the most exceptional circumstances. The legislators were obliged to accept his decision. They were obliged to appropriate the money to pay for the settlement, even though that settlement might upset state priorities—which he was instructed to ignore—or exceed the capacity of the public to pay.

This would be mildly revolutionary if the arbitrator were deciding only the size of the public budget for salaries and benefits. But arbitrators are beginning to set public policy—because that is where labor-management negotiations are moving.

Government employees' organizations have a further effect of some importance—an effect upon the merit civil service. The movement for a career civil service based on merit was the midwife at the birth of American public administration. Now government workers are turning their backs on it. They dislike the idea that "neutral" commissioners should establish scales of pay, set procedures for promotions or layoffs, act on appeals of aggrieved employees, or represent them at the collective-bargaining table. These, they believe, are the functions of public unions.

> To many (union leaders), civil service is synonymous with unilateralism and paternalism, which means the "boss" imposes his rule on the employees. Because they are appointed by the "boss," civil service commissioners are viewed as "management-oriented"; in a showdown, they almost always back up the supervisors and agency heads. [23]

To public administrators already embattled by legislators, clients, professional associations, intergovernmental relations, and private contractors, collective bargaining must seem like an awful burden. Now they must contend with their own employees acting as a pressure group in the affairs of political administration. The fact that employee pressure groups extend administrative pluralism—opening up the subgovernment to more participants—must offer little comfort. Especially when standing behind the door with their entrance fees paid up are the citizens who receive the policy.

CITIZEN PARTICIPATION

Bureaucrats are anxious to institutionalize citizen participation. They ask: How can we build this into the program? How many citizens do you want? Are five enough? Citizens accept institutional participation, but this does not prevent them from standing outside of the system and sniping at it. In general, citizens want to participate when government hurts, not when the bureaucrats tell them to. Perhaps

136

they recognize that if they are institutionalized into the program, they will no longer be "citizens." The whole history of citizen participation is this contest between the pragmatism of citizens trying to gain access to government on their own terms and the desire of public officials to deal with them on a routine basis.

The institutionalization of citizen participation ranges from the tokenism of "blue ribbon" advisory committees to full-scale community control. Carl Stenberg describes how American government has moved through three epochs in citizen participation. The fifties were characterized by the citizen as advisor-persuader, sitting on advisory committees for urban renewal, juvenile delinquency, planning, land use, and transportation. The committee might be organized as a task force, a housing commission, a board of zoning appeals, a planning commission, or a school board. The citizens were expected to represent the needs of the city or county as a whole, to build support and community understanding for controversial projects, and to hustle federal funds. The citizens were hardly indigenous neighborhood leaders; they were white planners, businessmen, and lawyers, with a few labor leaders and priests thrown in to make the committee "representative."

With the advent of the "Great Society" programs in the midsixties, governments began to institutionalize the citizen ferment that was brewing in the neighborhoods. Federal legislation for Model Cities and Community Action agencies required the "maximum feasible participation" of the poor and minorities. Elected, appointed, and self-appointed representatives of citizen movements filed onto policy-making councils. They were asked to help improve the quality of public services by defining their own needs. They oversaw social programs, multiservice centers, and community corporations based in their own neighborhoods. In some cases they actually ran the programs. Citizen participation was supposed to democratize the bureaucracy, stimulate political activity, build community organizations, and provide jobs for the poor. The citizens were expected to confine their participation to little programs, like Operation Head Start or people's parks. Traditional city services, such as zoning commissions, were taboo. As soon as the citizens got the taste of power over social services, they demanded a say in highways and housing, police review boards, and community control of schools. These demands tended to alienate the old-line bureaucrats, who charged that the militants did not represent the hard-core poor and that the community leaders were using citizen-participation programs for political patronage. Stenberg accurately characterizes this as the period of the citizen as adversary.

Since 1969, governments have experimented with a variety of mechanisms for encouraging grass roots participation. Cities have set up town hall meetings, advisory neighborhood councils, complaint bureaus, and ombudsmen in an effort to open lines of communication. Community-wide committees advise public officials on housing, recreation, health, police, and schools. Some cities have ex-

The War on Poverty included provisions for more citizen control over administrative policy at the grass roots of administration. Recipients of the program benefits lined up to vote for citizens who would represent their interests in local community action councils. COURTESY OF THE COMMUNITY SERVICES ADMINISTRATION.

perimented with the decentralization of policy making by allowing advisory groups in the community, working with career officials located in the field, to develop public programs such as their own land-use plans. Some of the most interesting organizations to emerge are the little city halls: small, nonbureaucratic organizations designed to bring government closer to the people and reduce citizen alienation. Boston, one leading example, has established sixteen little city halls. With about eight employees in each, the storefront operations organize their neighborhood, process complaints, refer citizens to line agencies, and provide limited services.

Most persons who have studied the institutionalization of citizen participation carefully distinguish between administrative decentralization and community control. Most plans for citizen participation are administrative; that is, they result in a shifting of power between layers of the bureaucracy without any genuine redistribution of power between citizen and government. The professionals are moved out to the neighborhoods, and citizens are informed, consulted, placated, manipulated, or used by bureaucrats to "put off" an unwelcome issue or "put on" the community about a controversial one. Citizen participation, in these cases, means citizen co-optation. Many government officials sense that most citizens do not want to participate, that those who do are not necessarily "representative," and that citizens are really more interested in the decisions of big governments than the affairs of small, decentralized ones. These officials turn to administrative decentralization because it provides a strategy for absorbing potential sources of discontent into the system without significantly disrupting the balance of power within the subgovernment.

Community control, by contrast, vests administrative power in

community representatives who make decisions under limited profession control. It creates autonomous subunits of government char-
tered by the central institution: cities within cities. This approach
guided the creation of the Ocean Hill-Brownsville Demonstration
School District. It has been applied to education programs in the
Anacostia section of Washington, D.C.; to agricultural development
in Selma, Alabama; to community-development corporations in
Cleveland and Harlem; and, one must observe, to zoning and building restrictions in every white suburb in America.

Community control poses a large number of unanswered questions. Would community control, by granting separate governments
for separate neighborhoods, be a step toward racial separation?
Would community control reduce the capacity of governments to
vigorously attack metropolitan problems? Would it reduce honesty,
equity, and professionalism in government? Would community control accentuate existing inequities in the tax base? What would the
poor tax to raise the revenues to run their programs? How does one
define the boundaries of "the neighborhood"? As Alan Altshuler
observes in his book on community control, there are at least two
points of view behind each of these questions.

One thing is certain. Community control produces constant
conflict and ferment. From the point of view of citizens, this may
seem like a good thing. To citizens who are battling the bureaucracy,
participation is not a finite thing, like an administrative decision, but a
process that never ends. If the bureaucrats try to channel citizen
participation, to make a beginning and an end to it, the citizen will
find ways to get around the system. The project officials may hold
community meetings, set up advisory boards, and publicize their
plans, but the day that they stop asking for participation and start the
project one hundred people they have never seen before will come
out of the woodwork and throw baby carriages in front of the bull-
dozers.

There are many approaches citizens can adopt that do not depend
upon the approval of the people in the system. Citizens can protest,
sue the government, or get at bureaucrats through the political process. These approaches are dynamic. Citizens can think up ways to
use them faster than political scientists can write them down.

Organized citizen protest has a long and honorable history. Martin Luther King used it to solidify the southern civil rights movement.
Antiwar activists used it to build a campus protest movement against
American involvement in Vietnam and to hound Lyndon Johnson
from office ("Hey! Hey! LBJ! How many kids did you kill today?") On
a lesser scale, protest has been used to organize community rent
strikes, to block urban renewal projects, to organize labor unions of
public employees, to publicize the demands of poor people, Indians,
and migrant workers. Social scientists like to characterize organized
protest as a form of political bargaining, a tactic employed by persons
who lack the resources or the access necessary to directly affect public
policy. Protest is "the weapon of the powerless." This characteriza-

139

tion fits neatly into the sociological perspective that defines poverty as a form of impotence.

Activists like Saul Alinsky see organized protest in a similar way, as a strategy for creating an organization where none exists among people who share only a common condition and a common complaint. Alinsky was convinced that citizens in protest could defeat any big public institution, provided they remained pragmatic and flexible. He advised protesters to use ridicule, to taunt bureaucrats to obey their own rules and morality, which would make them look stupid before the public audience. Alinsky wrote out this advice during his free time, in jail. *"The Prince,"* he said, "was written by Machiavelli for the Haves on how to hold power. *Rules for Radicals* is written for the Have-Nots on how to take it away."[24]

If protest is the resource of the have-nots, then sueing the government is the weapon of the haves or, in some cases, the have-nots who are represented by public-interest law firms. Citizens have sued public agencies to force government action (or inaction) on school desegregation, environmental protection, legislative reapportionment, consumer protection, highway construction, airport noise, secrecy in government, and a variety of other policies.

There are four recent developments that have widened citizen access to policy making through the courts. One is the development of public-interest law firms, run privately and as arms of public antipoverty programs, which put court action within the reach of those citizens most vulnerable to bureaucratic rip-offs and least able to prevent them. The second is the enactment of laws encouraging citizens to bring lawsuits against the government and giving them a basis to do so. The National Environmental Policy Act of 1970, which requires federal agencies to defend against ecological intrusions, has been a powerful weapon in the hands of citizens suing to block the federal bulldozer. The third development is the courts' allowance of a broader definition of what constitutes the personal and direct injury that any plaintiff must show as a precondition to filing a suit against an administrative agency. Finally, potential litigants have utilized the class-action suit, a case brought by one person on behalf of all persons similarly injured, wherever they may be. The courts have restricted this strategy, however, by requiring that a clearly definable class of plaintiffs exist in fact.

Political action is the ultimate approach for citizens who want to get at government bureaucrats. It is here that the most fascinating aspect of citizen participation appears. One must remember that a sense of frustration directed against government is not a prerogative of the citizen alone. Subgovernments look like bureaucratic castles to the chief executive too, so it is only natural that chief executives should see the advantages of a coalition with the citizen movement—something both could use as a club to punish unresponsive bureaucrats. Mayor John Lindsay built such a coalition by walking the streets of New York, cooling tempers in Harlem, and picking up votes for his election.

Herbert Kaufman, who six years earlier had written the book on *Governing New York City* with Wallace Sayre, put the citizen-executive coalition into administrative theory. One of the central political questions in public administration is: who should do the administering? Three alternative solutions exist, Kaufman said, which he characterized as the values of executive leadership, representativeness, and politically neutral competence. One can entrust the administration of government to elected officials and an administrative corps of well-educated generalists—the value of executive leadership. Alternatively, one can dish out administrative posts to the "common man," as the advocates of representativeness did during the era of spoils. The reaction against the spoils system in turn led the administrative branch into the period of politically neutral competence; without rule by experts, writes administrative historian Leonard White, "the government simply could not have supported the tasks that the country imposed on it in the twentieth century."[25]

Of course, the experts are no longer "politically neutral"—their participation in subgovernments makes them partisans for their own programs. The citizen movement, embracing the value of representativeness, senses this; so do the politically elected executives who are more often than not advocates of the value of executive leadership. Their alliance is based on a common threat—the entrenched bureaucrat—and a need for each other's resources. (Citizens have votes and campaign organizations, while the executive has experts and money.) Kaufman characterizes the alliance as "an uneasy, mutually wary relationship."[26] John Lindsay's sorry career as mayor of New York demonstrated just how estranged the love affairs between citizen groups and an ambitious executive could be.

ARE SUBGOVERNMENTS DEMOCRATIC?

Citizens and political executives denounce subgovernments as being "undemocratic" because they allow unelected bureaucrats to make policy while building a political base of power. Are subgovernments democratic? It all depends upon what sort of democracy you favor.

The roots of the problem go back two hundred years to the creation of the American government, when the founders were debating how to organize the new institutions of government. In a book titled *The Administrative Theories of Hamilton and Jefferson*, Lynton Caldwell explores two divergent points of view on this issue.

Alexander Hamilton favored a government of executives appointed by the wise, responsible to the public interest, ruling by control, centralization, and duration in office. In Hamilton's administrative theories, one can find the germs of the administrative principles of unity of command, the requirement that executives possess authority equal to their responsibilities, and the necessity for a permanent civil service. Hamilton was totally opposed to the notion of an independent bureaucracy capable of circumventing the wishes of their superiors by building a political constituency—he would not even allow administrators to report to the Congress. In Hamilton's ideal administrative state, the top political executives defined public policy, administrators executed it.

Hamilton sought to organize administrative power; Thomas Jefferson, on the other hand, was concerned with the control of it. He embraced plans for a civic democracy founded on extreme political decentralization and citizen participation in local affairs. His administrative theories stressed the need for simplicity in organization, flexibility in administrative arrangements, and temporary administrative machinery whenever possible. As an executive himself, Jefferson remained marvelously inept at instituting his own theory. While governor of Virginia, he remained the deferential executive and let the British antirevolutionary forces chase him out of both Richmond and his home at Monticello. As president, he became the active executive—purchasing Louisiana, declaring the embargo, and retaining all of the powers which the Federalist party had laid upon the central government. Before he died fifteen years later, he left instructions that no mention be made on his tombstone of his executive experience.

Neither Hamilton nor Jefferson played a major role in designing the constitutional arrangements which would mold the administrative system. Jefferson did not attend the constitutional convention, but fumed philosophically from Europe that the new government was too strong for liberty. Hamilton abandoned the convention in disgust because no one paid attention to his proposals for a powerful executive branch and later left the administration of President Washington discouraged because no one would accept his scheme for a prime minister (himself, of course) to coordinate the administrative and legislative branches.

The job of actually designing the constitutional system fell upon James Madison. Madison thought that he had found, through his study of ancient and modern constitutions, the source of governmental instability. Every government that failed, he thought, fell because it failed to solve the conflict between liberty and property—the values embodied in the conflict between the administrative theories of Jefferson and Hamilton. Too much Jeffersonian liberty created the sort of chaos that led to weak, ineffective government. Forms of administration strong enough to assure Hamiltonian prosperity tended to snuff out liberty.

Madison thought that he had found a formula for combining liberty with strong governmental administration. He constructed pyramids of power, carving the governmental institution horizontally and vertically to make it impossible for a single faction to capture control of every branch of government. By leaving the institutions of government deliberately weak and accessible, he invited the factions to participate in policy making. The genius of Madison's system was his realization that a large number of factions in a diverse nation could check each other through the balance of their competition in a diffuse governmental system. That, of course, is the essence of administra-

142

tive pluralism. And the system still retains most of the features that Madison made possible: participation open to organizing groups, constant competition between them, a wide distribution of powers and, most important, no final decision points—a governmental system in which policy never becomes fixed, but changes interminably, through an endless process of amendment, reform, compensation, and appeal. Over time, for a variety of historical reasons, the Madisonian system has come to dominate American public administration.

One of the central tenets in the Madisonian system is the recognition that government will be run by minorities: either the well-educated, as the founders preferred, or the well-organized. A modern disciple of the Madisonian formula, Emmette Redford, puts it this way. Public policy in a complex, technological society will be made and executed by people "occupying strategic positions in specialized organizations, operating only in part under directives from organizations directly representative of the people."[27] It is unrealistic to think that citizens or novice political executives can run a complicated modern government in a technological society, make it work, and make it democratic. The best that any state can hope for is a "workable democracy" in which the complexity of the problem and the opportunities for access create a situation in which a large number of groups are forced to compete with each other. And what about bureaucrats who try to play the tyrant and avoid the competition? Their programs will fail, because they will never be able to mobilize the group support they need to make their programs work. In the pluralistic state, the effective administrators will be the ones who can work within the competition to achieve some sort of consensus so that they can move ahead. Since they demonstrate skill at building consensus among competing groups, they will be rewarded with increased program responsibility. In a truly pluralistic system, power tends to gravitate toward these agencies because their administrators know how to survive within the system of administrative pluralism.

Some persons may be skeptical about the amount of real competition within the modern subgovernment. Consider as an example the most famous of all subgovernments: the military-industrial complex. The journalist who popularized the subgovernment concept, Douglas Cater, did so to expose the shortcomings of government by specialized minorities. But even Cater admits that it is inaccurate "to regard the subgovernment of defense as a secret conspiracy of malefactors."[28] Competition within the defense subsystem is intense. The debate over a new policy or a new weapon is generally more intense than the arrows of public discontent. What seems remarkable is the development, without any central planning, of institutional procedures that serve to neutralize outside opposition to military spending, while the competition among the military services and their legislative and industrial allies rages on. This may be the most workable measure of administrative pluralism in the twentieth century: the ability of subgovernments to internally replicate the Madisonian characteristics—participation, competition, distribution

143

of powers, and no final decision points—while maintaining some element of unity against outside attack.

The modern-day advocates of Hamiltonian and Jeffersonian solutions bristle at this definition. Madison, says political scientist Theodore Lowi, would rebel at the suggestion that subgovernments could be representative. Madison's definition of pluralism, according to Lowi, stressed the dynamic process of citizens in the act of forming and re-forming new groups around new issues. Madison never expected that organized factions would become permanently entrenched at the public trough. The military-industrial complex, says Lowi, is a perfect example of what happens when pluralism is corrupted by the participation of permanent groups. The groups—the defense industries in particular—conspire to confine participation to those willing to make the work of the subgovernment their life's career. They limit participation because they fear that the citizen novice or the executive generalist will upset the internal power equation. The initiated groups fight to maintain their "fair share" of the benefits, by becoming permanent beneficiaries of public funds, substituting self-preservation for the public interest, taxing the powerless to pay for their own excessive spending habits, and abusing their power in other ways. The military-industrial complex, say its critics, is a perfect example of the consequence of carrying the Madison-Appleby-Redford formula for democratic pluralism into a complex society: specialized interests conspire with their allies to promote the powers that be. The result is not democratic government, but an unworkable, entrenched system of administration immune from attempts to reestablish priorities that reflect real public needs.

The power of that criticism has created widespread demands for reform, from neighborhood councils to the Executive Office of the President. In general, the profession of public administration has favored Hamiltonian solutions to the problems of pluralism. Ironically, this is where public administration in America began eighty years ago: with a cry for more power to the executive to check the power of representative administration in the form of the spoilsman. Now the reformers cry for more power to the executive to weaken the power of politically competent bureaucrats and the subgovernments they have formed. Like the movement that set off the search for principles of administration eighty years earlier, the modern call for reform has set off a search for new methods of administration appropriate to the job of the modern public executive. It has revolutionized the study of public administration.

FOR FURTHER READING

The study of politics and administration is the mainstream of American public administration. Paul H. Appleby's *Policy and Administration* (University: University of Alabama Press, 1949) set out the general themes of the political approach to public administration. It is hard to appreciate this approach without an understanding of the historical development of governmental administration in the United States. Frederick C. Mosher summarizes the development of the American public service in Chapter 3 of *Democracy and the Public Service* (New York: Oxford University Press, 1968). Lynton K. Caldwell frames this development in the minds of two of the founding fathers in *The Administrative Theories of Hamilton and Jefferson* (Chicago: University of Chicago Press, 1944).

Structural arrangements in American government arise largely from political considerations. Harold Seidman shows how in *Politics, Position, and Power: The Dynamics of Federal Organization*, 2nd. ed. (New York: Oxford University Press, 1975). The advantages that career civil servants possess in the policy-making process are examined by Francis E. Rourke in *Bureaucracy, Politics, and Public Policy* (Boston: Little, Brown & Co., 1969), and are characterized as "subgovernments" by Douglas Cater in *Power in Washington* (New York: Vintage Books, 1964), Chapters 1 and 2. J. Leiper Freeman reveals how bureaucrats and congressional committee members tend to monopolize policy making, in *The Political Process: Executive Bureau-Legislative Committee Relations* (New York: Random House, 1965). Like these studies, most of the research on the politics of administration has focused on the federal government, although the findings of these studies are equally applicable to state and local government, where most of the administrators work.

The classic study of clientele-group–executive-bureau relations is Philip Selznick's *TVA and the Grass Roots* (New York: Harper & Row, 1949). Mosher explains the rise of professionalism in *Democracy and the Public Service,* Chapter 4, cited above. The structure of modern administrative federalism is laid out by Morton Grodzins in *The American System* (Chicago: Rand McNally & Co., 1966). The literature on government contracting is still undeveloped, but the student might consult Richard F. Kaufman, *The War Profiteers* (New York: Doubleday & Co., 1972) and move up to Clarence H. Danhof, *Government Contracting and Technological Change* (Washington, D.C.: The Brookings Institution, 1968). The issues surrounding collective bargaining and the public service are outlined in Sam Zagoria, ed., *Public Workers and Public Unions* (Englewood Cliffs, N.J.: Prentice-Hall, 1972). The context of citizen participation is set out by Herbert Kaufman in "Administrative Decentralization and Political Power," *Public Administration Review*, 29 (January/February 1969), pp. 3–15. For the arguments for and against extreme decentralization, see Alan A. Altshuler, *Community Control: The Black Demand for Participation in Large American Cities* (New York: Pegasus, 1970). Emmette S. Redford defends the pluralistic formula for reconciling democratic ideals and administrative necessities in *Democracy in the Administrative State* (New York: Oxford University Press, 1969).

During the fifties, the heyday of the political approach to public administration, scholars wrote a great deal about particular executives making particular decisions. One of the best collections of these case studies is Harold Stein's *Public Administration and Policy Develop-*

ment: A Casebook (New York: Harcourt, Brace & Co., 1952). The best analytical study of a single agency is Herbert Kaufman's *The Forest Ranger: A Study in Administrative Behavior* (Baltimore: Johns Hopkins Press, 1960), which merges the structural, behavioral, and political approaches in a single study of the U.S. Forest Service.

STRATEGIES

In general, the lessons contained in the first four chapters of this book tend to make the job of the public administrator more difficult. Knowledge about behavior, bureaucracy, and politics tells public administrators what problems to expect, but not what to do about them. The traditional principles of administration, while useful in a way, do not prescribe complete solutions to the most pressing administrative problems. As government becomes more complex, administrators begin to look for strategies that can make their programs work. There are four major groups proposing strategies. The policy analysts claim that they can create a better administrative system through reorganization, research, and economic analysis. The pragmatists promise to tell administrators how to use their power more effectively. The experts educated in the computer age think they can make management more scientific, while the behavioral scientists think they have a formula for making the bureaucracy more responsive to change.

POLICY ANALYSIS

When any public executive is placed in charge of an ineffective organization, the first temptation is to consider reorganization. The executive rightly suspects that the structure of the organization is an obstacle to the accomplishment of its goals. The administrative system is a curiosity produced by the unpleasant evolution of bureaucratic resistance to change coupled with all sorts of political compromises made in response to the demands of various special-interest groups.

Executives often begin their reorganization drives by announcing that their purpose is to "end waste" in government. It may be popular to raise the standard of efficiency and economy, but it is also misleading. "Reorganizations," says Harold Seidman, "do not save money."[1] Executives engage in reorganization in order to improve the effectiveness of the organization—ideally, to choose the best possible administrative methods, without regard to bureaucratic or political preferences, given the goals of the agency. Along the way, the executives also hope to increase their own power.

Why is reorganization associated with policy analysis? Policy analysis, narrowly defined, is the use of research techniques to analyze public policy. In practice, policy analysis has come to be associated with a number of administrative strategies that are based on rigorous methodologies, including program evaluation, economic analysis, and productivity studies. All of these strategies—along with reorganization—are backed by a common desire for administrative rationality: an administrative system based on reason rather than the emotional or political criteria that often influence administrative decisions.

THE NIXON REORGANIZATION

Most Americans, President Richard Nixon proclaimed in one of his more prophetic speeches, "are simply fed up with government at all levels."[2] As president, he could not correct the situation as long as bureaucrats were obliged to join subgovernments to make their programs run. Nixon's advisers told him that there was no reason why the president of the United States, the elected chief executive, the person held responsible for administrative failure, the most powerful man in the world, should not have as much authority over his government as corporation executives had over their businesses. Nixon agreed. He set as a top priority of his administration the reform of public administration in American government.

Now reform is not new to public administration. The American wing of the discipline was born out of the progressive "good government" reform movement. Periodically it sets out on another reforming binge. When it does, it has to solve two problems. The reformers have to decide how much power to give to the chief executive. (The answer, in general, is more. A renewed public service, in the eyes of the reformers, seems to require a dynamic chief executive.) Also, the experts backing up the reformers have to create management tools that the executive can use to run the reformed government. The Nixon reorganization illustrates the mechanics of enhancing the top executive's power at the expense of specialized bureaucrats. Here is how Nixon did it.

The president tried to make his own office the command center over the federal bureaucracy. He created the Domestic Council, the home-front counterpart of the National Security Council, and gave it a big staff and a big mandate: coordinate all of the domestic programs. Then Nixon created the Council on Economic Policy, which was supposed to coordinate the government's economic game plan. Overall, the size of the presidential staff expanded twofold under the influence of Nixon's Praetorian Guard. The expanded presidential staff pushed the venerable Bureau of the Budget out of its Executive Office Building and across Pennsylvania Avenue. Nixon changed its name to the Office of Management and Budget, consolidated its budget review functions into four program areas, expanded its management oversight functions, and had OMB dispatch managerial mod squads to unsnarl the federal bureaucracy.

The primary target of the reorganization plan was the federal bureaucracy. No president in modern times expressed a greater distrust of the federal bureaucracy than Richard Nixon. Aside from his fabled belief that the bureaucracy was trying to screw him, there was evidence that the organization of the executive branch was atuned more to the needs of special interests than to presidential priorities, making it difficult for the president to undertake new programs or phase out old ones. In this view, Nixon found a number of allies. John Gardner, a cabinet officer in the Johnson administration, testified:

> The federal government is designed to solve problems that no longer exist. It is a museum in which all our past purposes are displayed under the glass of anachronistic bureaucratic compartments.[3]

151

To solve the organizational problem, Nixon proposed to consolidate the eleven cabinet departments into eight. The Departments of State, Treasury, Defense, and Justice would remain, but the secretaries of Labor, Commerce, Interior, Agriculture, Transportation, Housing and Urban Development, and Health, Education and Welfare would disappear. Their functions would be stuffed into four new superdepartments: Natural Resources, Community Development, Human Resources, and Economic Affairs. The new secretaries would be given a "power package" of budgetary and management authority to run their new monoliths, which meant they would have the power to shift agency functions and abolish others. As the enemies of reorganization saw it, that was the problem. In any reorganization, the executive "unplugs the wires." The carefully nurtured contacts between bureaucrats, legislators, and constituents all come loose when jurisdictions are shuffled around.

That was Nixon's purpose—to unplug the wires. The five-thousand-volt wire that powers the subgovernment is the categorical grant-in-aid which conducts federal money to state and local officials for narrow, specialized programs. Bureaucrats convince their friends in Congress to lock into law the power of the agency to distribute funds for categorical problems, such as abnormal tide protection. Once the money is appropriated for abnormal tide protection, governments must spend it for abnormal tide protection. The executive is prevented by law from shifting money around or phasing out programs, a phenomenon known as the hardening of the categories. The subgovernment, as might be expected, fights to keep the categories hard.

Nixon proposed drastic surgery, by executive order and congressional legislation. By abolishing the categories, he believed that he could give the chief executives considerably more discretion over how to spend their funds. He proposed, first, to continue the practice the Johnson administration began of consolidating a number of categorical grants-in-aid into single block grants. The Public Health Service, for example, had a categorical grant-in-aid for each disease, such as hypertension, supported by the physicians who were specialists in curing it. Johnson had succeeded in consolidating these categories into a single "Partnership for Health" grant that allowed state officials to decide for themselves which health problems to attack. Nixon continued the practice and succeeded in making a single block grant out of the categorical job training programs of the Labor Department. In all, five grant-consolidation bills passed.

To further weaken the categories, Nixon proposed a plan for special revenue sharing. Like the block grant concept, state and local officials had to spend the money for certain broad, general purposes—such as education, transportation, law enforcement, or the construction of community facilities. Unlike block or categorical grants, however, special revenue sharing did not require state and local executives to put up matching funds or seek federal approval for their plans—a degree of discretion which the Congress found objectionable, thus refusing to enact any of the special revenue-sharing programs.

Congress did enact Nixon's proposal for general revenue sharing, the broadest attack on the concept of categories. Nixon's cabinet carried the promise of administrative discretion through revenue sharing to the nation's governors and mayors and, in passing, told them how much they would get under the distribution formula. The local politicians promptly spent their financial bonanza, then came running to Washington in September to demand that the Congress enact the program. Congress in turn authorized the Treasury to share federal tax revenues with state and local governments. Congress required no matching, no plans; it initially blocked out priority areas and prohibited the states from spending the money on certain functions, such as teachers' salaries, but even this requirement was eventually knocked out. One string, however, remain attached. Local officials could not receive revenue sharing funds unless they stopped discriminating against women and minority groups, even if this meant putting women on the all-male state patrol.

Despite their new-found freedom from the constraints of categories, the state and local executives did not demonstrate much imagination in the use of revenue-sharing funds. They poured the money into the old standbys: police, transportation, public buildings, and tax abatements. Congress began to wonder if it should not go back to the old categoricals and force the local executives to spend the money on the big national problems of poverty, pollution, and urban decay.

Back in Washington, where Congress was busy killing the departmental consolidation bill, Nixon increased presidential power over the existing departments. To broaden his control over the budget, the president began to impound money appropriated by Congress. Impoundment is an executive action that delays the expenditure of funds duly appropriated by the legislature. In theory, the legislature allows this. It passes laws authorizing the executive to delay expenditures when delay would promote savings or prevent deficiencies. In practice, President Nixon used impoundment to wipe out or reduce legal congressional appropriations—permanently. With a stroke of the presidential pen, Nixon could terminate programs for political reasons or manipulate the budget to further his economic policies. In 1973 he impounded 6.6 percent of the total federal outlay. Legislators and local officials went into the courts to recover the impounded funds and often won. In 1974, Congress passed the Budget and Impoundment Control Act, which severely reduced President Gerald Ford's ability to continue the practice.

While Congress stewed over impoundment, Nixon broadened executive control over agency performance. He established a government-wide management-by-objectives program, run out of the Office of Management and Budget. The MBO system required agency chiefs to state their program goals and allowed the White House to monitor their performance. To make sure that the bureau-

153

crats who wrote the objectives were responsive to presidential priorities, Nixon took steps to tighten up bureaucratic loyalty.

When any new president is inaugurated for the first time, it is customary for all political appointees in the departments to prepare letters of resignation. After his landslide election in 1972, Nixon announced that it was now customary for all high-ranking officials to submit letters of resignation at the start of a second term. Nixon specifically asked for letters of resignation from two thousand presidential and political appointees in top policy-making positions, including a number of persons serving fixed terms on government commissions. A mere formality, most thought. Nixon surprised everyone by taking the letters to Camp David, where he and his advisers accepted enough of the resignations to frighten the wits out of the bureaucracy. Nixon's press secretary, Ron Ziegler, announced that the resignations would improve relationships between the White House and the bureaucracy and hasten enactment of the presidential reorganization.

Of course the presidential appointees would still have to work with the same old career bureaucrats. So Nixon revived the proposal for a corps of generalists to serve as the top administrators in the federal bureaucracy. Old supergrade bureaucrats would be replaced by members of a new Federal Executive Service. To modify the effects of the Peter Principle in the federal bureaucracy, each career administrator would be given a three-year contract, renewable at the pleasure of the political executive. The federal administrators would be rotated from agency to agency to prevent their capture by special interests. They would be responsive to the public interest and, one presumes, to the White House. The plan was proposed to Congress, which cut the heart out of the proposal.

Some of Nixon's reforms might straighten out administration in the capital, but only one out of ten federal bureaucrats work in Washington. The rest work in the field, a maze of activity that makes headquarters administration look as plain and simple as the architecture of the buildings it occupies. Programs go out from Washington to the states and cities through federal regional centers. Before the Nixon era, each agency had its own regions, its own centers, its own boundaries, an overlay of federal jurisdictions so complex that a state official from Kentucky wanting to meet federal regional officials serving the state had to travel three thousand miles from city to city to find them all. Every president since Franklin Roosevelt had tried to force federal agencies to straighten out their regional boundaries; agency bureaucrats and local businessmen had always killed the plans. In 1969 Nixon ordered the departments to move their federal regional centers to ten central cities and ordered all agencies to adopt conterminous regional boundaries. He then established a Federal Regional Council in each area to coordinate federal programs; told the bureaucrats in Washington to decentralize program authority to the regions; and even threatened to appoint a presidential ambassador to each regional center to oversee program coordination.

The Nixon reorganization took place at the same time that policy analysts were making their greatest inroads into the federal bureaucracy. Even Nixon recognized the power of analysis. In the twilight years of his administration, he entrusted his main line programs to three professors adept in the analytical skills of policy analysis—Dr. Henry Kissinger in foreign affairs, Dr. George Schultz for economics, and Dr. James Schlesinger for defense. To understand the significance of this, it is necessary to put the Nixon reorganization in perspective.

REORGANIZATION IN PERSPECTIVE

The impulse for comprehensive administrative reform struck the American federal government three times before the reorganization proposals of the Nixon administration. In 1911, President Taft's Commission on Efficiency and Economy proposed progressive administrative reforms, including a proposal for consolidating the preparation of the federal budget, the proposal that led to the creation of the U.S. Bureau of the Budget. Ex-President Hoover came back to Washington to direct two ambitious reorganization commissions during the Truman Administration. Hoover made the usual pleadings for departmental consolidation, budgetary reform, and improved accounting procedures, which the Congress, in its usual fashion, largely ignored. The paragon of reorganization efforts was undertaken by the Brownlow Committee during the administration of President Franklin Roosevelt. Roosevelt asked two public administrators and one political scientist—Louis Brownlow, Luther Gulick, and Charles Merriam, respectively—to assemble a staff and apply the principles of administration to the federal government. In their 1937 report to Roosevelt, they recommended:

1. Establishing an Executive Office of the President, the core of which would be the White House staff and the Bureau of the Budget brought over from the Treasury Department and given expanded budgetary and management powers. Roosevelt instituted this recommendation by executive order.

2. The consolidation of all line agencies, including the independent regulatory commissions, into twelve cabinet-level departments. Here Roosevelt stumbled across the old-guard Congress, which had in its hands a rebutting report from the Brookings Institution showing Congress to be the source of administrative policy making with the president's role defined as that of a general manager. For political reasons, Congress rejected departmental consolidation.

3. Improved mechanisms for personal administration, fiscal management, planning, and congressional audits. This resulted in gradual alterations of the work of the Civil Service Commission, the Government Accounting Office, and the

Natural Resources Planning Board, as well as specific reforms in departmental management.

The history of administrative reorganization in the twentieth century has been one of glacial change. As a result, the federal bureaucracy was not prepared for the eruption of government programs during the turbulent sixties. The volcanic changes in the size and responsibilities of American governments came to rest on the ice pack of an administrative system that had not moved very far in the last century.

The administrative machinery simply melted under the weight of the new program responsibilities. New programs and bureaus sprang out of the baronies of Congress to meet the special needs of any clientele with bus fare to get to Washington. By 1968, the federal departments and agencies were administering nearly twelve hundred special categorical programs to lower units of government, primarily through the grant-in-aid system with its cumbersome requirements for matching funds and comprehensive planning. There were nine cabinet-level departments and twenty federal agencies administering education programs. Seven federal agencies competed to give away water and sewer funds. The duplication of programs was exaggerated at the state and local level. Big cities ran twenty to thirty separate employment training programs, funded by a dozen different bureaus, often competing to serve the same group.

The situation created a sense of drifting; a sense that things were not working, that government bureaus were doing too many things too poorly at too high a price. Costs seemed uncontrollable, outstripping revenues and resulting in higher taxes and inflation; archaic civil service rules crippled efficiency and frustrated young civil servants; and bureaucratic empire building resulted in overlapping services, red tape, and a general trend to concentrate revenues on nonproductive overhead costs that were not directly related to the delivery of services. Attempts to establish national goals and priorities were lost in the political system of checks and balances—from President Eisenhower's forgotten "Goals for Americans" to the endless presidential task forces of the 1960s. Administrators who took risks and exposed waste were put down. Mayors who tried to combine federal programs for a coordinated attack on urban problems were told that each program had its own special requirements and its own separate categorical grant-in-aid.

The federal government was being primed for an administrative shakedown. In 1964 Don Price and members of the public-administration community issued a report calling on the president to broaden the responsibilities of department secretaries. President Johnson tapped Ben Heineman, a railroad executive, to head the Advisory Council on Executive Organization. Heineman proposed such a radical restructuring of the federal bureaucracy that his report was classified and never released. President Nixon sought advice from Roy Ash of Litton Industries, an aerospace firm. Ash's report, similar to the Price and Heineman plans, became the basis of the president's reorganization. At the same time, task forces in the Budget Bureau prepared special studies and reports. State and local officials organized their own reorganization commissions. Although former President Nixon is associated with the reforms, their genius clearly came from many sources.

There were three common elements in all these proposals for administrative reform. First, the reformers wanted to break up the subgovernments so as to eliminate bureaucratic resistance to the priorities of the chief executive and his appointees. The announced purpose of this was to reorient government away from the special-interest group and back toward the individual citizens who voted for the chief executive. Bureau chiefs would cease to see themselves as members of subgovernments, beholden to special interests, and instead become concerned with the coordination of programs to meet public needs.

Second, the reformers wanted to make effective service delivery the first test of good administration. They suspected that old-line bureaucrats were less interested in effective service delivery than they were in empire building, internal efficiency, and making interest groups happy by spending more money. To achieve their goal, the reformers had to create new methods of measuring service delivery (policy analysis) and restructure the departments of government in line with the broad purposes to be accomplished (reorganization).

Third, the reformers adopted the rhetoric of decentralization. Yet it was a "decentralization" founded on the assumption of centralized political control. In effect the executives said: take the power away from the subgovernments and give it to me and I shall give it back to the people and their elected administrative representatives. Everyone wanted decentralization. The issue was which *kind*, decentralization to special interests or decentralization to administrative generalists.

Like his Republican forebear, Teddy Roosevelt, President Nixon was not prone to wait for congressional debate when administrative reform was wanting. By executive order the president took many actions designed to make the government more manageable. He reorganized the Executive Office, set up the regional centers, consolidated grants, realigned internal department programs, and increased secretarial powers and staff. He personally terminated many programs or shifted their functions to other departments. The most spectacular was the move to dismantle the Office of Economic Opportunity. When congressional committee chairmen, frightened of losing their ties to old-line bureaucrats, forced the president to withdraw the Department of Agriculture from the superdepartment plan, the president responded by appointing his agriculture secretary as presidential counselor for the proposed superdepartment of natural resources. Using his powers of appointment, the president brought more policy analysts into positions of power than had the two Democratic presidents who preceded him. Using his budgetary powers, he set the precedent that the president had far-reaching power to impound funds appropriated by Congress. He teased the nation's governors and mayors into lobbying through Congress the nation's first revenue-sharing bill.

Nixon almost accomplished administrative reorganization by executive power. But true reorganization cannot be accomplished by administrative reform alone; it also requires political centralization. It requires the various congressional barons, parochial bureaucrats, local politicians, and special interests to come into line with the new administrative arrangements. It requires the reorganization of legislative committees. By executive order, the president might force into existence a department of natural resources, but could that new department coexist with the old congressional committees on agriculture, interior, and commerce, the state departments of agriculture, the state land-grant colleges and their schools of agriculture, and agricultural organizations such as the Grange and the Farmer's Union?

The answer, if you asked a public executive in early 1973, was yes. Nixon did win a huge popular majority. People seemed so fed up with government malpractice that they might just accept the reforming impulse and demand that Congress and the interests go along. It could have resulted in the first broad-scale government reorganization in the history of American government.

Watergate intervened. The value of executive leadership was discredited by association with a burglary, washing away any chance Nixon had of achieving popular support for administrative reform. The high point of the reaction was the passage of the Budget and Impoundment Control Act of 1974, in which Congress set up machinery to prepare its own consolidated budget and prohibited the president from rescinding congressional appropriations without prior congressional consent.

Still, the need for broad-scale reform remained. Despite revenue sharing and the passage of several grant-consolidation measures, 80 percent of Washington's payments to the states and cities still flowed through 1,100 narrowly defined categorical grants-in-aid. And, in 1976, presidential candidate Jimmy Carter made a campaign issue out of his reorganization of the Georgia state government, his introduction of zero-base budgeting, and his promise to reorganize the federal government once elected. It is very likely that another president will raise the flag of executive leadership that Nixon soiled.

When that happens, he (or she) will have to solve two problems. First, the president will have to find the political power to make the reorganization work. That is the primary lesson of the Nixon reorganization. Administrative reform requires political centralization. Second, the top executives will have to acquire analytical tools allowing them to make reasonable choices based on limited analysis—and to do a better job than their bureaucrats. It serves no purpose to reorganize the government and give top executives the power to coordinate and evaluate administrators if those same executives do not know what they are doing. This is the second half of the equation for success in administrative reform. The first is reorganization; the second is finding the analytical tools to make it work.

Despite the temporary failure of executive leadership, administrators have been able to master new tools of analysis. They have research methodologies, program evaluation, methods of measuring productivity, cost-benefit analysis, PPB, and the findings of a small band of economic and political rebels gathered under the umbrella of the theory of public choice. Analysis broke into public administration during the 1960s when economists were hired to analyze financial resource decisions using economic models. They were hired because they had fancy methodologies that produced smart-looking answers to complex problems. To understand how this developed, it is necessary to turn back the clock to the first days of the Kennedy Administration:

PLANNING-PROGRAMMING-BUDGETING

Economics arrived in public administration in early 1961 when President-elect John Kennedy dispatched Robert McNamara, president of the Ford Motor Company, to the U.S. Department of Defense. McNamara asked the RAND Corporation, the air force think tank, to help him establish a planning, programming, and budgeting system (PPB) in the defense department and to analyze security requirements using cost-benefit analysis.

One need only contrast McNamara's budgetary practices with

Defense Secretary Robert McNamara sought to bring economic rationality to public administration through the techniques of cost-benefit analysis and planning-programming-budgeting. The PPB system was extended to the entire federal government by President Lyndon Johnson; since then there has been much controversy over its impact. COURTESY OF THE U.S. ARMY.

those of the previous secretaries of defense to appreciate how much he expanded the power of his office through economic analysis. The first secretary to try to unify the Department of Defense jumped to his death from an upper story of the Bethesda Naval Hospital in northwest Washington. The next president, Dwight Eisenhower, found the task so frustrating that he simply set a ceiling on defense expenditures and told his defense secretary to referee the battle between the military services over the budgetary pie. Expenditures appeared in line-item categories for the weapons, personnel, and equipment necessary to support each service's activities. This created a number of problems. Expenditures for the navy's Polaris submarine missiles were separated from the air force ICBMs, even though both contributed to the same mission. The air force generals overfunded their intercontinental B-70 bombers, starving the tactical jet fighters that the army needed for ground support. The army generals, in order to protect the total number of divisions, thinned out some divisions so that they had enough equipment to fight for only a few weeks. Costs of the really big items, such as the navy's aircraft-carrier program, were defended on a year-by-year basis without much reference to total costs. In essence, each service was allowed to do as it pleased so long as it kept within the budget ceiling.

McNamara instructed his assistants, including Charles Hitch and Alain Enthoven, to institute a program-budgeting system in the Defense Department by midsummer 1961. They relied upon recommendations in various reorganization proposals, including the Hoover Commission proposal and studies conducted by David Novick of the RAND Corporation. Hitch rearranged the defense budget into nine programs, including America's nuclear arsenal, troops and tactical support, continental defense forces, research and development, and so on, without regard to whether the air force or army ran them. He told the budget analysts to project the costs of each program five years into the future. Enthoven told the generals and admirals to defend their investments in each program in terms of the benefits it would produce and to compare the costs and benefits of alternative systems within each program.

The system tightened McNamara's control over defense decisions and achieved the elusive goal of military service unification. In that sense, the system worked. Whether the analysis led to the best decisions is a matter of much controversy. Critics cite the ill-fated TFX, a program to produce a jet fighter-bomber adaptable to the needs of both the navy and the air force; the jumbo C-5A transport; and McNamara's fascination with body counts that brought America closer to victory each year in Vietnam. At any rate, President Johnson was so impressed by PPB that he ordered all government departments to adopt the system "so that through the tools of modern management the full promise of a finer life can be brought to every American at the lowest possible cost."[4] Johnson put the actual implementation of government-wide PPB under the direction of his budget director, economist Charles Schultze. According to Schultze,

PPB requires agency executives to analyze their activities in the following ways.

1. State the agency's objectives and outline the programs necessary to accomplish those objectives. Hitch, for example, asked the air force and navy why the United States had a nuclear strike force. The defense chiefs replied that America's nuclear capability was designed as a credible deterrent to an atomic Pearl Harbor. Hitch then announced that all forces contributing to this objective would be classified as the Strategic Forces Program. He subdivided Strategic Forces into various subprograms, such as the Polaris submarines and the activities required to support them. Basically, defining the programs is a conceptual process, often agonizing, which requires administrators to analyze their activities in terms of the mission of the organization.

2. Calculate the output of each program in relation to the agency's objectives. The aim of this exercise is to bring operating programs into line with department objectives and to eliminate unnecessary activities. The problem is how to calculate output. Even something as solid as "credible nuclear deterrent" turns out to be unfathomable. The generals may talk about matching the enemy's missile payloads one for one, but in the long run the credibility of any nation's deterrent winds down to a matter of perceptions. How does one quantify perceptions?

3. Calculate total program costs. Most government programs run for more than a single year. Once initiated, they commit the government to make outlays for construction, personnel, and maintenance many years into the future. PPB requires the bureaucrats to state total program costs at the beginning in order to inform the executive about all of the potential costs that a decision to proceed would entail.

4. Undertake multiyear program planning. The executive has little opportunity to influence agency objectives by reviewing the annual budget, since upwards of three-fourths of the funds requested in that budget consist of commitments made through previous decisions in previous years—decisions that are essentially unalterable. Only through long-range planning and programming does the executive have a fighting chance to influence the direction of the agency.

5. Analyze alternative programs and search for the most effective means of achieving a high output at the lowest cost. Instead of viewing public programs as ends in themselves, with budgetary decisions based on whether the program should receive a small increase or a small reduction, the approach to PPB requires "a periodic review of fundamental program objectives, accomplishments, and costs while considering the effectiveness and efficiency of alternatives."[5] This is the heart of PPB: analysis and experimentation on alternative systems.

6. Integrate the analytic process into the budgetary process. The objectives, the measures of output, the program costs, the multiyear plans, and the alternative designs have to be fitted into the budgetary decisions for the upcoming fiscal year.

161

The last step—integrating PPB into the budgetary process—proved enormously difficult outside of the Department of Defense. It was not a problem with the concept, as Schultze describes it. Only a few old curmudgeons seriously argued that the need for analysis embodied in the concept of PPB was bad for the government. The problem was largely one of mechanics—of actually instituting PPB into the daily routine of the agency and making it fit into the daily routine of the budgetary process. To make PPB work, the budget bureau asked the agencies to prepare four things.

a. A budget categorized by programs. The old-line agency chiefs asked: What is a program? It is not an expenditure object, such as payroll or operating expenses. It is not an activity schedule, such as application processing or facilities operations. It is simply a summary of the agency's plans to accomplish its objectives. There may be many ways to state agency objectives, especially if the goals of the agency are vague or complex.

b. The multiyear program and financial plan. This is the planning document for current and future expenditures, and is supposed to provide a complete financial accounting of the agency's proposed activities. It calculates the impact of current budgetary commitments five years into the future, breaks each broad program into specific program elements, states how the performance of each program will be assessed, and suggests measures of program output. The plan also contains a crosswalk—that is, a translation of the program budget back into an old line-item budget—which is included to appease the legislators and bureau chiefs who are understandably anxious to know how well their pet organization is doing through PPB.

c. The program memorandum. "While the program and financial plan is a tabular record of cost and output consequences of proposed budgetary decisions, the program memorandum provides the strategic and analytical justification for these decisions."[6] In essence, the program memorandum recounts the strategic planning process which led to the submission of the budget. What critical decisions were made? What was the analytical base for these choices? What assumptions were made? The PPB system "tries from the start to force an *explicit* statement of broad program strategy as a basis for detailed budget decisions." [7]

d. Special analytical studies. Budget officers often ask the agencies to conduct in-depth studies of critical programs, such as programs that require interagency coordination. The studies provide an extra measure of analysis not found in the program memorandum. Each year a few major issues are selected for analysis.

The mechanics of PPB produced a mound of paper work and frustration which eventually led President Nixon's budget analysts to tell the agencies that they no longer had to submit the multiyear program and financial plans, the program memorandum, and the special analytical studies as part of their annual budget requests. This did not mean that analysis was dead. Hardly. The idea behind PPB— that budgeting could be improved by analyzing programs and their objectives over multiyear periods—is still very much alive. More agencies of government use the concepts of program budgeting today than when President Johnson made his announcement to the departments in 1965, and economic analysis is still very much in demand in public administration.

COST-BENEFIT ANALYSIS

One of the toughest problems facing public executives in complex agencies is how to influence program decisions that they do not fully understand. If they leave complex decisions up to the experts, executives lose the opportunity to shape the course of public policy. If they make the decisions themselves, they risk failing on account of their ignorance. Is there no relatively simple method by which executives and their staff can grasp the essence of complex programs?

The economists have an answer. They suggest that executives treat program decisions as economic problems involving the efficient allocation of public resources. That makes the job of the public executive amenable to microeconomic techniques and cost-benefit analysis.

Cost-benefit analysis originated in the field of water-resources development. Federal agencies such as the Bureau of Reclamation and the Corps of Army Engineers used the technique to evaluate prospective projects and narrow the area within which administrative rivalries could prevail over analysis. Here is a simplified example of some of the factors to be considered in comparing costs to benefits.

Dam A: A dam proposed to serve a large farming community would cost $62 million to construct. This is not the total cost, however. In building the dam, the government foregoes the opportunity to spend the money on other programs; it may also add to its total debt. To account for the fact that the government is in effect borrowing the money from itself, the analyst will calculate the equivalent investments costs by amortizing the $62 million over a period of 100 years at a standard interest rate. In addition, the analyst must add in the annual costs of maintaining and operating the facility. Altogether, the real costs of the dam in constant value dollars over 100 years would amount to some $275 million. The dam would reduce spring flood damage (annual benefits: $1.6 million) and provide irrigation water during the summer drought (annual benefits: $1.7 million). It would also provide recreation benefits and fish and wildlife enhancement (annual benefits: $1.9 million).

Dam B: Citizen groups in the valley, especially conservationists, object to the location of the dam. As an alternative, they propose a high-mountain dam which would cost $88 million to build, or an equivalent cost of $366 million over 100 years. This dam would produce additional flood-control benefits (total annual benefits: $1.9 million), more irrigation benefits ($1.8 million), and about the same recreation and wildlife benefits ($1.9 million).

Dam C: As a compromise, a smaller dam could be built at the end of the valley. It would cost $43 million or an equivalent of $188 million over a century. It would produce flood-control benefits of $0.9 million, irrigation benefits of $1.0 million, and recreation, fish, and wildlife benefits totaling $1.1 million.

All three of the dams would produce an excess of benefits over costs, apparently signifying that all are "worth" the federal investment. Each dam has its own advocates: the farmers prefer Dam A and citizen groups prefer Dam B, which would produce the highest level of benefits and not spoil the valley. Policy makers tight with the public purse find much to recommend Dam C, which is cheapest and could also resolve the controversy over the placement of the dam. From a purely cost-effective standpoint, however, Dam A is preferable, because it would produce the highest ratio of benefits over costs.

This elementary approach to the use of microeconomic models in government was developed by Charles Hitch and Roland McKean at the RAND Corporation before they went to work for Defense Secretary McNamara. In *The Economics of Defense in the Nuclear Age*, Hitch and McKean predicted that economic analysis would reduce interservice rivalry and bureaucratic conflict in the Pentagon by increasing the amount of information available to defense executives.

The theory of economic analysis is simple enough. It does not depend upon calculus or computers, despite their use by analysts. Hitch and McKean emphasize that "economic choice is a way of looking at problems" rather than a formula for calculating correct choices.[8] They describe five elements in the cost-benefit strategy.

1. Objectives. Cost-benefit analysis, like PPB, begins with the clarification of objectives. A careful description of all objectives, immediate and tacit, is fundamental.

2. Alternative program systems. Given the objectives, what are the various forces, material, or tactics by which the objectives might be accomplished? Two problems arise. One is imagination—which is why the RAND Corporation was set up to hire philosophers to read comic books. The second problem involves systems analysis. It is necessary to consider each alternative as a complete program or system—the composite of personnel, machines, and shape of their deployment necessary to make the alternative work.

3. Costs or resources. The total costs of each alternative system must be calculated. This is true even if two alternative systems differ only in a single respect—for example, a two-site versus a three-site ABM system. When planning for large, complex systems, the analyst must calculate all of the resources necessary to operate the system, including personnel and training costs. On smaller systems, such as dams, the analyst may concentrate simply on the specific dollar costs of planning, construction, and operation.

4. A model or models. Cost-benefit analysis is rarely the simple exercise illustrated above: the comparison of two or three alternatives that have clearly predictable consequences. Economists who analyze defense systems like to consider incremental changes in a complex program; they love to draw curves on graphs representing how those incremental changes affect costs and benefits. In planning the TFX, for example, it was necessary to find the optimal relationship between the electronic gear the manufacturers dreamed up for the plane, its costs, its benefits for a pilot flying blind over hilly terrain, and negative factors such as increases in the weight of the plane, which might make it too obese to land softly on an aircraft carrier without crashing through the flight deck. Models—paper models, computer models, wind-tunnel models—are essential for explicating reality and comparing the relationships between resources and objectives for each of many alternative systems.

5. A criterion. In principle, the choice of a criterion is simple. First, the program as a whole should be worth the investment—it should show a surplus of benefits over costs. Second, the alternative chosen should be the one that achieves the greatest margin of benefits over the least use of resources. In practice, such calculations are very difficult. The analyst will have to compare a number of benefits without any feasible method of reducing these things to a common dollar denominator. Moreover, the analyst will have to confront the fact that people have different preferences and, as such, they will tend to assign different values to the same benefit. Finally, the analyst may have to struggle with costs that are difficult to state as numbers or dollars, such as noise pollution from a particularly loud aircraft. All that economic analysis can do is to make intuitive knowledge more specific and help planners to think in terms of the efficient allocation of resources. Economic analysis is most useful, say Hitch and Mc-Kean, where executives "rely on the intuitive judgment of well-informed people (of whom the analyst may be one) to select one of the efficient systems in the neighborhood of the optimum."[9]

Cases of misapplication of economic analysis abound in government folklore, and illustrate the difficulties in making these five elements work together for the public decision maker. One of the toughest problems is measuring benefits. In a book edited by Robert Dorfman, *Measuring Benefits of Government Investments,* various authors suggest how to calculate benefits for programs that resist quantitative analysis, such as outdoor recreation, syphilis control, preventing high school dropouts, and urban renewal. The author analyzing outdoor recreation calculated the number and type of persons using the facility. More value was given to a child's spending a few hours in the wilderness than to an adult's rowing a boat in a city-park pond full of dead ducks. The benefits of syphilis prevention were calculated as income—personal earnings that would be lost due to disability, medical care, and the stigma of social disease. Programs for high school dropouts were also analyzed in terms of the increased lifetime income that the dropout would realize if he or she could be

165

encouraged to stay in school. Urban renewal was the most complex—benefits accrued from removing fire hazards, health problems, crime, and the intangible benefits of personal and social adjustment. As Dorfman concludes, the future of cost-benefit analysis clearly depends upon the ingenuity of analysts in discovering units of analysis for measuring public programs.

All of this reenforces the lesson that the best cost-benefit analysis utilizes judgment as well as statistical calculations. The lesson is well illustrated by one of the early applications of cost-benefit analysis in the defense department: the decision to build up the Minuteman missile forces. This was essentially a decision to favor a large number of missiles, with small payloads, over the giant liquid-fuel rockets that the United States had inherited from the Germans after World War II.

At the time, defense-policy makers had no advance knowledge on the strategic merits of Minuteman versus liquid-fuel rockets such as the Titan II. They had to make a choice based on existing information. So they used cost-benefit analysis. The Titan II cost more but carried a larger payload. The Minuteman missile cost less to deploy and, because it was solid-fuel, appeared (incorrectly) to have a substantially lower maintenance and operation cost.

Shortly after the decision to deploy the Minuteman missiles, the strategic defense environment changed drastically. The Soviets broke the nuclear test ban moratorium, exploded an enormous bomb in Siberia, and began work to make their land-based missiles secure from attack by hardening the silos and experimenting with antiballistic missile defense systems. The United States agreed to begin negotiations on limiting the number of missiles, but not the size of the payload. Meanwhile, technological developments opened the possibility of placing multiple nuclear warheads on top of a single missile, each warhead aimed at a different target.

All together, these events tended to favor missiles that could carry larger payloads. Big payloads were necessary to assure destructive capability over Soviet silos, carry the multiple-reentry vehicles, and counterbalance the limitation on the number of missiles. Yet there remained the decision that set up the Minuteman low-payload missile force, based on narrow cost considerations. The lesson, suggested by Defense Secretary James Schlesinger, is to expand systems analysis, make it flexible, include the total strategic environment of the organization—even if that means delay in beginning a new system—and "to stress what the best practitioners have always known: that judgment and educated intuition in handling quantitative considerations remain the critical inputs."[10]

PERFORMANCE AND PRODUCTIVITY

Once economic analysis became embedded in public administration, it became necessary to discuss certain fundamental questions about how to go about measuring the effectiveness of public programs. The

CHAPTER 5: POLICY ANALYSIS

application of analysis to productivity improvement in government illustrates some of these problems. Consider this case.

Rats symbolize the horror of the inner city. In medieval times, their appearance in large numbers forecast the plague. In the modern ghetto, rats attack babies in their cribs. As the last gasp of the Great Society, the U.S. Congress passed a bill establishing a categorical grant-in-aid to wage a war on rats.

Various cities established rat-control bureaus and applied for federal funds. Some rat bureaus were set up on a complaint basis. If a citizen called the city to complain about rats, the call would be transferred to the rat bureau which would dispatch inspectors to drive out to the area of complaint and try to kill the rats. The more complaints the rat bureau received, the more money and inspectors it requested from the city government.

Rats practice population control by regulating their birth rates in relation to the availability of food and water. When garbage is available, the rat population booms. The rat inspectors could not force the collection of garbage, since garbage fell under the Sanitation Department and rats were in Human Resources. As citizen frustration rose along with the summer rat population, more people complained. Interpreting this as a prelude to success, the bureaucrats at the rat bureau asked city hall for authorization to hire more inspectors to handle their heavy workload.

City hall, however, had come under the influence of policy analysts, and in any case there was no more money for rats. The analysts told the director of the rat bureau that he would just have to get more work out of his existing inspectors. The director gave each inspector a two-way radio and hired a dispatcher to relay complaints to inspectors in the field. This raised the productivity of the inspectors, who now visited more premises and killed more rats. It also raised the dissatisfaction of the citizens who lived with the rats and who realized that all of this busy rat trapping was having a negligible effect on the rat population.

Eventually the director was forced to abandon the complaint-and-dispatch system. He hired an animal biologist to take a rat census and assigned inspection teams to target districts. Each team included a representative from the Sanitation Department, and each team had a target—reduce the rat population a given percentage and make this reduction visible to the citizens in the target districts.

Public dissatisfaction with government performance is not confined to rats but has become a common problem for all public executives. Everyone complains—rich as well as poor. When public dissatisfaction and administrative costs rise simultaneously, the stage is set for a campaign to increase governmental productivity. The case of the rats illustrates the three basic methods by which public executives can measure and improve agency performance.

1. Resources consumed. "We spend more money on this program than any other city, so it must be good." Absurd as this may sound, the traditional method for gauging the performance of gov-

ernment work is to see how fast the agency can consume resources. An inefficient agency is defined as one so burdened by red tape and so hamstrung by clearance procedures that it cannot move its programs. To improve its performance, the agency streamlines its operations. As its reward for beating its deadlines, the effective agency is allowed to consume even more resources. Growth becomes the standard criteria of bureaucratic success. Of course, there is no guarantee that an agency which is consuming more resources is actually performing a vital public service. It may be very efficient at satisfying no public need whatsoever.

2. Workload. When there are no more resources to consume and complaints continue to rise, government executives can turn to measures of workload. Industrial managers have been raising productivity this way since before the time of Frederick Taylor. The objective, obviously, is to increase output against unit input, either by producing more at the same cost or by cutting costs without reducing the level of goods or services produced.

To do this, the executive establishes some simple measure of work performance. For a fire department, it might be the time that its engine companies take to respond to an alarm. For a sanitary commission, it might be the gallons of sewage treated. These results are then compared against the costs of producing the service. One can use labor productivity (wages or man-hours required to produce a given level of services), capital productivity (the cost of the equipment needed to produce the service), or a combination of the two. To provide a fair comparison, all costs must be reduced to a constant dollar value, which is why economists are usually found as analysts in productivity programs.

Workload productivity can be increased by restructuring the work force, as in setting up mobile fire-fighting companies that rove around the city; or by introducing cost-saving technology, as in automating a sewage-treatment plant. Sometimes it can be as simple as establishing a regular equipment-maintenance program to prevent costly breakdowns while the equipment is in use. Usually line employees are brought in to assist with the discovery of such improvements, since it is assumed that through experience they have learned how to pinpoint productivity bottlenecks.

This is basically where government productivity programs are today—trying to demonstrate that the agency can "do more for less money." It is a particularly useful approach in an era of no growth when the revenue spigot dries up. The main drawback to workload measures, as with resources consumed, is that they tend to state the unit of output in terms of improvements *inside* the organization. Remember the rats? No matter how fast the rat inspectors increased their workload (responding to complaints), they could not keep up with the rats and their baby machines. Workload measures, in this case, led to an assembly-line mentality which sped up the pace of work inside the organization without really making a dent in the fundamental problem which the agency was trying to solve outside the organization. For this reason, many policy analysts advocate that executives substitute measures of impact for measures of work output.

3. Impact. Impact, simply defined, is the total result that any agency creates in the world around it. Impact is generally stated in terms that the taxpayer can understand—fewer rats, safer streets, cleaner air. Instead of trying to process more complaints, the rat bureau tried to reduce rats in target districts by cutting off their supply of food and water. Impact is result oriented; it tests the performance of the agency in terms of the visible change that it produces.

As measures of productivity, impact and workload are similar in that both are balanced against basic labor or capital costs. Impact analysts, however, have been much more clever in their selection of performance indicators. In garbage collection, for example, they eschewed tons of garbage and instead took before-and-after pictures of randomly selected streets.

A special type of impact study, advocated by persons skilled at economic analysis, focuses on net output. The economists calculate the benefits that the program produces in the community at large. The benefits are usually stated in dollar values. The economists then calculate the cost of the resources used up in producing the service which, when subtracted from the benefits, gives them the net output. Finally, the net output is compared to the "opportunity costs," defined as the changes that the same investment of resources would have produced if invested in another program. This, the economists insist, is the only true measure of government productivity.

The great difficulty with impact is that it is nearly impossible to calculate. How does an analyst who is measuring the performance of a school system separate the impact of the school from the educational impact of television or home learning? Furthermore, how does one put a dollar value on the side benefits of school, such as its value in providing a day-care facility for the children of working parents?

Faced with such problems of calculation, analysts often fall back on simple measures, such as reading scores on national achievement tests. The problem with test scores—as with all simple measures of performance—is that they are so easy to manipulate. In one city a private firm received a contract to teach remedial reading to slow learners. The children's reading scores improved remarkably. The program was terminated when educators learned that the contractor was giving the children sample tests on which to practice.

In another city, when local officials became distressed by the statistical lag between the reading scores of their pupils and the national average derived from standardized tests, a psychologist working for the school board proposed a crash reading program. This productivity program had to be canceled when the teachers learned that the psychologist was planning to base all annual pay increases on a single criterion: how well the pupils of each teacher improved their scores on the reading exam.

The second case illustrates the terrible problem of incentives.

How does one create incentives to make the public employees produce more? The traditional solution is to pay employees more money, a contract established through productivity bargaining. Productivity bargaining, however, is nothing more than the old criterion of "resources consumed" in disguise. If the performance of government agencies is to be placed in a state of permanent improvement, then new incentives must be created. Some economists think that they have found the answer. They call it the theory of public choice.

THE THEORY OF PUBLIC CHOICE

The beauty of scientific analysis is its ability to lead analysts to conclusions which they did not know were there. What began as a simple attempt to apply economic models to government budgets and resource decisions has led to a brand of research that challenges the validity of the assumptions upon which the government is organized. It is called the theory of public choice.

Modern government is run under the assumption that groups are good or, more precisely, that "groups of individuals with common interests are expected to act on behalf of their common interests much as single individuals are often expected to act on behalf of their personal interests."[11] In short, individuals join groups to further their common interests. This assumption guided Locke as he formulated the concept of the "social contract," the agreement bringing civilized persons together to form a government and draft a constitution. The assumption is crucial to the theory of democratic pluralism, outlined by Paul Appleby, who viewed the public interest as a product of the activity of organized groups. Even Chester Barnard used the assumption of group cooperation—to formulate the foundations of modern organization theory. The public-choice economists challenge this assumption.

> [People] will *not* act to advance their common or group objectives unless there is coercion to force them to do so, or unless some separate incentive, distinct from the achievement of the group interest, is offered to the members individually on the condition that they help bear the costs involved in the achievement of group objectives.[12]

That is Mancur Olson, who offers proof for his statement in *The Logic of Collective Action.* The logic of the proof can be illustrated by an example based on one of the oldest forms of common association: the volunteer fire department.

In rural counties with old wooden houses and open barns, fire remains a persistent threat, especially in areas where ponds freeze and water pipes burst. So the citizens, acting in their own self-interest, agree to put out each other's fires. They form a volunteer fire department, purchase a fire engine, and wait for the siren that calls them to assist a neighbor. To finance the engine and the operation, the volunteer fire department sells subscriptions. As a special incentive, the volunteer fire fighters also hold dinners, dances, and raffles, where the price of the subscription is added onto the price of the

170

event. When you buy a subscription, you receive a sticker to put in your window.

In one upstate New York town, there was an old Yankee gentleman who had a cosy farm, several ponies, a tweedy wife, and a modest fortune. He was absolutely charming, but he never paid anybody. He was an economist's dream: the perfectly rational man who always wanted to maximize the services he received while minimizing the costs he paid for them. No matter how the volunteer fire fighters tried to cajole or embarrass him into paying for his subscription, he would always diplomatically elude their trap.

The game of pursuit and escape might have continued for years except for the neighbors. Observing the old gentleman's skill at avoiding the subscription fee, and the unfailing fact that the fire fighters always responded to a call for help regardless of whether the subscription was paid or overdue, the other farmers began to withhold their payments. Why, said the farmers, should they voluntarily pay for a service they were guaranteed to receive?

The result was an acute financial crisis in the volunteer fire department. The crisis was quickly resolved when the old gentleman's old home caught fire. The volunteer fire fighters voted not to put out the fire until the old man paid his subscription. He lost half of his home, but there was a long line the next day at the engine house as the other farmers paid their subscriptions.

The problem facing the volunteer fire fighters was that they were producing a public good without any of the advantages of a public agency. A public good, by definition, is provided to all citizens within a given jurisdiction. It is extremely difficult to exclude any one citizen from the benefits of the public good once it is produced. Once the benefits of fire service, police protection, national defense, traffic lights, or collective bargaining are provided for some, they become available for others to enjoy regardless of who pays the costs. Purely private goods, by contrast, can be divided, packaged, and distributed to only those users who are willing to pay for them.

In order to serve the common interest, the volunteer fire department, a community association producing a public good, had to coerce its members into paying for the service. In so doing, it ceased to be purely a voluntary association. It began to *institutionalize*, a process that has led most fire departments to attach themselves to local governments. They become a single organization, serving a single jurisdiction, with the power to tax, to regulate their public, and to outlaw rival organizations from providing the same service in competition.

This is what the public-choice economists see when they look at government as a producer of public goods and services. They see monopolies. Government programs are administered like public monopolies, with one fire department serving one city. In order to finance the costs of production, the government uses its taxing powers to coerce citizens into paying for the benefits they receive. Following this, the agency extends its jurisdiction over a wider territory,

171

claiming that by increasing the scale of the operation it can lower the per capita cost to consumers. As it moves into the new territories, the agency absorbs or outlaws competitors. Citizens are rarely allowed to choose between competing departments; they have to accept the services produced within their own jurisdiction. They are supposed to be content with the knowledge that their self-interest is somehow being satisfied by the agency providing the service.

Public administration begins with the assumption that agencies of government exist to satisfy the common interest of groups of people by providing them with public goods and services. This in turn leads to the assumption that the service has to be monopolized and the people coerced in order to satisfy the common interest. Both assumptions, say the public-choice economists, are fundamentally false. Citizens will not voluntarily join together to promote their common interest and government services do not have to be provided by monopolies.

Public-choice economists are advocates of consumerism in public affairs. They view the government as a giant factory producing goods and services, not as a mythical voluntary association—and they see citizens as consumers. The public-choice economists want to give the citizen-consumer more power over the bureaucrats in government by pumping a little free-enterprise theory into public administration. They are the trust busters of the public service who want to break up public monopolies so that citizens can vote with their pocketbooks by choosing between competing services. A market economy for public goods, they insist, would provide strong incentives to government bureaucrats to produce better goods and services more efficiently. In a word, the public-choice economists would give the citizen-consumer a *choice.* Here are two typical proposals.

The Voucher System

Primary and secondary education is characteristically monopolistic. The consumer receives education through a plant that serves its own monopoly clientele. All schools within a district are virtually identical, except for the occasional vocational or special education school. The schools—as many as two thousand of them in New York City—are administered by a central bureaucracy. The bureaucracy is controlled by professional educators, who have a stake in maintaining a large, uniform system that promotes their interests. It should be no surprise to find that most school systems grow inflexible and are not terribly responsive to new or diverse demands.

The public-choice economists suggest this solution. Parents, they say, should be given vouchers worth a certain amount of education. The student, in conjunction with his or her parents, would select the school he or she wishes to attend. The school would exchange the vouchers it collected from the parents for the public funds it needed to finance its operations. The school could be run by a private or a public agency, so long as it met minimum standards. One assumes that the

172

consumers of education would select those schools which most effectively responded to the public's needs. The other schools would simply wither away. The idea was tested but, due to bureaucratic and
political resistance, never caught on.

The Lakewood Plan

The most certain method of irritating a public-choice economist is to
argue the prevailing notion that, when it comes to government, big
equals better. Public-choice economists have worked for years to dispel the myth of economies of scale that has led to urban annexation
and city-county consolidation. They prefer small governments because small governments are more responsive to the needs of citizens
than large ones. Empirical evidence, they say, proves it. The
Lakewood Plan shows how it works.

Lakewood is a relatively small residential community in the
checkerboard-square megalopolis known as Los Angeles, just north
of the Long Beach Municipal Airport. As part of its plans for growth,
the city of Long Beach moved to annex Lakewood. Lakewood residents feared that they would be swallowed up in the Long Beach
bureaucracy, so they incorporated. They hired ten employees, and,
instead of creating municipal departments, they purchased all of their
services from other governments and contractors in the Los Angeles
area. Lakewood became the first complete "contract city" in America.

The unique feature of Lakewood was the fact that the city officials
who represented the residents were completely separated from the
officials who produced the services to satisfy local demands. In other
words, the Lakewood executives were in a position to bargain over
the provision of municipal services. They encouraged neighboring
cities, the county of Los Angeles, special districts, and private ven-
dors to compete with each other by submitting competitive bids to
provide alternatives services. They put the squeeze on the county,
which won most of the contracts, for special privileges. The county,
for example, in its contract for police protection, required all county
police officers working in Lakewood to live in Lakewood so that they
would become more responsive to local needs.

The voucher plan and the Lakewood plan are designed to provide
bureaucrats with a new set of incentives to produce better public
goods and services. This does not mean that the bureaucrats will
know how. How can bureaucrats improve their operations if they do
not know the sources of success? What produces better police protection? What helps a child to receive a better education? Too often the
bureaucrats simply do not know.

Policy analysis backs up the bureaucrats who want to find out. It
gives them a reason to authorize the research and program experimentation they need to succeed. Modern executives must be able to
establish objectives, weigh multiple criteria, compare costs to benefits, and measure performance. None of this is possible without
research; none is possible unless the executives can experiment with

alternative program designs. Here the skills of the economist, who is good at calculating trade-offs, give way to the contributions of many policy analysts, including economists, who can produce research findings relevant to the needs of public administrators.

RESEARCH FOR MANAGEMENT

Twenty-five years ago most administrators laughed at the suggestion that research scientists could make a significant contribution to the conduct of public policy. Scientists, administrators thought, belonged in the research laboratory. While the administrators laughed, the scientists completed a set of research studies that demonstrated the relevance of policy analysis to public administration. The rest of this chapter describes the kind of research that policy analysts do, and some of the controversies about its use.

The need for research stems from the assumption that the world is essentially counterintuitive. Things do not turn out as people expect them to. If things did, there would be no need for research, only for common sense.

A good example is the American war on poverty. In 1964 the federal government embarked on a crusade against poverty that began with the assumption that poverty was a culture, a set of attitudes, a sense of personal powerlessness. No one tested the assumption; it was presumed true. Ten years later an American university completed a major research study on the relationship of attitudes to poverty and found that there was no statistical correlation between a person's sense of efficacy and his or her chances for economic deprivation. Not surprisingly, the war on poverty did not produce any substantial redistribution of wealth in America.

Preliminary research of the kind illustrated by the policy-analysis model on page 175, would have helped. The policy-analysis model is a simplified version of the way in which policy scientists look at the governmental process. It is based upon models introduced into political science in the fifties by persons associated with the systems approach and refined by a number of later model builders like Ira Sharkansky and Thomas Dye. If you understand the model, then you can understand the kind of research questions that the policy scientists tend to ask.

The model has five basic elements, although the actual policy process is, of course, far more complex.

1. The environment. The environment is the world—the total setting within which the government struggles to function. In one sense, the environment provides the "givens" of public policy: the social, economic, demographic, technological, and organizational state of the nation. In another sense, the environment is where problems "get caused," problems like poverty, inflation, overpopulation, and pollution.

2. Political supports and demands. Political problems do not just

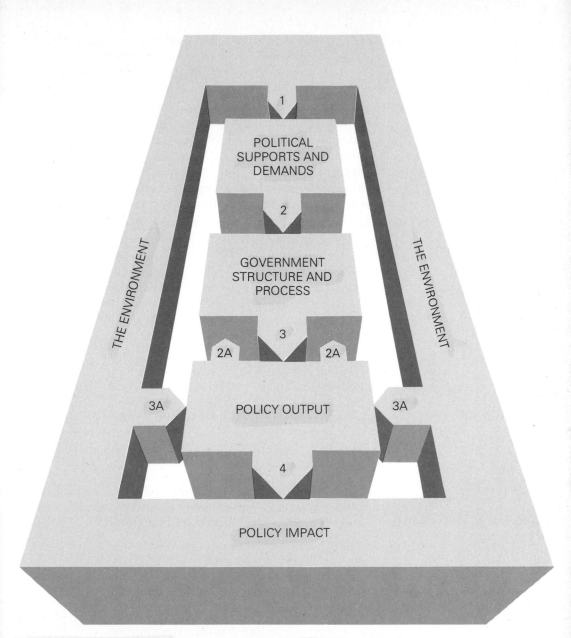

POLICY-ANALYSIS MODEL *Policy analysts distinguish between the output of government and the impact it has on society at large. The arrows in the model represent the most important research being done by policy analysts on (1) the underlying causes of public problems; (2) the process by which public policy gets made, including (2A) the effect the policy type has on the formulation process; (3) whether or not reorganization of government can improve policy output, or (3A) whether the quality of policy is determined by forces in the environment; and (4) the evaluation of the impact of government programs.*

happen; they are forced on the government by organized groups, political parties, and occasionally by citizens. Farmers demand higher prices for their hogs. The Rotarians want to know why the congressman they supported is not doing

175

something about inflation. Such groups represent the interests that provide most of the resources, revenue, personnel, and information upon which the government runs. As such, to a great extent they set the rules of the game.

3. Government structure and process. The government receives the political demands and converts them into public policy. It is widely believed that by changing the internal political or administrative structure of government one can produce changes in the quality of public policy. This belief is the motivation behind reorganization. Unfortunately, there is little empirical evidence to support this point of view.

4. Policy output. Policy is the action of government. It is the money that politicians throw at a problem in the hope of solving it, the decision to send troops to wage a war or bureaucrats to investigate a crash, the rule that regulates a railway. It is a series of miscellaneous activities, from prosecuting an accused criminal to picking up the garbage.

5. Impact. Impact is the end product of governmental activity. It stands for how well (or how poorly) the government hits the environment with its policy. It is also the headache of policy analysts, since it is so difficult to determine in a complex society what difference one government agency has made in changing human behavior or the general state of society. To make matters more complex, government policy also produces side effects. Governments unintentionally redistribute income; they establish or perpetuate inequities. They may create a larger problem by trying to solve a smaller one.

Through the babble of studies conducted by persons who claim to reside under the policy-analysis tent, one can discern four fundamental kinds of research addressed to four different questions.

- *What causes problems?* Many social scientists, natural scientists, economists, political scientists, and anyone else who is interested have conducted research on the roots of the ills that the government seeks to cure.

- *How does policy get made?* Traditionally, this has been the province of political science—understanding how political supports and demands filter through the governmental system and become policy.

- *Does governmental reorganization work?* There are those who believe that changes in the structure of government will produce changes in the quality of policy, and there are those who believe that other forces in the environment or in the policy itself determine the shape of public policy.

- *How do we know what works?* This is the area of program evaluation, where program evaluators attempt to relate the outputs of government to their impact (good and bad) on the environment.

The urgency of these questions—and the controversy over the answers to them—is best illustrated by reference to some actual research studies. The first three questions are examined in the remainder of this section; the fourth question is the subject of the following section on program evaluation.

What Causes Problems?

In 1965, as head of policy planning and research for the U.S. Department of Labor, Daniel Patrick Moynihan wrote a report addressed to the top policy makers in the Johnson administration calling attention to what he thought was the fundamental reason that black people could not break into the mainstream of American society. The title of his report was "The Negro Family: the Case for National Action."

One must remember that Moynihan wrote the report at the close of the civil rights era. Federal legislation assuring equal rights in voting, jobs, and housing would do little to improve the condition of blacks in America, Moynihan explained. The problem, he said, was

Policy analysts insist that public agencies will never be able to solve problems like unemployment without conducting research on the causes of the problem and the effectiveness of existing programs. The results of that research, however, are likely to be distorted or misinterpreted if they pose a threat to vested bureaucratic interests.
COURTESY OF THE COMMUNITY SERVICES ADMINISTRATION

177

the Negro family, or rather the absence of it. Drawing on census data and welfare and labor statistics, Moynihan sketched the following picture of the Negro family. One-fourth of all Negro marriages in cities were dissolved. One-fourth of all Negro children were born illegitimately. One-fourth of all Negro families were headed by females. Less than half of all Negro children reached maturity having lived with both of their parents. The result, Moynihan suggested, was a "tangle of pathology." The black child in a broken family was caught in a cycle of poor education, unemployment, crime, and alienation, a cycle that would only be broken, he said, by the strengthening of the Negro family. He suggested that all government programs reaching blacks—welfare, manpower, education, and others—be reviewed in terms of how they affected the Negro family. Although the report contained no specific recommendations, Moynihan later called for increased job opportunities for blacks and an income-maintenance plan to replace welfare, a system, many observed, that often required the black father to leave home before the mother could receive benefits.

President Johnson used the report as the basis for his 1965 speech calling a White House conference, "To Fulfill These Rights." After the speech, criticism of the report began to build. Critics questioned the statistics used in the report. The data, they said, did not prove conclusively that family conditions were the primary cause of economic hardship. The data did not support the idea of a "tangle of pathology." Some blacks called the report racist because it supposedly blamed the problems of the blacks on their own "pathologies" and not on segregation, discrimination, and white prejudice. It could be used, they said, as an excuse for a government policy of "benign neglect" while the society waited for Negroes to get their own house in order. When the White House conference met, civil rights leaders used it as a forum for attacking the assumptions underlying the report. Administration officials called the conference a "total disaster." Moynihan went back to New York to run for the city council.

It is impossible for the government to attack a problem unless it knows the fundamental causes to attack. This realization has given the government a voracious appetite for scientific research on public problems, from the hazards of smoking to the barriers between races. The Moynihan report illustrates the terrible difficulty of actually using research to reform public policy. Moynihan thought he was presenting "hard facts"—census data, after all, are facts. But the government had already made a substantial commitment of resources to solving unemployment through welfare, so those "facts" had explosive implications. They might mean an end to existing programs, which put the "facts" in the maelstrom of bureaucratic politics. Policy makers, Moynihan learned, will distort, deny, misinterpret, or selectively perceive scientific analysis to suit their bureaucratic self-interest or to protect existing programs. Moynihan left the government in 1965 in a bitter state of mind. Public executives, he complained, were not ready for serious policy research.

We spend most of our money on it [the negro problem], in health, in welfare, and on unemployment, and yet we know nothing about it . . . and one of the reasons is that we are not supposed to know anything about it. It's none of your business . . . and if it is getting worse, that's even less of your business. All you're supposed to do is keep on supplying welfare.[13]

Is the governmental game rigged against the advocates of policy analysis? To answer that inquiry, one must ask a larger question: how does policy actually get made? Wanting to be part of the policy-formulation process, the analysts are led by their natural scientific instincts to test models that explain how that process operates. For such tests, one can turn to political science.

How Does Policy Get Made?

From an administrative point of view, it is very useful to know in general how public policy gets made. Administrators do wonder how legal curiosities such as "maximum feasible participation" get stuck in agency mandates. They also realize that it is impossible to improve that policymaking without understanding how the process works and who influences it.

For decades, political scientists have been telling anyone who will listen that public policy is made under the influence of interest groups. There is not much agreement, however, on the matter of which interest groups are involved. One side claims that elites make policy. The other side claims that the process is essentially pluralistic.

The elitists assume that important policy decisions are controlled by top business leaders and the military brass who force their own preferences on the powerless and often apathetic masses.

Those who propound the doctrine of pluralism assume that people organize into interest groups, that the interest groups compete with each other, that they eventually form coalitions powerful enough to establish a policy, and that there are different coalitions for different policies.

In 1963 Karl Deutsch announced that both sides were wrong. Policymaking, he said, is primarily "a problem of steering."[14] As such, it is related more to the laws of communications than to the rules of interest-group politics. Deutsch explained the channels of communication and decisionmaking in his book *The Nerves of Government*. Policymakers, he said, receive so much information in such short periods of time that they are forced to create perceptual screens to filter out unwanted news. They confine their attention to feasible policies, recall information that is acceptable to them, and repress memories that are not. When the policymaking process breaks down, Deutsch suggests, one can usually trace the blowout to a communication overload.

The same year, a team of policy analysts, led by Raymond Bauer, released the results of a lengthy study on the politics of foreign trade. For nine years, through the Eisenhower and Kennedy adminis-

179

trations, the analysts had studied the debate over proposals to liberalize U.S. trade policy and lower tariff barriers. Their findings tended to confirm Deutsch's theory and discredit the positions of both the pluralists and the elitists.

The analysts found, for example, that few business executives or industries took sides on the tariff issue. The top military leaders played no role whatsoever. A public-opinion poll revealed that most tycoons favored freer trade; nevertheless, the protectionists (drawn from the middle ranks of American corporate and labor power) usually got their way. These findings were most discomforting to the believers in elitism.

The pluralists did no better. Not all of the interests organized. The protectionists were better organized than the antiprotectionists, perhaps because they represented fewer people. The two sides never met face to face to enact a compromise; the outcome in any given year was a result of whose definition of the issue prevailed. If foreign policy was in the news, the free-traders won. If local economic issues dominated the media, the protectionists won.

Bauer and his colleagues concluded that the communication process was the glue of foreign-trade policymaking. Because they were inundated with facts on the effects of foreign trade, members of Congress paid attention only to information with which they agreed. Lobbyists learned to contact only those lawmakers who favored the aims of their organization. To policy analysts disturbed by their lack of influence on other issues, this certainly sounded familiar.

And what about the search for an accurate model of policy formulation? It would be a mistake to assume that the pattern of participation in foreign trade—neither pluralistic nor elitist—was characteristic of all policy decisions. In fact, the analysts discovered that each policy tended to take on its own characteristic modes of decisionmaking and administration. Foreign trade is different from housing which is different from defense which is different from consumer affairs.

There is a pattern to this diversity. If one sorts through all of the government policies in search of commonalities, a pattern of piles emerges. According to Theodore Lowi, one leading typologist of policy formulation, policy may be characterized as essentially distributive, regulatory, or redistributive.

Defense contracting, public works, and grants-in-aid are all policies by which the government distributes benefits to special groups. *Distributive* is a term that arose from the administration of public-land policies in nineteenth-century America. Having bought up all the land from the Mississippi to the Pacific, the government proceeded to give it away to railroads, homesteaders, and land-development companies. The process underlying distributive policies can be characterized as mildly elitist. Pressure groups enter the policy-making arena and demand certain services. Legislative committees authorize the program; government bureaus distribute the benefits. The pressure groups, legislative committees, and bureaus concerned with any one program are closely allied; they do

180

not interfere in the affairs of other subgovernments concerned with other programs. To preserve this rule of noninterference, everyone engages in logrolling. Everyone supports everyone else's programs and the system is balanced to insure that every subgovernment gets a prize.

Trust-busting, civil rights, environmental protection, and consumer affairs are all examples of regulatory policies. In the regulatory arena, the government is confronted with two general groups whose interests are in conflict. To resolve the conflict, the legislature delegates power to an administrative agency, which is charged, under the rule of law, with regulating certain types of activity. Regulatory policies come to resemble the classic form of coalition building that is ascribed to pluralism. The interests meet face to face. When one side wins, the losers often appeal the decision to the legislature or try to recruit new allies to support their claims.

Few of these generalizations apply to redistributive policies. In the redistributive arena, the government is taking benefits away from one group and handing them to another. Unemployment compensation, social security, and national health insurance schemes are all basically redistributive. There are clearly winners and losers, but, unlike the regulatory arena, the winners and losers are not brought together to battle with each other over benefits. Instead, a centralized bureaucracy redistributes benefits through elaborate formal procedures designed to reduce the potential for conflict. The workers who pay the bill for social security never really encounter the elderly who receive the funds. A similar situation exists for welfare and the graduated net income tax, other redistributive policies. From an administrative point of view, they are dull.

Lowi is suggesting that the policy itself is the most important factor shaping the policy-formulation process. Bauer's study of foreign trade seemed complex, Lowi observes, because foreign trade was at that time a policy moving from the distributive to the regulatory arena. The recognition that policy outweighs process has explosive implications for the study of public administration.

Does Governmental Reorganization Work?

The policy-formulation studies by Bauer and Lowi are fundamentally anti-administrative. How is this so? One must remember that the study of public administration is based upon two fundamental beliefs. The first is the assumption that administration is a common process crosscutting all administrative agencies. The policy analysts assault this belief through their suggestion that different policies take on different modes of administration, that the political administration of distributive policies is different from the formalistic administration of redistributive policies. This is why modern schools of public affairs often create one program for health care, one for criminal justice, and another for the environmental sciences. This takes the science of administration back to where it was before Fayol, when to study the management of mines one majored in mine engineering, not management.

The second belief is more critical—the belief in administrative reform. Public administration lives off the assumption that one can improve the output of government by improving the structure of government. Many policy analysts dispute this too.

The Coleman Report, issued in 1966 by the U.S. Office of Education, exemplifies this dispute. The report confirmed the popular suspicion that poor children, especially blacks, start school less prepared than middle-class kids and that the performance gap widens steadily through the school years. What is worse, there is not a great deal that the school system can do to improve the education of the poor child by tinkering with school structure. Class size, the quality of school facilities, the type of curriculum—none of these make much difference in the child's performance. Non-school factors, such as the income of the parents, do.

Philosophers and historians have often argued the case for such broad economic determinism. Policy scientists such as Thomas Dye lent empirical research to this perspective. Dye viewed "economic development—urbanization, industrialization, wealth, and education—as the critical input variable that shapes the character of the political system and the kinds of policy outcomes it produces."[15] By comparing statistics from the American states, Dye found that the level of governmental spending for different policies followed the pattern of wealth. Rich states spent more money on education, health, and welfare than poor states. It did not matter what sort of a governmental system the state possessed. Even that, Dye found, could be explained in terms of the economics of the state.

Needless to say, this brand of economic determinism has not been well received among persons devoted to public administration. A large number of policy scientists insist that the organizational and political arrangements in government can be rigged so as to produce different policy outcomes or to favor the participation of one group over another, such as scientists versus lawyers. Says one analyst, James Q. Wilson:

> Government has an independent effect on public policy in ways that can be associated with the characteristics of that government, the party arrangements which animate it, and the values which permeate it. [16]

What is the evidence supporting this point of view? For one, there is Wilson's own study of police behavior. Wilson, a Harvard University political scientist, was interested in what happened when a city government decided to engage in a bit of administrative tinkering and professionalize its police force.

To professionalize its force, the government recruits young, well-educated criminal justice students, often from outside the city. It gives them lots of in-service training, promotes them according to merit, and encourages them to dispense justice without regard to personal considerations. The chief joins the International Association of Chiefs of Police.

How does this affect crime? Take juvenile delinquency as an example. Statistics show that the young person in a city with a professionalized police force is twice as likely to come into contact with the police and four times as likely to be arrested. On the surface, it seems normal that professionalization would increase police productivity. Except that similar policy studies, which carry the analysis into the impact area, fail to demonstrate any relationship (positive or negative) between the number of arrests and the crime rate among juveniles. The police professionals may arrest more juveniles, but only 3 percent of those who are stopped by professional police are ever tried and incarcerated, a message that is clearly received on ghetto streets. The evidence, as hard as it is to swallow, seems to suggest that while the decision to professionalize will change the behavior of police, it will not significantly change the behavior of the juvenile.

Wilson and his colleagues are willing to go that far—to show that governmental reform does affect the output of policy, but not policy impact. Other studies are both esoteric and amusing. One research scientist discovered that partisan governments with strong mayors are more likely to put fluoride in their water supply. Another analyst discovered that big-city political machines are more likely to raise taxes. (One explanation: when ward bosses walk the precincts, they generate demands for more services, which produces higher spending, which in turn creates the need for higher taxes.) Most of these studies are based upon empirical research at the local level, a necessity created by the need to compare evidence from many different jurisdictions.

Only a few policy scientists have been able to trace an empirical connection between governmental reform and policy impact. One is Elinor Ostrom. Like James Wilson, she is interested in police behavior. Her studies indicate that the size of the police force has a direct bearing not only on output (such as response time) but also upon policy impact (such as public satisfaction with the service). The smaller the police force, she found, the better the overall performance. That, say her critics, is due to the fact that smaller police forces are generally located in the suburbs where there is more money.

Faced with all of this conflicting evidence, professional public administrators can move in one of two directions. They can go sour on administrative reform and accept the determinism which says that organizational tinkering is unlikely to make much difference in the long run. Or they can call upon the policy analysts to sharpen their tools and, like Elinor Ostrom, produce research findings that indicate what does work. That brings in the program evaluators.

PROGRAM EVALUATION

Joseph Wholey, in his book *Federal Evaluation Policy*, defines program evaluation as "research—the application of the scientific method to public programs to learn what happens as a result of program activities."[17] Regardless of how it is defined, it is the hottest item in public administration since the consolidated executive budget. And for a good reason—what with all the citizen dissatisfaction with government, policy makers from the departments to the legislature want a tool that lets them know whether the programs they authorize "are contributing to the solutions of problems and if they are worth the money being spent on them." [18]

A workable evaluation program, Wholey says, will consist of four basic elements.

1. Definition of program objectives and measures of performance. Like every other policy-analysis technique, program evaluation begins with an explicit statement of objectives. Wholey insists that evaluation will fail if top executives cannot articulate their objectives and give the evaluators the guidance they need in defining appropriate performance criteria. Of course, the agency's legal mandate is probably vague; its actual objectives are probably complex. The only solution to this situation is for evaluators to use multiple criteria. In evaluating an education program, for example, the researchers would want to consider more than the performance of students on achievement tests. The researchers would want to look at drop-out rates, the professional reputation of the school, and the attitudes of the public toward it. They would want to balance these findings against the social, economic, and intellectual background of the students being served. They might want to compare the school to other systems in other cities or weigh its quality against its performance in the past. "Multiple measures are necessary to reflect multiple objectives and to avoid distorting performance. One can imagine schools developing and publishing a variety of measures of skills, knowledge, and satisfaction of students."[19]

2. Development of evaluation work plans. Before actually beginning the evaluation, it is necessary for the evaluators to establish a plan that lays out their research strategy three or more years into the future. The multi-year plan sets the priorities for the evaluation program by identifying the most pressing research questions. It should assess the methodological techniques available to answer these questions, the potential cost of the program, the number of agency personnel needed to execute it, and the overall feasibility of actually completing the studies as planned.

3. Design and execution of evaluation studies. Most evaluation studies are not done by the agency itself but are contracted out to universities or private research firms. The contractors usually have research interests of their own and will pursue them if allowed to select the general approach and methodology. To prevent this, the agency must prepare work statements that specify the purpose of the study, the performance criteria, the

methodology to be used, and a summary of what the agency already knows about the effectiveness of its programs. This, in turn, needs to be followed up with close contract monitoring.

4. Dissemination and use of evaluation-study findings. Evaluation is only effective to the extent that it results in improvements in the actual program. There are four reasons why policy makers may refuse to utilize evaluation research findings. One is simple organizational inertia; there is little that the evaluators can do to change this. The other reasons, however, are faults that the evaluators can correct. The policy makers may choose not to accept the research findings because they distrust the methodology, finding it simpleminded or improperly applied. They may ignore the study because it is irrelevant to the most pressing issues before the agency. Or they may take no action because they never heard of the study or, if they have heard of it, did not understand its implications.

How does one evaluate the effectiveness of a public agency, especially when its employees are out in the field, cut off from direct central control? Program evaluators have used a number of criteria for evaluating the performance of police departments: arrest rates, crime rates, response time, the professional reputation of the department, comparison with similar jurisdictions, and public attitudes as determined through opinion polls. COURTESY OF THE INTERNATIONAL ASSOCIATION OF CHIEFS OF POLICE.

Unfortunately, it costs money to overcome the obstacles of methodology, irrelevance, and dissemination. Wholey estimates that an effective evaluation will eat up about 1 percent of the total agency budget. Most agencies spend one-tenth that amount. As a result, they get a bargain-basement evaluation program.

There are a number of types of evaluation studies, ranging from cheap to exotic. The least expensive method is to compare readily available data collected before the program began against data collected after the program is underway. Police departments, for example, often evaluate their programs by comparing before-and-after statistics on crime rates. A more sophisticated evaluation includes time-trend projections, since one can assume that data such as crime rates will change on their own and that a pattern to this change can be found. A slightly different approach to evaluation can be set up through targeting—identifying planned goals, such as a 10 percent reduction in armed robberies, and then collecting enough data to evaluate whether or not the goals are met. Before-and-after statistics, time-trend projections, and targeted goals all suffer from one major deficiency—there is no guarantee that the results reflected in the statistics are due to the performance of the agency. A better method, in some ways, is to compare one neighborhood or jurisdiction that is served by the program to a similar area that is not. Under any of these approaches, the effectiveness of the evaluation is enhanced by increasing the complexity of the criteria used. A good police evaluation, for example, will compare data taken from reported crimes to data acquired through a public survey. ("Have you been a victim of crime? How safe do you feel?")

If money is no problem, then the best form of evaluation is *systematic experimentation*. The New Jersey Graduated Work Incentive Experiment demonstrates how this works. The federal government was searching for a cheap, effective substitute for welfare. A number of social scientists recommended the negative income tax, a scheme under which every American would be guaranteed a certain income. Opponents of the plan argued that heads of households so rewarded would lose their incentive to work. (For this reason, families headed by healthy men are generally ineligible for welfare.) The Office of Economic Opportunity decided to find out whether or not the negative income tax would work or whether it would encourage people to sit at home and live off the dole. The evaluators selected four neighborhoods in the Northeast and delivered to the families—including those headed by men able to work—eight different combinations of income and tax benefits. At the same time, the researchers set up a control group—similar kinds of families receiving no special benefits whose behavior was to be compared to the test group. Astonishingly, there was no difference at all between the experimental group and the control group in terms of the willingness of the men to work, regardless of whether or not they received the negative income tax.

Such experiments are costly to run and difficult to control. The evaluators must recruit experimental groups and control groups, set up performance criteria, measure preprogram performance, monitor changes during the experiments, account for extraneous variables, and guard against the "Hawthorne effect," the fact that the presence of the research team may encourage the subjects in the experiment to behave differently than they normally would.

This may seem awfully elaborate to bureaucrats who are used to evaluating from the seat of their pants, but to the policy analysts, it is only the beginning. Listen to the leading exponent of improved policy evaluation, Yehezkel Dror. Dror is probably the least readable social scientist since Talcott Parsons. In a series of three arduously written books, Dror sets out his plan.

Dror is worried about the gap between policy and technology. On the one hand, technology has created the methods by which people can control the environment, society, and individual behavior. On the other hand, policy makers lack the knowledge they need to effectively design and operate the systems that will do the controlling. Policy makers, Dror complains, are too accustomed to planning for tomorrow on the basis of what they did yesterday without reviewing their objectives or evaluating their results. Policy analysts, he continues, do not help this situation when they rely upon simple-minded analysis techniques.

Dror advocates an optimal approach to policy making and evaluation, one that begins with a search for the best possible policy through a review of problems, goals, values, alternatives, costs, and benefits, and continues with midcourse corrections once information on the performance of the program begins flowing in. Needless to say, this will require substantial changes in both the governmental process and the policy sciences.

Dror begins his policy revolution by insisting that policy analysts broaden their use of information. He is upset with the policy analysts because of their reliance upon the concept of net output, an economic showpiece too often used by public administrators to prove that their programs are cost effective without reference to how good the programs are. Net output is only useful when integrated with other standards of performance—past quality, planned targets, professional reputation, performance of other jurisdictions, and institutional survival.

Dror also wants policy analysts to broaden their use of extrarational information. He chides them for being preoccupied with rationality and numbers—a result, he suspects, of their desire to imitate the physical sciences—when some of the best available sources for policy analysis are those which are extrarational and non-quantifiable. In one of his more fascinating proposals, he urges policy analysts to pay attention to intuition, exceptional leaders, value preferences, and acute perceptions of reality. This might help policy makers expand their use of tacit knowledge, personal experience, and history. Dror would also invite philosophers to explore the implications of alternative futures and draw upon executives who have an

187

unusual capacity to make correct decisions or survive change. Their friends call such executives creative, intuitive, or lucky; their enemies call them Faustian. Dror does not care; he would use these exceptional people too.

Of course, none of this is possible without a general restructuring of the governmental process. In Dror's optimal approach, policy makers would have to reformulate their procedures for setting objectives and monitoring results.

> The more policy sciences indeed does develop, the more should the policy-making system be redesigned to avail itself of policy sciences knowledge and the more should politics be reformed to permit full symbiosis between political power and policy sciences knowledge.[20]

To achieve this symbiosis of knowledge and power, Dror outlines schemes for improving the evaluation of past policies, for better consideration of the future, and for extensive social experimentation. He shows how policy analysis can be used at the early stages of policy formulation when issues, alternatives, and goals are still pliable. He would reorganize government to encourage more innovation and risk taking, especially on political and administrative heresies. There would be more policy-research organizations like the RAND Corporation, which Dror once worked for. He has great plans for involving citizens in the policy-making process, educating adults about it, and developing the capacity of elected politicians to use policy sciences. On top of it all, he would establish what looks like a council of philosopher-kings to supervise the executives and issue explicit "megapolicy decisions." They would decide how many risky programs the government would undertake and determine the optimal mix of programs with concrete objectives and those which build up resources for yet undefined problems awaiting us in the future.

Dror's optimal approach seems awfully utopian, especially to policy evaluators who have to struggle with more mundane problems, such as how to keep their evaluation budgets from being cut back again. To persons who take an incremental approach to policy making, Dror's ideas are absolutely dangerous.

THE INCREMENTALISTS' DISCLAIMER

What is the proper role for policy scientists in the administrative process? Can the public service be reoriented so as to make greater use of empirical research and economic approaches? One test is to apply the optimal model to an actual policy.

Suppose that the executive directing the nation's price-control board decided to apply the contents of this chapter to the problem of controlling inflation.[21] He would start by clarifying his objective, in this case, to control prices. He would then consider all of the secondary effects that inflationary control might produce on employment, the balance of payments, the supply of commodities, the stock market, persons on fixed incomes, and so on, knowing that the side effects of his program could cancel out progress toward his primary objective. Policy scientists from economics and other academic disciplines would be called in to develop suitable techniques for measuring inflation, to investigate the root causes of inflation, and to evaluate the potential impact of various controls. Using the general policy-making model as their guide, they would then advise the executive on the political or administrative alternatives with the highest payoff as well as warn him about the economic conditions beyond his control.

The executive would then create a model of the national economic system through which he could calculate the costs and benefits of the proposed alternatives. He would calculate the total costs over the life of each program and assess whether the benefits of all such programs together were worth the government's investment of time and money.

Finally, the executive would choose a strategy insuring the best results at the lowest cost. With the policy scientists, he would devise criteria for evaluating the impact of the strategy and the productivity of his employees. His staff officers would prepare a budget for each program, projected five years into the future, accompanied by documents describing the programs and the strategic choices made. Once authorized, the programs could begin.

Some social scientists find this model of policy formulation unrealistic. Says one:

> It assumes intellectual capacities and sources of information that men simply do not possess, and it is even more absurd as an approach to policy when the time and money that can be allocated to a policy problem is limited, as is always the case. Of particular importance to public administrators is the fact that public agencies are in effect usually instructed not to practice [this] method. That is to say, their prescribed functions and constraints—the politically or legally possible—restrict their attention to relatively few values and relatively few alternative policies.[22]

That is Charles Lindblom, writing in 1959, in what is now considered to be one of the classics in public administration.

Lindblom predicted at that time that the science of policy analysis would outrace the ability of public administrators to use it. This would create a monstrous gap between what social scientists preached and what public administrators were capable of practicing. Public administrators, who desperately need scientific guidelines to help them make decisions, would turn away from the policy sciences so long as they continued to stress the clarification of objectives, the explicitness of evaluation, the comprehensiveness of review, and the quantification of values for mathematical analysis.

Lindblom proposed an alternative set of guidelines, which he called the Science of Muddling Through. It is a model of incremental policy making, or, in the jargon that Lindblom supplied for the social scientists, a model of successive limited comparisons. It assumes that a historic chain of decisions exists which the executive can use as a basis for his future choices. The process may be illustrated with reference to the problem of the executive directing the price-control board.

Using Lindblom's approach, the executive would set a principal objective, no doubt stated in general terms so that conflicting interests could agree upon it—something like "keeping prices level." He would disregard most other social values, such as unemployment, unless they threatened the survival of his price-stabilization program. Those problems would be attacked by executives in separate but adjacent bureaus. As a second step, the executive would consider various courses of action that were in the neighborhood of what the government was already doing or had done in the past. He would select one, expecting not to achieve his goal completely, but to move a little closer toward it. In so doing, he would estimate the probable consequences of taking this action, based on his own experience, intuition, and a little empirical social science if it was applicable, easily accessible, and understandable. Making such estimates is not difficult, because the government has accumulated experience on programs that are roughly similar. If the executive's action produces the expected results, he can begin the process again and make further incremental changes. If the results do not conform to expectations, he

The growing popularity of policy analysis has been accompanied by much debate over its relevance to administrative problems. Yale professor Charles Lindblom (left) insists that policy analysis requires more time, money, and information than public administrators possess. Lindblom advocates an incremental approach to policy making, which he says is more realistic and better suited to democratic values. One of the leading writers on policy analysis, Yehezkel Dror, argues that Lindblom's proposal for a "science of muddling through" will never work because there is no viable base upon which one can incrementally build future policy. Dror, a professor at the Hebrew University of Jerusalem, advocates an optimal approach to policy making that seeks out the best possible policy, regardless of the past. COURTESY OF THE HEBREW UNIVERSITY OF JERUSALEM AND THE YALE NEWS BUREAU.

can retreat back to his previous strategy without having to risk the entire price-control program.

Well, you can imagine the howls of protest from policy scientists devoted to pumping the governmental system full of information and training executives to use it. Admittedly, said Yehezkel Dror, "most public policy in modern societies is made by incremental changes in older policies." This is due to "respect for the past and skepticism about human ability to change the future." Such attitudes are common in periods characterized by rapid change when people "long for stability" and search for incremental-change models, even though that change makes "such models continually less useful for deciding what to do. When the results of past policies have been unsatisfactory, those results count for little in deciding what to do next, since incremental changes in them cannot produce significantly better results."[23] Dror parts with the incrementalists because he does not believe that a historical base exists upon which good public policy can be based. A sense of crisis, in which the unexpected is the norm, leads Dror to adopt the optimal approach to policy making and administration.

Dror continues. Lindblom's objections to policy analysis, he says, are out of date. Information and intellectual capacity do exist, due to advances in management science and empirical research. Reorganization is removing the last legal barriers to broad policy planning. As to the lack of time and money, says Dror, if you do not spend time and money on policy analysis, you will not have a policy that works.

These things may be available, says Lindblom, but they are certainly not well accepted by governmental executives. Dror's brave new world of policy analysis will require radical restructuring of the government and a new set of rulers chosen from among the intelligentsia. This last point leads the critics to their ultimate indictment. *Even if policy planning is feasible, they say, it is not desirable.* Social scientists may have noble intentions, but they make poor social planners. Their empirical tests are not only silly, they are dangerous.

As evidence, Daniel Moynihan cites the ill-fated poverty program and its provision for maximum feasible participation of the poor. The presidential committee that wrote the basic legislation creating the poverty program came under the domination of social scientists who believed that poverty was caused by the inability of the poor to organize themselves and press their demands upon the government. Put bluntly, the social scientists did not know what they were doing. The fuzzy theory that powerlessness caused poverty was based on incomplete research and sloppy analysis. The only causal relationship the reformers could have verified through research, Moynihan insists, was the fact that the middle-class-inspired requirement for the "maximum feasible participation" of the poor would cause *conflict*, which it did, severely damaging President Johnson's plan to eradicate poverty in America. When Moynihan tried his own hand at writing policy, in his report on the Negro family, he confirmed his own thesis. Like the poverty program, it produced conflict and disorder.

191

Moynihan's diatribe against the architects of the war on poverty applied to other programs touched by policy scientists. Social science was badly discredited by association with the controversy over bussing and school desegregation. American policy analysts "won" the war in Vietnam every Christmas with their dubious body counts and kill ratios. The U.S. government, said Moynihan, possessed as little knowledge about how to motivate Vietnamese peasants to resist Communism as it had formulas for ending American poverty. Urban renewal, touted by social planners in the 1950s as the salvation of the cities, became a bad joke in the ghetto, where it was labeled "Negro removal." And what did the policy scientists do when their formulas bred conflict and disorder? The reaction among many was "to welcome it. How grand to live in such interesting times!"[24]

As long ago as 1953, Lindblom and a colleague who is Mr. Pluralist himself, Robert Dahl, laid out this message in a book titled *Politics, Economics, and Welfare.* They rejected the grand planning strategies of socialism and liberalism as inappropriate to governmental administration in a pluralistic society. There is great social value, Lindblom later insisted, in having interest groups rather than social scientists evaluate social policy. Each group understands its own interests from its own perspective. It does not have to grapple with the obscure value conflicts that plague planners of grandiose social schemes. Each interest group knows what it wants and can be expected to protect its own survival.

Yes, say the policy scientists, the organized groups will protect their own interests. But not all of the interests are organized. Blacks, minorities, and consumers are not represented by powerful pressure groups at the councils of government. Out of the clash of special interests in an organized society will not emerge the public good—but a collection of large, unassailable, unresponsive special interests, armed with government power and money, trying to buy off poorly organized groups with a small piece of the action. It happened in urban renewal, where social planners insisted that private groups compete for limited federal funds under comprehensive guidelines that purported to favor "comprehensive" planning. The result was a lot of real estate developers who used government power to tear up neighborhoods and build concrete castles and parking lots in the air. Governments that embrace the doctrine of pluralism will never be able to produce effective change. That includes the social planners who agreed to promote pluralism in order to gain admittance to the inner councils of policy making, the scholars who wanted to bring pluralism to the poor, and the experts who tried to convince the American military that the United States was somehow obliged to ingrain participatory democracy into Vietnamese village life.

This sort of academic rhetoric really frightens the pluralists, who believe that it will lead to an omnipotent executive governing society like a high-court justice through the rule of law, backed by policy analysts trying to coordinate society through their empirical superiority. Lindblom in particular has struggled to convince the academics

192

that it is not necessary to appoint the wise to plan and coordinate everything. "People can coordinate each other without anyone's coordinating them, without a dominant common purpose, and without [written] rules."[25] He calls the process partisan mutual adjustment—the hidden hand of incrementalism. Moreover, incrementalism makes better use of information than the policy sciences, with all their emphasis upon collecting data. Incrementalism assures that decisions will be made on the basis of concrete information presented by the interests who have the most to gain or lose in the process. If not all of the interests are organized, then government can help them to get organized or give them special access.

Even if the government could feasibly plan everything, Lindblom concludes, he would choose incrementalism. It is simply a better method for resolving conflict. Authoritative social planning requires people to bow to a superior will. Incrementalism allows the people to resolve their value preferences by participating in a mutually agreed-upon process of mutual adjustment. He calls policy scientists back to political philosophy, where government is not an exercise in economic efficiency, but a process of distributing power so as to reconcile the various partisan interests that try to coexist within the same society.

The incrementalists' disclaimer raises serious questions about the relevance of policy analysis to modern government—whether the reforms based on reorganization, economic analysis, and research methodologies are not inappropriate, given the nature of the administrative process. Of course, the analysts would change that by making administration more rational. The incrementalists find this both unfeasible and unwise. At any rate, this much is clear: analysis will not win everyone over just because it can claim to be rational. The history of PPB proves that. To work, analysis requires power—the sort of power embraced by the advocates of reorganization and the sort of power that resides, often unused, in many administrative offices.

FOR FURTHER READING

Policy analysis is the newest approach to creating solutions for administrative problems. As such, any recommendations about the literature are highly tentative. Before plunging into the field, the novice is advised to read a few overviews, such as the short survey by Alice M. Rivlin, *Systematic Thinking for Social Action* (Washington, D.C.: The Brookings Institution, 1971). Richard I. Hofferbert reviews quantitative studies and case histories in *The Study of Public Policy* (Indianapolis: The Bobbs-Merrill Co., 1974) while the full academic treatment is provided by Ira Sharkansky, ed., in *Policy Analysis in Political Science* (Chicago: Markham Publishing Co., 1970); the first two sections by Sharkansky and Dye present the most commonly accepted frameworks for studying public policy.

The Nixon reorganization is the subject of the book by Richard

193

Nathan, *The Plot that Failed* (New York: John Wiley & Sons, 1975). Charles Hitch explains the rationale behind the introduction of PPB and cost-benefit analysis into the Pentagon in *Decision Making for Defense* (Berkeley: University of California Press, 1965). It is an excellent short introduction to the use of economic models for policy analysis. The best survey of PPB is by Fremont Lyden and Ernest G. Miller, eds., *Planning-Programming-Budgeting: A Systems Approach to Management* (Chicago: Markham Publishing Co., 1968). Cost-benefit analysis is outlined by Robert Dorfman, ed., *Measuring Benefits of Government Investments* (Washington, D.C.: The Brookings Institution, 1965) and Stephen Enke, ed., *Defense Management* (Englewood Cliffs, N.J.: Prentice-Hall, 1967). The *Public Administration Review* published a symposium on productivity in volume 32 (November/December 1972, pp. 739–850. The basic outlines of the public-choice approach can be found in Robert L. Bish, *The Public Economy of Metropolitan Areas* (Chicago: Markham Publishing Co., 1971).

A good example of the use of social science research in public administration is the book by Lee Rainwater and William Yancey, *The Moynihan Report and the Politics of Controversy* (Cambridge, Mass.: MIT Press, 1967), which contains the entire Moynihan report on the Negro family. Theodore Lowi outlines his typology of policy formulation in "American Business, Public Policy, Case-Studies, and Political Theory," *World Politics* 16 (July 1964), pp. 677–715. Lowi's article is actually a book review of one of the most ambitious studies of policy formulation, done by Raymond A. Bauer, Ithiel de Sola Pool, and Lewis A. Dexter, *American Business and Public Policy: The Politics of Foreign Trade* (New York: Atherton Press, 1963). For a closer look at the influence of governmental reform on public policy, see James Q. Wilson, ed., *City Politics and Public Policy* (New York: John Wiley & Sons, 1968). One of the best sources for books on program evaluation is the Urban Institute, which produced the study by Joseph Wholey et. al., *Federal Evaluation Policy* (Washington, D.C.: The Urban Institute, 1970).

By now the newcomer should be ready for the more turgid attempts to frame general theories of policy making and evaluation. Karl Deutsch suggests a model based on communications and political control in *The Nerves of Government* (New York: The Free Press, 1963). Yehezkel Dror pleads for a more rational approach to policy formulation and evaluation in *Public Policymaking Reexamined* (San Francisco: Chandler Publishing Co., 1968). The dissent against all of this rationality is led by Charles E. Lindblom, whose position is well summarized in "The Science of 'Muddling Through,'" *Public Administration Review* 19 (Spring 1959), pp. 79–88.

EXECUTIVE POWER

6

Policy analysis provides a model for those who believe that public administration can be made rational. When policy analysis fails, one often finds that an infatuation with measurement took precedence over political caution. Policy analysis often fails because the executive lacked the political instincts to correct the intemperance of the analysts.

When John Lindsay left Gracie Mansion after two terms as mayor of New York, the press asked him: what do you think was your greatest accomplishment in eight years as chief executive of America's largest city? Lindsay replied: *management and administration.* In his last term, he said, he had reorganized the city government, modernized the budget system, set up a productivity program, installed project managers, and brought in policy analysts and policy evaluators to monitor program performance. He had introduced systems analysis and computerization and recruited bright, young people to middle-management positions in the city government. The city's collective bargaining officers had settled 680 labor contracts. Improvements in management and administration, Lindsay said— that was his greatest accomplishment.

The press corps was incredulous. They remembered the strikes, the crime, the cost of government, the taxes, the police corruption, the snowstorm that the city could not dig itself out of, and the intergovernmental relations that Lindsay never had with Governor Nelson Rockefeller. Here was the man who had people asking, Is New York City governable? announcing that he had solved the city's management problems with a bag of administrative tricks. Despite his modern management techniques, Lindsay possessed a solid reputation as a man who could not make the city run.

What accounted for the gap between Lindsay's perception and the impressions of the press? Lindsay certainly had mastered the science of administration; what he lacked, quite simply, was the power to make it work.

196

Is power a necessary element in public administration? Many experts believe so. It is foolish, they say, for the executive to rely solely upon formal administrative procedures. The success of a program frequently depends upon the skill of the executive at persuading people who are outside of the executive's organizational tree; even the ones inside the executive's span of control may have to be persuaded to accept the executive's sense of priorities. When the executive presents the budget, solicits advice, sets up programs, or takes risks, the skills of influence usually count for more than administrative procedures. Here the executive needs pragmatic, short-range political strategies. He or she may attempt to behave rationally and follow procedures, but nothing will happen until the rationally selected procedures are pursued politically.

The scholarly literature on executive power in public administration is awfully thin. Political scientists, who usually study these things, have concentrated on policy analysis, which contains very little politics. A few economists have objected to the lack of politics in political science—the incrementalist disclaimer discussed in Chapter 5. As for the study of administration, despite Appleby's insistence that public administration is politics, the discipline has no extensive regard for the political dynamic from a practical point of view. There are enough *descriptions* of politics, but few applications that tell managers how to deal with these challenges.

This chapter pulls together what information is available, adds a few new ideas, and applies the knowledge to the problems of budgetary control, information gathering, administrative oversight, bureaucratic risk taking, and administrative ethics. Our study of executive power in public administration begins five centuries ago with a political adviser from Florence.

MANAGEMENT AS POWER

Niccolò Machiavelli was a public administrator. For fourteen years he served as secretary of the chancery of foreign affairs in Florence. From that position he attempted to organize a citizen militia for the city, represented Florentine interests on some thirty foreign missions, and oversaw diplomatic correspondence. He lost his job during a change in administration. The new rulers, the Medici family, imprisoned Machiavelli, tortured him on the rack, then allowed him to retire to a small farm in the Tuscan countryside outside Florence with his wife and children. There, at the age of 44, he wrote *The Prince*.

In spirit, at least, Machiavelli was a democrat. Unfortunately, he found just government nearly impossible to administer, given local conditions. Italy was governed by a plethora of independent city-states with little to hold them together. Rulers could not always trust those who served them. Other governments, notably the French and Spanish monarchies, intervened in Italian politics. People asked: is Italy governable?

Machiavelli's experience turned him into a skeptic. That is, he believed that the words of rulers were a screen for their true intentions, which in turn were always based upon their own self-interest. *The Prince* is a discourse written to the Medici executives, instructing them on the rule of Italy given these conditions.

Machiavelli recognized that the people needed to be reassured with words. The exercise of power requires ceremony (the modern term is *legitimacy*). Power, after all, is the ability to make another person do what he or she would not otherwise do. People resent naked power; they want the executive to make an appearance of being righteous and constitutional in order to make the dose of power palatable.

Machiavelli thus advised the executive to take care to appear merciful, faithful, humane, upright, and religious. He advised the executive to make speeches before local guilds or societies and to give awards to persons demonstrating great ability in commerce or agriculture. He advised the executive to concentrate on one or two achievements "and keep the minds of the people occupied with them."[1] The executive should maintain a reputation as a winner, he said, but should guard against liberality, which would weigh down the people with excessive taxes and bring the executive hatred in return for his kindness.

In maintaining a reputation, Machiavelli stressed appearances. He knew the power of an image in soliciting consent and respect from the people being controlled. But Machiavelli also knew that if executives who made a show of being righteous actually became merciful, faithful, and so on, it would lead to their downfall. "Everyone sees what you appear to be, few really know what you are, and those few dare not oppose themselves to the opinion of the many."[2]

Appearances aside, Machiavelli believed that the highest temporal morality required the executive to maintain the stability of the state and protect it against external invasion. He disliked tyrants and advised against meanness, cruelty, and becoming hated, which violated his temporal morality and constituted poor administration. He thought the best executive was the one who was feared. "Fear preserves you by a dread of punishment which never fails. . . Men have less scruple in offending one who is beloved than one who is feared."[3]

How does one become feared? By being decisive in the employment of one's advantages, by not being afraid, "on proper justification and for manifest cause," to proceed against the security or property of others.[4] Every office contains formal advantages; the willingness of executives to use those advantages, even ruthlessly, fixes their reputation in the minds of others.

Machiavelli offered advice for managing a subordinate. "Study him, honor him, enrich him, do him kindness, share with him the honors and cares; and at the same time let him see that he cannot stand alone. . . . When you see [him] thinking more of his own interests than of yours, and seeking inwardly his own profit in everything, such a man will never make a good servant."[5]

CHAPTER 6: EXECUTIVE POWER

He advised the executive to form a cabinet, made up of the wise men in the state, and to reward with preference above the others those who freely spoke the truth. "A prince, therefore, ought always to take counsel, but only when he wishes and not when others wish. He ought to be a constant inquirer and afterwards a patient listener."[6] He warned executives against yielding their affairs to a single prudent subordinate. Things may be well managed for a while, but not for long, because such a subordinate would in short time usurp the executive's job.

Machiavelli wrote this advice in 1513. Four hundred forty-six years later, Richard Neustadt, a political scientist who had served on Harry Truman's White House staff, brought it up to date. Like Machiavelli, Neustadt wrote his treatise for a chief executive: President Kennedy, a modern-day Medici.

Neustadt warned Kennedy about executives who "failed to make their choices serve their influence." They forgot the risks to their own influence "because they saw the issues through the eyes of their advisers."[7] The advice might be technically correct, but disastrous in terms of its effect upon the ability of the executive to govern. The advisers could not be expected to share this sensitivity to the limits of influence; this is essentially a matter of the executive's own self-interest. When it comes to executive power, says Neustadt, no one is an expert but the executive.

Subordinates, Neustadt insists, act upon their own conception of their own interests. Because people hold different offices, because they have different constituencies, they are bound to disagree about what is the common interest. The essence of an executive's job is thus to induce others "to believe that what he wants of them is what their own appraisal of their own responsibilities requires them to do in their interest, not his."[8] Neustadt calls this the power to persuade. He perceives that an executive who *commands* a subordinate to do something has in effect admitted his (or her) own failure—his failure to *persuade* the subordinate.

An executive can persuade others only if they believe that he "has skill and will enough to *use* his advantages." The executive strengthens this belief by maintaining his professional reputation and public prestige. Professional reputation is what other executives and politicians believe he is capable of doing. Ideally, an executive who values his reputation would make "vivid demonstrations of tenacity and skill." If this is not possible, "his need is to keep [people] from thinking they can cross him without risk, or that they can be sure what risks they run." At the same time, the executive must convince them that he will not "leave them in the lurch if they support him."[9]

Neustadt characterizes prestige as "a jumble of imprecise impressions held by a relatively inattentive" public.[10] Prestige gives the executive leeway—leeway to take risks, leeway to exploit opportunities. Without public prestige, the executive has no leeway to draw upon his power to make unpopular decisions. Prestige also gives the executive leverage over others, persons who are reluctant to cross the executive because they fear that their recalcitrance will bring public disfavor, or persons who desire that their cooperation be rewarded by public opinion.

To Machiavelli and Neustadt, executive success requires that the executive seek power, establish a reputation, and skillfully employ his or her advantages. Neither trusted advisers, analysis, or reason. Both recognized that reasonable persons differ in their own conceptions of their own duties, and that such differences have to be resolved through the tools of persuasion, control, and influence.

To establish a reputation, executives have to know their advantages and how to use them. Executive advantages might include wealth, goods, symbols, values, violence, or security. They might be the formal advantages of offices, or they might be favors owed. Both Machiavelli and Neustadt agreed that, in general, the best executives are those who use their advantages to engender a slight sense of fear among colleagues and subordinates. The rest of this chapter reveals how executives use their advantages to gain power and protect against its loss.

THE POLITICS OF THE BUDGETARY PROCESS

In 1946 the air force and the Atomic Energy Commission (AEC) decided that the United States should build a nuclear-powered airplane, which would be able to stay aloft for a month on a fistful of uranium. Of course there would be technical obstacles—the crew would have to be shielded from the nuclear reactor by six feet of solid concrete or its equivalent, there was the messy problem of nuclear exhaust, and what to do if the plane crashed.

To determine the feasibility of a nuclear plane, the air force and AEC hired an advisory committee, consisting of forty scientists and engineers assembled by the Massachusetts Institute of Technology. The committee said yes, an atomic-propelled plane could be built. The Joint Chiefs of Staff liked the idea. So two military contractors received instructions to produce an acceptable propulsion system powered by an atomic engine.

When the Eisenhower Administration came into office in 1953, it attempted to balance the budget by cutting back on excess defense spending. Eisenhower's defense secretary found the nuclear plane program and dubbed it a shitepoke. "That's a great big bird that flies over marshes, you know, that doesn't have much body or speed to it or anything, but it can fly."[11] All funds for the nuclear plane were sliced out of the 1953 budget.

The secretary of the air force took money out of his contingency funds to keep the nuclear plane alive. Then the navy told its contractors to begin to study the feasibility of building a nuclear seaplane. *Aero Digest*, a trade publication, announced that "America can build an A-plane now. . . . All that is lacking is the approval from Washington."[12] *The American Mercury, the New York Times, Life,* and

Newsweek joined in prodding the government, and an influential senator expressed concern that red tape was holding down the nuclear plane. Meanwhile, the navy launched its first atomic submarine, which encouraged the air force to pump more money into its campaign to put a nuclear airplane into the air.

Despite the optimism of the air force and its allies, the civilian defense chiefs remained skeptical. The chances of flying a nuclear plane in the near future, they said, were "almost nil."[13] Furthermore, the nuclear plane was taking money away from the more important air force missile program. After a meeting with President Eisenhower and his budget analysts in 1956, the defense secretary ordered that the nuclear plane be scrapped.

The following year the Russians launched Sputnik, shocking America's faith in its technical superiority. This was followed by a report in *Aviation Week* that the Russians had test-flown a nuclear plane. The news media called for government action, Congress held hearings, and the air force and AEC continued to spend money on technical studies. As of 1959, they had spent $1 billion. With such a substantial investment, one congressman asked, why couldn't the administration move ahead and complete the project? With the military brass and atomic scientists assuring the lawmakers that the money could be spent, Congress put $150 million into the 1960 appropriation act to finance the nuclear plane.

The following year the military brass asked for another $150 million. President Eisenhower, in his farewell budget message, cut that amount in half. President Kennedy then cut the half in half. After Defense Secretary McNamara announced that the program was not cost effective, Kennedy announced, in his 1961 national security message to Congress, that he was terminating the program. When the aerospace industries complained, the defense secretary responded by labeling any possible future flight of a nuclear plane a stunt and dismantled the bureau that was in charge of the program.

The budgetary skill of the air force executives was truly amazing. For fifteen years, against the solid opposition of their political superiors, they kept alive a program for a plane that never flew. They won outside support, built confidence, marshaled technical arguments, and tapped fresh sources of funds. Their skill at budgetary politics gave them the power to spend, which in the administrative world is the power to act. The go-ahead to act is fundamentally a political decision, a fact that has frustrated most attempts to make budgetary decisions more rational by subjecting them to objective standards. There is very little agreement over what constitutes a fair and objective standard, as any executive whose program has been gored by an objective standard will reveal.

Budgetary skill is the subject of *The Politics of the Budgetary Process* by Aaron Wildavsky, who is the enfant terrible of public administration. From his academic post at Berkeley he blows huge holes into the schemes of naive reformers. His book is the most frequently cited work on public administration written by an administrative scholar.

201

In The Politics of the Budgetary Process, *Aaron Wildavsky reveals the strategies public officials use to get their budgets passed and explains why attempts to reform the budgetary process by making it more rational have always failed. The book is one of the most popular in public administration. Wildavsky is Dean of the Graduate School of Public Policy at the University of California at Berkeley.* COURTESY OF THE UNIVERSITY OF CALIFORNIA AT BERKELEY.

An agency budget, says Wildavsky, "is almost never reviewed as a whole every year in the sense of reconsidering the value of all existing programs as compared to all possible alternatives."[14] The issues involved in budgeting, such as the choice between different programs that promise a cure for cancer, are too complex for that. Instead, budgeting becomes historical, repetitive, and sequential— by which Wildavsky means that budgets from previous years are taken as a base and problems are dealt with one at a time largely in terms of the effect they would have on the base. Problems are often simplified so that decision makers have only to look at the personnel and overhead required to solve the problem rather than examine the technical issues involved. The budget officials often experiment; that is, they "make only the roughest guesses while letting experience accumulate."[15] They are satisfied if things seem to work out without anyone's screaming trouble. Budget officials simplify, experiment, and satisfice. Budget making, Wildavsky concludes, is essentially incremental.

To make the budgetary process work, each group must act as an advocate. Agency officials are expected to advocate increased spending. Budget examiners are expected to defend their executive's chief priorities. Legislative committees are expected to guard the public purse, or promote the congressional interest, or act as a court of last appeal for the aggrieved. Like the advocacy process in a courtroom, the truth is supposed to emerge from the clash of special interests. In the budgetary process, the outcome will likely reflect a collective judgment as to the *fair share* of the expenditure pie to which the administrator seems entitled. Wildavsky prefers the advocacy system. "It is much simpler for each participant to calculate his own preferences than for each to try to calculate the preferences of all. . . . How can anyone know what is being neglected if everyone speaks for someone else and no one for himself?"[16]

To be a good advocate, the executive must be schooled in the budgetary tricks of the trade, which Wildavsky calls strategies. The strategies are designed primarily to push the agency budget past legislative committees, although most of the strategies are also applicable to fiscal survival within the executive branch.

In the beginning, the executive must find and serve an appreciative clientele. Agencies that have the toughest rows at budget time are usually agencies with no clientele—such as prisons, agencies for foreign aid, or the weather bureau. Successful agencies parade their clientele, letters of appreciation, or unfunded applications for aid before the legislative examiners. Advisory committees are especially useful—they always ask for more. Smart bureaucrats divide up their programs so that the glamorous ones can be identified, like cancer research at the National Institutes of Health. If the other programs sound esoteric, like enzyme research, the executive can always claim that they might lead to an early cure for cancer.

In serving the clientele, executives must never admit that they have given in to pressure; they should always avoid the image of having been captured by the client. It is best to have the clientele pressure the legislators for better services, forcing the lawmakers to turn to the bureau. When they do, says Wildavsky, throw the demands for fiscal restraint out the window and make them pay through the nose.

Executives must cultivate confidence in themselves and their agencies. According to Wildavsky,

> bureaucrats are expected to be masters of detail, hard-working, concise, frank, self-effacing fellows who are devoted to their work, tight with the taxpayers money, recognize a political necessity when they see one, and keep the Congressman informed. [17]

It also helps to play it straight. Few things hurt a budget presentation more than the discovery of a buried bone the agency was trying to hide. Many bones of contention can be settled informally between the agency staff and the committee staff. Some can be headed off by friendly visits with individual legislators where the bureaucrat demonstrates his or her friendliness and interest. Other times bureaucratic skill is required in saying no to a suspicious legislative request— our hands are tied, we may be able to do it in the future. Nothing helps as much, Wildavsky concludes, as the opinion of others "that the agency official is a man of high integrity who can be trusted."[18]

Effective budget presentation takes practice. Many executives hold mock hearings at which the executive rehearses his or her presentation and subordinates play the role of legislators who ask embarrassing questions. The object of the rehearsal is to guard against surprises and allow the executive to appear spontaneous and unprepared while saying all the right things. The following exchange demonstrates how much it hurts when the executive really is unprepared.

> Representative Rooney: I find a gentleman here, an FSO-6. He got an A in Chinese and you assigned him to London.

Mr. X: Yes, sir. That officer will have opportunities in London—not as many as he would have in Hong Kong, for example—

Representative Rooney: What will he do? Spend his time in Chinatown?

Mr. X: No, sir. There will be opportunities in dealing with officers in the British Foreign Office who are concerned with Far Eastern affairs.

Representative Rooney: So instead of speaking English to one another, they will sit in the London office and talk Chinese?

Mr. X: Yes, sir.

Representative Rooney: Is that not fantastic?

Mr. X: No, sir. They are anxious to keep up their practice.

Representative Rooney: They go out to Chinese restaurants and have chop suey together?

Mr. X: Yes, sir.

Representative Rooney: And that is all at the expense of the American taxpayer?[19]

At the hearings, executives are expected to play by the rules of the game. The basic rule is to avoid being surprised. That is why executives will dispatch their aides for a friendly chat with the staff on the congressional committee. That is why questions get planted at committee hearings. That is why executives, just for insurance, arrive at the hearings backed by an army of subordinates. Executives are expected to know their budget backwards.

One of the most difficult situations for an executive is having to defend a budget proposal that was forced upon him (or her). He wants to tell the legislators that he wants more, but the rules of the game require him to defend the budget. The lawmakers ask the executive to reveal his original requests. Citing administrative loyalty, he refuses. They press. He hesitates. They insist. He spills everything. It is all a game.

The executive must show some results. "Outside of overwhelming public support, there is nothing that demonstrates results better than tangible accomplishments."[20] J. Edgar Hoover would appear on Capitol Hill each year with statistics showing that the Federal Bureau of Investigation had recovered stolen cars and cash worth more than the bureau's annual budget. Space officials shuttled congressmen and executives to Cape Kennedy to watch launches. See it, they would say, it works!

What about programs whose benefits are intangible? Officials claim that their program is priceless—who can put a dollar value on human lives (medical research) or on preserving freedom (the U.S. Information Agency)? A result may be just around the corner. Some agency officials, faced with no results whatsoever, may at least claim that they are doing it efficiently, free of corruption, with hardly any personnel turnover whatsoever.

Since all budget calculations begin from the base—last year's appropriation—the executive must have the ability to protect the base from a budgetary trimming. When city councils start looking for fat in the education budget, the school superintendent announces that the first program to go will be high school football. When the navy was told to list the shipyards they would shut down first if forced to, they put the politically sensitive yards on the top of the priority lists. Other agencies pass the buck (and the blame) by telling the examiners to choose—but only submit the best programs for review. The air force resists budget cuts by telling the examiners: so much money has been invested in this program that it would be a shame to stop spending now that the results are coming out. If the program is a failure, the air force presents figures demonstrating that it would cost more to close down the program than to see it through and accept the product that does not work. As a last resort, the agency can alter the form of the budget, burying questionable expenditures such as travel and public relations in a program budget and insisting that any cut in the program would ruin productivity.

The executive must also have the ability to justify new increases in the base each year. This is the cardinal rule of incrementalism. If you do not ask for more, you will get cut. Legislators and budget examiners expect the executive to ask for more money; if he stands pat, they feel he is not doing his job. There is the camel's nose—a small, temporary expenditure. Like the sultan who allows his camel to poke its nose under the tent to avoid the cold, the legislator who admits such an expenditure will soon find himself sleeping aside the entire beast. One can spend money to save money: build it now, because it will cost more later. Or: this program saves the public more money than it costs the government. Salesmanship helps—a fancy program name like Polaris accompanied by favorable media coverage. But nothing helps as much as a crisis—a gas shortage to push energy programs, inflation to push economic controls, crime in the streets to push law enforcement programs. If no crisis exists, then the new program can be tied to the continuing crisis of national defense. (One of the key arguments in favor of the interstate highway system, for example, was the assertion that it could carry heavy military hardware in case of an invasion.)

What about the poor executives who cannot present a new program? All is not lost. They can "round up" budget requests so that $1.86 billion becomes $1.9 billion. Or they can adopt the navy tactic of putting new wine into old bottles. The navy likes to retain the names of ships, even if an old vessel has been mothballed and replaced by one that costs twice as much. The admirals like to disguise this as a repair-and-maintenance program.

A ROLE FOR ANALYSIS

Does the fact that the budgetary process is so political rule out the use of policy analysis? Or is there some way to balance the need for power with the need for rationality in administration?

The debate over this issue has been played out around the status of that economic strategy which was supposed to reform the budget-

205

ary process and "identify our national goals with precision": PPB.[21] To review, PPB was brought to the federal government by Defense Secretary McNamara and extended to the entire government by President Johnson. It required bureau chiefs to clarify their mission, identify their key programs, define objective measures of performance, compare the costs of alternative systems, and project those costs five years into the future.

Aaron Wildavsky and his friends predicted that PPB would fail, primarily for two reasons. First, PPB was politically unacceptable. Legislators and bureaucrats opposed PPB because it threatened to untie the wisdom accumulated through a half century of central budgeting. Legislators feared that a budget organized around programs would upset the tight lines of specialization that separated the work of legislative committees. Bureaucrats feared that any restructuring of the budgetary process would deprive them of the fair share of the budgetary pie—fair share being defined in terms of what they got last year. Neither had much faith in the promise that PPB could reform budgeting by improving the choice of objectives. In fact, the incremental system that governs the budgetary process deliberately avoids the calculation of objectives in preference to the process of negotiated bargains. Budget makers were more comfortable with negotiated bargains produced through the advocacy system than with the rational pursuit of optimal output. They thought that advocacy produced wiser public policies. One noted analyst concluded, "the concepts which took root in economics and planning will have to undergo considerable mutation before they can be successfully transplanted in political soil."[22]

Second, the political resistance to PPB was aggravated by the disagreement over technique. "No one," said Aaron Wildavsky, "knows how to do program budgeting."[23] Bureaucrats would fight over the definition of programs, which often resulted in compromises like "Expanding Dimensions for Living." That was vague enough to satisfy everyone. There were battles over how to measure benefits. How did one measure the value of a human life saved, for example? The technicians suggested net lifetime earnings. The bureaucrats said this was appalling—trying to reduce human beings down to their purchasing power. Some of these controversies were politically motivated—officials bent the statistics to protect a point. But a large part of the problem arose because there were too few technicians skilled at program budgeting. A lot of the program development activity was thus left up to old-line managers who did not believe in it, who did not want to understand it, and whose bosses did not support it either. Wildavsky surveyed the literature on PPB. All of the writers talked about how it was misused in one agency or failed to win support in another. "I have not," he wrote, "been able to find a single example of successful implementation of PPB."[24]

The critics point to the memorandum of 1971 issued by the Office of Management and Budget countermanding President Johnson's 1965 executive order setting up PPB as proof that the system was "dead."[25] The policy analysts point to the creation of the Congressional Budget Office, the revival of zero-base budgeting, and the fact that many departments, such as defense, continue to use PPB (even if they do not submit it to the White House) as evidence that analysis is very much alive.

As is generally true, the truth is contained in a contradiction. Analysis penetrated the arena of political bargaining. Charles Schultze, who helped write the executive order setting up PPB, thinks he knows why this happened. Schultze explains that the analytic approach embodied in PPB is attractive to executives engaged in budgetary bargaining. In this explanation, he denies neither the ideals of the analysis nor the objections of its critics.

First he defends the need for analysis. "The most frustrating aspect of public life," he says, "is the endless hours spent on policy discussions in which the irrelevant issues have not been separated from the relevant, in which ascertainable facts and relationships have not been investigated but are the subject of heated debate, in which consideration of alternatives is impossible because only one proposal has been developed, and, above all, discussions in which nobility of aim is presumed to determine effectiveness of program."[26] Schultze cries for a little help. Give executives a little help in identifying agency goals, in measuring program costs and projecting them beyond a single year. Give executives help in putting goals into action and analyzing whether the agency is reaching its goals.

Schultze agrees that the advocacy process is essential in insuring that all interests are represented in budgetary decisions. He thinks that incrementalism is necessary to achieve mutual agreement on a single budget that embraces widely differing values. So where does analysis enter the picture? Analysis, including program budgeting, introduces a new group of advocates into the bargaining process. Schultze calls them *partisan efficiency advocates*. "At each level of the decision process these participants become particular champions of efficiency and effectiveness as criteria in decision-making."[27] They help to raise the level of the debate. In the maelstrom of politics, the analysts help to create a center of rationality.

Who needs the analysts? The executive at the top of the organization, says Schultze. It may be true that analysis works better at the bottom of the organization, where the criteria of efficiency begins to replace the complexity surrounding policy decisions, but the *need* for analysis is greatest in the office of the executive. The specialists have their expertise; the executive has little. He needs analysis as a type of shorthand—a method of calculation that will let the executive in on the business of the experts.

Analysis "improves the capability of the agency head to shape the program of his agency and increases his power relative to his operating subordinates."[28] Analysis reduces the executive's feeling of impotence when confronted with the tyranny of detail. It gives executives the strength to resist the demands of their experts. It gives them a reason to enlarge their staff. It expands their power.

207

Analysis has succeeded in penetrating the political process because it has been used by executives who know how to make it enhance their power. Moreover, they know how to use analysis to analyze complex problems at a high level of abstraction and make trade-offs between competing objectives without becoming entangled in technique. The people around Robert McNamara, by contrast, were mainly preoccupied with technique. McNamara himself was a technician who had risen to power through the Ford Motor Company because he was very good at doing one thing: cost-effectiveness analysis. It is no wonder that his management techniques, and the decisions associated with them, became the focus of the daily resistance to analysis in general.

Even Aaron Wildavsky agrees that analysis brings power to executives. But he would add a caveat. The federal budget, says Wildavsky, smothers analysis. Budgeting is a political, incremental, short-range process. Analysis requires inquiry, initiative, and imagination. So he would separate analysis from the budget process. Of course, the analysts object to Wildavsky's qualification. No system of analysis, they say, will work unless it is integrated into the budgetary process where all the important commitments are made.

The controversy over PPB points up how important it is for executives to be able to distinguish between analysis that is relevant to their needs and analysis made superficial or incomplete by an overdependence upon technique. It also points up how important it is for the advisers to be able to relate their advice to the political needs of their superiors. Fortunately, there is a theory of advice that helps clarify such things.

KNOWLEDGE AND POWER

Executives need advice. They need information on the impact of their decisions and the actions of forces around them. On paper, the solution seems simple enough. Set up a special intelligence-gathering unit, staff it with bright young analysts, establish a team of top executives to review the intelligence estimates, and wait for the facts to start rolling in.

Unfortunately, there are too many examples of this type of system's breaking down: Pearl Harbor, the Bay of Pigs, and the Russian wheat deal, to mention a few. Either the correct message never gets through in undistorted form, or the executive team members refuse to believe the message because it does not fit their preconceived notions. Effective advice getting involves more than standard operating procedure; it requires astute executive skill at avoiding the causes of intelligence breakdowns.

Remember Pearl Harbor? Every top civilian and military official in Washington during the autumn of 1941 knew that war was imminent. The possibility of a Japanese attack on the American base at Pearl Harbor was discussed and dismissed. The executives felt that the Japanese would never open a second front by attacking an American

The attack on Pearl Harbor was a total surprise to American public executives, despite the fact that their intelligence agencies had received numerous advance warnings about the Japanese plans. An advocacy system for collecting information is the best safeguard against such intelligence breakdowns.
COURTESY OF THE U.S. ARMY.

territory after they had already begun to move against the Dutch and British in the Far East. It was strategically inconceivable.

That autumn, intelligence officers deep in the organizational system broke the Japanese code. Far Eastern code analysts intercepted dispatches which, properly interpreted, revealed the Japanese plans. The analysts passed on this information to their superiors, who ignored it; they even tried to contact the top military brass, which dismissed the analysts as long-haired intellectuals. The message never got through.

Ten days before the attack, after Japanese-American peace negotiations collapsed, military chiefs in Washington warned field commanders in Hawaii that war with Japan could begin at any time. Nevertheless, when field intelligence units managed to lose track of the Japanese fleet, the commander did not call for new reconnaissance to find it. It did not occur to him that the Japanese might be steaming toward Pearl Harbor.

On December 7, at 3:00 A.M. Hawaiian time, the Japanese ambassadors in Washington asked for an appointment with the secretary of state—a certain sign that war was about to begin. A copy of the request was placed on the desks of the army and navy chiefs of staff. The army chief of staff was out horseback riding. The navy chief took no action.

At 4:00 A.M. the American destroyer U.S.S. Ward sighted a Japanese submarine off the island of Oahu. At 6:30 A.M. the submarine opened fire on the Ward. The military commanders at Pearl Harbor did nothing.

At 7:00 A.M. the army shut down its five mobile radar units, as it did every morning at that time. When an army private turned on one radar set for practice, he saw a huge flight of planes. He telephoned his lieutenant, who told him to forget it. The Japanese "surprise" attack began at 7:55.

Two lessons emerge from the information failure at Pearl Harbor. One is the danger of allowing preconceptions to displace analysis. The other is the likelihood that bureaucratic structure will distort and block out information that might help restore an image of reality. In two separate books on the subject, Irving Janis and Harold Wilensky analyze these failures and suggest strategies to combat them.

The intelligence breakdown at Pearl Harbor began with a preconceived notion: the illusion of invulnerability. Top executives deliberately discounted warnings that challenged that notion; in a number of cases, the persons who offered the warnings were informed that such dissent was not proper behavior for loyal members of the establishment. Janis calls this "groupthink": the conformity to group norms that makes bunglers out of a team of otherwise shrewd, calculating executives. This is usually accomplished through a false illusion of unanimity on the executive team, self-censorship, the emergence of self-appointed mindguards, a stereotyped view of the enemy as excessively stupid or evil, and the group's unswerving faith in its own morality no matter what it decides. Preconceived notions not challenged eventually become slogans: Air Power Will Win the War in Vietnam, Credible Nuclear Deterrent, Sino-Soviet Bloc, Poverty Is a State of Powerlessness.

The distortions created by the drive toward group conformity frequently are exacerbated by organizational structure. Specialization was a distorting factor at Pearl Harbor. Hierarchy and centralization cause similar problems.

Specialization tends to result in the blocking of important information. Says Wilensky: "signals of the pending attack on Pearl Harbor lay scattered in a number of rival agencies; communication lines linked them but essential messages never flowed across the lines, let alone to the top."[29] The reason, he says, was the excessive organizational rivalry that generally accompanies specialization. Even if one group of specialists discovers the truth, the clash of special interests may bury it. If the executive forces rival factions to resolve their differences, he may get nothing, especially if dissent was reconciled by mutual exhaustion rather than a commitment to find the truth.

Hierarchy also distorts the upward flow of information. It tends to encourage the concealment of information, especially news that might not fit the preconceived notions of the top executives. Subordinates in the hierarchy sense that the information they pass on will be used to evaluate their performance and will affect their status in the ranks. The normal reaction is to play it safe, to transmit only happy news that will be well received at the top. The Greeks elevated this to an art in their slaying of military couriers who brought word of defeat.

To combat the evils of hierarchy and specialization, top executives often centralize the intelligence-gathering function, and thereby generate a third source of distortion. The primary cost of centralization, says Wilensky, is the production of inaccurate or misleading information. It happens this way. To improve their power, the centralized intelligence staff exploits the executive's wariness of information gathered through specialization and hierarchy by developing its own sources of information, independent of officials in the body of the organization. Clandestine sources are favored, since this gives the information an aura of mystery and inside scoop. The intelligence the staff gathers may be quite different from the information possessed by line officers. To the extent that the executive insists upon consensus in intelligence estimates, the staff will conceal or discourage disagreement arising from within the organization. This can help to perpetuate the most incredible fantasies at the highest level. Anyone who does not believe that this happens is urged to study the doctoring of intelligence estimates that led White House officials to believe, shortly before the Tet offensive, that they were winning the war in Vietnam.

None of these organizational deficiencies can be wholly resolved by structural reform. To get good intelligence, Wilensky says, executives must beat the system. It does not matter what kind of a system—good intelligence invariably depends upon extraformal sources that cut against whatever formal system the executive has got.

> Some gains in the quality of intelligence are possible from a reorganization of the intelligence function; but much of an organization's defense against information pathologies lies in the top executive's attitude toward knowledge—a product of his own education and orientation, his exposure to independent sources, and his capacity to break through the wall of conventional wisdom.[30]

Both Wilensky and Janis favor an advocacy system for intelligence gathering. The executive is best served when the organization sets up several independent groups composed of people who are pulled away from their organizational homes. The executive should encourage competition between the groups, receive their recommendations firsthand, and guard against directives that would have the groups resolve their differences before presenting their advice. To encourage advocacy within each group, the executive can invite experts in to challenge its assumptions, rotate in field officers and specialists to participate in its work, and shuttle members through different subgroups while giving them special tasks. To guard against groupthink, the executive should never state his or her preferences in the beginning and should continue to solicit outside advice from both amateurs and experts. As a final safeguard, the executive can call the group back to reconsider their recommendations. The first-century Germans, Janis reports, were so serious about reconsiderations that they made each major decision twice: once while everyone was sober, again when the group was drunk.

What about the advice givers? How can they be assured of getting

211

their advice through to the executive? In an advocacy system, the advisers cannot dump the facts onto the executive's desk and say that their work is done. In a study of the politics of advice based on a history of the U.S. Council of Economic Advisers, Edward Flash outlines the conditions underlying successful advice giving from the point of view of the adviser seeking an audience.

The expert must first understand that all advice is competitive. The most successful chairman of the Council of Economic Advisers, Walter Heller, told President Kennedy in 1961 that a tax cut would be the best way to fulfill the president's campaign pledge to "get the country moving again." It was sound economic advice. Unfortunately for Heller, Soviet Premier Khruschev had just blasted the president over the status of Berlin. Military chiefs told Kennedy that a mobilization of force, perhaps backed by a tax increase, would display America's resolve to defend West Berlin. It was sound military advice.

In short, good advice is not measured by inherent standards of truth that all persons of good will immediately recognize. Different agencies produce different advice, and any advice that is not controversial is probably not worth giving.

Good advice is advice that can be acted upon. This means that the advisers have to anticipate the effect of their advice in light of political issues and opportunities. Successful economic advisers such as Heller understand the role of their advice in the political system. They understand the stakes involved in political issues, are able to readjust their advice and functions to fit the situation, and are able to fight for their recommendations. They are pragmatic and flexible.

In his own book, Heller relates the success of the economic advisers to their ability to educate the president. Kennedy brought his father's economic views to the presidency; he was determined, for example, to maintain a balanced budget. Heller slowly converted Kennedy to the "new" economics, making him the first president to embrace Keynesian economics publicly. It worked because Heller understood Kennedy's political needs and Kennedy understood Heller's economic lessons.

Such a symbiosis of knowledge and power is a rare and beautiful event in public administration. As Flash reports it, it is essentially a political relationship, not an intellectual one. The advisers possess certain resources, which the executive can turn into political advantages. The advisers possess knowledge that the executive lacks, the mystique of their techniques and the prestige of their profession. Whether or not the executive accepts these things depends largely upon the ability of the advisers to shape the tone of the discourse and to define the issues the executive must face. The initiative is largely theirs. When advisers lose, it is due not so much to poor intellect as to the fact that the executive has a different set of values or priorities and decides not to make use of the advisers' resources at that time. Heller, incidently, lost his initial bid for a tax cut. But the military did not get a tax increase, and the following year Congress, at Kennedy's initiative, approved a tax reduction bill.

It is very hard to institutionalize these relationships—either the politics of advice or strategies for avoiding intelligence failures. The joining of knowledge and power almost always depends upon extraformal arrangements. So do many other special problems of administration. The next section reviews strategies that executives have used to create an extraformal system to supplement the formal bureaucracy.

BEATING THE SYSTEM

Few executives are as clever at beating the system as Franklin D. Roosevelt was. His style of bureaucratic confusion is a model in public administration.

To begin with, Roosevelt accepted the formal bureaucracy. As assistant secretary of the navy and governor of New York he knew that it was essential, he had learned its strength, and as president he established the famous Brownlow Committee to bring administrative science to the federal government.

Franklin Roosevelt was a master at creating the sort of bureaucratic confusion which insured that his subordinates would bring all of their problems back to him. He often placed two or more administrators in charge of the same program, a bit of manipulation known as the strategy of calculated competition. Here Roosevelt confers with one of his closest assistants, Harry Hopkins. COURTESY OF THE FRANKLIN D. ROOSEVELT LIBRARY.

213

At the same time, Roosevelt knew that he had to beat the bureaucracy in order to maximize his influence. When it came to his own power, FDR distrusted administrative formulas. Here is what he did.

As part of his work-relief program, Roosevelt put Harry Hopkins in charge of starting up a multibillion-dollar federal job program that could hire four million unemployed within sixty days. Hopkins complied. At the same time Roosevelt recruited Harold Ickes to establish a similar program in the Interior Department. Since Ickes was the more cautious spender, Roosevelt told his Treasury secretary to watch over Hopkins's spending habits and gave him such powers of interference that Hopkins nearly resigned. When Republicans began to complain about "leaf raking" federal jobs, Roosevelt told his postmaster general to watch over the whole bunch to make sure that they did not stir up too much political trouble.

Roosevelt was afraid that he would lose control of basic decisions if he appointed a single administrator to run his favorite programs. One of his pet projects was the Tennessee Valley Authority. Roosevelt stacked it with a three-headed executive and put the trio in Knoxville, away from the distractions of Washington. Two of the commissioners ganged up on the third, who left the commission spitting out charges of corruption and mismanagement at his colleagues. Roosevelt apparently liked the arrangement so well that he appointed two men to head the office in charge of economic mobilization for the war. One man rode herd on industrial production, the other one drummed up labor support. Production lagged, but Roosevelt kept the system. It was as good, he said, as a law firm headed by two partners.

Roosevelt showed a preference for running the departments through his undersecretaries. Roosevelt ran the State Department through Undersecretary Sumner Welles, but kept Cordell Hull on as secretary—even though Hull was often excluded from major foreign policy decisions—because the venerable gentleman had enormous prestige on Capitol Hill. Roosevelt ran the Justice Department through J. Edgar Hoover, director of the FBI, and would telephone Hoover when he wanted hasty action on some matter. When the attorney general, Francis Biddle, complained about being undercut, Roosevelt apologized, complimented Biddle on his fine work, then called Hoover again after a decent interval.

Executives employ strategies such as these for many purposes. Roosevelt's primary intention in violating administrative orthodoxy was to make certain that the important problems got through to him and were not stopped up in channels by some nervous bureaucrat. Unorthodox strategies will also shake up a department that is going underground in order to hide some activity from a disapproving executive. They work well in interorganizational battles, when an executive is fighting another executive who heads another bureau. They work to get a program authorized, funded, and running while avoiding both the bureaucratic inertia and the political bombardment that can ruin it. Sometimes the strategies are used simply for administrative self-protection. Here are some strategies made popular by successful executives:

Strategy of Calculated Competition "There is something to be said," Roosevelt observed, "for having a little conflict between agencies. A little rivalry is stimulating, you know. It keeps everybody going to prove that he is a better fellow than the next man. It keeps them honest too."[31]

Roosevelt generated conflict by appointing ambitious persons to public office, giving them general assignments, keeping their grant of authority incomplete and their jurisdiction uncertain. He would then appoint another person to a similar office and tell the person to do the same job. The system was designed to insure that one of the parties would feel injured and run to Roosevelt with his or her problem. Roosevelt thrived on these complaints, on bits of administrative gossip or macabre stories about his subordinates' escapades. It made him feel he was on top of things. All this violated the canons of orthodox administration and wore down Roosevelt's executives too, a few of whom resigned. But it kept FDR in the driver's seat. It is the only system of delegated authority that pushes everything to the top.

The Bureaucratic Dip Reformers in public administration often want to consolidate departments into superbureaus and surround the executive with a staff that can perform his or her work. Such reforms rely upon the dictum that a good executive should supervise no more than a dozen persons, all of whom report directly to him or her. Unfortunately, this often cuts the executive off from the bureaucrats on the firing line whose actions determine the success or failure of the executive program.

Roosevelt accepted the staff, but never let that prevent him from dipping into the bureaucracy when he wanted something done. He would locate the bureaucrat who was actually running the program, contact him directly, tell him what he wanted done, and follow up. It inflated the bureaucrat's ego and made a friend for the chief executive. Strategic use of the telephone can expand the chief executive's span of control enormously.

"Should I Appoint Strangers?" According to the orthodoxy of merit, the executive is supposed to recruit subordinates on the basis of their professional qualifications. This often means that the executive has to appoint subordinates whom the executive has never met before or with whom he or she has little personal rapport. Sometimes it helps to break the rule and select a friend, as Mayor Richard Daley of Chicago did by appointing the son of the majority leader of the city council to the city's Board of Zoning Appeals. When an alderman, who was also a political science professor, criticized the appointment, Daley exploded.

> I made this appointment because I've known Tommy since he was a baby. I know his mother, a fine American woman. . . . Should I appoint strangers?[32]

215

The Task Force When President Kennedy risked a nuclear confrontation over the Cuban Missile Crisis, he appointed a special task force to advise him and coordinate operations. He appointed friends he could trust—including his brother, his speech writer, his appointments secretary, a campaign adviser, and a member of his Harvard brain trust—and he appointed experts to represent the top military and diplomatic points of view. The task force allows the executive to hear diverse points of view and, because the members are removed from the bureaucratic setting, may become the source of new ideas. The president's brother reports: "We all spoke as equals. There was no rank and, in fact, we did not even have a chairman. The conversations were completely uninhibited and unrestricted."[33] The president sat in as factions in the task force argued the relative merits of a Cuban invasion or a naval blockade. Kennedy chose the diplomatic route, backed by a blockade; the Russians withdrew the missiles. All agreed it was Kennedy's finest hour.

The Power Broker Robert Moses was "only" a public administrator, serving at the pleasure of six governors and five mayors who for forty-eight years kept appointing him to the most important New York State building commissions and authorities. At one time he controlled seven commissions and authorities simultaneously. It would not be an exaggeration to say that Moses built New York City. He controlled the construction of its highways, parkways, bridges, playgrounds, beaches, and public-housing projects; planned the suburbanization of Long Island; and even built the United Nations. He used the positions to which he was appointed to become a broker—a middleman—who made the deals with the bankers, politicians, and labor unions, trading what he had for their support. His resources were money—projects worth billions of dollars in bond sales, honest graft, and payrolls—and his talent for Getting Things Done, a precious resource in the eyes of the mayors and governors who had to show off their accomplishments at the next election. To get things done, Moses followed a few simple rules. He drew up his own plans and he never compromised them. He either drafted the law under which he worked or he defied it. He made sure he had popular support on his side. By any means possible, even threats or misleading information, he would get a project started. "Once you sink that first stake," he said, "they'll never make you pull it up."[34]

Do It! Suppose that an executive is going to shake up the bureaucracy with a major change in policy. Does the executive call in the bureaucrats with their mania for meetings and delay? Here is Henry Kissinger's advice:

> Because management of the bureaucracy takes so much energy and precisely because changing course is so difficult, many of the most important decisions are taken by extra-bureaucratic means. Some of the key decisions are kept to a very small circle while the bureaucracy continues working away in ignorance of the fact that a decision is being made in a particular area. One reason for keeping the decisions to small groups is

216

that when bureaucracies are so unwieldy and when their internal morale becomes a serious problem, an unpopular decision may be fought by brutal means, such as leaks to the press or congressional committees. Thus the only way secrecy can be kept is to exclude from the making of the decision all those who are theoretically charged with carrying it out.[35]

The Art of the Memorandum If the policy needs clearance from higher-ups, write a memorandum. "The primary rule of the memorandum is to expect no action from its recipient."[36] Chances are that superiors will be too cognizant of the risks of approval or too busy writing their own memoranda.

Skill in writing memoranda depends upon the writer's ability to translate inertia into approval. The author drafts a memorandum informing the superior of plans to take a certain action on a certain date *unless otherwise directed*. Silence constitutes one's authority to act. To assure silence, announce that the proposal does not change anything, that it is just a variation on present policy, or type the order out on computer paper (anything that comes off the computer will automatically be accepted as standard operating procedure). To insure that the superior reads the memorandum, type the covering letter on chartreuse paper, send it as a telegram, or mark it Top Secret.

The Participation Game It is said that Lyndon Johnson, the legislative wizard, once passed a bill through the U.S. Senate even though no one save himself had seen a printed copy of the complete act. There is little question about Johnson's genius at the participation game. In developing policy, Johnson would show his colleagues only those pieces in which they had a special interest. If they were sore at what they saw, he would offer a compromise and was quick to point out the features that helped them. He rarely revealed the master plan. Why let them criticize the entire proposal when they got upset just thinking about the part that affected them?

Worst Foot Forward Busy executives rarely want to be troubled by a new issue. One way to soften the impact of a new proposal is to convince an ally of the merit of putting out a worse plan first. Executives and legislators invariably hate the first plan they see. A worse plan allows their anger to escape, shocks them into thinking that something may have to be done, and makes the proposal that follows look like a moderate solution to their problems.

Indecent Exposure Some proposals stink. The best way to kill a bad proposal is to expose it prematurely, before its supporters have had a chance to smooth out all of their differences. Outsiders will take sides on the differences, pressure different members of the group, and split up the supporters.

The Isolated Executive When Richard Nixon became president, he tried to copy Franklin Roosevelt's administrative strategies. He appointed unfraternal twins to every important White House post, never really defined their duties, and promised to cut back on the total White House staff. He was preoccupied with details, and used his advantages to promote bureaucratic loyalty.

Nixon's desire to succeed, however, fell prey to his personal preference for solitude and his tendency toward self-pity. The twins departed, and so did dissent. A tight hierarchy emerged with H. R. Haldeman at the top. The White House came down with a case of constipated feedback, a managerial malady in which the wishes of the chief executive are enlarged as they move down through the hierarchy, while information that might contest the wisdom of those wishes backs up. The decisions to burglarize the Watergate and then to cover up the burglary were two perfectly natural consequences of the managerial methods of the Nixon administration. They demonstrate how hard executives have to fight—even with their own personalities—to beat the bureaucratic system in order to keep themselves informed about the outcome of their policies.

Are these strategies contradictory? Of course they are. Politics is a contradiction. A distrust of uniformity in administration underlies all successful strategies for creating executive power. Harvey Sherman summed it up in the title to his book on public administration: *It All Depends*. Successful administration is the ability to avoid administrative formulas, and successful executives are those flexible enough to fashion their strategies to fit each situation as it occurs.

BUREAUCRATIC RISK TAKING

Anytime executives try to beat the system, they take a risk. Who are the risk takers, and what is the secret of their success (or failure)?

- William Henry Seward, secretary of state in the Lincoln Administration, purchased the state of Alaska from the Russian government for $7 million. He was ridiculed and the newspapers called the purchase Seward's folly. Seward seized an opportunity that had the potential for high payoffs but gave the appearance of being so risky that no one would take the responsibility. This kind of risk taking is known as the Bold Stroke.

- In the last days of the war, Hitler appointed a new general to command the Paris garrison. The general had qualified for the post by initiating the scorched-earth policy against Russia. Hitler instructed him to reduce Paris to a field of ruins if the Allies moved on it. German troops began placing explosives on bridges, factories, and monuments, and the German high commander made plans to bomb Paris and asked for permission to send in Panzer divisions to crush the French resistance. The general, Dietrich von Choltitz, delayed the bombing and the Panzers and he dispatched a Swedish diplomat to cross the German lines and ask the Allies to attack Paris so that he could give it up unscarred. Legend says that Hitler called von

Choltitz to ask, "Is Paris burning?" After the surrender of Paris, the German commander in chief urged Hitler to prosecute von Choltitz as a war criminal. The general's friends in Germany delayed the trial and protected members of his family, who could have been punished in his place under the *Sippenhaft* law.

Von Choltitz's actions are known as Breaking the Chain, a frequently practiced form of bureaucratic risk taking in which an executive breaks the chain of command by deliberately refusing to execute an order that is patently illegal, immoral, impossible, or absurd. These cases are rarely publicized, because the organizational titans who gave the command are *(a)* reluctant to acknowledge that they ordered such a thing, *(b)* reluctant to acknowledge their inability to prevent insubordination, or *(c)* both.

■ New York City's police force has been called the best that money can buy. In the 1960s police recruits were pressured by veteran officers to accept payoffs from bookies and numbers runners. Frank Serpico refused. He tried to get higher-ups in the police department to clamp down on the payoffs, but they turned the other way. Serpico and another policeman went to Mayor Lindsay's office, but he wouldn't touch the issue. Finally they went to the police internal investigation unit, which caught a few small fish. The payoffs continued, so Serpico and David Durk, after five years of trying to work within the system, took the story to the *New York Times*. The *Times* put it on

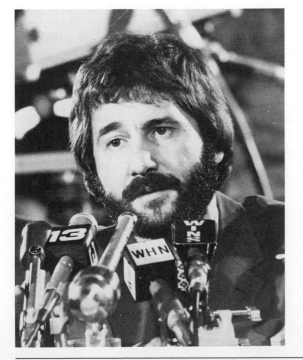

There are three kinds of bureaucratic risk taking: whistle blowing, breaking the chain, and the bold stroke. Here patrolman Frank Serpico blows the whistle before the Knapp Commission appointed to investigate police corruption in New York City. For five years Serpico worked to put an end to payoffs to city police officers. UPI PHOTOGRAPH.

page one. As a result of the story, Mayor Lindsay appointed the Knapp Commission, which held hearings that led to the resignation of the top police executives and created an atmosphere in which businessmen stopped making payoffs and honest cops felt they had someplace to go. This is known as blowing the whistle, and it occurs whenever anyone publicly reveals some corrupt, deceitful, or illegal practice within an organization. Blowing the whistle is like calling a foul in a basketball game—it stops the play (at least temporarily) and calls attention to the evil deed. Most people fear that the players will then expel the referee. After his revelations, Serpico went back to the front lines, where he was shot in the head by a dope peddler. His fellow police officers donated fifty pints of blood and the money to pay the informant to put the finger on the trigger man. The movie *Serpico* gave the impression that he was set up, but in fact you do not have to risk your life or give up your career to blow the whistle. Lots of risk takers come out ahead of the game because they know how to play their advantages.

In all three cases, the risk takers were successful. Despite the fact that they were confronted with institutional resistance, public discontent, and fellow officials who disagreed strongly with their actions, these risk takers won. The first step in risk taking is to learn how to win. Here are a number of strategies employed by successful risk takers.

The most dramatic strategy is *The Divorce,* a controversial, well-publicized break with organizational policy that has all the drama of an estranged couple battering each other in court. The press loves it. Like a messy divorce, there is little hope of reconciliation. Thus, the risk takers must accomplish their objective in one stroke as they divorce themselves from the organization. When Attorney General Elliot Richardson resigned in protest over the order to fire Watergate Special Prosecutor Archibald Cox, another bureaucrat stepped in to execute the order. Richardson failed to break the chain of command, although he certainly did raise the political costs to President Nixon. It is hard to imagine what more Richardson could have done to call attention to his cause, given his determination to resign.

Because the divorce offers a limited opportunity for success, veteran risk takers often prefer to stay within the organization as long as they can and use a strategy called *Raising the Costs.* This strategy is based on the assumption that political support behind questionable policies is paper thin and that the top dogs issued the order in the hope that someone else lower down in the organization would silently execute it. There are several ways to raise the costs to the person who gave the order. Threatening to resign is one way. Another is simply to raise the monetary costs, insisting that the questionable order cannot be executed without tooling up, adding personnel, or practicing. Sometimes it is enough to climb the chain of

220

command, asking "Are you sure?" while pointing out all of the possible consequences. In special cases the costs may be raised after the order is executed. After Nixon sacked Archibald Cox, Justice Department executives hired a Texas hanging judge who was twice as tough.

A similar tactic is simply to *Drag Your Heels*. Everyone loves to quote Harry Truman's vision of the presidency under Dwight Eisenhower:

> "He'll sit here," Truman would remark (tapping his desk for emphasis), "and he'll say, 'Do this! Do that!' *And nothing will happen.* Poor Ike—it won't be a bit like the Army. He'll find it very frustrating."[37]

The first time public executives are told to "do this," they can forget the order and say that they never got around to it with all of their other pressing duties. The second time they are ordered they can send the order back for further clarification and instructions and say that their hands are tied because of regulations. Only after their superiors press an order upon them a third time can they be reasonably convinced that the higher-ups really want it done. Then they can give the job to Charlie, who has never finished a job since he joined the agency twelve years ago.

If all of these tactics fail, executives can open a war of protest. One of the best protest tactics is the *End Run*, an appeal to an outsider who can put enough political pressure on the superior to modify or change the objectionable policy. For the bureaucrat, the outsider might be a congressman, a governor, a lobbyist, a lawyer, even the superior's preacher or spouse: anyone who might have some influence. The contact with the outsider is handled discreetly, and often goes like this: "Our mutual friend (the superior) is pursuing a policy which could really damage him (or her) in the long run, and I think he should be told, but I'm not in a position to do so. Can you help?"

On the surface these seem to be blocking strategies, since they serve to reinforce the bureaucrat's position as a negator. A negator's first reaction to any new idea is to tell everyone why it cannot be done. Legal myths are very important to the why-you-can't bureaucrat, who is clearly not a risk taker but a cautious team player against whom these strategies can be used.

Because of the lock that negators have on any organization, many risk takers feel the need to go outside the usual channels. Such tactics may begin with *Calculated Leaks* and eventually lead to *Public Appearances*. The calculated leak is a familiar tactic. Someone allows potentially sensitive information to leak out of an organization which is trying to conceal it. This is usually done secretly. Alternatively, the risk taker may put in a public appearance, testifying before Congress or on television. One assumption underlies both tactics: that the practice being exposed by leak or appearance is so obnoxious that mere publicity will snuff it out.

Ernest Fitzgerald, an air force cost analyst, exposed military cost overruns in a public appearance before a Senate committee.

Fitzgerald revealed that for over two years his superiors had been concealing cost overruns of $2 billion from the Congress, the president, and the secretary of defense. The generals removed Fitzgerald from the C-5A program and told him to study bowling alleys in Thailand, where, appropriately, Fitzgerald discovered a $100,000 cost overrun. After that, the military abolished Fitzgerald's job. Fitzgerald was guilty of opening his mouth when he was expected to play along with the team. He appealed his dismissal to the Civil Service Commission, which eventually gave him his job and back pay.

A final tactic is the *Organized Protest*. Younger bureaucrats seem to prefer this strategy, which works best when there is no new evidence to lay before the public. Employees opposing a policy organize to negotiate their resistance with the top executives, often without much outside publicity. In 1969, Gary Greenberg, a trial attorney in the civil rights division of the Justice Department, organized sixty-five fellow employees to protest President Nixon's decision to delay the desegregation of southern schools. The lawyers refused to present Nixon's position in the district courts and drafted a declaration of organizational independence, citing legal ethics and their oath to uphold the law of the land. Informed that "around here Attorney General John Mitchell is the law,"[38] Greenberg was ordered to resign. Even so, the federal judges tightened up the desegregation guidelines.

The public was misled into thinking that Greenberg and Fitzgerald lost their battles because they lost their jobs. In fact, both accomplished their purposes—the courts stayed tough on desegregation and the Congress got tougher on cost overruns. Greenberg went off to New York to practice law, whereas his superior, John Mitchell, was found guilty of crimes against the Constitution by a jury of his peers in Washington, D.C. It would be hard to say that Greenberg's career suffered more than Mitchell's in the long run.

In the short run, of course, both Greenberg and Fitzgerald were punished for their actions. There are a few legal protections that shield risk takers against such retaliation. In reinstating Fitzgerald to his job, the Civil Service Commission made the point that a federal agency cannot fire an employee for exposing waste in government. In a different case, the U.S. Supreme Court held that neither federal nor state agencies may punish employees simply because they disagree with government policy. Long ago, the U.S. Congress passed a code of ethics stating that federal employees are legally obligated to "put loyalty to the highest moral principles" above loyalty to their organization and to "expose corruption wherever discovered."[39] A number of government agencies have established bureaucratic ombudsmen to whom employees can take their stories without fear of immediate retaliation, and all agencies have grievance procedures that protect employees from arbitrary dismissal, although it is still easier to harass risk takers than to remove incompetence.

The legal protections are nice, but they are no substitute for the political protections that accompany successful risk taking. The best protection against retaliation is to have the right person use the right strategy at the right time. Correct timing is essentially a matter of waiting until the cause is clear and the risk taker is in a position where he or she is legally or morally obliged to speak out. Bureaucrats are obliged to blow the whistle when they are under oath, when appearing before a congressional committee, or when there is a statutory requirement to do so, as in the code of ethics. They are obliged to break the chain of command when they receive orders that are clearly contrary to the law, and they can make a good case for it when the action contemplated will cause serious harm to the society as a whole. All of these are proper causes for risk taking.

It also helps to have the right person take the risk. Even though the cause may be honorable, the person taking the risk may not be. Veterans draw the following picture of the worst risk taker:

- Those who have not done their homework, who do not fully understand the policy, the interests threatened, the magnitude of the harm, the rules, laws, and ethical standards involved; or those who have not verified the accuracy of their information about the situation.

- Those who might be motivated by a personal vendetta, by the promise of direct personal gain, especially money, or by the desire to save their jobs.

- Those who do not understand the risks themselves or who are unwilling to accept those risks.

It really boils down to a question of credibility. Bureaucrats who speak out at the right time, over the right cause, using the right strategies, will appear credible to their audience. In fact, they will increase their influence by taking the risk, since their method of doing so will enhance their reputation for courage and success.

All of the strategies of executive power, from bureaucratic risk taking back to the politics of the budgetary process, are double edged. They can be used by persons whose purposes are sinister as well as by persons pursuing a higher morality. With enough close group support, inhumane executives can convince themselves that they are in fact behaving morally. How will these political strategies be used? It all depends upon the general moral climate in the state.

MORALITY AND ADMINISTRATION

Suppose that an executive takes a certain action and claims that he or she is following a higher moral principle. To uphold the claim, it seems likely that this moral standard would have to be widely accepted and that other persons, if put in the same situation, would reach a similar conclusion.

Well, what about moral principles? Are there any moral absolutes against which the essential goodness of any administrative action may be measured?

Historically, public executives have followed four paths in their search for a morality of public administration. The oldest is the Judeo-Christian ethic, which was brought to Europe by an administrator of inquisitions who had undergone a sudden conversion. Its acceptance was hastened because of its compatibility with Hellenistic traditions of self-government, advanced by the mixing of temporal and spiritual authority during the Middle Ages, and integrated into public policy as a result of the crusade against slavery and the institutionalization of humanitarianism in the welfare state. In its simplest form, the Judeo-Christian ethic commands the public administrator to "do good," to be honest, and to respect the sacredness of human life. The apostles testified to the abuse of executive power—in the person of Herod Antipas, for example—in order to promote the lesson that good leaders will act as servants to those over whom they have authority. For many centuries, religious morality intermingled with public policy. Most recently, the southern civil rights movement, led by Dr. Martin Luther King, drew both its tactics and moral cohesion from the church. Assaults upon the abuse of power, conflicts of interest, corruption in government, and administrative policies that create human suffering, while not always traceable to religious morality, are certainly highly compatible with it.

The second moral influence on public administration arose as a result of reforms undertaken around the eighteenth century to democratize political and administrative power. Administrative power, both in the church and state, had become increasingly centralized and subject to abuse by executives who could rule public agencies without interference. Armed with the doctrine of legislative supremacy, the reformers attempted to create a new set of constituencies for public administrators that would check their obligations to the chief executive. The consistencies included the legislature, the law, one's clients, and the concept of the "public interest." The reforms were supported by the doctrine of natural rights—the belief that society was governed by fixed moral laws, that those laws endowed each individual with certain inalienable rights, and that the purpose of government was to secure and promote those rights. In sum, the doctrine encouraged administrators to place their own natural sense of morality above the policies of the organization, a doctrine that is quite compatible with religious ethics and that encourages resistance to government policies which degrade human life, retard equality of opportunity, or substitute coercion for democratic consent.

Neither religious morality nor democratic doctrines provided a complete set of ethics for the administrative state. As a result, modern administrators turned to a third standard: utilitarianism. Utilitarianism is the theory of the greatest good for the greatest number, the exaltation of administrative methods that produce the greatest store of results. Good administration is viewed as the production of public goods and services, the exact distribution of which is buttressed by mathematical calculations, attitude surveys, and cost-effectiveness analysis. The good bureaucrat is viewed as one who works to improve the effectiveness of the program while minimizing its harmful effects. Anything that impairs the effectiveness of the program is viewed as morally wrong. Utilitarian doctrine is frequently used as a basis for moralistic campaigns against waste in government, the wrong that heads the hierarchy of utilitarian sins. One can understand why busy executives prefer the morality of utility—it supports the puritan ideals of self-sacrifice and hard work, encourages loyalty to the missions of government, is biased against ideas that might threaten the accomplishment of those missions, and provides moral justification for the sacrifice of personal feelings to the organizational requirements of economy and efficiency.

All three of these moral standards—the Judeo-Christian ethic, democratization of power, and utilitarianism—have been invoked by administrators bent on justifying righteous campaigns. And all three have been violated by administrators campaigning in other directions. Religious ideals have never stood in the way of the security of the state (or the church, for that matter). One remembers the American cabinet secretary who sought guidance at chapel before recommending the bombing of Hiroshima. Democratic administration is certainly not a universal ideal, and frequently is sacrificed to the more pressing problems of war, poverty, and overpopulation. The morality of administrative utility runs aground on the fact that most governmental programs are inherently inefficient and unprofitable. Education can never be made as efficient as the printing of books, and anti-pollution programs can never be made as profitable as the manufacture of automobiles. In effect, none of these approaches creates moral absolutes; they create loose standards that can be adjusted to fit the problem at hand or the attitude of the executive.

The result is a moral double standard that promotes ethical confusion in public affairs. On the one hand, the public executive is expected to be an ethical giant and abide by the standards of religious morality, democratic ethics, and the principle of utility, all at once. At the same time, executives are excused for moral transgressions made in the service of that state—provided that they are successful. This double standard is no accident. Since it is recognized that public officials may have to waive certain moral standards under circumstances such as war, it is necessary to subject those same officials to exceptional moral scrutiny to insure that they are ethical enough to receive the public trust. No wonder so many stumble over the line between moral allowance and ethical misconduct.

The problems of ethical relativity in public affairs have led many to fall back on a fourth, more realistic moral standard for the work of the executive—the doctrine of administrative competence. It looks strange alongside the ethics of religion, democracy, and utility, but experience shows that it provides a firm standard for judging the morality of administrative activity.

The doctrine of administrative competence has been advanced by persons who expect public executives to behave morally but who also recognize that public executives are motivated more by considerations of power than by moral virtue. This system of enlightened self-interest was advanced during the Renaissance by men like Machiavelli, who, one must remember, was never Machiavellian. Machiavelli never preached that the public executive was above moral restraint. In *The Prince*, he frequently refers to ethical standards. In Florence, he fought the Medici family in the hope of establishing a more democratic form of government. As a realist, however, he recognized that the leader who enforced the temporal morality might have to twist it to do so. He recognized that well-meaning rulers might become bad executives if they allowed morality to stand in the way of the preservation of their power.

To Machiavelli, the greatest sin that a moral ruler could commit was *incompetence in the use of executive power*. The problem, of course, is what one means by competence. Machiavelli thought that competence was the ability to preserve the power of the state, that is, to understand the effects of one's own actions upon one's own influence. The science of public administration has taken that definition one step further to say that an understanding of the effect of one's actions on one's influence can be acquired by knowing its impact upon the public that receives it.

The creation of such a standard underlies the modern "social equity" movement in public administration. Its advocates would, for example, assess the impact of educational policy by calculating its effect upon the children who receive the service. This represents a move away from the more traditional measures of competence, such as the principle of merit, which examines only the qualifications of the people administering the policy. Traditional measures of competence such as merit, the advocates of social equity fear, simply promote the standard of utility. (The administrators of Hitler's extermination camps, after all, were highly qualified to run the camps, which had the effect of improving enormously the technical efficiency of the camps.)

In selecting impact as the key test of administrative competence, the advocates of social equity are motivated by a sense of injury. They sense that public policy is never neutral, even when bureaucrats strain to treat everybody equally. Consider educational policy as an example. The advocates of social equity are disturbed by the fact that residents of richer counties receive better educational services than the residents of the inner city. They are discouraged by the finding that equal expenditures for education do not solve this problem, that equal expenditures still produce unequal results, and they are frustrated by the discovery that efforts to balance educational opportunity through other techniques, such as bussing, produce new inequities, such as white flight to the suburbs.

> Much governmental action in the United States has been not simply discriminatory, but massively and harshly so. Much governmental action has also, however, been directed toward achieving equality; paradoxically, action to secure assimilation and uniformity also has sometimes been insensitive and coercive.[40]

CHAPTER 6: EXECUTIVE POWER

The advocates of social equity suspect that bureaucrats try to ignore the inequities they are creating by claiming political neutrality and measuring their programs by the standards of efficiency, economy, or effectiveness. This, say the advocates, simply strengthens the existing inequities. By focusing attention on the effect of government programs, they hope to encourage public administrators to actively promote a more equitable distribution of public services and develop a deeper sense of concern for the impact they have upon all classes of people, especially those who lack power.

The case of strategic bombing illustrates the effect that an ignorance of consequences has upon the opportunity for moral administration. After World War II began, proponents of air power in Britain urged their government to initiate a policy which they called area bombing. The proponents suggested that by bombing working-class districts in German cities the allies would disrupt the German economy and destroy the morale of the German people. After winning the support of top political leaders and scientists, they carried out a policy of indiscriminate attacks upon civilians, culminating in the Allied attack on Dresden in the closing weeks of the war. Dresden was a lovely medieval German city, jammed with refugees from the East who assumed that the city would not be bombed because it contained no war industry. The Allies sent 800 bombers against Dresden, producing a fire storm that killed as many as 135,000 human beings. Altogether, Allied bombing killed between 300,000 and 600,000 Germans, depending upon whose estimates one accepts, at a cost of 150,000 British and American airmen killed or injured. After the war, teams of social scientists and military experts canvassed Germany to assess the impact of air power. Their conclusion? Area bombing, they found, made a negligible contribution to the Allied victory.

Neither moral absolutes nor ethical sensitivity restrained the most civilized nations on the earth from fire bombing civilians. A knowledge of consequences—the fact that the Allies were not ending the war by killing the working-class people of Germany—would have been a restraint. It would have refuted the argument that there was any purpose to the bombing, save the wolfish self-satisfaction of retaliation. From a Machiavellian point of view, the striking point about strategic bombing was the stupidity of those who advocated it. It was bad morality and it was bad administration. Morality did not prevent the bombing. Competent administration—defined as a knowledge of consequences—would have.

In a world full of ethical contradictions, executive competence stands out as a stronger shield against moral transgression than moral restraint. Good administration begins when executives accept the responsibility for the consequences of their actions. Bad administration begins when executives seek to isolate themselves from it. Isolation leads to incompetence, the only absolute administrative sin in an age of ethical relativity. (The only situation in which ignorance can promote morality is in the case of hopelessly cruel executives, who would be prevented by their own incompetence from executing their immorality upon the state.)

Lord Cherwell, the British war government's chief science adviser and the prime mover behind area bombing, was an excellent administrative tactician. He understood the politics of advice and had great skill in pressing his beliefs on others with the power to execute them. He had taught at Oxford, so one must assume that he acquired some knowledge of philosophy and ethics, even if by accident. Still, he was incompetent; he knew how to drop bombs but not how to measure their impact. In effect, he was caught in the jaws of a technology he knew how to execute but not how to manage.

Out of World War II came a new appreciation for the technology of management. A knowledge of executive control, including some sensitivity to morality, is essential. But it has its limitations, especially in the face of modern technology. It is awfully hard to run a large, complex institution with only a knowledge of politics. One also needs some methods for gaining control over the technology in the institutional core.

FOR FURTHER READING

The original advice to executives on how to maintain power is contained in Niccolò Machiavelli, *The Prince and the Discourses* (New York: Modern Library, 1950). Compare this to Richard Neustadt's advice to modern chief executives in *Presidential Power* (New York: John Wiley & Sons, 1960). Aaron Wildavsky shows how smart bureau chiefs beat the budgetary game in *The Politics of the Budgetary Process*, 2nd ed. (Boston: Little, Brown & Co., 1974); this is probably the most popular book in public administration today. Wildavsky's book should be read in conjunction with Charles L. Schultze, *The Politics and Economics of Public Spending* (Washington, D.C.: The Brookings Institution, 1968). Schultze attempts to carve out a role for rationality in the political policy-making process. On the problems and politics of advice, see Harold L. Wilensky, *Organizational Intelligence: Knowledge and Policy in Government and Industry* (New York: Basic Books, 1968) and Irving L. Janis, *Victims of Groupthink* (Boston: Houghton Mifflin Co., 1972).

A good introduction to the different ways that chief executives beat the bureaucratic system (and are beaten by it) is Richard Tanner Johnson, *Managing the White House: An Intimate Study of the Presidency* (New York: Harper & Row, 1974). Advice and strategies for risk takers, along with cases of bureaucrats who have stood up to the organization, are offered in the Ralph Nader study *Whistle Blowing* (New York: Bantam Books, 1972). Few books on morality and administration have been written in the last twenty years; the outlines of the morality problem can be found in the symposium by H. George Frederickson, ed., "Social Equity and Public Administration," *Public Administration Review* 34 (January/February 1974), pp. 1–51.

Overall, the literature on executive power is pretty thin. The advanced reader invariably must turn to memoirs and case histories. Take your pick. Three of my favorites are the Rowland Evans and Robert Novak exposé, *Lyndon B. Johnson: The Exercise of Power* (New York: New American Library, 1966); the novel based on the life of Louisiana governor and senator Huey Long by Robert Penn Warren, *All the King's Men* (New York: Modern Library, 1953); and the Robert Caro study, *The Power Broker: Robert Moses and the Fall of New York* (New York: Alfred A. Knopf, 1974).

MANAGEMENT SCIENCE

During the debate over whether or not the United States government should try to protect itself from a nuclear attack by deploying antiballistic missiles, one leading scientist told a congressional committee that the technical issues surrounding the choice were so complex that no policy maker could hope to master them. The scientists suggested that the ABM system would not work, but not even they could be sure. The policy makers finally made the decision on the basis of intuition. Since they could be wrong no matter what they did, they decided in the end to go ahead with the system and err on the side of safety.

In circumstances such as these, the government seems to be a captive of its technology. Because the technology was there, the government had to use it; because the policy makers did not understand the technology, the requirements of the system were determined by technicians, not executives.

Quite often, public officials find themselves in a race with technology. It is difficult to keep up with technology because the natural sciences have joined with engineering to accelerate the pace of change. Fortunately, the natural sciences also have collaborated with the administrative arts to produce management science, an approach to administration that gives the officials a fighting chance to win the race. Management science has three centers of emphasis— some general guidelines for solving administrative problems through scientific analysis, a bag of specific techniques designed to help administrators calculate the solutions, and proposals for reshaping public organizations in order to make them more responsive to technological change. This chapter examines each point of emphasis in turn.

CYBERNETICS

The theory underlying management science is cybernetics, or, as it is often called, the science of messages. Cybernetics is to twentieth-century management science what Weber's theory of bureaucracy is to the traditional principles of administration. Each embodies a set of assumptions about the world of administration, a perspective that determines the shape of the knowledge to follow.

The word *cybernetics* comes from the Greek word for steersman and was chosen to emphasize the process of communication and control in the animal and the machine. In public administration, cybernetics is the study of how organizations as man-machine systems use communications to ensure, at least temporarily, their survival.

The term *cybernetics* was first heard in the councils of science in the 1940s, around the seminar tables of Harvard Medical School after the evening meal. The scientists who attended these seminars were concerned by the increasing fragmentation in their fields, the fact that a biologist was no longer a biologist but a coleoptcrist, for example, and that a physicist was now a topologist, or some other kind of specialist. In their discussions, the scientists stumbled upon what they felt to be a common set of problems "about communication, control, and statistical machines, whether in the machine or in living tissue."[1] The scientists were astonished by the parallels between rapid computing machines and an ideal model of the human nervous system. They assembled other scientists, who were interested in mathematical logic, antiaircraft weapons engineering, and heart disease, and discovered that the parallels remained. Soon psychologists, sociologists, anthropologists, economists, more engineers, and mathematicians joined their ranks. In 1947 one of the leaders of the group, an M.I.T. mathematician named Norbert Weiner, summarized their findings in a book titled *Cybernetics* and, three years later, in a companion volume, *The Human Use of Human Beings*.

Weiner drew a model of how all systems—living and mechanical—attempt to control their actions. To paraphrase his own words, when we desire an organization to pursue certain objectives, the differences between the objectives and the actual policies of the organization are used as a new input to steer the organization toward its chosen objectives. Control engineers call this process *feedback*. In essence, the organization engages in a constant *scanning* process to check its progress toward its objectives. It collects information on its current position (*inputs*) and sends this information to a central processing unit (*memory*), which compares the new message with its knowledge of previous actions and issues new instructions to tell the organization how to close in on the objective (*output*). Ideally, the central processing unit is programmed to move the organization smoothly toward the objective and to avoid oscillations caused by oversteering. If oscillation begins, or if the objective moves off faster than the organization can pursue it, the system retreats to a neutral or stable position.

Weiner insists that this model provides an analogy that allows scientists to compare the operation of a machine, such as a computerized antiaircraft gun's chasing a target, to the human nervous

231

system's working in conjunction with the brain to move an arm. Both operate in similar ways. Most important, the analogy allows the management scientist to think about the man-machine symbiosis that is the basis of the modern organization. Symbiosis means the union of two specifically different systems—a human and a life-imitating machine, for example—which join together to accomplish a specific mission.

Here is a fictional illustration, taken from a novel by Michael Crichton. Suppose that a man suffers from temporal-lobe epilepsy. The attacks produce convulsions within the brain which cause the man to become so violent that he commits criminal acts. A hospital might develop a miniature computer, driven by a small plutonium power pack, which could monitor the patient's brain waves. When it sees an attack coming, it sends a shock to the brain—in effect, a message that will override the seizure. The computer and its source of power can be sewn into the man's body. He becomes a perfect cybernetic man: a human brain permanently linked to a computer. The computer, in its area of specialty, controls the brain. The brain, indeed the man's body, becomes "a terminal for the new computer . . . as helpless to control the readout as a TV screen is helpless to control the information presented on it"—a terminal man.[2]

The shocks to the brain to stop the epilepsy might produce a feeling of extreme pleasure. In that case the temporal lobe in the man's brain will be rewarded by a computer-created high every time it thinks about having a seizure. The more the brain automatically learns to create the symptoms of a seizure, the more frequently the man receives the euphoric shocks, until the whole man-machine system begins to oscillate, the electrical stimulation becomes constant, and the man is driven into the primitive rage of a permanent temporal-lobe seizure. The doctors' efforts to maintain the man's mental equilibrium through control and communication fail. Although the computer and the brain fight to survive, the man destroys himself through his spasms of violence. Weiner characterizes this as *entropy*.

Weiner observes that entropy has a natural tendency to increase. The universe is running down: ashes to ashes, dust to dust. Everything eventually dies and returns to a common sameness; the natural state of affairs is disorganization. In a universe made up of atoms, there are only small enclaves of resistance—cells, animals, organizations—which strive to hold off nature's uncompromising push towards deterioration and disorder. They survive only through enormous acts of will, in particular, because they have the ability to discriminate in collecting information. Information destroys entropy. Only by learning how to process information can a system steer its way to survival. As entropy is a measure of the tendency of a system to disintegrate, its information-processing capacity is a measure of its organization. A developed system uses information to collect and transform resources so that it approaches a state called negative entropy, where its natural tendency to run down is arrested.

CHAPTER 7: MANAGEMENT SCIENCE

Organizations are unnatural. They survive only so long as they can maintain negative entropy, a process that does not occur accidently but requires conscious, deliberate action. In the view of the management scientists, this situation can be achieved when the organization, its people and machines, replicate the functions of a cybernetic system, collecting information and using it to systematically comprehend and influence the relevant elements of the environment. To do this, the organization must establish a planning-and-control system. That is the view of the public organization that cybernetics inexorably leads to. Cybernetics has profound philosophical implications for new directions in technology, for religion, for the value of human enterprise. For public administration, it implies a preoccupation with organizational planning-and-control systems.

The most popular framework for planning-and-control systems is offered by Robert Anthony, a Harvard professor of management controls. Anthony suggests that the failure or success of any organization will depend on its ability to accomplish three key activities: strategic planning, management control, and operational control. To begin, the executives must establish a center of strategic planning which is capable of making decisions on the "objectives of the organization, on changes in these objectives, on the resources used to attain these objectives, and on the policies that are to govern the acquisition, use, and disposition of these resources."[3] Anthony believes that strategic planning is an irregular process subject to its own laws, unstructured, creative, analytical, and long-range, drawing upon information from outside sources that is incomplete or in need of interpretation. It becomes a bit more structured, however, as the strategic planners begin to calculate the resources needed to accomplish their goals and program these calculations into the budget plan. Strategic planners are people with experience: staff specialists and career bureaucrats inside the system, perhaps a few selected politicians. Top-level political executives, Anthony claims, generally do not participate in the strategic-planning process. They may pass judgment, along with other elected and appointed officials, on the work of the expert strategic planners, but most of the time they are engaged in the second key activity, management control.

Once the strategic-planning process has begun, the executives must establish a system of management control which assures "that resources are obtained and used effectively and efficiently in the accomplishment of the organization's objectives."[4] Anthony characterizes management control as primarily people oriented, that is, to coordinate and persuade. He implies that the people involved in management control have considerable discretion in planning their own procedures, mix of resources, and methods of measuring how close the agency is moving toward its general objectives. Their activity is more regular, less complex, and more dependent upon integrated information systems.

After the plans have been set and the resources obtained, it is

233

necessary to establish a system of operational control to assure "that specific tasks are carried out effectively and efficiently."[5] This assumes that the tasks to be accomplished and the methods of performing them are fairly well defined, so that operational control becomes a matter of proper work engineering, scheduling, quality control, and a reporting system that allows the higher echelons to monitor the progress of the organization towards its objectives.

Implicit in Anthony's typology is the belief that organizations ought to do more strategic planning. An organization cannot be effective so long as it lacks a single control center that can develop strategic plans. The catalog of deficient organizations includes public agencies that define "strategic" decisions as the sum total of what all the bureaucrats are already doing, and the organizations that hire long-range planners. According to Anthony, long-range planning is usually not strategic planning but long-range management control on programs already underway.

How relevant is Anthony's framework for public agencies in a political setting? For one thing, it smacks of Taylorism and the old, discredited politics/administration dichotomy. Anthony admits that the distinction between policy making and administration "fits our distinction between strategic planning and management control."[6] Another problem: centralized strategic planning might injure democratic administration by placing organizational control with a small group of career bureaucrats. Like the hero of *The Terminal Man*, public organizations have more than one control center. Policy making is a process of collaboration involving bureaucrats, politicians, and clients. It does not really fit Anthony's centralized model. Public organizations, especially in a pluralistic state, do not utilize central control centers to achieve their survival.

The defenders of cybernetics would point out that governments normally do not survive. Their departments do not resist entropy. Consumed by the misallocation of organizational energy, they cannot accomplish complex tasks. In departments that are accustomed to carrying out complex missions, such as the military, Anthony's suggestions are well received. Such departments attempt to survive, in Anthony's words, by creating a center of strategic planning which uses information to steer the organization toward the accomplishment of its goals. As for the problem of integrating bureaucrats and politicians within the strategic-planning exercise, this probably requires no more collaboration than already exists within the specialized little worlds of modern subgovernments.

INFORMATION SYSTEMS

According to management scientists, administration is the process of converting information into action. The conversion process requires decision making, and the prerequisite of effective decision is some method of gathering and processing information.

234

A number of public agencies are quite adept at collecting and processing information—the U.S. Air Force, for example, which has designed a computerized tracking system that is the heart of the North American Air Defense Command system headquartered beneath the mountains of Colorado. Radar stations situated around the perimeter of the continent and satellites fixed in orbit track the path of every aircraft, missile, satellite, even space debris that crosses over Canada and the United States and relay this information to the NORAD computers. Technicians seated at computer consoles do not need to check through all of this information; the computers do it for them by performing the task of information discrimination. The computer remembers the origin, speed, and destination of every object that is scheduled to fly over the continent, compares the messages it receives to this memory, sorts out the unexpected, flashes it up on a large display screen, and thus provides the warning that could trigger Armageddon. Unfortunately, the computer was not programmed to recognize the moon. One night the moon rose, as it always does, and bounced back signals sent out from an American radar station 240,000 miles away, which in turn told the computer that it had located an unidentified flying object rising over the eastern horizon. The computer told the defense chiefs that America had been attacked by a fleet of ballistic missiles. One of the defense officials, apparently, had the good sense to recognize that the system had locked onto the celestial orb.

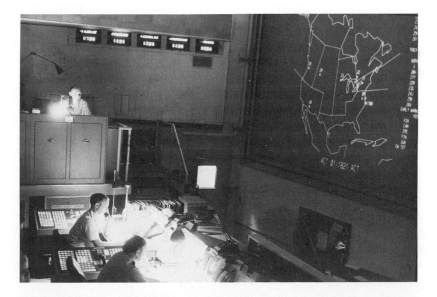

Management science requires the use of large amounts of information for strategic planning and operational control. The command center of the North American Air Defense Command is one of the most complex information-processing systems in public administration. A computer–radar–earth-satellite system keeps track of all objects crossing the continent and charts the unusual on the large display screen.
COURTESY OF THE U.S. AIR FORCE.

It is already possible to automate the human decision maker as well as the collection and filtering of data. During the launch of *Gemini VI*, two seconds after the rocket engines had ignited, the computer controlling the lift-off discovered that an electrical plug had shaken loose from the *Titan II* rocket. A workman had also left a dust cover in a fuel line, an error which would have put the astronauts into the Atlantic instead of earth orbit. Without consulting the flight director, the computer shut down the rocket engines, saving the mission. The rocket settled back onto its launching pad.

The implications of such a totally automated system inspired Arthur C. Clarke to design the ultimate information-processing machine—in fiction. Hal, a heuristically programmed artificial intelligence computer, is so smart that he makes all of the decisions necessary to keep the spaceship *Discovery* on course toward the moons of Saturn while maintaining the life-support systems that keep the astronauts alive. Unfortunately, Hal is also programmed to lie to the crew about the true nature of the mission, a psychological contradiction that causes him to make a nervous mistake, a simple error, for a human. To preserve his image of infallibility, Hal covers up the error by disposing of the evidence. The evidence is the astronauts.

Information-processing systems consist of a common set of elements—some method for collecting raw data and feeding it into the system, programs (called software) that instruct the computer (called hardware) to consolidate or filter the data, and terminals that give the decision maker access to the information or the ability to manipulate it. Simple data retrieval systems, such as the FBI's list of stolen cars, are not considered information systems unless they are programmed to alter the shape of the data. The most advanced types of information systems, such as NORAD, have been built for operational control.

A special type of information system has been designed for higher decisions, particularly at the level of strategic planning. Called a management information system (MIS), it is designed to formally organize the information that managers need to plan the future course of the organization and to make decisions on the optimal allocation of resources. Management information systems have been widely adopted by business executives who use them to analyze the performance of the firm, forecast future economic conditions, and signal variations from desired plans. Management information systems have moved slowly into public administration, in areas such as metropolitan government and defense planning. The resistance to the use of MIS in public administration often can be traced to the tendency of information specialists to make two assumptions which public executives know to be false.

Information specialists often approach the organization with the idea that managers do not have enough information upon which to base their decisions. From the managers' point of view, this is not the crucial problem. They feel that they suffer from an overabundance of information. Since they have more information than they can use, they need a system that filters and condenses data so that only those bits of information they need arrive on their desks. The primary function of the management information system is not information gathering, but information discrimination.

Information specialists also tend to assume that more information and better communication of it will in itself lead to better decision making. In many public agencies, the reverse is true. The introduction of more information makes things worse, either because the managers have not acquired the skills necessary to use the information or because the organization is torn by internal rivalries. In a politically torn organization, more information will fuel the distrust among factions by encouraging the belief that the information will be used as a weapon in the struggle for power. The factions, therefore, will try to manipulate the data being fed into the information system in order to protect their own position while discrediting their enemies. An information analyst must have the ability to distinguish between decision-making problems caused by poor management or organizational hostilities as opposed to those problems caused by a lack of relevant information.

There is no simple method for avoiding these problems in the design of a management information system, but the following model is at least a first step.

1. Analysis of the decision system. The first step in designing an MIS is to analyze the objectives of the organization and determine the type of decisions that must be made to achieve them. Flow charts and decision tables are useful methods of representing these things. They will reveal important decisions that are not being made or that are being made by default, and interdependent decisions that are made independently. An accurate model of the decision process also provides the basis for analyzing information requirements.

2. An analysis of information requirements. Information requirements in an organization vary, depending upon the type of decision being made. For routine managerial decisions, the proper sources of information are probably well established. For more complex decisions, the managers may know what information they need but not how to work it into an optimal decision. Simulation of the decision can help to clarify this situation. Finally, there are those highly complex decisions where no one can agree on what information is needed. Here it is necessary to conduct research of the sort discussed in the chapter on policy analysis, searching to identify the information most relevant to the causes and solutions of the problem. Complex problems such as these usually require the organization to search for new, untapped sources of data.

3. Aggregation of decisions. Decisions with similar information requirements should be identified and grouped together under a single unit or person. Such reorganization leads to information efficiency and helps the manager become more of an expert on a complex subject.

237

4. Design of the information-processing system. This is the system for collecting, storing, retrieving, and reporting the data—the mechanics of MIS. The designers of the system have to select the programs for processing the data and the type of computers that will do it. Three observations are worth making. First, the choice of where and how to gather the raw data is strategic and not mechanical. If garbage is fed into the system, then garbage will come out of it. Second, the system must have the capability to "answer questions that have not been asked by reporting any deviations from expectations. An extensive exception-reporting system is required."[7] Both of these point to the third observation. A manager who only knows how to listen to an information system, but has no idea how it works, will not be able to use it. Not only will such a manager be unable to perform the calculations necessary to make complex decisions, he or she will be unable to catch errors the MIS might make.

5. Design of the control system. The management information system will be deficient in many ways—if not now, then later. A standardized procedure must be established for reviewing deviations from expectations, for determining whether they are due to faults in the information system, and, if so, for correcting the system. This requires cooperation between the computer specialists, the information specialists, and the managers.

OPERATIONS RESEARCH AND SYSTEMS ANALYSIS

The great obstacle to rational decision making in administration has been lack of information upon which to base optimal decisions and predict their consequences. As a result, many scholars in public administration have gone off to study bureaus, groups, habit, or the politics of administration—but not decisions. Among the scholars who have studied decisions, many utilize practical case studies, which naturally lead them to focus on the intuitive or unquantifiable aspects of administrative choice.

In 1947, Herbert Simon, one of the deans of public administration, published a book in which he urged public administrators to build a theory that focused on administrative decisions. But even Simon admitted that there were cognitive limits to rationality. He said that it was impossible for managers to achieve a high degree of rationality in making decisions because the amount of information they would need to evaluate was too great. Then, in 1960, Simon seemed to suddenly change his mind; traditional methods of management decision making, he said, were as outmoded as the pick and shovel for construction work. In a set of lectures published under the title *The New Science of Management Decision*, Simon issued a utopian forecast that scientific method would replace habit and intuition in administrative decision making. What had broken the information problem? The computer revolution, Simon said, with its enormously expanded capacity to process and organize information for managers. The science of management decision making had been rescued by the dawn of cybernetics and the management information system. From now on, Simon said, managers would be able to make decisions scientifically.

How would they do it? Here is the problem that brought scientific decision making to public administration. After conquering France and driving the British from the continent at Dunkirk, Hitler prepared to march the German army through Britain. Before the land invasion, Hitler dispatched the German Luftwaffe to soften the English into submission. He said he would strangle the English like a peasant breaking the neck of a chicken. The German bombers outnumbered the British interceptors ten to one; moreover, the Germans thought they could be over their targets only a few minutes after the British spotted them coming across the channel. All Churchill had was his small fleet of interceptors, some antiaircraft guns, and an untested invention the scientists called radar. If Churchill deployed these defenses through intuition or trial and error, and was wrong, England would be crushed in less than a month. It was like parachute jumping; he had to do it right the first time.

When governments sense that their survival is really threatened, they turn to scientists and their methods to relieve the problems menacing the state. The British scientists said that the optimal utilization of radar, guns, and planes could be determined scientifically. Just as the scientists had discovered radar through scientific investigation, so they would improve the performance of the radar operators under fire through scientific experimentation. They had to perfect a ground-control system that could guide the British interceptors to their targets; the requirements of the system, said the scientists, could be determined scientifically without reference to the administrative problems involved. After pinpointing the air routes the Germans tended to use, they could deploy the guns and integrate the gunfire with radar sets at the gun sites. All of these things were treated as scientific problems susceptible to rigorous experimentation and mathematical vivisection. Hitler thought that his air minister could destroy the British through force of strength, but the Luftwaffe was so badly beaten that Hitler had to call off the invasion. It is said that radar and operations research magnified the British strength by a factor of twelve, quite in contrast to Hitler's romantic, impulsive attitude toward military strategy.

Great Britain and the United States quickly established scientific teams in all of the military services. The Americans termed their work operations research (O.R.) and used it to guide merchant marine convoys across the North Atlantic, to pinpoint military targets for strategic bombing, and to lay mines in Japanese ports and shipping lanes.

Operations research is simply the use of "any scientific, mathematical, or logical means" to help the executive "achieve a thorough-going rationality in dealing with his decision problems."[8] The scientific method is plunged wholesale into public administration, the words not even changed to protect the innocent. Administrative decisions are transformed into scientific questions with scientifically correct answers. Scientists from various disciplines are called in to prescribe those answers and assure that the solution chosen achieves the most efficient use of resources.

Any operations research project, including the defense of Britain, contains the following steps:

1. Formulate a clear definition of the problem. This includes a description of the decision to be made, the particular values to be maximized, the variables in the problem, and the restrictions or constraints on the variables.

2. Construct a model that is representative of the system under study. The model allows the scientist to study the problem in the laboratory before testing the solution in the real world. Model builders usually represent the static and dynamic elements of the problem with mathematical formulas, which set out the relationships between the elements of the problem, the restrictions upon the variables, and the time horizon.

Modeling is really easier than it sounds. One famous O.R. problem to come out of World War II concerned a new bomber that always seemed to get shot down. The manufacturing company back in the United States proposed an elaborate test program to locate the source of the fault. An O.R. group in Britain had a better idea. They went into the country where the planes were based and counted the flak marks, identifying where each aircraft had been hit. When they placed this data on a paper model of the plane, a pattern emerged. No flak marks appeared behind the wings. The scientists surmised that any plane hit behind the wing never returned; a close inspection of the aircraft revealed that fuel lines passed along this point behind some weak armoring.

3. Perform the analysis. After modeling the problem, the O.R. team collects the data necessary to calculate the solution to the problem. Normally this step requires the analyst to optimize one objective while holding others within permissible levels of performance.

4. Test the model and the solution in a real-world setting under tight controls to see how well the solution works. Pilot projects or systematic experimentation can be used to reveal whether or not there are hidden flaws in the model, the solution, or the definition of the problem.

5. Establish controls over the implementation of the solution. At the least, this should include some system for monitoring the results of the solution and some plan for adjusting the solution if results deviate from expectations.

6. Implement the solution and the control system throughout the organization. In the bomber problem, the planes were rede-

240

signed. The O.R. team stayed on until they were convinced that losses had dropped to a normal level.

Persons who use operations research bring what is known as a systems approach to the consideration of problems. In the jargon of the systems analyst, problems are viewed as a complex whole comprised of interrelated parts and diverse activities that must be coordinated if organizational goals are to be met. No element of the problem can be omitted from organizational scrutiny: every obstacle, every opportunity, every bit of information with a potential impact on the mission must be programmed into the organizational system. This requires the executive to identify the total system purpose, to inspect the fixed constraints placed on the system by its environment, and to devise appropriate performance indices for measuring the success of the system at accomplishing its goals. The executive must also calculate the resources needed to accomplish the mission and identify management strategies that will make the system run. The system itself is broken down into a collage of subsystems: managers, groups, employees, formal structure, the technology utilized, and the tasks performed within each subsystem.

Systems analysts see systems everywhere: clockwork mechanisms, biological systems, social systems, governmental systems, ecosystems, organizational systems. In every case the system collects information and resources from its environment and systematically transforms those resources into a product in such a way that the organization can fulfill its purpose while staving off decay. Why should public agencies be any different?

The systems approach leads to systems analysis, which, like operations research, is simply a thoroughgoing scientific approach to analyzing the operations of the system. Systems analysis comes in many forms. When linked to economics, it takes on the form of cost-benefit analysis, which was developed by the defense executives to analyze the allocation of financial resources within the defense system. When linked to mathematics, it can provide a model for discovering the best way to lay out the work of the organization. Gradually, systems analysis has penetrated public agencies not accustomed to treating problems scientifically. These recent developments are documented in a book edited by Alvin Drake, *Analysis of Public Systems*. Part of the volume describes how New York City called upon analysts at the RAND Corporation and the Massachusetts Institute of Technology to apply "formal modeling for the improvement of the delivery of public services."[9] One analyst studied the work of the switchboard operators at the New York City police department, using mathematical models to develop a staffing plan that insured that a citizen dialing 911 in an emergency would not get a busy signal. Another team of analysts spent four years developing a computer simulation representing the 14,500 fire fighters and 400 fire units in the city's fire department. The simulation allowed the team to prepare a location plan that put the fire units as close to the potential sources of fire as possible. The fire fighters union even used the simulation to bargain for roving tactical control units that would move into high fire areas during peak alarm periods and help even out the workload.

Other analysts showed how systems analysis could be applied to services in other government agencies: regional blood banks, airport traffic control, automobile insurance regulation, law enforcement assistance, water pollution, air pollution, even the development of a new airport for Mexico City. Despite these advances, despite the fact that operations research was a child of public administration, many public executives remain suspicious of management science, especially in programs where politics is important. But management science is coming to politics too. The following case introduces the sections on specific management science techniques.

MATHEMATICS AND PUBLIC ADMINISTRATION

The use of quantitative methods is nowhere further advanced in the social sciences than in survey research and analysis, often called polling. Typically, it has not been considered part of public administration. Recently, however, management experts wielding the tools of operations research have applied their skills to the administration of political campaigns.

The term "management" in elections is generally synonymous with manipulation. The fear of electoral management began after Goebels used mass propaganda tactics to solidify the German Nazi party. In his novel *The Ninth Wave*, Eugene Burdick, a political scientist, speculated on how the principles of mass hysteria could be utilized to swing a California state political convention to an unqualified candidate. In *The Four-Eighty* Burdick revealed how a candidate could be programmed to say the right things to any group, based on a computerized picture of every voter's fears and desires. The novel, also set in California, was based on an actual computer program designed for John Kennedy, which told him how to get elected president by stressing his Catholic religion and foreign policy. In 1970, in a senatorial campaign that was the inspiration for the movie *The Candidate*, management scientists introduced operations research into political campaigning, once again in California. That candidate was Congressman John Tunney, son of the former world heavyweight boxing champion. Management scientists applied linear programming techniques to the scheduling of Tunney's personal appearances, his advertising, his registration drives, his canvassing of precincts, and his get-out-the-vote efforts on election day.

Everyone knows that half the money and time spent by politicians on campaigning is wasted. The problem is that nobody knows which half. Nobody, that is, until two systems analysts developed a mathematical model for achieving the optimal distribution of scarce resources in candidate Tunney's campaign. The model is now used by public relations firms that specialize in scientific election management.

242

Here is one of the problems the analysts solved. Officially, over 50 percent of the voters in California register as Democrats. But they often vote Republican. The analysts interviewed the voters in a number of precincts that had a reputation for ticket splitting and discovered that between 2 and 35 percent of the registered Democrats were leaving their party, while between 1 and 20 percent of the registered Republicans were voting with the Democrats. The analysts knew that Tunney could reduce Democratic defections by personally appearing in the high-defection areas and by running paid advertisements there during the middle of the campaign. Obviously, Tunney could not appear everywhere; the analysts had to concentrate Tunney and his advertising in the areas with the greatest potential for defection. But how could they identify those precincts scientifically? A state-wide, district-by-district public opinion poll would be prohibitively expensive.

The analysts recognized that they had resolved the problem into a standard linear programming exercise. First, something was being *dispersed*. Registered Democrats and Republicans were going to the polls and scattering themselves into the voting columns of opposing candidates. (The analysts used the previous gubernatorial election, in which a large number of Democrats defected to Ronald Reagan, as the data base.) Second, there were *constraints* on the problem—a limited range of possibilities. In this case the analysts knew that no more than 35 percent of the Democrats were defecting. Third, every linear programming problem contains an *objective function*, something that the analysts are trying to maximize. In this case the analysts wanted to know the maximum number of defections possible in each precinct in the state.

The analysts constructed a mathematical model to predict the probability of Democratic defections, turned on their computer, fed in data from the previous gubernatorial election, and stood back as the computer ranked all 20,000 precincts in the state from the highest to the lowest number of possible Democratic defections. The result was used to plan Tunney's campaign, in which he won election to the U.S. Senate with 53 percent of the vote.

Linear programming is the most elementary mathematical technique used in public administration. It is normally used for problems involving transportation, procurement, distribution, or scheduling, although a clever analyst can also use it to solve problems of probability, like campaign management. Linear programming works best when the manager has a single problem with a limited number of variables and a fairly well defined set of constraints. If the problem is more complex, then the analyst must turn to other mathematical techniques.

Dynamic Programming Many problems in government are dynamic; that is, they are marked by continuous change. They involve a long chain of choices—in effect, a series of linear programming problems—over a long period of time. Each choice reduces the

243

number of remaining options. The choice of routes for the pony express is often used as an example of dynamic programming. The managers of the pony express had to place their way stations along the one route that would move the mail from Missouri to California in the shortest possible time with the maximum safety to the riders. There were hundreds of possible routes; as each leg of the route was selected, the subsequent choices would be reduced. To solve the problem, a modern analyst would visualize all possible branches in the trail from St. Joseph to Sacramento. The analyst would then assign a probable value to each line between the branches, a value representing the objectives of speed and safety. By adding up the values along every connecting set of lines, the analyst could identify the best possible route.

Stochastic Programming Models   Both dynamic and linear programming models assume that the executive has all the data needed to measure the problem and that the data is accurate. Is this practical? What about real-life problems where the executive is uncertain about the weight of some elements in a situation?

Stochastic programming, which is conjectural, attempts to deal with such situations. It works when one knows the limits of uncertainty and the probability of any one thing happening within those limits. Analysts examine the nature of uncertainty in the problem and choose a mathematical model to deal with it. They might assume, for example, that the chance of any one event occurring within the limits of uncertainty are as good as any other, and choose a model based on the random distribution of numbers. They would then locate an appropriate computational technique to solve the problem, given the data which exists and the probable ranges for the rest.

Statistics and Probability   Much of the analysis done in public administration relies upon statistics and the theory of probabilities, which are associated more frequently with policy analysis than with management science. Sampling and statistical inference techniques allow the analyst to estimate the characteristics of a large population by drawing information from a smaller one. The sample is usually selected randomly from the total population being studied. A complex theory of probability underlies the use of statistics to infer future events. Regressional analysis and correlation techniques are used to ascertain one thing when another is known, such as predicting the number of elk that will perish in Yellowstone National Park on the basis of the relative depth of the winter snowfall. Correlation coefficients are formulas used to determine the *degree* to which the two things are related, or the probability that the calculated prediction will be correct. Multivariate analysis, an extension of regression analysis, gives the analyst the ability to measure the combined effect of a number of independent variables on one dependent variable. Altogether, these techniques allow managers to increase the amount of information on hand for decision making and to estimate the consequences of their actions. It reduces guessing. It means that the executive can no longer venture the opinion that one thing "causes" another without considering the rigorous standards that exist for defining cause and effect.

Bayesian Analysis   One hears a great deal about Bayesian analysis in public administration. The Bayes Theorem, which was published by the Royal Society in 1763, provides an analytical method for combining subjective information with formal data to produce a single set of probabilities. Interest in Bayes was revived by twentieth-century analysts who wanted to put intuition and perception back into management science. In essence, Bayesian analysis is a method of decision making in an uncertain environment. It calls upon the executive to assign probabilistic weights to uncertainties according to his or her own personal prognosis. Since different executives may have different perceptions of reality, the optimal solution to any problem will depend in part upon the preferences of the people involved.

Regrettably, public administrators are often driven away from operations research because of the mathematics involved. This situation is aggravated by management scientists who write textbooks full of technical jargon, puzzling formulas, and industrial examples with little bearing on public decisions. As a result, many public executives equate all of management science with the mathematical techniques used to solve complex problems—and thus ignore it.

SIMULATION

Not all management science techniques require an advanced degree in mathematics. Any executive with a high school knowledge of algebra and the money to hire a computer programmer can design a simulation. Some public administrators think that simulators are the greatest invention since Lionel came out with the model train.

Man-machine simulators are used for training. During the Apollo Program, NASA operated two life-size mock-ups of the command module and lunar lander. The astronauts practiced their voyage in the simulators, which simulated motion (through noise and vibrations) and full flight operations (controlled by a complex computer program). The astronauts looked out the windows of the spacecraft to see the moon and earth, and even practiced landing over a three-dimensional view of the lunar terrain, an effect created by the use of large models and sophisticated television equipment.

Closer to the needs of public executives are games used to simulate the administration of government. Urban games, for example, allow students to run an entire city government. The voters, the parties, the special interests, the industries, the real estate developers are all simulated by a computer program.

Computer simulation has been used extensively to solve operational problems in government. The Port Authority of New York and New Jersey used computers to simulate the flow of motor vehicles through their toll booths. The print-out told them how to set up work shifts and how many lanes should be open in each direction each hour at each location.

Simulation has been used to predict the need for long-range governmental services. The city of San Francisco developed a computer program that simulated housing in the Bay Area—its growth, its deterioration, and the factors that influenced it, such as income and population. The simulation was used as a tool for planning urban renewal projects.

The basis of the simulation is a model of reality that takes into account the major factors that have an impact upon the problem and relates them to one another in a systematic fashion. Part of the attraction of simulations for public administration is the challenge of drawing and testing the model. Here is how it is done.

1. Identify the basic components of the system. What makes the problem get worse and what makes it get better? The analyst will usually start by drawing a paper picture that traces out the sources of the problem, the variables that cause fluctuations in it, the factors that cannot be controlled, and the factors that can.

2. Establish an index for monitoring the problem. The index is a quantitative indicator reflecting the objectives of the program managers. Existing indexes are often available. For air pollution, the index would be chemicals or particles in the air. For urban renewal, it might be homes and buildings, their density and condition. For solid-waste disposal, it might be tons of garbage. Usually the indicator will have a geographic dimension, which allows the analyst to monitor the problem in several different districts.

3. Study the historic trends of the various elements of the system. This allows the analyst to generate some propositions about the relationships between the elements—for example, the effect that population growth might have upon housing density in a simulation of urban development. By analyzing past trends, the analyst can also make some predictions about the probable range of values of key elements in the future.

4. Draw in the feedback loops that describe how the elements relate to one another. A feedback loop is a situation in which a change in one variable triggers a change in another, which in turn triggers a response in the first. The classic example is the wage-price spiral. The chain of events may be quite involved; there may be many feedback loops within any one system.

5. Reduce the relationships to numerical terms and choose appropriate mathematical methods. This step is both analytical, since it requires the analyst to be precise about relationships that may be poorly understood, and mechanical, since it invariably requires a computer program that can calculate all of the relationships simultaneously.

6. Test the model. Before running the simulation, in which trends are projected far into the future, it is necessary to test the accuracy of the model. Frequently the analyst will simulate scenarios that have

already occurred to see if the model conforms to events as they happened. Or the analyst will run the simulation backwards, starting with today and projecting trends back into the past to see if the results are historically accurate.

There are a number of mathematical techniques that can help the designer overcome problems in step five. *Queuing theory* consists of a set of prepackaged mathematical formulas that can be used to simulate situations in which a group of people or machines are queued up, waiting to be serviced. It has been used to synchronize traffic lights, to open and close teller windows, to schedule vehicles for maintenance, and to organize emergency-room services at hospitals. The analyst determines the number of people or things to be serviced, the rate at which they arrive (it is assumed that they do not come all at once), how long they can wait, the amount of time necessary to serve them, and the number of servicing units. Given this data, the analyst can develop a schedule for the use and staffing of the servicing units, with the help of standardized tables.

Some elements of a simulation cannot be predicted because they are too complex; others are simply unknown. If probabilities cannot be obtained, then the designer may use *Monte Carlo* techniques. These techniques are a lot like spinning a gambling wheel. Within certain limits, the probability that any given event will occur is established through the theory of random chances. The use of Monte Carlo techniques borders on stochastic programming, defined in the previous section.

By simulating reality, the public executive can learn the outcome of future events before they happen, providing one is willing to make assumptions about future conditions. Simulations can be run through computers for all possible assumptions, good or bad. It was probably inevitable, then, that someone would simulate the world and predict the future of humanity. The seer was Jay W. Forrester, a professor of management at the Massachusetts Institute of Technology. Forrester cut his teeth on a simulated factory, then a simulated city. Today a city, tomorrow the world!

In the computer, Forrester's World Dynamics Model was a maze of mathematical relationships. Its basic assumptions were fairly clear, however. Forrester believed that global population growth, the production of food, the availability of natural resources, industrialization, and pollution all could be related to each other and to a variable he called the quality of life—a composite of food, pollution, overcrowding, and the general standard of living.

The feedback loops in Forrester's model were fundamentally Malthusian. Thomas Malthus was a nineteenth-century British economist who proclaimed the doctrine that population would always increase faster than the food supply. The Irish confirmed this thesis. After discovering the virtues of the potato, the Irish increased their population by some three million people. When rain and a potato fungus set in, one million starved to death and one million fled the nation.

Forrester's model seemed similar. The best efforts of humans to control their future led to unintended results. In one early run through the model, Forrester predicted what would happen if governments tried to solve problems of starvation and overcrowding by increasing the standard of living. As industrialization increased, so did population. Pollution increased faster than anything else, as the reserves of clean fossil fuels were depleted. Severe pollution killed off crops and fishes, thus reducing the production of food. As a result of the attempt to increase the standard of living, more people would starve.

Forrester turned the model over to the Club of Rome, a world-future society, which paid Forrester's colleagues at MIT to increase the complexity of the model and make new predictions years into the future under a variety of assumptions. The gloomiest prognosis revealed a breaking point around the year 2020. By then, increases in pollution and population along with dwindling natural resources would overtake the engine of industrialization. The population curve would climb like a roller coaster, then plunge. Even after the holocaust the quality of life would continue to fall. The computer revealed a relentless decline in the quality of life beginning in 1975.

There were howls of protest against this doomsday simulation. The Club of Rome was accused of all varieties of sin: taking a Malthusian view of nature, which has already been discredited in industrialized nations; ignoring alternative sources of energy; and building a model that contained no cell for human adaptability. Since then, the Club of Rome has backed off from its most pessimistic predictions. At any rate, the world model revealed what great fun simulations could be in public administration.

NETWORK ANALYSIS: FAD OR TECHNIQUE?

In the formative years of management science, network analysis was hailed as the hottest new trend in space age management. At the launch of the first nuclear submarine carrying Polaris missiles, which had been built using network analysis, the technique was heralded as the management science breakthrough of the decade. Network analysis supposedly made the Polaris system operational two years ahead of schedule without any cost overruns. The technique received as much publicity as the submarine itself.

Network analysis is a systems-design technique for identifying and integrating the various subsystems in a program. It rejects the traditional method of organization, which is to group people together who perform purportedly similar functions and direct their work from the top down. It discounts theories of human relations and decision making, because they are too ambiguous to solve the complex problems of measuring the progress of an organization towards its objectives. Instead, network analysis focuses on the flow of work.

In *The Measurement of Management*, Eliot Chapple and Leonard Sayles describe how the flow of work can be used to administer the modern organization. The flow of work is the management scientist's organization chart. It is people oriented, not machine oriented, and asks "who does what with whom, when, where and how often."[10] It assumes that every process relevant to the completion of a job has a beginning and an end. Patterns of activity can be plotted; individual performance can be measured against the time necessary to complete the job. Job specifications can be written describing the responsibilities of each person or contractor in the flow of work, with the aim of eliminating many of the irrelevant tasks that add nothing but overhead to the costs of the organization. The managers have their authority set in terms of the flow of work, just like the others. Their techniques of control are not budgetary, nor a matter of correct attitudes toward people, nor of correct principles of organization. Rather, the managers monitor and measure the flow of work, especially at the points where stress occurs or where people have difficulty meeting project deadlines. The managers try to hold the organization on schedule and, where necessary, redesign the work flow to make it more effective.

The development of the Polaris missile program, which began in 1957, is accepted as the genesis of network analysis in public administration. Admiral William Raborn was responsible for building the missiles and the submarines. The problems were enormous. For one thing, the program resembled the tower of Babel, with too many specialists speaking too many technical languages. For another, it was difficult to assign distinct areas of responsibility or measure individual contributions to the program. Since Raborn had to coordinate the work of private contractors, he needed an information system that could provide him with reliable estimates of program progress.

Management scientists generally organize operations on the basis of the flow of work. The specific technique for doing this (PERT) was developed by the U.S. Navy Special Projects Office for controlling development of the Polaris missile and the nuclear-powered submarines that carry them.
COURTESY OF THE
U.S. NAVY

He also needed some method of checking on critical jobs that could hold up the entire program if not completed on time. On top of all this, there was the simple, disillusioning fact that no one really knew what a Polaris missile system looked like. It had never been built before.

The navy set up a special projects office to coordinate the work of its technical bureaus. Admiral Raborn asked the office to survey the management innovations coming out of Chrysler, General Motors, and Dupont. The survey team returned with the news that their reputations for managerial effectiveness were overblown. While the survey team was gone, the bureaus began to schedule the development of the Polaris system. Some of the activities were compressed into impossibly short time intervals. Parts of the program were already behind schedule. Although the program extended years into the future, encompassing thousands of tasks, the special projects office did not know how to coordinate it and meet the deadline for a completed weapons system.

To plan and control the development of the seventy thousand odd components that made up the Polaris program, including the missiles, guidance systems, submarines, maintenance systems, and the training of crews, the special projects office set up a special project team. The team developed a network-analysis approach, which became known as the Program Evaluation and Review Technique (PERT). Here is what the team members did.

1. They identified all the jobs in the program, terming each job an event.
2. They identified which events would have to be completed before others could begin. As each sequence of events was identified, it was plotted along a long roll of paper. This was called network building.
3. They asked experts to determine how long it would take to complete different events in the project, using three estimates: optimistic, pessimistic, and most likely.
4. All of this data—the time estimates, the events, the sequencing—was fed into a computer programmed to identify the logical arrangement of events for each major phase of the project. The print-out produced a map of project activities, which they called the PERT chart.
5. The PERT chart was used to plan and control the progress of the Polaris program. It was revised as project deadlines were changed or broken.

In addition to establishing deadlines, the project team called for cost estimates for each event. These estimates were programmed into the computer, creating what was known as the PERT/cost-control system, a watchdog that barked when time or money was lost or gained.

Finally, the project team experimented with different schedules for completing different activities. By simulating the development of various phases of the project, the team could identify those activities which could be stretched out to save money or those activities which could be compressed to meet critical deadlines. The simulated runs also allowed the project team to beat the time estimates of the experts. In one instance, twenty-five simulated runs on the computer showed the team how to cut the estimated time for one activity by 67 percent.

When industry picked up the technique, another dimension was added: the critical path method. Industrial analysts would study each phase of their project, plotting out the paths of events that would have to be performed in sequence. Many such sequences would appear; the analysts would identify the longest one, calling it the critical path. They spent the most time reviewing the progress of events along the critical path, since this represented the minimum amount of time required to complete that phase and any deadlines missed along the critical path would delay the entire program.

Some people think PERT was oversold. One air force titan called it "a load of shit."[11] A top executive from Lockheed told the special projects team:

> No management system is going to get me to admit that I am going to miss my scheduled delivery dates. This system is going to listen to some pessimistic Lockheed engineer say that Lockheed is likely to miss delivery, but not to me. I sign the contracts. I hire and fire Lockheed engineers. I've got all the information I need in my desk.[12]

One skeptic suggested that PERT was a managerial innovation only insofar as it created the *appearance* of managerial competence. As a technique, he said, it was overblown. Schedules were missed, errors went undetected. It cost too much—upwards of 1 percent of the entire program, said industrial spokesmen. But it gave an illusion of managerial competence that enhanced the power of the special projects office. The office was independent, no one harassed it, it was well funded, its programs got top priority, and it could push industrial contractors around. Admiral Raborn was applauded and the Polaris program had little trouble acquiring the political backing it needed to stay healthy.

If the program's success was a myth, then why have so many public and private agencies adopted PERT and CPM? Network analysis is used to launch spacecraft, plan urban renewal projects, and develop weapons systems. The Office of Management and Budget uses it to reduce the time necessary to process grants-in-aid. The Soviet Union uses it in its five-year plans. A restaurant-and-hotel tycoon even used it to plan President Nixon's gala second inaugural.

How does one distinguish between a management science fad and a management science technique with real analytical power? According to its advocates, PERT "worked" because it accomplished its objectives: it permitted managers to monitor progress toward a goal and reorder the sequence of events as the project moved along. As will be seen, this is a poor test of the power of technique. A better test looks at the impact of the technique on the shape of the organization and the nature of the administrative process within it. This leads to the third center of emphasis in management science: proposals for making public organizations more responsive to change and more amenable to management science.

TECHNOLOGY AND ADMINISTRATION

One nation has developed an ingenious information-and-decision system. At the capital of the nation, a data bank contained the age, marital status, health, and location of every human being living in that country, the number qualified to bear arms, the casualties from the last war, the number of operational weapons, the volume of foodstuffs to be produced that season, the number of animals and their condition, and the amount of food in storage. Towns with many widows or poor people were noted.

Each year, the information experts summarized the state of the nation for the chief executives, who allocated resources to the military, the needy, and the people who ran the government. In an emergency (the country suffered flash floods), a monitoring system transmitted information on the disaster into the data system. Within hours, information summaries went to the executives, who decided how much food, medicine, and clothing to dispatch to the distressed area. The data system contained the plans for rebuilding highways, buildings, and bridges. The mathematical computations to determine the optimal load factor for a new bridge were done on the data-processing system, down to the last decimal.

The people kept one-third of their labor, one-third went to support the executives and national trust, and one-third went for arms, welfare, and public works. Housing, health care, and food production were subsidized by the government. Materials and information passed along an amazing system of tunnels, bridges, and roads.

In 1532 the nation was invaded by 180 soldiers led by Francisco Pizarro. He kidnapped the ruler, Atahualpa, then assembled the information experts and asked them to explain the amazing collection of string the Incas called the *quipu*.

The Incas showed Pizarro a long rope with colored strings attached to it representing precious metals and warriors. People and supplies were counted on separate threads. Knots in the threads represented numbers in a decimal-decade system, in units of ten to ten thousand. Information was collected through units of ten: ten families under a quipu clerk, ten clerks under a quipu administrator, and so on. Fine threads attached to a main thread indicated an exception to a rule.

Pizarro asked for gold. The priests tied the knots and sent out runners, who brought back the national trust. Then Pizarro strangled the Inca. The empire died.

How did the Incas invent the quipu? Above the valley of Cuzco, on the plateau atop the Andes Mountains, are Inca temples com-

252

memorating the legend of the two founders who came out of the sun to start the civilization. Nearby are the amazing ruins of Tiahuanaco, and not far away, by modern standards, are the prehistoric grooves in the earth that resemble giant runways from the air. Archaeologists know that a great civilization existed in the Andes before the Incas. What were its origins? Did outsiders of superior intelligence show the Incas a management information system and allow them to copy its basic features?

The lesson from the quipu seems startlingly clear, regardless of how one feels about theories of outside influence. The Incas had somehow acquired a technique of management science but had not learned how to use it to manage the future. In Anthony's terms, they were preoccupied with operational control. The priests who kept the quipu served the Inca; they were not allowed to innovate. It was a cybernetic civilization, using information to resist decay, but it was also a closed system that was not programmed to deal with change. When the Spaniards arrived, the Incas treated Pizarro as a god, relying on religion and llama entrails to explain his presence, just as a modern executive might fall back on intuition or the flip of a lucky coin. The Incas possessed a management technology, but they could not manage technology.

To what extent are modern nations that adopt management science like the Incas? This is the crucial test: a truly powerful management science technique will enlarge the capacity of the organization to respond to change. There are two indicators which show that this has happened:

- Public executives will not use management science exclusively to maintain the efficiency of the status quo, but will invite scientists to work at the top to discover solutions to unforeseen problems. The British, who allowed their scientists to participate in strategic planning, repelled their invaders; the Incas, who used their experts for the purpose of control, did not.

- The use of management science will change the shape of public administration, replacing traditional methods of organization and supervision with strategies more flexible and responsive to change. This almost always happens when management scientists are allowed to apply their tools to the total organization.

Neither of these things will happen unless public executives know how to anticipate the effects of technological change and organize scientists into research-and-development teams. To anticipate the effects of technology, the executives must be prepared to perform three functions. First, public executives must be able to *forecast* the technological discoveries that will affect the success or failure of their programs. Forecasting techniques include *demand assessment* (which presumes that technology is created by demands in the society for food, fuel, and other commodities); *theoretical-limits tests* (to push a new invention or phenomenon, such as the laser, to its theoretical limits and visualize its uses); *parameter analysis* (which tries to show that the future price of present systems will rise past the probable costs and limitations of new systems and make the new ones a bargain); *scientific surveys* (to project new trends into the future to see where the lines of discovery cross); and *competitors' actions* (what the Russians will invent next).

Second, public executives must be able to *assess* the second-and third-order impact of technologies that are used in the course of government operations. The goal is to reduce suboptimalization, which means doing one thing well at the expense of everything else. Technology assessment got a big boost when Rachel Carson discovered that agricultural pesticides killed birds as well as bugs. But not all secondary effects of technology are damaging; it just seems that way.

Third, public executives must learn how to borrow or *transfer* technologies. Technology transfer allows scientific progress in one area to be transferred to another sector wherever relevant. Military and space programs have been particularly adept at transferring technology. Cynics, however, point to the $10 billion frying pan, Teflon, which was developed by aeronautical scientists to protect reentry vehicles. In fact, there has been considerable technological spin-off in areas including computer systems, miniaturization, and management techniques.

None of these functions will work very well unless scientists are organized into research-and-development units within the organization. The study of R & D management began during World War II, shortly after the publication of the traditional *Papers on the Science of Administration*. R & D management begins with the axiom that the traditional principles of administration proclaimed in the *Papers* will be a flop in an agency stocked with scientists and engineers, since these people do their best work in a managerial vacuum. Since the top executives generally are unwilling to forgo all managerial controls, a compromise is struck that might be called creativity engineering. It is a contradiction in terms, but no more so than the contradictions inherent in R & D management.

For example, R & D managers will see the need to centralize administrative functions in order to free scientists and engineers from the dirge of routine work which always seems to triumph over the time available for creativity. The executives thus acquire a great deal of administrative power, but if they exercise it—by writing categorical job descriptions, setting up permanent bureaus, establishing some sort of hierarchy, or otherwise routinizing operations within the R & D shop—they are likely to snuff out that creativity. The resulting style of supervision can be best characterized as collegial. R & D managers are not gang bosses, although they may wish at times they were.

Despite the R & D dictum that no management is good management, the R & D executive has to show results: a product worth the investment of resources. This requires some sort of planning-and-control system to establish goals and monitor the work of the experts, at least for the development half of the R & D equation. The goals are generally stated as program objectives and the work of the experts monitored through project teams. The emphasis upon program objectives has a dual advantage: it focuses on results, yet it does not lead to a managerial system that interferes with creative flexibility.

In order to establish program objectives, top executives must calculate whether the investment in any R & D program is worth the potential benefits. They also have to control costs on programs already underway. Although it is difficult to predict costs and benefits when no one has ever seen the final product, rough estimates can be made on the basis of previous experience. Simultaneously, R & D programs are expected to invest money in "spin-offs" which lead to practical applications of their work. The American space program suffered budget cuts largely because it could not convincingly demonstrate applications of space technology.

Then there is the awful issue of trust and secrecy. R & D executives claim that scientists and engineers produce better results when their work is compartmentalized and security is maintained. Scientists, on the other hand, argue that technological breakthroughs require open communications, especially between scientists from different nations. This view irritates R & D executives, who want to maintain a monopoly on technological progress. The rule for R & D projects, in both government and industry, has been one of closed inquiry rather than open communications.

The most important organizational innovation to come out of the research-and-development field is program management. Like other R & D innovations, the program management craze is spreading outside of the R & D framework to a variety of public agencies.

PROGRAM MANAGEMENT

The impact of technology, the application of systems analysis, and the growth of large-scale organization have combined to create demands for new methods of management. Managers need to integrate the old functions of administration, such as planning and budgeting, into new centers of ability by using the systems approach to accomplish a specific mission within a fixed period of time. The resulting organizational style is program management, also known as project management, systems management, or matrix management.

James E. Webb, administrator of the National Aeronautics and Space Administration during the Mercury-Gemini period, is a leading advocate of program management. In his view, conventional organizational forms are too inflexible for space exploration. They cannot adjust to rapidly changing technology and they cannot contend with the intangibles inherent in NASA's mission. Conventional management is also alien to the large number of scientists and professionals working in NASA, persons accustomed to a great deal of independence on the job. Recognizing that neither machines nor techniques will solve these management problems, Webb concludes

255

that constant reorganization is the key to creating a new organization that can respond to a turbulent environment without sacrificing the space mission or the time schedule for accomplishing it. At the same time, Webb recognizes the need for a conventional organization to perform special support functions: engineering, budgeting and program analysis, purchasing and contracting, quality control, administration and public affairs.

To solve these problems, NASA officials hired one hundred project and program managers. Webb placed them at strategic points throughout NASA's functional organization and its nine centers in the field.

Webb sent one program manager, George Low, to Houston and made him "responsible for over-all planning, coordination, and direction of all aspects of the Apollo spacecraft program through the supervision of industrial contractors and other elements of NASA which are assigned parts of the project."[13] Low became a focal point for the NASA-wide mission of sending at least one man to the moon and bringing him back by New Year's Eve, 1969.

Many of the persons working on the moon program reported directly to Low as head of the Apollo program office—the control

George Low (standing, left), manager of the Apollo spacecraft program, listens in as technicians at Cape Kennedy prepare to launch Apollo X. The success of the spacecraft program depended upon people over whom Low had no formal control—including the officials in charge of launching the spacecraft (seated at the consoles), the overall program director from Washington, D.C. (standing, middle), and the chief spokesman for the astronauts (standing, right). Program management is one of the most important innovations to emerge from management science. COURTESY OF NASA.

CHAPTER 7: MANAGEMENT SCIENCE

officers who ran the PERT charts and tested the spacecraft, and the project managers who prepared the spiderlike LEM for the lunar landing and made sure that the astronaut's suits, medical kits, maps, and Tang were on board. Altogether, Low directly supervised twenty subsystems and five division chiefs.

The success of Low's mission, however, really depended upon his ability to coordinate the work of his program office with people over whom he had no formal control. First of all, Low's program office did not design the spacecraft. That had been done by the venerable Maxime Faget, Director of Engineering and Development at the Houston center. The astronauts who would have to fly the spacecraft were in a separate office under the direction of Donald Slayton. The technicians who would oversee the flight of the spacecraft from the mission-control center were under the flight operations office. Beyond that, there were the scientists who prepared the lunar experiments, physicians in charge of survival in space, as well as the other program managers for the Mercury, Gemini, and Skylab programs.

That was just at Houston. At Cape Kennedy, the spacecraft would be in the hands of other technicians and executives. Operations at the Kennedy Space Center were designed in the form of what is called a matrix organization—technicians and administrators in permanent departments providing routine services while being coordinated by launch managers who stood outside of the organizational pyramid.

In addition, Low had to integrate the development of the spacecraft with the program managers and office directors in Huntsville, Alabama, who were building and testing the rockets. He had to remember to report to the directors of Manned Space Flight. There were two—one in Houston and one in Washington. And he had to work closely with the Apollo program director in Washington, D.C., whose job it was to oversee the program from the headquarters' point of view and make certain that Low had all the money and support he needed to meet his goal.

To a traditional O & M specialist, these organizational relationships look like the wiring diagram for a Japanese computer. They look confusing because traditionalists have been conditioned to look for formal lines of authority and official divisions of responsibility. In the Apollo program, those lines of authority were not as important as the fact that Low and all of the other officials were working on the same objective and that the spacecraft—which Low was developing—was the primary means of accomplishing that objective.

From George Low's point of view, it was relatively easy to get the support he needed from people over whom he had no formal control. He got the support he needed because he enjoyed four advantages. First, he had the advantage of perspective. Because he had responsibility for a total system, he saw how each piece fit together. Second, he had the advantage of urgency. His program had a deadline and an objective that would show visible results. If someone failed to do his or her job, that too was extraordinarily visible, as when the *Apollo 13*

257

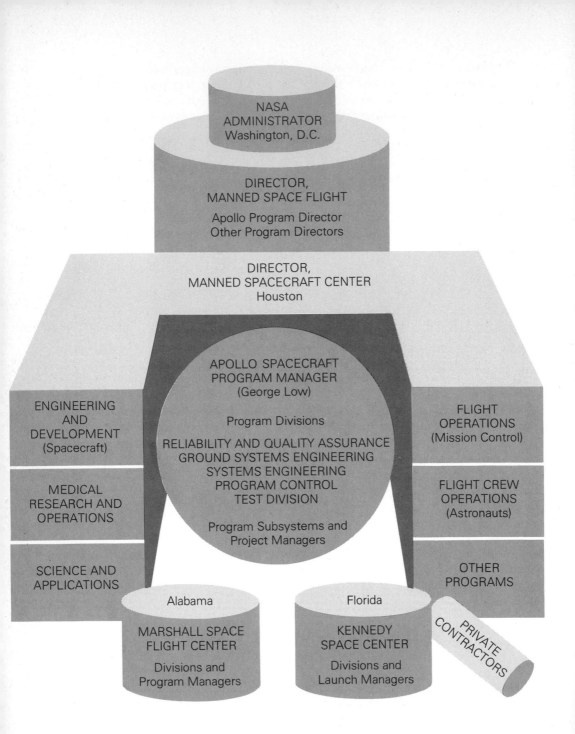

NASA
ADMINISTRATOR
Washington, D.C.

DIRECTOR,
MANNED SPACE FLIGHT

Apollo Program Director
Other Program Directors

DIRECTOR,
MANNED SPACECRAFT CENTER
Houston

APOLLO SPACECRAFT
PROGRAM MANAGER
(George Low)

Program Divisions

RELIABILITY AND QUALITY ASSURANCE
GROUND SYSTEMS ENGINEERING
SYSTEMS ENGINEERING
PROGRAM CONTROL
TEST DIVISION

Program Subsystems and
Project Managers

ENGINEERING
AND
DEVELOPMENT
(Spacecraft)

MEDICAL
RESEARCH AND
OPERATIONS

SCIENCE AND
APPLICATIONS

FLIGHT
OPERATIONS
(Mission Control)

FLIGHT CREW
OPERATIONS
(Astronauts)

OTHER
PROGRAMS

Alabama

MARSHALL SPACE
FLIGHT CENTER

Divisions and
Program Managers

Florida

KENNEDY
SPACE CENTER

Divisions and
Launch Managers

PRIVATE
CONTRACTORS

Under program management, a single administrator is responsible for a specific mission that has a beginning and an end, and must coordinate all of the activities necessary to accomplish that mission, including those which cut across functional or organizational boundaries. To accomplish the objectives of the Apollo spacecraft program, the Apollo program manager had to supervise activities in his own program office while coordinating the work of other administrators at Houston; Cape Kennedy; Huntsville, Alabama; and Washington, D.C.

service module blew up between the earth and the moon. Third, the power of the program manager was temporary. People in other offices were less reluctant to go along with the program manager because they knew that it was nothing permanent. After they made their contribution, they could get back to the work on their own desks. Fourth, the program managers were carefully selected, as were the other NASA employees. They were recruited on the basis of their talents to manage through persuasion, to lead through ability, and to coordinate the work of specialists from diverse fields. They were recruited because they could cooperate.

The power of these advantages are most apparent in the organization that uses the matrix form of project management. For a variety of reasons, the organization has to retain large, functionally organized departments staffed with highly specialized employees who provide basically the same uninterrupted services day after day. At the same time, the organization has to show results on some very specific priority programs. So the executive hires a few project managers and puts them off to the side. The project managers are given only a small staff and must depend upon the functional departments for their resources. The departments in the matrix provide the skilled employees, who may work on many projects at one time. The project managers become the focal point for scheduling, planning and engineering, cost control, performance control, and contracting. The Kennedy Space Flight Center, which treats every launch as a project in an organizational matrix, is run this way. So are many other organizations which may have from a handful to several hundred projects, each with its own project manager drawing upon the permanent departments.

The setup for Apollo fell at the other end of the program management spectrum. The Apollo spacecraft program manager had to coordinate large numbers of outsiders; at the same time, many people were hired into his own program office. This model, called program management, works best in an organization that has a few big, complex missions. NASA's Office of Manned Space Flight appointed program managers for Mercury, Gemini, Apollo, Skylab, earth resources, the space shuttle program, the joint space mission with the USSR, and the unmanned Viking flights to Mars. As each program was completed, the program employees moved into another program, to a functional office, or to a new job in another organization.

Substantively, there is little difference between a project manager in a matrix organization and a program manager in an organization like NASA. Concentrating on the project and its problems, both act as the focal point for the mobilization of resources to accomplish a specific objective. Both force functional specialists to funnel their work through the project and its objectives. And both are single individuals who have the perspective to integrate the resources of the organization into a dynamic system that can master the totality of the job that needs to be done.

As science and technology become more central to public administration, public agencies are likely to take on more of the characteristics of research-and-development organizations. Thirty years ago one rarely found techniques like program management practiced outside of government research laboratories. Today, what was once pronounced as favorable for managing scientists is now advocated as essential for all public agencies that feel the pinch of technological change. This, with the advent of computers, automation, and management science techniques, is radically changing the shape of modern public administration.

SIMON'S UTOPIA AND THE ALCHEMIST

The computer is the symbol of management science. It processes the information that managers need to make decisions scientifically, it forecasts the race toward automation that makes human skills obsolete, and it foreshadows the rise of new forms of organization and new styles of supervision. Herbert Simon has announced that "the computer and the new decision-making techniques associated with it are bringing changes in white-collar, executive, and professional work as momentous as those the introduction of machinery has brought to manual jobs."[14]

Computers are used for process control, regulating the operation of sewage treatment plants and traffic lights. They are used in direct support of operations—in welfare agencies, for example, where the computer checks the eligibility of the applicant and calculates the amount of the award. Computers reduce paper work by preparing tax bills and payroll checks; they speed up the design of roads and bridges by performing complex engineering calculations; they manipulate the massive amounts of data necessary to plan parks, transit systems, or the location of new schools; they can even analyze the budget by breaking down the per-unit cost of operations. Computers order inventories, run railroads, track hurricanes, calculate public opinion, and launch spacecraft. There is no serious doubt about the capacity of computers to perform these functions. Once a public agency has established a routine process for handling a repetitive task, it is a simple matter, given modern technology, to instruct a computer instead of a human to perform it. The difference between a computer linked to a cash register reordering inventories and a computer program linked to a spacecraft that controls launches is merely a matter of complexity.

Simon is not only talking about computers that perform these functions, he is talking about computers that can think, computers that can innovate, computers that can behave like managers. Simon believes that computers can be programmed to do strategic planning, far beyond the rules of routine. Computers, he says, can be taught to solve novel, ill-structured problems.

In solving problems, human thinking is governed by programs that organize myriads of simple information processes—or symbol manipulat-

260

ing processes if you like—into orderly, complex sequences that are responsive to and adaptive to the task environment and the clues that are extracted from that environment as the sequences unfold. Programs of the same kind can be written for computers.[15]

Social scientists describe this thought process as *heuristic*. There is a pattern to heuristic decision making, akin to cybernetics, in which executives scan their past experience in a search for new solutions. This is the arena in which intuition, judgment, and rules of thumb currently hold sway.

How does one set up a computer to solve heuristic problems? In essence, the programmer places large amounts of information on-line under the control of the central processing unit at all times. In theory, every management decision is put in the computer memory bank so that it is always available. When a new problem arises, the programmer instructs the computer to scan its past experience, within certain parameters. The computer then puts bits of old decisions together into a new formula for success. A simple example is the computer that plays chess. It remembers every game it ever played, every move it ever made and the consequences. It is programmed not to repeat errors that led to previous defeats, but always to make the optimal move.

The application of computer technology to heuristic decisions, Simon claims, will revolutionize organizational decision making. In

Transit officials in Oakland, California, monitor the operation of the Bay Area Rapid Transit System, which is completely automated. The computer even controls the brakes of the trains. Computer-age technology has had an enormous impact on public administration, restructuring the shape of agencies and encouraging the use of scientific decision-making techniques. COURTESY OF THE BAY AREA RAPID TRANSIT SYSTEM.

essence, it will mean an end to intuition. Intuition will join the other methods of decision making that humans have discarded as they have climbed the technological ladder—fatalism, superstition, religious authority, deductive reasoning, and common sense. The computer revolution will change the method of human thought just as surely as the invention of the printing press accelerated linear thinking and the invention of telecommunications created a village of the world. Persons who think that computers are too dumb to think, say the futurists, are like the citizens of Rome who, believing that slaves lacked the capacity for independent thought, were surprised when the gladiators revolted.

Of course, the predictions could be wrong. Alchemists served the rulers of medieval society for several hundred years after some initial success in recovering quicksilver from what appeared to be dirt. They maintained their special position as advisers to the ruling class by announcing annually that they were on the verge of a breakthrough that would distill gold from lead. One of the first heuristically programmed computers, programmed to play chess, was beaten soundly by an eleven-year-old novice.

Worse than failure may be the image of computer success: a machine at the hub of an organization supervising the work of ten thousand clerks. The scientifically created organization resembles a bicycle wheel. At the center is an information-processing computer with lines of communications like spokes on a wheel radiating out to local offices on the rim of the organization. Computers are not limited by the principle of span of control. They can process information and coordinate ten thousand employees as efficiently as an old-line manager could supervise twelve. The image is not a hypothetical one. Airlines, commercial lending institutions, police, welfare bureaus, employment offices, and government purchasing agencies have already begun to eliminate the hierarchy of field offices made obsolete by the computer.

Will computer control result in greater centralization of authority? The pessimists point to organizations where the introduction of the computer resulted in more managerial authority at the top, where unskilled employees were laid off and the responsibilities of the remaining personnel were reduced and standardized. The theory proclaiming imminent centralization runs as follows.

In the past, large organizations were fairly decentralized because people at the top really never had the time, information, or skill to closely monitor the work of subordinates. Field units were relatively autonomous so long as central control proved inefficient. In other words, the will to centralize existed, but the technology of control did not. Enter the computer. The computer gives the executives at the top the ability to continuously evaluate—or spy upon, depending upon one's point of view—the work of employees in the field. Given such information, the pessimists say, the top executives will be unable to resist the temptation to become totally involved in day-to-day operating decisions.

CHAPTER 7: MANAGEMENT SCIENCE

The optimists begin with exactly the opposite assumption. They insist that managers have traditionally poked into subordinates' affairs because the managers could never devise an effective monitoring system. The computer, with its amazing information-processing capacity, solves this problem. Once the managers at the top are confident that they can effectively monitor performance, they will delegate authority to lower managers, who will be instructed to use any means necessary to accomplish general goals within the constraints of time and money. This is the concept of the cybernetic trigger. Employees are freed from supervision so long as they produce results within predetermined perimeters. Executive intervention is "triggered" by the information system only when the perimeters are crossed. The cybernetic trigger has an added advantage—it frees top executives to work on more creative tasks: strategic planning, defining the mission of the organization, building political support, and helping out subordinates when they have problems. The optimists argue that this is what the executives wanted to do all along.

Underlying the realization that computer technology is changing the shape of public administration is a general sense of concern for the impact that this will have on the supervision of employees. This concern triggered a debate between Herbert Simon and Chris Argyris in the pages of the *Public Administration Review*. It all began when Argyris, a leading human relations specialist, accused Simon of fomenting a rational-man theory, which would lead to more hierarchical, less humane organizations. Management science, said Argyris, is not really different from Frederick Taylor's old time-and-motion studies; both produce an intolerable tendency toward centralization of authority. "In Simon's organizations," said Argyris, "it is management that defines the objectives and the tasks, management that gives the orders . . . it is management that rewards and penalizes."[16]

Simon replied that Argyris suffered from a pre-occupation with power. This is common, said Simon, among those associated with student unrest on campus. They tend to acquire an image of "them," the managers, driven by a paramount need for power, forcing their view of the world on students and workers, all alienated, all frustrated, all cut off from the joys of affiliation and self-actualization. This is a false image, said Simon, unsupported by an empirical evidence. "One wonders how the companies [Argyris] describes stay in business. . . . In the world that I observe, there is much less need for power, and consequently much less alienation than in Argyris' world. I see a social system making use of hierarchical organizations to reach a high level of productivity and to produce a large quantity of freedom."[17] Simon accused Argyris of being against any kind of structure at all.

"I am not against structure," Argyris replied, but one must recognize "that formal structure inhibits people's energy for commitment and initiative. . . . It is the design and administration of organizations that do not encourage the discussion of emotions and emotionally loaded substantive issues that is the shackle."[18] He accused the management scientists of ignoring human problems, of ignoring the people who fought management information systems because the computers reduced their ability to use intuition, or the employees who demanded more freedom from the mechanisms of organizational control. "There is precious little in the work of rational-man theorists to overcome [these] problems."[19]

"Argyris paints a romantic picture of man," said Simon, "an inexhaustibly creative creature who only needs to be given a blank wall of infinite size in order to paint on it an unimaginably beautiful picture. Unlimited freedom is not the best condition for human creativity. Gothic cathedrals were created not out of unlimited freedom, but out of the stern physical constraints imposed by gravity acting upon masonry walls, and the equally severe social constraints of the Catholic liturgy."[20]

A static society, not creativity, would be the legacy of the rational-man theorists, said Argyris. Management scientists "make change in organizations seem hopeless," they unintentionally support the powers-that-be, and their generalizations "tend to become coercive of human behavior."[21]

Simon replied that Argyris's argument was just part of "the general antirationalism of the contemporary counter-culture. . . . Nothing in human history suggests that we can save mankind by halting descriptive research on the rational aspects of human behavior."[22]

Fears about the control of technology are not all antirational ignorance. Technological progress is ruthless. It demands that people change their lives, begin new careers, adopt new attitudes, and change their methods of supervision. Quite often the employees affected by change are left out of the planning process—for the obvious reason that if they were included they would sabotage the change. It is extraordinarily difficult to balance the right to one's own private behavior against the demands for organizational adaptation.

Such a balance is made more difficult by the tendency of management scientists to view the world as a machine. Management scientists often assume that controversies over goals and values are less important than controversies over operations and fashion their techniques of analysis to control the latter. From this perspective, management science owes a great legacy to Frederick Taylor, who believed that he could make work more efficient with his stopwatch and time-and-motion charts. Taylor's fault was that he treated employees like machines—to him the worker named Schmidt was nothing more than a human forklift with a tendency toward fatigue. Cybernetics resurrects the engineer's view of humanity, with its stress on the analogy between complex machines and the human brain.

The debate between Simon and Argyris really resolves itself into a question of human motivation. Any government can plug in a computer. But how will people adjust to it? Will people have the adaptive capacity to accept responsibility, to innovate, to cooperate, to change? Or will they become captives of the technology they seek to manage? Argyris and his colleagues are searching for new theories of organization development which would assure that technology serve human values, rather than making employees serve the technology necessary to maintain an auspicious level of personal consumption. That is why Argyris ends the debate with a plea for "much more research . . . to integrate the two views [and encourage] the bridging that must occur."[23]

The bridging has begun. Administrative scientists have recognized the human element in management science. The systems approach, after all, insists that managers take *all* aspects of their task into consideration, and human beings are certainly one big aspect of any task. Not by coincidence, in 1962, management scientists and behavioral scientists held two separate conventions in Pittsburgh, Pennsylvania, the same week, in adjacent hotels. They exchanged papers and ideas. Behavioral scientists interested in human motivation talked to management scientists skilled in information technology. Both groups were interested in the new styles of supervision required by management science, and the proceedings of both conventions were printed in a single volume.[24] After that, every important text in management science has been concerned with both the behavioral and the technological aspects of management science.

FOR FURTHER READING

The best overview of management science is still the textbook by Richard A. Johnson, Fremont E. Kast, and James E. Rosenzweig, *The Theory and Management of Systems*, 3rd ed. (New York: McGraw-Hill Book Co., 1973). The underlying theory of management science, cybernetics, is developed in Norbert Weiner, *The Human Use of Human Beings* (Boston: Houghton Mifflin Co., 1956). Robert N. Anthony presents the basic framework for applying management science to modern organizations in *Planning and Control Systems: A Framework for Analysis*.

At this point, the student should be ready to look at more detailed explanations of the systems approach and operations research. C. West Churchman has written two popular introductions, *The Systems Approach* (New York: Delta Publishing Co., 1968) and, with Russell L. Ackoff and E. Leonard Arnoff, *Introduction to Operations Research* (New York: John Wiley & Sons, 1957). A management science text that merges mathematical lessons with general theory is David W. Miller and Martin Starr, *Executive Decisions and Operations Research* (Englewood Cliffs, N.J.: Prentice-Hall, 1960). One of the few books to concentrate on management science in government agencies is by Alvin W. Drake, Ralph L. Keeney, and Philip M. Morse, eds., *Analysis of Public Systems* (Cambridge, Mass.: MIT Press, 1972).

One of the best ways to keep up with development in management science is to study the applications as they appear in the journal *Operations Research*. The best way to learn about simulations is to study an actual one; the most popular is described in Donella

Meadows et. al., *The Limits to Growth* (New Hyde Park, N.Y.: Universe Books, 1972). The theory underlying network planning can be found in Eliot D. Chapple and Leonard R. Sayles, *The Measurement of Management* (New York: Macmillan Co., 1961). David I. Cleland and William R. King explain how to integrate these techniques into an operational program in *Systems Analysis and Project Management* (New York: McGraw-Hill Book Co., 1968). Fremont Kast and James Rosenzweig present a useful set of papers on the general problems of research-and-development management in *Science and Technology and Management* (New York: McGraw-Hill Book Co., 1963). The use of computer systems underlies the entire management science approach. A good overview of the computer element is Donald S. Sanders's book of readings, *Computers and Management* (New York: McGraw-Hill Book Co., 1970). Herbert A. Simon speculates on the impact of computers on the administrative process in *The Shape of Automation for Men and Management* (New York: Harper & Row, 1965).

ORGANIZATION DEVELOPMENT

8

Thirty years ago scholars began to worry out loud about the "remarkable growth in the number, size, and power of organizations of many kinds, ranging through all areas of life."[1] Kenneth Boulding called it an organizational revolution—a complete overhaul of the established system, resulting in the flow of power to giant economic and governmental organizations. It was no longer possible, Boulding said, to talk of individual choice or personal ethics. Society was governed by organizational decisions and organizational morality.

To a number of writers, this "organizational revolution" appears to have resolved itself into two distinct epochs. The first epoch, spurred by the growth of industrialism and the rise of nationalism, saw the development of bureaucracy from a position of neglect to one of vast power. The expanding bureaucracies were designed to produce utilitarian goods and services without interruption and, as the sociologists observed, to ignore their errors.

The second epoch is largely a product of the interplay between bureaucracy and technology. Bureaucracies form the organizational base for the beginning stages of technological development; it is difficult to imagine the railroads, for example, being run along the principles of a feudal organization. However, as the level of technology becomes more complex, bureaucracies become less and less useful. Bureaucracies are not flexible enough to handle complex problems in the face of rapid technological change. Bureaucratic societies that have achieved a high degree of technological sophistication stand at the gateway of the second epoch, an epoch which many feel will be marked by new forms of organization and new styles of supervision.

Organization development has sprung up as a movement to help organizations and the individuals in them become more comfortable with the need for flexibility and change. Warren Bennis defines organization development as "a complex education strategy intended to change the beliefs, attitudes, values, and structure of organizations so that they can better adapt to new technologies, markets, and challenges, and the dizzying rate of change itself."[2] Most OD advocates are strongly antibureaucratic and want to replace this traditional form of organization with a new, postbureaucratic society. They are also driven by a personal desire to make life at work more humane for the individual employee than it has been under the bureaucratic state.

ADJUSTING TO POSTBUREAUCRATIC ADMINISTRATION

Only 150 years ago most individuals spent their lives in rural communities free from the presence of complex organizations. A few small, relatively weak organizations existed: armies, trading companies, and a few primitive bureaus. For most people, the family, the village, and the church remained the dominant institutions in their lives.

The earliest paintings from the industrial revolution reflect the amount of pain in the transition to organizational life. Farm life was portrayed as idyllic, without the mud and flies. Factories were painted as an inferno where flame and smoke alternately lighted and shaded human cells. The literature of industrialization, from Dickens to Zola, describes a hopeless contest between the spirit of individualism and corporate necessity. Embedded upon the consciousness of persons of reason was a common fear: that the individual was becoming a cipher in an impersonal rabbit-warren bureaucracy. Those fears are most completely documented by William H. Whyte in *The Organization Man*.

Whyte attacks what he calls the social ethic—the principle that people leave their families, their personalities, and their creativity to take the vows of organizational obedience. People who uphold the social ethic are "the mind and soul of our great self-perpetuating institutions."[3] Few will ever become top executives, but all are motivated by the desire to succeed and receive approval. The organization rewards them by satisfying their transient material desires, a form of impulsive greed that gives rise to what David Riesman has called the lonely crowd. At the same time, the organization immobilizes its people, since the only marketable skill they are allowed to develop in return for their economic security is loyalty. Their lives at work degenerate into meaningless routine and the eternal staff meeting. They are trained by the organization to avoid face-to-face relations, to fear punishment by higher authority, and to avoid risks or innovations. Above all, says Whyte, their lives become subordinate to the Good of the Cause, the preservation of the organization so that it might fulfill the purpose of its creator, now deceased, whose portrait hangs on the wall.

The "organization man" thesis, which dominates literary predictions of the future by authors such as Orwell, Huxley, and Burgess, has achieved the status of a self-fulfilling prophecy. Yet according to futurists and administrators, it is a dying system that will be left in the wake of the second epoch of the organizational revolution.

269

The leading futurist in the organization development field is Warren Bennis. According to Bennis, bureaucracy has served its purpose—to provide civilization with a great social machine for reorganizing rural life into industrial society. Bureaucracies are highly efficient organizations for mobilizing thousands of people into routine tasks: fighting trench wars, building Model-T Fords, licensing automobile drivers, distributing agricultural products. They thrive on the sort of institutional planning that can develop only where organizations are allowed to pursue fixed goals within a relatively stable environment. When rapid change erases that stability, the bureaucratic form loses its utility.

Bennis traces the roots of the new organizational revolution to rapid technological and social change. Rapid change brings down the ladder of authority, impeding bureaucrats who wish to subject each new problem to the organizational routine. When things change rapidly, decisions must be made at the point in the organization where information and technical competence meet, regardless of the consequences for the rule of authority. The man-in-a-slot organization crumbles. A leading futurist, Alvin Toffler, observes:

> It is not surprising to find that wherever organizations today are caught up in the stream of technological or social change, wherever research and development is important, wherever men must cope with first-time problems, the decline of bureaucratic forms is most pronounced.[4]

Organizations that use technology to cope with change require better-educated employees to manage the new systems. Better-educated employees are different from ordinary employees in many ways. They join professions, are mobile, and are more freethinking and vocal. Since their loyalties to the organization are compromised

Warren Bennis was a professor of psychology and business administration at the Massachusetts Institute of Technology when he first proclaimed his "end to bureaucracy" thesis. He later became president of the University of Cincinnati. Bennis predicted that bureaucracies would give way to flat, temporary organizations with democratic styles of supervision and a system of responsibility based on ability rather than authority. COURTESY OF THE UNIVERSITY OF CINCINNATI.

by their loyalty to professional standards, they are less likely to find themselves trapped within the organization. From the new navy to the modern factory, organizational leaders can no longer expect the obedience of employees that is necessary for the maintenance of bureaucratic life.

What will the postbureaucratic organization look like? Probably it will be very similar to the research-and-development organizations described in Chapter 7. It will be flat, which is to say nonhierarchical. It will be temporary, which means that the most important organizational structure will be the team brought together to solve a special problem. Ability will replace formal authority as the basis of power—ability based primarily upon professional knowledge. The style of supervision will be democratic. Says Bennis, "democracy becomes a functional necessity whenever a social system is competing under conditions of chronic change."[5] He defines organizational democracy as a system of open communications, candid confrontations, and decision making by consensus, where ability outweighs authority. Bennis believes that organizational leaders will adopt this kind of system not because it is more humane, but because they have to in order to insure the survival of their organization in a dynamic environment.

Who will replace the old bureaucrat? Scholars believe that the new administrator must be self-motivating, innovative, capable of exercising self-direction, mobile, comfortable with constant reorganization, and skilled at working in temporary groups. The new administrator will possess internalized standards of excellence, founded in professional values and personal ethics, and will be motivated by the challenge of work itself rather than wage slavery. The death of bureaucracy will bring greater job freedom and responsibility to the individual in the modern organization.

The death of bureaucracy, nonetheless, is not inevitable. There is a very real alternative to the optimism of Bennis and Toffler: the nightmare of Orwell, Huxley, and Burgess. The inevitable technological change that may rid civilizations of bureaucracies might instead give the bureaucrats the tools they need to survive. In countries with no real history of administrative tolerance, where executives view individual creativity as an excess of organizational permissiveness, technology might be used to centralize control and to monitor behavior. In the past, bureaucracies were too inefficient to detect and discourage deviance. Technology can erase that inefficiency.

The transition from bureaucratic to postbureaucratic society will be difficult. To understand how difficult, recall the trauma of the first epoch of the organizational revolution. The lives of the peasants who abandoned their farms to work in the factories were set to the rhythm of the growing seasons and the rising of the sun. They had to adjust to the routine of the factory, dominated as it was by the standardized work week, the straw boss, and the time clock. The industries acted as agents of transition, spreading the Algier myth and the Protestant ethic, and training the workers. (One company used textbooks praising the joys of neatness and punctuality to teach its Polish immigrants how to read English.) Government helped with its public schools, holding out the promise that hard work would at least make life better for one's children, while the city and the labor union helped by creating some sense of community among displaced workers.

And what of the modern managers and employees confronting the new pressures for change? Will they, in Eric Fromm's words, attempt to "escape from freedom"? Despite the fact that life in a society of adhocracies seems to be healthier than the old organizational routine, persons do not readily adapt to the new organizational freedom. Empirical studies reveal that many people prefer to be directed. Managers who derive their ethics and values from the bureaucratic era are uncomfortable with the push toward more democratic styles of supervision in postindustrial society. Perhaps the managers are paralyzed by their need to control others. Perhaps, faced with the prospect of a new organizational revolution, they suffer what Toffler calls future shock. Toffler suggests that people cannot endure constant reorganization, temporary work assignments, and physical mobility without some personal stability zone in their lives, some enclave of permanence and stability.

Organization development is popular because it associates itself with the agents of change. Most OD specialists are too cautious to promise a full-blown postbureaucratic civilization through OD, although one occasionally hears someone hope that OD "can act as a force to loosen the pervasive grip of the concept of industrial rationality which underlies our society."[6]

The message underlying OD is fairly simple. If people can be taught to be indifferent and accept organizational routine, then they can be taught to be flexible and creative. It is simply a matter of unfreezing old habits, learning new behaviors, refreezing them, and creating the sort of climate within the organization that keeps people from slipping back into the old bureaucratic mold. Inevitably, this sort of change must be created by the organization itself. Along the way, OD specialists have some theories and techniques that may help the organization respond to the need for behavioral change.

THE INDIVIDUAL AND THE ORGANIZATION

The old behavioral theories discussed in Chapter 2 were quite deterministic, viewing the individual as a static product of role expectations, patterned behavior, and the need for organizational equilibrium. The new behavioral scientists, whose theories underly organization development, reject this deterministic view. They have created a theory of the individual in the organization which promises change and adaptation. Abraham Maslow, Chris Argyris, and Douglas McGregor are the behavioral scientists whose theories are most widely accepted.

Maslow begins with the elementary problem of human motivation, the same problem that had prompted the earliest experiments in human relations fifty years earlier. Managers continually try to discover what drives people, why some people are lazy while others strive to do their best.

Maslow opens by explaining that every human has the same needs. These needs are instinctive, products of the human situation. His denial that motivation is wholly a carrot-and-stick affair places him at odds with B. F. Skinner, who sees humans totally as products of their particular environment. If each human is wholly a product of external stimuli, then motivation can be controlled by the person who controls the rewards and punishments. Maslow, in contrast to Skinner, believes that human motivation arises from certain driving needs common to all persons.

If every human has the same needs, then why, executives ask, does motivation vary so greatly among different individuals? Partly because, Maslow replies, the driving needs are arranged within the human psyche as a hierarchy. Because different individuals are at different stages in their own hierarchy of needs, their motivations appear to be different.

Maslow identifies five primary needs within the hierarchy. At the lowest level are physiological needs, which motivate humans to seek food and rest and shelter. At the second level are the safety needs, which include the need for emotional security as well as for physical safety. Humans encounter the first social needs at the third level—the need to be loved, to give love, and to feel oneself part of a group. Maslow calls the third level the belongingness and love need. Beyond this, at the fourth level, is the need for esteem—for a feeling of personal worth and to have others recognize it by granting status, respect, and admiration. At the fifth level is the need for self-actualization. Maslow characterizes the self-actualized person as one who has an exceptional ability to perceive reality, who accepts givens, is spontaneous, problem centered, and has a need for privacy. Arrival at the need for self-actualization is the hallmark of the healthy individual.

It is necessary, Maslow says, to satisfy the lower needs before moving up the hierarchy to a higher need. He calls the first four needs deficit needs, because one leaves them behind as part of one's personal development. Satisfy the need for safety and food and one is driven to seek love and companionship. When the drive for love is fulfilled, the individual begins to seek out esteem.

Only the fifth need—self-actualization—is a permanent need, in the sense that one does not graduate to a higher need but continues to be motivated to satisfy this one. Maslow calls it a growth need. He believes that it is present in every normal person, waiting for the deficit needs to be fulfilled before its latent drives begin to appear.

What is the relevance of this hierarchy of needs to public administration? That answer was provided by Chris Argyris in 1958 when he decided to test human progress towards self-actualization against conditions in modern organizations. After contrasting behavioral theory with organizational practice, he concluded that "there is a lack of congruency between the needs of healthy individuals and the demands of the formal organization."[7] Organizations demand that workers be submissive, have a short-term perspective, develop a few simple unchallenging skills and relinquish control over the pace of their work to superiors. These demands have the effect of shunting off personal growth, halting it at one of the lower needs.

Argyris relates the story of a knitting factory in upstate New York that contracted with the Rome Institution for Mentally Defective Girls to employ over sixty women whose mental ages ranged from six to ten years. They turned out to be ideal workers. Managers praised them for being punctual, holding down absenteeism, not indulging in gossip, and setting a regular rate of production. When faced with slack production periods, the company would lay off proportionately more regular workers than mentally defective women.

In short, Argyris is saying that most organizations tend to create conditions under which workers must halt their progress up the hierarchy of needs. Individuals, in response, spend their energy constructing elaborate psychological defenses against the abnormal organizational demands. Individuals respond in four ways, says Argyris. They become apathetic and disinterested; they exhibit excessive ambition to climb the organizational ladder; they construct special defense mechanisms, which range from rationalizations to daydreaming on the job, or they leave the organization and join the ranks of the underemployed. The work groups to which the employee belongs support these responsive styles. The groups might sanction a restricted pace of work, emphasize money and status, preserve a separation of management and labor, or encourage new workers and their children not to expect much from their chosen vocation.

Management observes such behavior and concludes that their employees are lazy, apathetic, money crazy, and make too many errors. In response, management adopts strategies that tighten central control and rely upon tough leadership methods to pressure employees to work harder. This is often accompanied, Argyris observes, with a phony human relations program that gives the appearance of involving employees in their work—the work situation which in fact is the cause of their apathy, anxiety, and stunted personal development.

The human energy necessary for personal growth is depleted by personal defense and the executive desire for control. Argyris sees this as the principal problem in modern organizations. The psychological energy that might be directed toward self-actualization and organizational change is fired instead against the organizational aims. It is wasted. It produces a vicious circle in which work conditions foster individual withdrawal and management aggravates those conditions by its attempts to reduce indifference and breed organizational loyalty.

One can generally tell whether an organization is suffering from these ills by examining the attitudes of management toward its employees. In organizations where personal development is stunted and executive control is stressed, managers are likely to embrace a set of beliefs that Douglas McGregor calls Theory X. These beliefs are as follows:

1. "The average human being has an inherent dislike of work and will avoid it if he can.

2. "Because of this human characteristic of dislike of work, most people must be coerced, controlled, directed, threatened with punishment to get them to put forth adequate effort toward the achievement of organizational objectives.

3. "The average human being prefers to be directed, wishes to avoid responsibility, has relatively little ambition, wants security above all."[8]

These beliefs are self-fulfilling. If the manager believes that the employees hate work, and treats them accordingly, then the employees will hate their work. It will not matter whether management adopts a style of supervision that is hard or permissive. Both hard and permissive management, McGregor felt, were usually built on a Theory X view of individual behavior.

McGregor made a plea for a new set of assumptions about individual behavior in organizations, which he felt would lead to the creation of conditions such that the growth of individuals could become integrated with the goals of the organization. These assumptions, which he called Theory Y, are as follows:

1. "The expenditure of physical and mental effort in work is as natural as play or rest.

2. "External control and the threat of punishment are not the only means for bringing about effort toward organizational

While a professor of industrial management at the Massachusetts Institute of Technology, Douglas McGregor framed one of the best-known theories in the behavioral sciences: that of theory X and theory Y. Theory X is the assumption that people hate work and have to be forced to do it; theory Y is the view that people will seek responsibility and exercise self-control under the proper conditions. COURTESY OF MIT.

275

objectives. Man will exercise self-direction and self-control in the service of objectives to which he is committed.

3. "Commitment to objectives is a function of the rewards associated with their achievement."(The satisfaction of ego and self-actualization needs are more significant rewards than money.)

4. "The average human being learns, under proper conditions, not only to accept but to seek responsibility.

5. "The capacity to exercise a relatively high degree of imagination, ingenuity, and creativity in the solution of organizational problems is widely, not narrowly, distributed in the population.

6. "Under conditions of modern industrial life, the intellectual potentialities of the average human being are only partially utilized."[9]

McGregor insisted that "the limits on human collaboration in the organizational setting are not the limits of human nature but of management's ingenuity in discovering how to realize the potential represented by its human resources."[10] If management would accept the assumptions of Theory Y, these too would become self-fulfilling. Employees would accept more responsibility and the managers would be motivated to search for new strategies of supervision, neither coercive nor permissive, which would allow the individual to achieve self-actualization and the organization to reach its goals.

MOTIVATION AND SUPERVISION

On a blackboard Tom Landry's [football] teams would always win, but the human element is hard for him to deal with. He tells a man exactly what to do but he forgets what motivates a man to do it. With robots he'd be undefeated.[11]

Dealing with the human element in administration is like trying to find the Holy Grail. Everyone searches for an effective system of motivation and supervision, but no one can find it. Once the new behavioral scientists had set out their basic assumptions, they went crusading for a new system of motivation and supervision. Like the earlier zealots from the human relations movement, the behavioral scientists looked for the perfect system of supervision in the small group. The scholars who took the lead were Frederick Herzberg and Rensis Likert.

Herzberg is best known for his thesis that work itself is the primary source of motivation in organization. Executives, he suggests, cannot solve basic problems of employee motivation by increasing pay and fringe benefits. These executives may expand the health plan, offer longer vacations, build in protections against arbitrary dismissal, and pipe music into elevators and offices. But dissatisfaction will not disappear.

To find out what workers really want, Herzberg and his followers

276

interviewed thousands of employees in a half-dozen nations with a remarkably simple set of questions: "what do you like most about your work? what do you dislike most about your work?" The employees in Herzberg's surveys said that they enjoyed *achievement*, the satisfaction of seeing the results of one's own work; acknowledgment by others of it, or *recognition*; the creative and challenging aspects of the *work itself*; *responsibility* for one's own work or the performance of others; *advancement* into jobs with higher responsibility and status; and opportunities for personal and career *growth*. Herzberg called these "satisfiers."

Herzberg discovered that the factors traditionally associated with human relations motivational techniques—salary, status, and fringe benefits—were consistently cited by employees as barriers to effective performance. Herzberg describes eight general facets of work which the employees most disliked about their jobs. They cited dissatisfaction with *company policy and administration* when it was screwed up; *supervision* when it was incompetent or unfair; *working conditions* when the physical environment was poor and ugly; *interpersonal relations* where two people could not get along; *salary* when expectations of an increase went unfulfilled; *status* when they did not have enough; *job security* when it was threatened; and *personal life* when the employee's family or friends were upset about some facet of the job. Herzberg called these "dissatisfiers."

The most striking result of Herzberg's studies was the fact that hardly anyone said that they loved their job because of their salary or status or job security or any of the other dissatisfiers. Borrowing a convenient analogy from Maslow's hierarchy of needs, Herzberg suggested that the "dissatisfiers" were only important as deficit needs. If they were missing, then the employees would feel cheated and dissatisfied. But their presence, Herzberg insisted, would neither make workers happy nor motivate them. It would merely spur the workers to seek achievement, recognition, responsibility, and the other satisfiers. If the executives satisfied the lower needs, then failed to respond to the higher ones, they would still find themselves supervising unmotivated employees. To executives who have spent enormous amounts of time, money, and effort in attempts to motivate workers through fringe benefits, this must seem terribly depressing.

Herzberg's prescription for making work the primary source of motivation is remarkably simple: enrich the job. This is done by expanding the responsibilities of the employee while offering rewards that reinforce his or her sense of accomplishment. It does not mean burdening an employee who already has a worthless job with more insipid tasks. Job enrichment requires the executive to reorganize the pattern of work, abolishing the assembly-line mentality, giving each employee a complete job, increasing accountability, removing controls, allowing greater job freedom, and making job reports available to the employee as well as to the supervisor. As the employees progress, new and more difficult tasks are introduced and the individuals acquire skills enabling them to become more proficient in complex tasks. All of this is designed to appeal to the six satisfiers—a change in the nature of work that stresses achievement, recognition, responsibility, advancement, and growth.

Some of the most famous experiments with job enrichment have occurred in automobile factories. To break the boredom of assembly-line work, employees would sabotage their products. They would place marbles in the side door panels of new automobiles, slash the upholstery, cut ignition wires, break keys off in the door locks. Sabotage became a challenge, a way of enriching their job. To combat this discontent, a number of factories restructured the work. At the Volvo plant in Kalmar, Sweden, the executives threw away the overhead conveyer belt and the division-of-work principle. The workers formed teams, and each team built one section of the car. Absenteeism, turnover, and discontent went down. The quality of work went up.

The behavioral sciences emphasize the importance of the work team or small group. This extends to the theory of supervision. Rensis Likert has formulated the best-known theory of group supervision, called the linking-pin concept.

In a traditional bureaucracy, hierarchy creates the system of supervision; the supervisor sends orders through the foremen to the workers. In the postbureaucratic organization, the scalar chain of command is replaced by teams; the foremen are replaced by managers or conveners. Any manager is a member of at least two teams: the management team, which includes the top supervisor, and the work team, which each manager convenes. In other words, each manager is a linking pin, linking the work of one group to the work of another.

The effectiveness of the linking pin as a manager depends not upon formal authority, but upon what Likert calls the interaction-influence principle. The work team will not respect the authority of the linking pin as a convenor unless that person interacts with the team and allows himself or herself to be influenced by the team. If the workers know that they can influence the linking pin, and sense that the linking pin can influence the management team, they will allow the linking pin to exercise more authority over them. Likewise, the amount of influence the linking pin has on the management team depends largely upon how much authority the supervisor perceives the linking pin to have on the work team.

This finely balanced system will collapse if the manager tries to exploit team members, be benevolent, or merely consult with them. Likert advocates a participative system of group supervision in which the linking pin advocates open communications, mutual trust, decision making by consensus, shared responsibility, and group goal setting. Such a system demands some rare skills in building group effectiveness and diagnosing group problems. Clearly, it requires more than a philosophic acceptance of the goodness of Theory Y and a nodding approval of job enrichment and linking pins. It requires some major changes in managerial style and organizational structure.

Here is where organization development comes in. The earliest attempts to promote organizational change through organization development aimed to help individuals interact effectively in groups. Then, the OD specialists hoped, managers would be able to mobilize their work groups and, ultimately, change the structure of the entire organization. How is this possible, especially in a government institution where everyone has grown accustomed to authority and direction?

ORGANIZATION DEVELOPMENT AND THE GROUP

One of the most famous administrative novels is John Hersey's *A Bell for Adano*. In it Hersey outlined behavioral science principles that would not become popular in public administration for another twenty years. Reviewing the novel in the *Public Administration Review*, Rowland Egger commented that "Hersey has said more that is valid for all who are honestly attempting to discharge their administrative mandates than is contained in all the pompous tomes which have so far appeared on the subject of public administration."[12]

Adano is a small town on the coast of southern Italy. During World War II, on the day that the armies land and liberate the town, Adano becomes a ward of the Allied military government command. Major Victor Joppolo of the U.S. Army, previously of the Bronx and the New York City Sanitation Department, walks through the town to the palazzo and steps into the mayor's office. His sergeant hands Joppolo the manual of procedures for civil affairs officers. It is very complex, so Joppolo sits down and begins to read. At noon he is still reading the instructions for the first day of operations. He stops reading, tears up the pages, walks out into the piazza and raises the American and British flags, then goes back into his office to wait for the people of Adano.

Joppolo gathers the town officials in his office. He tells the municipal employees that he will retain all of them, except for the Fascist mayor, who has fled into the hills.

> Adano has been a Fascist town. Now that the Americans have come, we are going to run the town as a democracy. You are servants now. You are servants of the people of Adano. And watch: this thing will make you happier than you have ever been in your lives.[13]

Joppolo asks the townspeople what they want. More than anything, they need a bell. The old bell, which was seven hundred years old, has been taken from the palazzo by the Fascists and melted down for gun barrels. Joppolo decides to talk to a friend who is in charge of the port of Adano about replacing the bell.

As a section of the Forty-ninth Division passes into Adano, a mule cart blocks the path of General Marvin. Marvin orders the cart dumped into the ditch and the mule shot through the head, then roars into Joppolo's office and orders him to "keep the goddamn carts out of this town."[14] When Joppolo informs the town officials that

279

mule carts will be banned from Adano and the streets and bridges leading into the town, the officials do not protest. As they leave, Joppolo promises to do everything he can to have the order revoked.

A delegation of mule cart drivers tells Joppolo that without the carts, the people will die of thirst and hunger and the villagers will not be able to get to their work in the fields. Joppolo listens to their story and, to the astonishment of the drivers, rescinds General Marvin's order.

Joppolo encourages the people of Adano to go back to work. The fishermen refuse to go out because they have always been supervised by a town bureaucrat. When Joppolo puts them in charge of their own work, the fishermen sail out through the harbor, even though it is full of mines. Joppolo commandeers five carloads of wheat sitting at a railroad crossing, and the bakers go back to work. A liberty ship delivers a roll of muslin and the villagers begin to manufacture clothes. And, of course, Joppolo organizes a sanitation department.

The officials of Adano commission the town painter to prepare a portrait of Joppolo from a photograph and present it to him as a big surprise. The same day a U.S. Navy truck delivers the ship's bell from the U.S.S. *Corelli.* There is a party that night. Joppolo's sergeant waits until it is over before telling him that General Marvin has learned that Joppolo countermanded the order about the carts and has transferred him to Algeria. As Joppolo drives from the town the next day, he can hear the bell ringing the morning hour.

Joppolo is a Theory Y administrator who comes to a Theory X town. He sees his primary mission as changing the process of government among the people of Adano so that they will be able to solve their own problems. He pays attention to people's needs, as with the bell, and he knows how to integrate their needs with the organizational problems that have to be solved, such as sanitation and baking bread. He allows himself to be influenced by the townspeople so that he in turn can influence them—men like the fishermen—to go back to work. Their willingness to respond to Joppolo is increased when they *perceive* that he has influence with his superiors, even though in the case of the carts he countermanded the order on his own.

Joppolo is an agent of change in Adano. Through the example of his leadership, he tries to break down the old status hierarchies and suspicions and show the villagers the power of collaboration. He tries to increase trust among the villagers. He expands their responsibility, makes them take pride in good work, and increases their sense that they own the organization. Although he keeps the Fascist town officials, who are organization men, at their jobs, he tries to change their managerial style. Unlike General Marvin, who relies upon the formal chain of command to get things done, Joppolo wants to strengthen the power of the work groups as a first step toward organizational democracy for the town of Adano. He wants to leave them with more than a bell.

Modern organization development begins with the same assumption that Joppolo makes in Adano: that effective work groups are the key to organizational renewal. The first techniques of organization development, as it grew out of the behavioral sciences, treated the group as the basic unit in the organization. By improving the group process, the behavioral scientists hoped to give individuals the capacity to diagnose and solve organizational problems on their own.

Two fundamental techniques among the proliferation of OD tools and fads are the T-group and the Tavistock study group. Both start from the remarkably simple observation that people learn more from studying their own behavior than by listening to lectures. Carl Rogers, one of the pioneers in the behavioral sciences, frequently claimed that "anything that can be taught to another is relatively inconsequential, and has little or no significant influence on behavior. The only learning which significantly influences behavior is self-discovery."[15]

T-groups, or training groups, rely upon learning through self-discovery. The T-group is simply an artificial group of individuals brought together in a learning laboratory. Under the supervision of group trainers, the individuals spend an intensive period, often a week, isolated from the rat race, studying their own behavior. There is no structured agenda, so that relationships within the group develop spontaneously. The trainer lets the group drift into its own ambiguous agenda. Although every group experience is unique, Leland Bradford, an OD consultant, has identified some common episodes in the T-group process.

The participants generally fumble through the opening sessions, since the trainer refuses to provide any guidance. Often a cleavage develops between those participants who are interested in exploring the group's behavior and those who feel threatened by the situation. The ambiguity of the situation provides "an open invitation for private manipulation of the group by an individual or clique."[16] The trainer encourages the participants to confront these problems openly. Confrontation may be traumatic, especially when participants learn the thoughts that others have formed about them. This is probably the most difficult episode for the group. It soon becomes apparent that some of the participants will have to alter their behavior if all of them are going to function together as a group. The participants will have to establish some system of feedback that will support modifications in individual behavior. If they succeed, the group will begin to coalesce, developing a sense of cohesion that is based on trust and candor rather than on the constraints of formal structure, hierarchy, and routine.

The role of the trainer in the T-group is crucial. In essence, the trainer attempts, like Joppolo in Adano, to present a model of ideal behavior. By providing such a model, the trainer helps to promote trust within the group; to provoke members into being open, candid and authentic in their relations with each other; and to encourage members to accept their differences of opinion and use democratic

281

methods to resolve them. "The T-group trainer deliberately utilizes his authority in order to get the members to relate to one another in ways which modify the hierarchy and allow collaboration."[17]

As a result of the T-group experience, the participant is supposed to develop personal insights into the group process—a sensitivity to emotions, greater skill at perceiving the consequences of one's own behavior on others, an understanding of what motivates people to act as they do, and an increased ability to regulated relationships with others. The T-group sharpens individual communication skills and promotes decision making by consensus. It encourages individuals to drop their facades—those ritual roles that suppress emotion, reenforce rank, and give an appearance of impersonal rationality—and to replace the facade with a spirit of collaboration and participation in organized problem solving. Participants often leave the T-group with an intense sense of group solidarity and an intense apprehension about the immediate problems of reentry into the real world and its bureaucracies.

Developments in British human relations have produced a somewhat different approach to laboratory learning. This is the Tavistock approach, based on the work of Wilfred Bion. In addition to the overt behavior of the members, Bion observed, a significant part of the activity of the group is hidden, unspoken, and in a sense subconscious. This activity might be characterized as the basic assumptions that the members make.

Bion identified three basic assumptions that all work groups make. One is dependence, the tendency of the members to seek security through the protection of a leading member of the group. The second is fight-flight, the assumption that the group has met to preserve itself and that this can only be done by fighting or running away from something. The third is the assumption that the group is meeting to create something, to bring forth a new idea or a new leader which, in the best traditions of psychoanalysis, Bion identified as a sexual act. Whenever two people get together on behalf of the group, they essentially are engaging in an act of creation. Bion called this pairing.

Every work group makes these assumptions: combat teams, football teams, task forces, and so on. It is as if behind each work group there is a second, phantom group that no one ever speaks about. The operations of this phantom group are neither intrinsically good nor bad. If they contribute to the group's task, then they are functional. If they draw energy away from the pursuit of the task, then they are dysfunctional.

When individuals come together in a T-group, they will tend to concentrate on the members' overt behavior. The purpose of the Tavistock study group, on the other hand, is to reveal the basic assumptions the group is making and analyze their impact upon its work.

This creates quite a unique role for the consultant in the Tavistock study group. Unlike the T-group trainer, the Tavistock consultant does not act as a "model" of good group behavior. To do so would be to accentuate the group's dependency assumptions as they search for the security of a leader. So the consultant speaks as the subconscious voice of the group, issuing pronouncements designed to give each participant insights into the functions which he or she is performing for the group. The consultant might "drop in a comment such as, 'The group is assiduously denying its feelings about. . . .' The consultant makes a statement from his own perspective about group process, whether or not members wish to hear it."[18]

Laboratory training, of which the T-group and the Tavistock study group are two leading types, has been used extensively in public administration—not only to improve personal behavior and supervisory style, but also for such special purposes as fighting racism, changing police behavior, making hospital workers more sensitive to the needs of patients, organizing community groups, studying power, rehabilitating criminals, and combating drug addiction. Laboratory training is a valuable learning tool because the performance of an organization will only be as good as the performance of its groups. For years, students of public administration have learned how to "run" agencies by preparing budgets and evaluation studies. Now OD also teaches these people how to improve the work of small groups, where most of the actual work of the agency is done.

The problem with laboratory training becomes obvious when the individual returns to his or her occupation. Laboratory training is divorced from the organizational situation. The trainers and consultants may be successful in building trust and giving insights into the group process, but this does not change the conditions in the agency that taught the employee to be less than candid, avoid responsibility, adopt facades, or fear authority. A one- or two-week exercise, no matter how much it improves one's mental health, cannot permanently unfreeze an individual who must return to the bureaucratic jungle.

In the long range, successful organization development requires alterations in the formal pattern of management within the organization. It is as necessary to restructure the organization as it is to reform individual behavior. This is where modern OD is moving—out of the laboratory and into the organization. Modern OD is much more concerned with organizational intervention strategies than with any of the group-learning techniques. This does not mean that group dynamics is unimportant; laboratory training is still used and OD consultants still exude the T-group style. Nevertheless, the techniques of group dynamics are now subordinated to the problems of total organizational change.

OD AND THE ORGANIZATION

A common suspicion among old-line bureaucrats is that OD advocates are too humane to succeed in the real world of organizational life. The techniques might work to improve people performance in groups, but can they really be used to reform a tradition-bound bureaucracy, like the American navy?

Organization development techniques were used, as one admiral said, to bring the navy into the twentieth century. In the mid-sixties, there was an enormous gap between the naval recruit and the naval institution. The naval recruit was twenty-one years old, hairy, smoked grass, and hated authority. The naval institution was hierarchical, traditional, and white, a policy established in 1913 when Woodrow Wilson segregated the armed forces. It was also complex, electronic, and atomic. The navy needed bright, creative sailors to run its ships and man the weapons systems. But it could not keep them; 70 percent resigned after their first tour of duty.

The navy blew apart in 1972. On board the *Kitty Hawk*, bound to Vietnam, a brawl broke out between blacks and whites. A few days later, 120 blacks on the carrier *Constellation* staged a sit-down strike. The captain refused to negotiate with the men.

The chief of naval operations, Admiral Elmo Zumwalt, used the incident to enforce the naval chain of command. The officers responsible for the incident, he said, "were just as obstructionist as a man who puts an order in a drawer and forgets it."[19] Zumwalt called in his captains and chewed them out for not following through on his program to unfreeze naval traditions.

Who was Elmo Zumwalt and what was he doing to the navy? In 1970, after leaving his post as commander of the navy in Vietnam, he jumped over thirty-two senior officers to become, at forty-nine, the youngest chief of naval operations ever.

> I approached this job like I've approached each of my other jobs, under the assumption that it's my last, and that I can always join the civilian community if it doesn't work.[20]

Zumwalt started his tour by upgrading working conditions in the navy, what OD specialists like to call improving hygiene factors. He established homeporting in Greece so that men at sea could have their families near them, abolished the rule against long hair and beards, and put topless dancers in the NCO clubs. He opened up lines of communications in the navy, telling ship commanders to hold gripe sessions with their men and setting up a naval ombudsman. All of these reforms came about because Zumwalt listened to the sailors. He and his assistants cut through the navy hierarchy to locate sensitive recruits and wise old sailors; brought them together in small groups, secluded in a conference room in Washington; and asked them to diagnose the organizational ills of the navy. On the basis of their recommendations, Zumwalt would issue his famous Z-grams, telegrams that went out to each individual in the service. One commander said, "Since these Z-grams came out, some men seem to feel that they are working directly for the chief of naval operations."[21] Altogether, Zumwalt sent out over 120 Z-grams.

To make the new navy work, Zumwalt established an elaborate Human Resource Management Program. The program consultants

CHAPTER 8: ORGANIZATION DEVELOPMENT

Strategies of organization development have been used by public executives who are committed to creating change in their organizations. Admiral Elmo Zumwalt, shown here with one of his human resource councils, used T-groups, action research, and process consultation.
COURTESY OF THE U.S. NAVY.

insisted that every officer and sailor go through T-group exercises to improve their sensitivity to race relations. They set up special programs to help men with alcohol and drug problems. But hygiene factors and T-groups do not a complete organization development program make. Organization development also requires institutional change.

Zumwalt knew that long-range change in the navy would require planned alterations in the basic pattern of leadership. To accomplish this, he dispatched process consultants to the big navy ports and told them to help commanders improve human resource conditions and requirements. The consultants began their visit by asking officers to conduct an organizational survey. The officers would set aside five days for an intensive seminar, during which the results of the survey would be fed back to them and the process consultants would help them develop plans for a comprehensive human goals program. The plans could include team building, goal setting, problem solving, and personal or group skills improvement. Six months later the process consultants would return to the port, conduct an evaluation exercise and set up another seminar, if necessary.

Institutional planning is the key to successful organization development. OD begins with group dynamics and ends with institutional planning. Only in this way can the goals of organization development—responsiveness to change, higher productivity, and a more humane climate of work—be frozen permanently into the institution. One of the first models to combine the complete methodology into a single, systematic framework was the managerial grid, put forth by Robert Blake and Jane Mouton.

Blake and Mouton observed that many managers considered

problems arising from human motivation distinct from the problems of meeting production schedules or organizational objectives. Moreover, many managers associated organization development solely with laboratory training and people problems. Blake and Mouton developed the managerial grid to overcome this people-production dichotomy, to use OD to improve organizational performance, while avoiding the abrasive emotional encounters typical of T-group sessions.

The managerial-grid program is designed to move the organization to the upper right-hand corner of the grid, where the managers in the organization maximize both their concern for people and their concern for production, a situation characterized as team management. The grid itself is nothing but a checkerboard square on which managers can plot their concern for people on a vertical scale against concern for production along the bottom line. Some managers rank low on both scales, a situation that Blake and Mouton characterize as impoverished management. Some managers rank high on people but low on production (country-club management), while others are high on production and low on personal skills (task management).

The program for climbing the grid consists of six phases involving all of the managers in the organization and taking as long as two years. Phase one is a type of laboratory training session in which the managers are brought together to analyze their behavior as it relates to their jobs. The discussion is confined to work-related situations; the managers may be asked to assess their effectiveness in dealing with simulated agency problems.

In phase two, the participants enter special team-building seminars. The teams are made up of executives, supervisors, and professionals who are responsible for the same task. They may have never worked together as a team before. In the phase-two sessions, the work teams study their behavior in relation to the management of their work and its relevance to agency objectives. They try to develop strategies for breaking down barriers to team effectiveness. The ground rules of candor and authenticity learned in phase one become operating standards for the teams in phase two.

In phase three, new teams are formed, made up of persons who work on different tasks but whose general cooperation is essential to the effectiveness of the organization. These people may distrust each other. After areas of conflict are identified and confronted, the teams attempt to establish open lines of communication so that organizational energy is spent solving problems rather than wasted on secrecy, suppressed anger, or the politics of self-interest.

Phase four is devoted to setting organizational goals. The top executives meet to review the mission of the agency, establish objectives, and develop a strategic plan.

Phase five is devoted to problem solving. Special task forces are established to develop solutions, implement plans, and assign responsibility for specific tasks. All of the managers, representing all levels in the organization, participate on these task forces (although their participation is limited by the fact that the top executives have already made the strategic decisions).

Evaluation and assessment take place in phase six. Special teams review the organization's development, correct errors, and pinpoint areas of opportunity where new objectives can be met in the future.

In practice, the phases are rarely distinct and sequential; the formal program using paid outside consultants rarely goes beyond phase one or two. The grid model is useful because it clarifies the stages of planned organizational change: laboratory training, team building, objective setting, implementation, and evaluation.

The Zumwalt reforms and the mangerial grid illustrate many of the intervention strategies used by OD consultants. The grid contains team building, the navy program used action research and a form of process consultation. All of these are drawn out of the bag of OD techniques that OD consultants carry to work.

In team building, the OD consultant works with small groups of people who are an organizational family—persons in the authority structure who work on mutual problems. "Team building interventions," say two specialists, "are typically directed toward four major substantive areas: diagnosis, task accomplishment, team relationships, and team and organizational processes."[22] In essence, the consultant and the client attempt to improve team performance by bringing together the right people at the right time over the right issue, and encouraging them to modify their behavior. The team is asked to diagnose its own performance and identify problems which, for various reasons, may have remained ambiguous or unspoken. The team is encouraged to improve its procedures for accomplishing its task, procedures that all the members of the team perceive as fair and equitable.

Action research is a method of increasing the amount of information available to the team or organization as it attempts to diagnose its own problems and improve its performance. The consultant collects information about the ideas and attitudes of participants, using standard survey research techniques. The participants know that they are going to have to account for the results. The data is fed back to the team, which must then formulate plans to resolve the problems revealed by the data. Later, the survey method is used to evaluate whether any real change has transpired as a result of their work.

Process consultation is what it says it is. The OD specialist acts as a consultant to help the manager improve the various processes of decision making and communication that go on in the organization. It is essentially a soft consulting role, in that the process consultant does not offer authoritative advice based on his or her special wisdom. The "key assumption underlying process consultation is that the client must learn to see the problem for himself, to share in the diagnosis, and to be actually involved in generating a remedy."[23] That is, the process consultant is not there as a doctor called in by a sick patient who wants someone to diagnose the illness and prescribe the remedy. The process consultant is there to raise questions, encourage

287

candor, and help the members of the organization confront their own problems before these problems become acute.

Warren Bennis has described the work of the OD consultant as professional, marginal, ambiguous, insecure, and risky. If the top executives in the organization are not committed to solving their own problems through self-analysis, then the OD program will fail. If the OD consultant is successful, then the organization will probably kick him out as soon as it gains control over its own affairs. This is certainly a more passive role than management consultants have played in the past.

The OD process has been applied extensively in private organizations. Elliott Jaques describes how it was applied by the British Tavistock Institute to the Glacier Metal Company, an English firm that had radically altered its technology and scale of operations during the Second World War without ever changing its style of organization or supervision. The program developed for Esso Standard Oil in 1957 is considered the pivotal experience in American OD, since it was here that OD specialists began to move away from sensitivity training and toward the planned-change strategies exemplified by the managerial grid. The Zumwalt regime in the navy demonstrates that these approaches have penetrated the public service.

THE EFFECTIVE ORGANIZATION

How does an OD specialist diagnose organizational maladies? How does he tell a sick organization from a healthy one? Consider the case of Robert Townsend, who was brought into the Avis Corporation as its general manager to brandish his style of guerrilla management upon the rent-a-car business.

What sort of organization did Townsend find when he arrived? According to his own description, Avis was a corporation devoid of central leadership, encumbered by a prying board of directors, stifled by independent departments unconscious of the organization's objectives (there were none), and suffering from the curse of monster watching: "if Time Inc. puts its executives in fancy offices, that must be the way to be big." Townsend set out to rebuild Avis and make it operate "as if people were human."[24]

Townsend began by firing the personnel department, the public relations department, the advertising department, the purchasing department, the computer priests, and his executive secretary. Then he chopped up the layers of hierarchy that prevented people from working with each other. He forbade nepotism, company airplanes, memo writing, mandatory staff meetings, most new reporting forms, mistresses on the payroll, and jargon. He refused to let the board of directors raise his salary. He spent six months helping the company executives define an objective that was twenty-three words long, and then fought to ensure that all work in the company was related to the objective.

Townsend made Avis healthy, or at least more profitable. Al-

CHAPTER 8: ORGANIZATION DEVELOPMENT

Organization development is designed to raise the level of trust and openness among work groups while increasing the responsiveness of the organization to its environment. The U.S. General Services Administration has designed a building to house the effective organization—an air dome built into the natural environment. Inside, the government offices would sit on raised platforms; they would have neither roofs nor walls. COURTESY OF THE GENERAL SERVICES ADMINISTRATION.

though his actions hardly fit the soft OD model, Townsend did move the organization back toward its "essential properties." Chris Argyris, one of the leading behavioral scientists, believes that healthy organizations have essential properties, just as groups and individuals do. Like any living system, the healthy organization is "created and controlled through the interrelationship of all the parts."[25] To Argyris, the locus of control is the distinguishing feature of the healthy organization. Members of such an organization share in the formulation of objectives, they are aware of how their unit contributes to the total effort (Argyris calls this the "pattern of parts"), and the objectives of each unit are geared toward the whole as opposed to the self-interest of the unit. This requires a great deal of openness and trust between members of the organization. The payoff, says Argyris, will be an organization with a high degree of flexibility and an unusual ability to control its core activities and influence forces in the environment that affect it.

When psychological energy is directed away from the essential properties, the organization becomes ill. A sick organization, says Argyris, is one in which authority is concentrated in a single unit that tries to control all the parts. The unit, usually the general manager's office, treats the organization as a "plurality of parts"; that is, each part is given discreet functions and limited objectives, and the manager assumes that the interests of the parts are narrow, self-serving, and unrelated to the whole. Because the parts are so independent, the central office cannot fully control the course of the organization. The organization becomes rigid, inflexible, and a victim of outside events; its approach to problem solving and goal setting is generally short-range.

One can measure the extent of organizational disease by testing the adaptive capacity of the organization. Edgar Schein, an organiza-

THE EFFECTIVE ORGANIZATION

tional psychologist from Harvard University, describes six symptoms of an organization that has lost its ability to adapt. How does your organization measure up?

1. "Failure to sense changes in the environment or incorrectly sensing what has been happening."
2. "Communications breakdowns, or a failure to get relevant information to those parts of the organization which can act upon it or use it."
3. Resistance to change within the organization that cannot be overcome, which Schein calls "failure to influence the conversion or production system to make the necessary changes."
4. Disastrous secondary effects following an attempt at change, or no follow-through, which Schein describes as "failure to consider the impact of changes on other systems and failure to achieve stable change."
5. "Failure to export the new product, service, or information." Perhaps the agency improves itself, or does something well, but nobody outside the agency hears about it.
6. "Failure to obtain feedback on the success of the change."[26]

An effective organization, by contrast, is one that can sense change, communicate it to the relevant unit, readjust its operations while anticipating and avoiding mistakes, sell its clients and supporters on the response, and make any necessary readjustments. Schein, along with Warren Bennis, suggests four measures for testing the degree to which an organization has achieved the "essential properties" of institutional health.

1. "Adaptability—the ability to solve problems and to react with flexibility to changing environmental demands."
2. "A sense of identity." The members understand the goals of the organization and feel that their own personal development is tied to successful accomplishment of those goals. Their own sense of identity clearly matches the image that outsiders have of the organization, and they see the same strengths and weaknesses in the organization that outsiders do.
3. "Capacity to test reality—the ability to search out, accurately perceive, and correctly interpret the real properties of the environment, particularly those which have relevance for the functioning of the organization."
4. Integration. Personal goals are integrated with organizational goals, and the organization can become as complex as it needs to be without losing its ability to internally integrate the institutional parts.[27]

In general, OD theorists believe that the bureaucratic form of organization, built around the formal principles of administration, will tend to be an unhealthy organization in a changing society. The

290

rules of hierarchy, authority, specialization, and efficiency will drive the organization away from its essential properties. The more that an organization is able to temper the effects of bureaucratic structure, the better the chance it has to approach the essential properties. Advocates of this point of view offer examples of successful organizations, such as the American space program, which were able to respond effectively to change by reducing their reliance upon the bureaucratic methodology.

Many theorists, including Warren Bennis, have predicted an end to bureaucratic hierarchy. In a period of organizational turbulence, they say, power will have to devolve to the persons with the greatest ability to solve the problems at hand. The able administrator will be one who combines technical skill with an ability to interact effectively in groups. The new managers will break down the bureaucratic barriers of specialization and hierarchy by assigning persons to teams. Each team will be an integrated system of skill and ability. Team objectives, not individual job descriptions, will become the basis of organizational motion. The teams will come together to accomplish a task and then disband. The total institution will become a cybernetic organization, scanning its environment for information and adjusting its course continually in pursuit of its objectives. Adjustment in course will require organizational arrangements that are temporary. Personal trust, candor, and motivation will affect the flow of information (or lack of it) as much as information technology.

The futurists paint a rosy picture of the effective organization of the future, but hardened bureaucrats pass it off as utopian. They suspect that OD advocates have reached for a type of organizational renewal that is beyond the capacity of the government to create.

THE LIMITS OF ORGANIZATION DEVELOPMENT

Efforts to change the style of public administration, to enrich the jobs of public servants, and to push employees toward self-actualization often bump into unfavorable work conditions, civil service regulations, and a hostile bureaucracy. In part it is the fault of hidebound bureaucrats who resist change. In part it is the fault of the behavioral scientists who are often too naive.

One of the best-known failures of organization development in public administration occurred within the bureaucratic bane of modern government, the U.S. Department of State. In 1965, the undersecretary for administration hired Chris Argyris to direct a series of laboratory training sessions for foreign service officers. Argyris, in a small pamphlet describing the intervention, observed that a number of secretaries of state had tried unsuccessfully to make the foreign service officers "accept and enlarge their responsibility." The foreign service, Argyris predicted, would continue to resist such change until "the interpersonal milieu is altered."[28]

The nature of that interpersonal milieu became apparent as the foreign service officers expressed their feelings in the laboratory groups. Many officers, especially the young idealists, wanted to become independent, aggressive, risk takers. But the foreign service bureaucracy—a "living system" beyond the control of its members—created a set of rewards and punishments that dulled initiative. Argyris learned that conditions of work in the State Department rewarded those passive individuals who withdrew from interpersonal conflict, suppressed ideas that others would view as threatening, relied upon their superiors to take the initiative, and did not question the hierarchy.

At the conclusion of the laboratory training sessions, Argyris recommended that the senior executives in the State Department undertake a long-range change program focusing upon their own behavior and leadership style. This would be followed by revisions in the department's personnel evaluation, promotion, and inspection policies so as to encourage self-actualization among foreign service officers.

Except for the administrative missionary who launched the seminars, all of the executives in the State Department viewed Argyris's comments and proposals as highly threatening. Unfortunately, the missionary left, and when it came time for the top executives to prepare the budget, they left out the Argyris program.

Why did the State Department executives view this as threatening?

In essence, because Argyris was questioning the political rules of administration. Politically and administratively, the State Department is highly fragmented. The foreign service officers have their own hierarchy, the political executives have theirs, there are factions within both, and each faction has its special ties to different congressional committees, interest groups, White House staffers, and foreign governments. As Robert Golembiewski observes, it may be technically desirable to pursue the objective of "building trust among individuals and groups throughout the organization." In practice, however, "this is a very tall order," since each of the factions and the groups they represent "tend to have mutually exclusive interests, values, and reward systems." Moreover, outside groups, such as the Congress, have "a definite interest in cultivating a certain level of distrust within and between government agencies so as to encourage the flow of information." Golembiewski concludes that the pluralism inherent in public administration creates "an array of hurdles" for OD programs—hurdles that do not exist in the business world, where OD was first developed.[29]

But isn't this pluralism, as Golembiewski characterizes it, the very sort of fragmentation that Argyris deplores in his model of organizational health?

Yes, it is. But Argyris makes certain assumptions about curing the effects of that pluralism which most hardened bureaucrats reject. In general, OD specialists tend to assume that problems of fragmentation and self-interest can be washed away through trust, candor, and open communications. To seasoned bureaucrats, this is nothing more than the old Rousseauean assumption that humans are good people made bad by poor institutions, a brand of spiritual liberalism that has

292

dominated the academic community for two centuries. Bureaucrats working in the fires of government find this assumption absurd.

What do they assume?

They assume that government agencies are working with scarce resources—not just money, for which the demand always exceeds the supply, but the ability to fulfill demands from outside groups who want the agency to grant them a special deal, such as permission to buy weapons from the United States. Over the years, each section of the bureaucracy develops elaborate procedures for protecting itself from demands it perceives as unreasonable. The procedures are usually diplomatic; foreign service officers are trained to be tactful rather than candid and open. When Argyris suggested that the State Department reform this interpersonal style, the executives in the department treated the Argyris proposal as just another unreasonable demand.

But Argyris was talking about reforming relations between people within the department. Wouldn't this have had a positive influence on the effectiveness of the organization?

It is very hard to tell, since there is no hard evidence to prove that OD "works." Nearly every major behavioral theorist presents some two- or four-factor theory: Theory X and Theory Y, the theory of satisfiers and dissatisfiers, the managerial grid, the mix model—all affirming their belief that improved supervision and teamwork will lead to organizational effectiveness. In fact, the causal arrow may point in the other direction. An increase in organizational effectiveness may cause the OD situation to develop. Victor Vroom suggests that executives who are placed in charge of highly productive groups will tend to elicit more participation, encourage more teamwork, enrich the jobs, and allow self-direction—not because they are intrinsically Theory Y managers, but because they perceive a high level of effectiveness in their work teams.

But in the absence of such teamwork, isn't it likely, as Argyris says, that there will be a lack of congruence between the demands of the organization and the needs of healthy individuals?

Like the debate over cures, this is largely a question of faith. No extensive body of empirical evidence exists that would support the contention that individual needs are frustrated by organizational demands. Labor leaders, in particular, are skeptical about the efforts of upper-middle-class reformers to "help workers realize their potential." The behavioral sciences out of which OD emerged sound a lot like the old middle-class Protestant ethic of hard work and duty as the road to personal salvation. OD specialists seem determined to push people into newly structured, "meaningful" jobs; in other words, to imbue them with the middle-class belief that humans cannot lead meaningful lives unless they excel at work.

Regardless of what causes what, aren't more organizations taking on the characteristics associated with OD?

Some are, some are not. It all depends upon the particular circumstances affecting the agency. When the American space program enjoyed a challenging objective and a fat budget, it relied heavily upon the OD approach. When its budget was cut back and it started phasing out programs, it reverted to more bureaucratic controls. A similar chain of events occurred in the navy. During the Zumwalt era, which was a time of great turbulence, the OD approach was quite popular. When things calmed down and Zumwalt left, the navy slipped back toward its traditional patterns of administration.

Under what circumstances is OD most likely to succeed?

We can only guess, but there seem to be four factors of major importance. One is the problem of scarce resources—OD seems to work best in times of plenty when the agency is prepared to satisfy what Herzberg calls the "hygiene" factors, such as salary, and move on to the "motivators," such as personal growth. The second is the problem of change—there is more demand for OD in times of turbulence than when the agency is settled into a comfortable routine. Third, the nature of the task appears to make a major difference. Obviously, the task of putting people on the moon presents different opportunities for teamwork than a mail-sorting room in a post office does. Finally, the setting of the agency—both social and political— seems to be an important factor. For example, the success of the OD approach in Japanese industries is due in part to the social tradition established in that country which favors a high degree of consultation and group participation before a problem is even defined, much less before any action is taken.

How can a person predict the impact of such things?

The success of any approach to administration, including OD, depends largely upon the particular conditions with which the agency is faced. Only by studying the administration of different agencies in different settings can one begin to anticipate whether the situation requires a rational, a political, a scientific, or a behavioral approach. It is best to study a wide variety of agencies in many different countries.

Have public administrators done this?

They have begun to, in particular by studying whether or not Western administrative strategies fit the conditions present in non-Western nations. This is the subject of the next chapter.

FOR FURTHER READING

To gain a feeling for the mood of the organization development movement, the newcomer might begin with the popular Theory X and Theory Y in Douglas McGregor, *The Human Side of Enterprise* (New York: McGraw-Hill Book Co., 1960). The need for organization development in an era of rapid change is argued by Warren G. Bennis and Philip E. Slater in *The Temporary Society* (New York: Harper & Row, 1968). The Bennis "death of bureaucracy" thesis is summarized by Alvin Toffler in *Future Shock* (New York: Bantam Books, 1970), Chapter 7. Abraham H. Maslow presents the idea that self-actualization is the highest human need in *Motivation and Personality*

(New York: Harper & Row, 1954), while Chris Argyris explains why individual self-actualization is impossible in traditional organizations in *Personality and Organization* (New York: Harper & Row, 1957). The most important efforts to develop a sophisticated new theory of motivation and supervision are found in Frederick Herzberg et. al., *The Motivation to Work* (New York: John Wiley & Sons, 1959) and Rensis Likert, *New Patterns of Management* (New York: McGraw-Hill Book Co., 1961).

There are many theories about how one actually constructs an OD program in an organization. One of the best reviews of the various behavioral science interventions for organizational change can be found in the book by Wendell L. French and Cecil H. Bell, *Organization Development* (Englewood Cliffs, N.J.: Prentice-Hall, 1973). Leland Bradford, Jack Gibb, and Kenneth Benne explain the personal approach to organization development in *T-Group Theory and Laboratory Method* (New York: John Wiley & Sons, 1964). Robert R. Blake and Jane S. Mouton link personal change to organizational productivity in *Corporate Excellence Through Grid Organization Development* (Houston: Gulf Publishing Co., 1968). The peculiarities of the British Tavistock approach to organization development are reviewed by Edward B. Klein and Boris M. Astrachan in "Learning in Groups: A Comparison of Study Groups and T Groups," *The Journal of Applied Behavioral Science 7* (Number 6, 1971), pp. 659–83. That journal is a good source of new techniques in this rapidly changing field. When the change program is complete, managers should be able to compare their agencies to the effective organization characterized by Edgar H. Schein in *Organizational Psychology*, 2nd ed. (Englewood Cliffs, N.J.: Prentice-Hall, 1970), Chapter 7. Schein's book is a good overview of the field. So is Warren Bennis's *Organization Development: Its Nature, Origins, and Prospects* (Reading, Mass.: Addison-Wesley Publishing Co., 1969), part of the six-book Addison-Wesley Series on organization development. Most of these books are based on the application of organization development to the private sector.

Criticisms of the behavioral sciences occur in bits and pieces, ranging from left-wing attacks on behavioral modification techniques, well represented by Anthony Burgess's novel *A Clockwork Orange* (New York: W. W. Norton & Co., 1962) to the question of whether OD can overcome the political side of administration. For a review of the latter, see Robert R. Golembiewski, "Organization Development in Public Agencies," *Public Administration Review* 29 (July/August 1969), pp. 367–77.

CONTEXTS

The first eight chapters of this book presented the basic principles, problems, and strategies of public administration. Theoretically, it should be possible to stop at this point. However, when one applies this knowledge to the solution of practical problems in the context of the real world, two difficulties arise. First, the strategies of "good administration," which on the surface may seem applicable to all situations, produce unexpected results when applied in non-Western nations. This fact has encouraged many scholars to explore the relationship between administrative strategies and local conditions. Second, the strategies and principles presented so far turn out, upon even cursory inspection, to be contradictory and often incompatible. Administrative experts speak with many tongues, a most confusing state of affairs that is having a profound effect upon the development of the profession. Together these difficulties have destroyed hopes for a universal science of administration and led experts to consider a contingency approach that views each administrative strategy in the context in which it is used.

COMPARATIVE PUBLIC ADMINISTRATION

9

Scholars of comparative administration have given special attention to an important phenomenon: the influence of local conditions upon the chances for administrative success. Concern with local conditions grew out of experience with technical assistance programs in Asia, Africa, and Latin America. The first technical assistance experts approached these developing nations with a disarmingly simple set of assumptions. The developing nations, they observed, wanted to climb the economic and social ladder, to share the jobs, wealth, and security possessed by citizens in the "developed nations" of Europe and North America. The new countries, however, lacked the institutions (and the money) to sustain rapid growth. Someone had to supply the missing ingredients: the planning agencies; organization and methods studies; the personnel, reporting, budgeting, accounting, and auditing systems; and the other tools of administration needed to make development work. Or so they assumed.

The outcome, from the mountains of Chile to the hamlets of Vietnam, was frustration. White, middle-class public administrators failed to bring administrative reform to countries that were neither white nor middle class. This failure produced what is probably the single most important intellectual breakthrough in the modern study of public administration: the discovery that local conditions have an enormous impact on opportunities for administrative reform. Out of this realization came a theory, called the ecology of public administration, which holds that any public organization must conform to its social, political, and economic environment—or suffer.

In the short range, the ecological approach pretty well destroyed the idea that there were any "universal" principles of good administration that could be applied with equal force in all countries, rich or poor. It meant that professional public administrators, instead of beginning with an ideal model of administrative efficiency, had to begin with local conditions *as local officials saw them* and fashion administrative solutions to fit. In the long run, this ecological approach held out

Modern public administration comes to a tribe of Turkana men and women in northern Kenya. The U.S. Peace Corps dispatched this community development officer to organize an irrigation project.
COURTESY OF ACTION/PEACE CORPS.

the promise that public administrators might be able to create a model of administrative contingencies, one that showed local officials how to make trade-offs between different administrative strategies applicable under different administrative conditions.

This chapter traces the evolution of comparative administration toward a model of administrative contingencies. It begins a generation ago when the first experts stepped off the plane to be greeted by the perplexing local conditions in developing countries, then catalogs the work of development administrators: the foreign experts and the local executives trained in Western methods who were charged with bringing modern public administration to developing nations. It shows how the ecological theory came to be revealed and led to attempts to judge administrative methods in terms of the local conditions.

ADMINISTRATIVE PROBLEMS IN DEVELOPING COUNTRIES

The earliest talk about administration in developing areas was dominated by a single theme: the romance of living in a foreign culture and the frustration of trying to accomplish anything within it. Everyone told the same funny stories about the same ludicrous problems of administration and how the developing countries fell so far short of standards established in efficient, Western societies. Even the simplest act—such as an attempt to visit a local official—became entangled in a web of tiny frustrations. The Spanish have a word for it—*mañana*. Everything is done "tomorrow."

Out of the early misadventures rose a common theme: certain administrative problems were endemic to all developing countries. From different administrators in different nations, one heard similar complaints.

299

- "Executives in developing countries are incapable of delegating authority. They want to control everything. Even the simplest administrative decision has to be approved at the top."

- "Carefully written development plans just gather dust. Officials in developing countries have no interest in the actual administrative details necessary to accomplish the plans."

- "Corruption is out of control. Development funds are siphoned off to hire friends or relatives. In some cases the money simply disappears."

- "So much time is wasted on the *forms* of management—paper work, big staff meetings, field trips. But when it comes to the guts of management—communicating objectives, defining responsibilities, delineating staff and line operations—they are just hopeless."

- "There is too much secrecy. The circulation of management information is severely restricted within the agency. You even need special permission to get copies of public documents."

- "Nothing works. How can you run a government department when the telephones don't work and mail isn't delivered?"

These complaints dominate the early Western literature on development administration. One still hears local officials as well as visiting experts talk about them as obstacles to effective administration in developing countries.

As there was general agreement on the basic problems of administration, so there was also general agreement on their fundamental causes. The failure of things administrative, said experts such as Ferrel Heady, could be traced to five underlying conditions.

1. The administrative structures in developing nations are generally imitative rather than indigenous to the society. Many developing countries borrow administrative models from other nations, even though the models do not fit. One writer notes that

> the organization of offices, the demeanor of civil servants, even the general appearance of a bureau, strikingly mirror the national characteristics of the bureaucracies of the former colonial powers. The *fonctionnaire* slouched at his desk in Lome or Cotonou, cigarette pasted to his underlip, has his counterpart in every provincial town in France; and the demeanor of an administrative officer in Accra or Lagos untying the red tape from his files would be recognizable to anyone familiar with the Colonial Office.[1]

In part, the imitation stems from the power of the colonial experience; in part, it grows out of the general impatience with administrative details. But in large measure the borrowing occurs because local officials in developing countries are led to believe that Western management practices will somehow give them more control over the affairs of their agencies. This preoccupation with management control encourages local officials to borrow the most primitive practices from the administrative parent. The result is often an administrative system that is neither modern nor indigenous.

2. Despite all the emphasis upon change, there is wide-scale resistance to development programs the effects of which the government cannot control. The symbols of change, such as computers and modern economic planning, are widely accepted. The actual development programs, however, are likely to be run by a very small class of educated civil servants who are incapable of overcoming the nibbling resistance to social change coming from within a very traditional and pragmatic society. Consider the economic reforms instituted by the Peronists in Argentina, a plan roughly similar to the one that preceded the downfall of the Allende government in Chile. In both cases public executives sought a more equitable distribution of wealth, to be achieved, they said, painlessly. The executives developed a program that required the freezing of prices, an increase in workers' wages, and expanded expenditures for public works. New jobs and higher wages would increase consumer demand; businesses would view demand as an incentive to gear up to maximum capacity and eliminate inefficiencies. Even though the profit on individual items might drop, business profits would rise because of increased volume. That, at least, was the plan. In fact, the costs of production rose despite government price controls—largely because of increases in the price of raw materials purchased abroad, particularly oil. Buyers could not find goods at the artifically low prices. Goods were available "under the counter," but only if the buyer agreed to pay the seller a higher, illegal price. Local businessmen kept two sets of books—a phony set to show public officials and a real set for their own managers and stockholders. Fearing government scrutiny, business interests invested their illegal profits in speculative holdings, such as real estate, rather than plowing the profits back into production. The government tried to sustain honest entrepreneurs with low-interest loans, backed by paper money, which in turn increased inflation and the costs of imported materials. Whatever the cause— and one can accuse the government of poor planning, the business interests of corruption, or the people for being panicked into buying black-market goods—the fact remains that in a society where pragmatism is a prerequisite of survival, public officials typically encounter more resistance to development programs than they can overcome.

3. Loyalty to the organization or its mission is not a powerful ethic among bureaucrats in developing nations. Public employees receive few incentives to work hard and be loyal to the organization. This is especially true among those at the lower grades. The pay scales are pitiful, government housing is generally substandard, the employees are rarely professionalized, and the jobs lack prestige in the eyes of the public. Even so, government jobs are a precious commodity where unemployment is high. Bureaucrats are expected to share their good fortune with family and friends from their village or tribe. The organization may become a social security system bloated with

hangers-on who really are not expected to do any work. Civil service regulations, imposed from above, are convoluted in order to allow appointment through such criteria.

The preeminence of personal over organizational loyalties encourages corruption on a massive scale. Bribes, paid from client to bureaucrat for services rendered, seem to have become a common cost of administration in the new nations. Many developing countries allow public executives to operate farms, factories, or commercial firms in addition to their government jobs—private enterprises that generally do business with government agencies or stand to gain from government regulation. As a cost of doing business in a new nation, many foreign businessmen have been told to kick back up to 25 percent of the value of the contracts they receive to various "agents," who in turn divide up the money among government officials. Some of the most spectacular cases of corruption occurred in Vietnam. During the height of the war, under pressure from American officials, Vietnamese executives would find a particularly corrupt public servant and have him shot. The example hardly deterred corruption, and may seem to resemble the old Inca practice of dragging victims to the altar of sacrifice to appease the gods of light and darkness. Needless to say, there is much debate in development circles over just how much corruption, given local conditions, is necessary to oil the wheels of administration.

4. There is an acute lack of skilled personnel available to carry out government programs. In nearly every former colony, the corps of foreign personnel, built up during the colonial era, departed more rapidly after independence than a staff of qualified replacements could be found and trained to take their place. Subsequent political instability reduced the staff of qualified officials even more, as suspect officials were jailed, shot, or exiled. The shortage of managers is most acute at the technical level. Shortages of skilled office personnel who can handle reports and process documents—or even type—are a serious problem. Fortunately, most new nations possess a small pool of educated civil servants qualified to run the top positions, but generally there is no large cadre of office workers, experts, bureau chiefs, technicians and field officials to implement the plans dreamed up by the talented ministers.

5. The bureaucracy enjoys an unusual degree of autonomy. The absence of widespread organizational talent creates a situation wherein those who possess administrative or technical expertise enjoy unusual power advantages in the society. The administrative elite may, in developing nations, congregate in the public service, particularly in programs for social progress, economic development, and, alas, the military. Restraints on bureaucratic power created by the legislature, the judiciary, organized pressure groups, and the press—an essential feature of administration in Western nations— simply do not exist in many developing societies. Moreover, there is generally no long-standing ethos requiring citizen participation in administration. As a result, most administrative actions take place in

a vacuum where officials are allowed to convolute administrative methods to serve personal goals and where the methods cannot be checked through the contributions of outside groups, except for the small band of foreign experts, who often have little appreciation for local conditions.

Development administration began from this perspective. Developing countries were seen as aberrations of the true administrative faith or, at best, as problems to be solved. Development administrators saw themselves as wise men bearing the gifts of a universal model of bureaucratic excellence, ready for implantation in the developing society, if only the local bureaucrats would accept it.

This perspective, one must note, was not confined to the Third World, but seemed to arise wherever professional experts met local conditions, in San Francisco as well as in Santo Domingo. The American journalist Tom Wolfe describes what happened in San Francisco during the "war on poverty." Bureaucrats working for the Office of Economic Opportunity—lifers in the civil service, uniformed in wash-and-wear semitab-collar short-sleeved white shirts, with felt-tipped markers, wax pencils, and ball-point pens lined across the pocket like campaign ribbons—were told to start a war on poverty in the Western Addition, Hunters Point, and Potrero Hill. The bureaucrats had money for manpower training, Head Start, Neighborhood Youth Corps, and sewing machines to manufacture black-made dashikis in a ghetto enterprise, money the bureaucrats would dispense to ghetto organizations that represented the poor. Only the ghetto, because it was just developing, contained no administrative organizations with black accountants, legal clerks, and O & M specialists. The poverty officials were puzzled.

> They didn't know where to look. They didn't even know who to ask. So what could they do? Well . . . they used the Ethnic Catering Service . . . right . . . they sat back and waited for you [the blacks, the poor] to come rolling in with your certified angry militants, your guaranteed frustrated ghetto youth, looking like a bunch of wild men. Then you had your test confrontation. If you were outrageous enough, if you could shake up the bureaucrats so bad that their eyes froze into iceballs and their mouths twisted up into smiles of sheer physical panic, into shit-eating grins, so to speak—then they knew you were the real goods. They knew you were the right studs to give the poverty grants and community organizing jobs to.[2]

The poverty officials behaved just like the first development administrators, expecting the poor to behave like "natives" and accept the administrative methods of development with gratitude. What the poor did was accept the money but not the methods. In Chicago, the poverty bureaucrats got maumaued by the Blackstone Rangers, a mean, tough gang of street thugs who terrified the people in the Woodlawn section of Chicago and controlled the streets after dark. The poverty officials realized that this was a group that really represented the neighborhood, so they gave the Rangers a million dollars to become job counselors in a manpower development training program. The Blackstone Rangers used the money to recruit teenage dropouts and to teach them hand-to-hand combat, how to make zip guns, and all the other skills that would help them survive in the Woodlawn community. When the congressional committees in Washington, D.C., got through investigating this episode in the War on Poverty, they concluded that the Rangers had created all the problems of a typical technical assistance program—corruption, excessive centralization, and political instability.

The approach of the poverty officials, like the perspective of many development administrators, was ethnocentric. That is, they were preoccupied with professional methods of administration and did not think that the uneducated had anything to contribute to the store of administrative wisdom. A small intellectual war has been going on for two decades over this problem. On the one hand, there are experts who feel that development will never succeed until new nations adopt modern methods of administration. On the other hand, there are those experts who believe that developing countries will never progress unless local officials define their own problems, set their own goals, involve their own citizens, and choose only those methods from the catalog of administrative techniques that fit local conditions. The history of comparative administration is the story of a very slow movement away from the ethnocentric approach, with its emphasis upon bureaucratic efficiency, to the adaptive approach, with its emphasis upon local efficacy.

THE JOB OF THE DEVELOPMENT ADMINISTRATOR

The study of comparative administration was launched twenty-five years ago with the belief that developing countries were not developing because they could not execute their development programs. Administrative experts traced the genesis of program failure to a series of administrative problems that were seen as common to all developing countries. From this perspective it was a short walk to the assumption that these common problems had common solutions, solutions torn from the fabric of Western management and exported by administrative experts to the newly developing areas.

In effect, everything described in this book was fair trade for export. But not everything was used. Development administrators selected those management methods which were harmless enough to win the approval of local executives yet powerful enough to act as a catalyst for administrative reform. It seemed like a sound assumption—use Western methods to help new nations develop their administrative systems, which in turn would make social and economic development possible. The assumption was widely accepted by local administrative reformers schooled in Western methods and by the foreign experts who advised them. As will be seen, events did not conform to expectations.

The following is a list of the most frequently exported management strategies, listed in the order of their importance. The list is

CHAPTER 9: COMPARATIVE PUBLIC ADMINISTRATION

based on a survey of some two hundred cases and recommendations frequently cited by experts in the field.

- Improvement of the public service, primarily through training programs, civil service reform, or the creation of national institutes of administration.
- Administration in the field, primarily in the areas of community development and local government.
- Modern management techniques, including organization development, management science, and the growth of public enterprises.
- Planning.
- Institution building, the process by which administrative experts seek to increase the capacity of public organizations to accomplish their objectives while surviving in a turbulent environment.
- Organization-and-management studies.
- Building political support for administrative reform.
- Financial and budgetary management.

The Public Service

Professional public administration in America began with the movement for a merit civil service, so it was only natural that Western experts and local administrative reformers would join forces to press for the creation of a professional civil service for the developing nation. The experts usually started with the problem of training, which was perceived by many to be the universal panacea for the problems of development administration.

Kenneth Younger states the case for training in his study of public administration in Nigeria. As the country approached the transition to self-government, expatriate administrators left their posts and returned home. The Nigerians did not have a pool of experienced managers to take their place. Younger argued that only through an extensive program of management training, supported by foreign experts, would the Nigerian government be able to maintain the level of public services achieved by the British.

The response was a crush of management training programs of all shapes and sizes. The Nigerian government upgraded the training programs run out of the Ministry of Finance and encouraged colleges and universities to expand their technical training programs. In Vietnam, an American university (Michigan State) established an institute to provide advanced training to high-ranking civil servants. It offered courses in public administration, finance, constitutional law, economics, and accounting. In Pakistan, the government established a civil service academy combining a nine-month training program with a six-month internship. Its supporters claimed that it would create a new spirit of professionalism in the public service that would reduce regional animosities.

With the training programs underway, the development administrators turned to the recruiting and staffing procedures within the government. They usually began by developing a central civil service agency, based on the American model, with the authority to upgrade personnel administration throughout the government. The agency would draft a code of civil service regulations and procedures, try to establish a position-classification system, salary and compensation scales, and a standardized method for handling grievances. It would encourage agencies to upgrade their recruitment, promotion, and performance appraisal procedures, improve supervisory practices, and engage in manpower planning. The personnel agency would promote ethical standards. It might run a few training programs and possibly become involved in collective bargaining.

As a final step toward professionalizing the public service, the foreign experts would encourage the new nation to establish a national institute of administration that could serve as a bridge between Western administrative developments and local administrative reform. The institutes operate advanced training programs through national academies, serve as national centers for the collection of administrative data, undertake research, consult on substantive problems, and serve as centers for administrative reform.

The results have been disappointing. The general consensus seems to be that, from the most extreme cases of corruption to countries where a relatively promising civil service has been allowed to degenerate, civil service reform in developing nations has not had a significant impact upon the behavior of government employees. Perhaps it was too much to expect—that training and civil service reform could overcome the more fundamental problems of poverty, education, and factionalism, which encourage corruption, inefficiency, and the practice of hiring employees on the basis of personal loyalty rather than merit.

Administration in the Field

The success of development policies depends largely upon the ability of local officials to translate national objectives into operating programs at the grass roots of administration. As a result, development administrators have become deeply involved in community development programs and to a lesser extent in the improvement of local government.

Community development programs have been used to improve social and economic conditions in nations as poor as India and as rich as the United States. As an international movement, community development also became the vehicle for exporting experts to foreign countries, outsiders dispatched from the United Nations Food and Agricultural Organization and the American Peace Corps, to mention two. All sorts of technical assistance officers, including administrative generalists, were drawn into the effort. In India, for example, community development programs offered technical assistance to rural poor in the areas of agriculture, animal husbandry, rural cooperatives, crafts and industries, civil engineering, medical assistance, self-government, and special programs for women and children.

Community development programs, by definition, emphasize self-help. The experts are there to provide technical and material assistance, but only for the purpose of showing citizens how to accomplish their own aspirations by themselves. Community development officers build up local institutions, such as self-help cooperatives, so that these institutions can carry on the development programs after the experts have left. The goals of community development, says a United Nations handbook, "go beyond the achievement of mere efficiency . . . their purposes are to develop skills in community work in groups."[3]

The emphasis upon community participation was evident in India's community development program, one of the most ambitious. The program was administered through a new territorial unit called the block, each containing about one hundred thousand people. Each village in the block elected a *panchayat* council, which sent representatives to a block development board, which in turn elected a president and sent representatives to a district development council. At the same time, the Indian minister of community development established a hierarchy of commissioners, block officers, and village workers whose job it was to provide technical assistance to the various villages, councils, and boards.

Unfortunately, local traditions often blocked substantial economic and social progress through community development. Kussum Nair, an Indian journalist, reports on one project in the province of Mysore—a showpiece financed in large part by the Ford Foundation. Through community development, most of the land in the block was put under improved methods of cultivation and irrigation, creating a substantial surplus of cash in the district. When Nair arrived, she found the farmers spending the surplus by sipping coffee in small hotels, men who had turned their wives out into the fields to work in their absence.

The reform of local government is no less challenging. Old local governments, because of their heritage of political and social autonomy, usually could not assume the new functions associated with development. New units of government, created to administer local development policies, seemed alien to local residents and commanded little support. Special obstacles to administration arose in metropolitan areas, in places like Calcutta, which has the reputation as the worst city in the world. The pressures for autonomy, coupled with the loyalties of local officials to special movements, plus the purely physical difficulties of communication, created problems of intergovernmental coordination that appeared insurmountable.

Technical assistance officers have offered lots of advice and fre-

307

An American official shows a Vietnamese peasant how to use a mechanical soil tiller to plow his rice field. Development administrators learned that Western methods were not always suited to local conditions in non-Western nations. COURTESY OF THE U.S. ARMY.

quently served as expatriate administrators in local governments. In general, the experts have tended to favor centralization—the consolidation of local governments into broad administrative units with increased financial and technical control from the central government. In the United Arab Republic, for example, the functions of local government were taken over by national ministries in Cairo until a system of provincial administration, run by provincial governors appointed by the central government, could be set up. Recommendations that might favor decentralization have been mild by comparison—moves to give local units of government more representation on national planning bodies and calls to grant an increased measure of autonomy to large metropolitan areas. Even such moderate doses of decentralization seem to work only in those localities that have the will and resources to help themselves. National executives are understandably reluctant to decentralize power to districts caught up with fiestas, subsistence farming, or political revolution against the central government.

Modern Management

The exportation of modern management techniques constitutes one of the two fastest-growing approaches to development administration. The systems approach was used for planning secondary education programs in Brazil. A programming and evaluation system was set up for implementing rural development programs in Kenya. It is hard to tell whether the popularity of modern management is due to the applicability of the methods or the fact that things like computers provide status symbols that can be used to assert the power of the agency.

. Computers have been installed for financial management and data processing in West Africa and for land-use planning in the Philippines, to cite two examples. They often break down—either because the technicians who make the repairs must service more than one country or because the national electric supply drops and surges beyond the tolerance of the machine. It is often cheaper to hire people to do the same work and the argument that computers are more accurate is diluted by the inability of local operators to debug their computer programs. Still, computers are much in demand.

The computers and the modern management techniques that accompany them are not wholly inappropriate to the needs of developing nations. In "islands of development," such as airports and nuclear power generating plants, where the government is able to concentrate its skilled technicians who speak the same language, the techniques of management science may work fairly well. The administrative achievements of such islands of development have encouraged a number of nations to establish public corporations to administer development projects. The Brazilian government, for example, established a federal development authority, called SUDENE, which administered an integrated regional development program for northeastern Brazil by coordinating other public agencies and offering tax credits to new industries.

One can even find traces of organization development infiltrating the Third World: T-groups in India, group dynamics in Malaysia, and sensitivity training in Latin America. The governments of East Africa hired outside experts to conduct a combined team-building and MBO program in order to improve the administration of the public authority that operates the three-nation telephone, telegraph, and postal service. As in the West, successful OD programs require strong central support—in particular, a willingness to encourage subordinates to accept the administrative responsibilities pressed on them by the trainers. In countries where managerial control and the rules of social deference stunt personal initiative, OD programs do not work too well. The same generalizations apply to management by objectives, which has been used with a fair degree of success for both population control and food production programs.

Planning

During the heyday of technical assistance, many foreign advisers served on the staffs of planning agencies in developing countries. The Ford Foundation and Harvard University, for example, sent an advisory group to the national planning board in Pakistan. The experts helped prepare the five-year development plan, provided advice on economic and fiscal policy, and trained Pakistanis to take their places.

Ideally, national planning boards in developing countries are organized to accomplish five tasks: data collection, program planning,

309

research, program coordination, and reporting. The key function is program planning—the preparation of coordinated plans for everything from food production and industrialization to education and fertilizer. The accomplishment of this task depends upon the other four. If the country has no institutions for collecting economic, demographic, budgetary, or physical data, or no capacity for completing special research studies, then plans are drawn up in a vacuum. If the reporting system is weak, the plans are not circulated. If the planning agency cannot coordinate the departments, it loses its power to act as a general staff agency. Beyond this, the planning agency may encounter problems of political subversion, bureaucratic breakdowns, droughts, famines, and unexpected little wars. The best planners in the agency may leave to take better-paying jobs with private firms. The agency may use up all of the available financial resources in the first six months of the five-year plan. All of these things have happened, leading to the general disillusionment with comprehensive, long-range, multisectoral planning.

National planning boards are no longer the glamour agencies they used to be. The emphasis has shifted to multidisciplinary teams that prepare development plans in the field, particularly for programs such as food production and population control. The administrative expert rides along as one member of a task force made up of economists, engineers, scientists, and anthropologists, as one among many experts. The task force attempts to get a firsthand view of local conditions and to coordinate the planning process out in the field with the local officials who actually have to execute it.

Institution Building

In public administration circles, institution building is largely a theoretical model describing how institutions develop. It suffers from the common theoretical ailments: jargon and ambiguity. Institution-building conferences become a repository for all the experts who hate the old ethnocentric approach and who dislike techniques, such as personnel administration, that are exported without reference to the institution's ability to accomplish its task. Although everyone talks about institution building, few agree on what it requires, especially in terms of administrative techniques. Some people even call it a fraud; something that administrative scholars invented to enhance their status as advisers on foreign-aid missions and to con research money out of various governments.

Nevertheless, institution building seems destined to become the new wave in development administration. Along with modern management, it is the fastest-growing approach. Institution building embodies a general strategy of planned change for the entire organization in which the survival of the institution becomes the first test of success. Institutional survival, governments are told, can be achieved only if the organization develops a "support environment" that is friendly to its programs. To build an institution, organizational leaders must build "linkages" to politicians, business and labor leaders, universities, and the public. Institution builders must also increase the capacity of the institution to utilize available technology. They eventually will have to strengthen internal administration, perhaps with traditional administrative techniques. Sometimes institution building is used to improve the work of agencies that provide key administrative services, such as civil service agencies or ministries of community development. Institution building can involve reorganization, requests for new legislation, increased planning, and technical assistance. Institution building is everything.

Institution building as a management strategy got a big boost from the American assistance programs to India. Since 80 percent of all Indians live in rural poverty, the government of India decided that it needed land-grant universities to bring agricultural progress to the Indian farmer. They asked the United States to help. Announcing that the success of the American cow college was due to its ties to the U.S. Department of Agriculture, college alumni, state politicians, and farmers, American research teams set out to recreate the complete land-grant institution in India, from its ties to the Indian Department of Agriculture right down to the old football team.

Organization-and-Management Studies

When theory sounds impractical, development administrators can always rush back to traditional administrative advice. Experts in the United Nations, for example, have encouraged developing countries to adopt various administrative reforms: to limit the proliferation of agencies, ministries, and autonomous enterprises; to group functions of government into homogeneous units; to identify clearly administrative functions and duties; to develop central administrative staff services; to decentralize operations; and to design new types of agencies to administer multipurpose programs.

The design of new types of agencies is most interesting. In the Philippines, miracle rice was introduced by an unusual collection of semiautonomous agencies and private groups. Some countries utilize two administrative systems side by side that check and balance each other, such as the French did in Vietnam. Some countries use the military to administer domestic programs. Much more research needs to be done on these indigenous organizational forms.

Building Political Support

Nearly everyone agrees that successful administrative reform requires strong political support. In Thailand, for example, budgetary reform succeeded because the prime minister moved the budget bureau into his own office, not because the bureau adopted modern techniques. Despite this fact, development administrators have been reluctant to barge into the political sphere, and their methods of building political support for improved administration have been touched with caution. Outside experts sponsor travel by political executives to other nations in order to enlighten the government about the need for reform. They conduct seminars for key executives, meet with top political executives before undertaking technical assistance programs, and they may help to draft the statutes under which development programs exist. Political involvement may become stronger, however, as public administration moves further into institution building with its emphasis upon the cultivation of the "support environment."

Financial and Budgetary Management

The scarcity of resources in developing countries would seem to make careful financial and budgetary management a necessity. Administrative experts have helped developing nations build up their central budgeting offices, perfect revenue estimates, improve tax collection, locate new sources of revenue, and test new methods of distributing it, such as revenue sharing. The experts have also tried to export program budgeting, cost-benefit analysis, and modern accounting standards, proposals that have led many critics to question why the United States continues to export administrative techniques that do not work well at home. If American administrators have difficulty projecting costs and measuring program performance, how can administrators in developing nations—where there is much less information available on such things—be expected to overcome the obstacles to rational budgeting?

Conclusion

All of these administrative strategies are at the mercy of local conditions, a fact that has not changed since the era of colonial administration. No matter how "adaptive" the outside expert tries to be, there is still a basic incongruity between the image of the professionally administered state and the way things actually get done in a developing society.

George Orwell, before he became the famous English author, worked as a subdivisional police officer in Moulmein, Lower Burma. Observing law enforcement in the empire at close quarters, he found colonial administration a dirty job and quickly determined that English interference in Asian affairs was an evil thing. Unfortunately, as a police officer, he was also an obvious target. The Asians jeered, insulted, and laughed at him. He could not decide whether to love his captive natives or "drive a bayonette into a Buddhist priest's guts."[4]

One morning an elephant, during its regular attack of "must," went wild in a bazaar, killed a cow, and destroyed a municipal garbage van. Its owner, the only person who could control it, set out in pursuit of the elephant, but unfortunately in the wrong direction, which removed the Burman owner by twelve hours' distance when police officer Orwell arrived on the scene. The women of the quarter were chasing the children away from something they ought not see. Orwell discovered an Indian, a black Dravidian coolie, still warm, whom the elephant had killed by grinding him into the mud with its foot. Immediately, Orwell dispatched an orderly to a friend's house for a weapon on the chance he might have to protect himself. The orderly returned with an elephant rifle and five cartridges. The citizens of the neighborhood, who had previously shown little interest in the ravaging elephant, ran through the streets shouting excitedly that a police officer was going to shoot an elephant.

Orwell did not want to shoot any animal, nor this elephant in particular. To shoot a working elephant, after all, was as serious an act as destroying a huge and costly machine. His reluctance was confirmed when he found the elephant grazing in a soggy paddy field as peacefully as a cow.

> But at that moment I glanced around at the crowd that had followed me. It was an immense crowd, two thousand at the least and growing every minute. It blocked the road for a long distance on either side. I looked at the sea of yellow faces above the garish clothes—faces all happy and excited over this bit of fun, all certain that the elephant was going to be shot. And it was at this moment, as I stood with the rifle in my hands, that I first grasped the hollowness, the futility of the white man's dominion in the East. Here was I, the white man with his gun, standing in front of the unarmed native crowd—seemingly the leading actor of the piece; but in reality I was only an absurd puppet pushed to and fro by the will of those yellow faces behind. I perceived in this moment that when the white man turns tyrant it is his own freedom that he destroys. He becomes a sort of hollow, posing dummy, the conventional figure of a sahib. For it is the condition of his rule that he shall spend his life in trying to impress the "natives," and so in every crisis, he has got to do what the "natives" expect of him. He wears a mask, and his face grows to fit it. I had to shoot the elephant.[5]

Orwell's story contains the theme frequently heard among returning development administrators: the enormous difficulty of trying to make professional management fit developing societies. At a United Nations conference on administrative reform, administrative specialists from around the world agreed that "it was not possible to identify one particular strategy or standard which should be adopted as a general model. . . . In each country, the best strategy would be dictated by the special circumstances."[6]

THE PRISMATIC SOCIETY

Persons educated in industrialized nations carry an image of good administration around in their heads. Usually it is an image of the smoothly run state, an image rooted in the Weberian bureaucratic ideal: agencies with clearly defined objectives and straight lines of authority, responsive to their public, efficient in their operations. Carried to its extreme, this image leads to the view that proper management is subject to principles as inviolate as the laws of gravity and

313

that societies which do not conform to these laws will perish through economic and political stagnation. Despite the fact that the bureaucracy is only one of several possible forms of organization, despite all the talk about adaptive management strategies, it is still awfully hard for a Western expert confronted with an inefficient, corrupt government agency not to recall that Western image and say, "If only their performance could be improved through proper administrative techniques, these problems would disappear and the country could triple its output."

In 1916 an American missionary went to China to help the Chinese peasants improve their farming methods. The image of agricultural management he carried in his head was based on progress through technology. But when he began to talk to the Chinese about buying tractors and improving their output, they turned away. They did not want tractors; they could not afford tractors. The missionary had to invent a new image of agricultural management, an image based on local conditions. After that, he was able to help the Chinese modify their own tools to meet the needs of Chinese agriculture.

The missionary's son, Fred Riggs, who was born in China, became a professor of public administration. He lived in New York, Bangkok, Manila, and settled in Honolulu. Drawing upon his early experiences in China, he developed a model of comparative administration that helped Western experts see administration through the eyes of their hosts. His insights—often called a prismatic theory—are highly controversial, both in style and content. Nevertheless, his theory is a widely respected alternative to the Euro-American image of the developed bureaucratic state.

To comprehend Riggs's theory, one must first understand that it draws upon an approach to political science known as structural functional analysis. All societies must perform certain functions—someone must act as Solomon to decide disputes, someone must cure disease, someone must bury the dead and pick up the garbage. Anthropologists tell political scientists that nearly all societies perform these functions, with only a few trifling exceptions.

After having identified the common functions of social and political life, political scientists are in a better position to explain the confusing array of *structures* that perform them. The variety of structures is enormous—Saudi Arabia has a king and Mexico has a president, Zaire has witch doctors and Los Angeles is full of psychoanalysts. They perform the same essential functions, despite the fact that their styles of organization differ dramatically. The governor cutting the ribbon that opens a superhighway and the witch doctor sprinkling magic water over a flood-control project are performing similar functions. Parliaments, cabinets, presidents, dictators, and independent commissions that issue laws all perform the function of laying down rules. There are structures for the economic functions, such as markets; structures for the social functions, such as families; and structures for all sorts of political functions with the purpose of allocating power.

314

Fred Riggs, who was born to American missionaries in China, is interested in the collision of Western administrative methods with non-Western values. He uses the prism as an analogy to explain the paradoxical nature of public administration in transitional societies. Riggs currently teaches halfway between East and West in the department of political science at the University of Hawaii. COURTESY OF THE UNIVERSITY OF HAWAII.

The traditional society, such as a traditional Eskimo village, contains only a few structures—the family and the chieftain. A few structures perform all of the necessary functions, enforcing rules, settling disputes, and caring for the health and safety of the community.

Humans who live in suburbs and skyscrapers are surrounded by a universe of structures—P.T.A.'s, labor unions, legislative committees, city managers, fire departments, university departments, and assorted churches, exotic and traditional. Each structure performs a rather specific function.

As any society develops and casts off its old ways, the old structures are broken down and replaced by new, more specialized structures. To Riggs, the differentiation of structures is the essence of development anywhere that rapid change occurs, from the Chinese Republic to the American space program. The process of differentiation is analogous to sunlight passing through a thunderstorm and emerging as a rainbow. Riggs characterizes most traditional societies as sunlight in its natural state, where the functions of society are gathered together into a few critical structures—mixed together, as it were, like pure, white light. (The light is actually *fused*, to use the correct term from the science of optics.) The storm acts as a *prism* to transform the light into a rainbow—to separate the various bands of color, make them more specific, just as the structures in the transitional society must be cracked apart to accommodate the specialization of functions necessitated by the automobile, the city, the radio, and the other products of modernization.

More than anything else, the developing society needs to discover methods for integrating the operations of the newly emerging structures: the banks, the schools, the parliaments, the national political parties. The need is made more acute by the fact that, in a transitional society, the old structures continue to exist alongside the new. The oxcart and the automobile travel along the same road. A visitor can drive a few miles from city to country and pass through two thousand years of social and technological history.[a]* The developing society is enveloped in a storm of transition. The more turbulent the change, the greater the need for integration. If the society can survive the turbulence, the result will be newly diffracted structures, more differentiated, better integrated, and well arranged, like the rainbow at the end of the storm.[b]

Riggs is interested in the process of change: what happens during the period of transition—the prismatic state—when new structures appear and the society struggles to integrate them.[c] To Riggs, who loves to deal in analogies, the prismatic country is caught like light inside a prism: not fused, not diffracted, just in the process of breaking down. It has not completed the process of integration. The new structures are not coordinated; they are not autonomous; they do not fit together. Only half born, the new structures continue to perform functions associated with traditional society. This is the key to understanding the developing nation—the modern is a screen behind which traditional life carries on. When the American West was developing, men on the frontier constructed flat wooden storefronts along the main streets of town to give the appearance of a modern community. But when a cowpoke walked through the doors, he entered small tents hidden behind the facade. Things were not what they appeared to be. Extensive structures and procedures existed, but they were not expected to work in reality. Riggs calls this discrepancy *formalism*.[d] It is the essence of his theory and the basis for understanding the essentially paradoxical nature of prismatic societies.

The following story, told by the Indian author R. K. Narayan, may help to illustrate the essentially prismatic nature of developing countries. Although written in the form of a novel, it is based on a true story about a man known as the Financial Expert.

Narayan sets the story in the fictional village of Malgudi, located in southern India in the triangle formed by Madras, Mysore, and Coimbatore. Most people there suffer from a terrible shortage of cash, not just for the general necessities of life, but for the inevitable obligations created by births, deaths, and weddings; harvest festivals; celebrations welcoming a season; religious rites honoring various gods, saints, and redeemers; and the New Year's celebrations, twice a year, once for the solar and then for the lunar new year. Ready cash for these obligations is provided by professional moneylenders, who dispense funds from beneath a large banyan tree in the center of the village. Although the villagers are chronically in debt, due to their own extravagant habits and the usurious interest rates charged them, the moneylenders are viewed as friends because they take an interest in one's personal affairs.

It is the dream of social reformers in the area to establish cooperative banks that will encourage thrift and halt the practice of reckless borrowing. Eventually the government sets up the Central Coopera-

---

*The small-letter footnotes are references to the special terms that Riggs uses to describe the characteristics of prismatic societies. Definitions for these terms appear on pages 320–21.

CHAPTER 9: COMPARATIVE PUBLIC ADMINISTRATION

tive Land Mortgage Bank, located in a new building across the street from the banyan tree. The bank officials encourage the villagers to save, and lend money at low interest rates to those in real need. To prevent reckless borrowing in the village, the bank devises various rules, regulations, and formalities that delay the processing of the loan application and insure that the loan, once granted, is spent on necessities, such as land or seed. All of this is accomplished through an elaborate loan application form, which, if properly drawn up, almost always draws out the desired loan.

The villagers, understandably, are anxious to borrow money at the low interest rates offered by the bank. However, few of them can read or write, much less fill out the loan application forms. At this point, the financial expert, Margayya, intervenes. Ambitious, but without social standing, he learns the rules for loaning money as a peon in the bank. When the bank secretary expels him for shady financial dealings, Margayya moves to the banyan tree with ink, pen, blotter, a small register, and loan application forms from the bank. There he sits, filling out forms for the villagers (for a fee), selling them application forms (which the bank gives out free), and making small loans to the villagers which they use as collateral to wedge out bigger and bigger loans from the cooperative bank. The villagers love him. The cooperative bank secretary plots to expel him from the banyan tree.

Still anxious to increase his status within the village, Margayya consults a local priest to determine how to make more money. The priest advises him to please the gods through a special rite—mixing the ashes of a red lotus with milk drawn from a smoke-colored cow. Margayya performs the rite and shortly thereafter meets a sociologist named Dr. Pal, who has written a scholarly book titled *Bedlife, or the Science of Marital Happiness*. The book makes Margayya blush, so he publishes Dr. Pal's manuscript under the discreet title of *Domestic Harmony* and sells it as pornography.

Sales are sensational. Margayya becomes rich. With his house full of money, Margayya sets up his own bank, lends money, and offers depositors high interest rates. He becomes a financial expert and lectures on the subject of capital. All goes well until Dr. Pal spreads a rumor that Margayya is a fraud. The villagers rush to Margayya's home to retrieve their deposits. The bank crashes. Within a matter of hours, Margayya is bankrupt. Courts, lawyers, and inventories consume Margayya's possessions. After four months, left with nothing but a pen and an ink bottle, he returns to his old place beneath the banyan tree.

Narayan wrote this story in 1950, nine years before Riggs began to set down his theory of prismatic society. Even though neither person was aware of the other's work, many of the characteristics of the prismatic theory can be found in the story. After reading the next section, you might want to reexamine the story to see if you can find them.

THE ECOLOGY OF PUBLIC ADMINISTRATION

Structures modern in appearance do not operate in the same manner in the transitional society as they do in the modern. The developing nation will create a bureau, copying its structure from the modern society, then assign the bureau many functions that Western experts would not classify as administrative.[e] Only a few civil servants, those who are Western educated, will view administration as being somehow different from economics, sociology, or political science. For the rest, the process of Western differentiation—separating knowledge into separate fields—will not have transpired. Administration, politics, economic welfare, social obligations—all of these things are meshed together in their own image of the prismatic bureau. Some societies do not even have a word for administration in their language and must borrow the word "administration" from the Western nations, just as they borrow the structure of the bureau.

Riggs insists that those experts who would modernize prismatic societies must first acquire a new image of organizational phenomenon. They must learn to see administration from the point of view of the administrator in the transitional society—from within the prism, as it were. The expert cannot use Western terms to describe what are essentially non-Western processes. A bureau in a transitional society is not a bureau in the Western meaning of the word. This is why Riggs invented a new vocabulary. He calls the transitional bureau a *sala*, a Spanish word that means not only a formal office where business is transacted, but also a chamber in one's home where traditional family functions are performed.[f] The operation of the sala can be under-

A modern English class is taught in a traditional Thai pavilion. Public administration in developing nations is characterized by the mixing of the old and the new, by the appearance of Western procedures intermixed with codes of traditional behavior. Fred Riggs developed much of his theory of prismatic society while studying in Thailand.
COURTESY OF ACTION/PEACE CORPS.

stood only in the context of the social and economic functions that it performs, that is, in terms of its *ecology*. Riggs describes five forces, translated into Western categories, that shape behavior in the prismatic bureau.

Economic Functions

The structures that perform economic functions in prismatic societies resemble a market wherein all persons have free access to the buying and selling of goods. Such structures include banks, supermarkets, car dealers, trade commissions, railroads, and chambers of commerce. In reality, however, the presence of market structures is a screen for a great deal of informal bargaining over such things as prices, salaries, interest rates, and the value of land. Formally, for example, interest rates are exorbitant, but many borrowers with sufficient political or social status can obtain special access to lower rates.[g] Economic structures in prismatic societies perform a variety of social and political functions, such as the redistribution of income by allowing different prices for different customers.[h]

Prismatic Elites

One curious feature of the prismatic economic system is negative development, a situation in which economic growth leads to personal insecurity and a lower standard of living. If an individual gains economic power, he or she may subsequently lose political or social standing.[i] Developing societies are often dominated by a single elite —the well-educated inheritors of the colonial system who epitomize traditional religious, political, or warrior values. As an outgrowth of change, new communities and new leaders emerge—rapidly, in continually changing patterns so confusing and so unstable that the position of the old elites is undermined.[j] The old elite, anxious to retain its dominant position, is reluctant to grant too much power to the leaders of the newly emerging communities. In theory, the developing society promotes the achievement ethic and the opportunity to enter into the elite class; in reality, the elite restricts such opportunities to those who embody the traditional values and can be trusted to maintain the status of the powers that be.[k] Like the Asians who were forced to leave Uganda, the subordinate elites are allowed influence not as a matter of right, contract or authority, but "through the back door," like servants always serving at the pleasure of the dominating elite.[l]

The Social System

In effect, new groups are mobilized within the prismatic society faster than the society can assimilate them.[m] There is not enough wealth, housing, employment opportunity or political power to accommodate all the newly educated citizens who emerge each day from traditional village life. What resources the society possesses are tightly

A GLOSSARY OF RIGGSEAN TERMS

Because of the paradoxical nature of public administration in prismatic societies, it is difficult to use Western words to describe things that are Western in form but not in substance. For this reason, Fred Riggs created a new vocabulary to describe the ecology of public administration. The terms are presented in the order in which they appear in the text. The letters identify the place in the text where the concept is introduced.

heterogeneity *(a)*, conflicting modes of life coexisting within one country that result in polarized, mutually hostile communities.

diffracted *(b)*, a term used to describe a society in which new structures are both differentiated and integrated; a developed society.

prismatic *(c)*, a term used to describe a society in which the differentiation of new structures occurs faster than the society can integrate them.

formalism *(d)*, the existence of extensive forms and procedures that are not expected to work in practice; the degree of discrepancy between prescribed form and actual practice.

overlapping *(e)*, a situation in which institutions formally give the impression of performing specific functions, e.g., education, but actually perform a variety of traditional functions.

sala *(f)*, the prismatic bureau, an office that merges administrative tasks with traditional functions; taken from the Spanish word meaning both an office and a personal room in a home, church, or public hall.

canteen-bazaar *(g)*, an economic system that formally resembles a market but actually works like a traditional economy. The canteen represents special stores serving privileged or captive clients; the bazaar represents the open market where the buyer must engage in protracted bargaining over the price of goods.

price indeterminancy *(h)*, a situation in which the price of goods, services, or.money is based on the relative status of the parties to the transaction.

agglomeration *(i)*, the development of new classes in society, but in embryonic form, insecure, with a single elite imposing its domination over them.

kaleidoscopic stratification *(j)*, a chaotic, continually changing society made up of overlapping communities and classes; taken from the term describing an optical toy.

attainment *(k)*, the mixing of ascriptive criteria and achievement ethics as the basis for recruitment to positions in the society.

intrusion *(l)*, the method by which new elites, lacking legitimate access to power, have to push or cajole their way into the traditional centers of power so that they can buy protection from the bureaucracy.

poly-communalism *(m)*, the mobilization of several separate communities without their assimilation into the society.

clects *(n)*, the prismatic association, an organization combining modern forms of association with a traditional communal orientation; taken from the words *clique* and *sect*. The clect draws its membership from persons with political or economic ambitions possessing a common social background who are discriminated against as a group.

status-contract nexus *(o)*, the formula for determining personal access to property and power; a combination of traditional inheritance and legal rights.

double talk *(p)*, the prismatic code that allows an official to decide whether to over-conform to a rule or not enforce it at all, depending upon the status of the client.

blocked-throughputs *(q)*, a situation in which the linkages between inputs and outputs in a prismatic system are deliberately scrambled to allow officials the power to treat each situation as an exception to the rule.

poly-normativism *(r)*, a myth system that mixes mystical and rational approaches to problem solving.

dissensus *(s)*, the absence of agreement on the goals of the state or on who should rule, which leads to the use of coercion, violence, money, or charisma as the basic methods for achieving goals.

bifocal scope of power *(t)*, a measure of the difference between the formal authority of an official and the actual scope of his or her effective control.

interference complex *(u)*, the ability of bureaucrats to intervene in the judicial, legislative, and executive processes because of an imbalance of power that favors the bureaucracy.

dependency syndrome *(v)*, a situation in which a disproportionately large share of the total national product is consumed by a small elite, making all others in the society dependent upon the elite for their personal security.

---

controlled by the dominating elite. Since competition for privileges is so intense, the modernized citizens band together to fight for special privileges for their own social group. Membership in the group is restricted to persons who share a common traditional background and therefore can trust each other. An example would be the Chinese chambers of commerce—in Bangkok or Manila, not China. Such groups develop dual purposes. They have a communal orientation, drawn from traditional customs, as well as the particular aspirations of their members for special economic privileges. Riggs calls these uniquely prismatic groups *clects*.[n]

Prismatic Symbols

All societies develop various rules, backed up by myths or symbols, which lend legitimacy to the distribution of privilege and power within the society. Property rights, for example, are a form of privilege that must be legitimized through the symbols of contract and private ownership. In prismatic societies, persons from groups with high status may enjoy access to all sorts of privileges to which they have no legal rights; the rights possessed by persons of low status are rarely protected by permanent legal arrangements.[o] The prismatic society will appear to promulgate a legal rule and then allow a wide variety of variations in its enforcement.[p] Legal rules are treated as obstructions to be by-passed informally.[q] The standard explanation for the variance is that the enforcers must make an informal exception because they do not have (and do not want) the information upon which to make a rational decision. The ambiguous quality of the rules is compounded by the extraordinary mixing of traditional myths with rational standards, with officials borrowing rituals from their ancestors while imitating the legal processes set up by the colonial parent—whatever is appropriate to the situation at hand.[r] Since there is little broad-scale agreement upon the basic norms of society and many groups remain unassimilated into the nation, it is terribly difficult to get everyone to agree to abide by standard legal formulas. Control must be grabbed—through coercion, violence, money, or charismatic rule, but rarely through constitutional authority.[s]

Prismatic Power

Prismatic society is characterized by an unusual preoccupation with acquiring and maintaining power. Administrative methods in the prismatic society are typically used to extend the scope of one's own personal power without reference to the goals of the agency. Formally, the authority of the executive is restricted by the law, but any individual may extend his or her effective control through a variety of extralegal strategies.[t] It is not uncommon for bureaucrats to interfere in political policy making, a privilege they enjoy because of the unusual weight of bureaucratic power in the prismatic state.[u] The realities of power require new entrepreneurs, whether economic or political, to transfer a substantial portion of their wealth or loyalty to the elite in return for protection from the elite.[v] Once again Riggs stresses the feature that guides the image of the prismatic state—the contrast between formal authority and effective control, between form and reality. In the prismatic society, things are not what they appear to be.

All of these forces converge on the administrative structures of the developing society—the sala. Sala officials are power maximizers; they try to exploit the ambiguity in any situation to serve their own power. Management control is sought as an end in itself, and thus administrative methods are selected on the basis of whether or not they advance the personal power of the administrator. Administrative power is not checked by legislators, judges, or pressure groups. The more powerful the sala officials are, the easier it is for them to place personal goals above the need for organizational efficiency.

Riggs concludes that "the degree of administrative efficiency of a bureaucracy varies inversely with the weight of its power."[7]

Nowhere is this more apparent than in the enforcement of rules. In short, there are rules for everything and there are rules for nothing. Formally, sala officials have at their disposal a confusing battery of rules, which are applied unmercifully to clients that the sala official does not trust. Because the rules are so contradictory, the only way to make the government work is to suspend the rules, which sala officials will do for persons of sufficient stature or for personal political advantage. In effect, every official action involves an exception to a rule. A Western management expert might suggest eliminating the conflicting rules, which would surely not exist had the developing society not felt obliged to imitate the complex rules and procedures of Western nations. If the duplicating rules were eliminated, however, the sala officials then would be left with one rule to apply for everyone—and they would become mere instruments of authority, without the power to enforce and waive the rules at their own pleasure. It is apparent, Riggs suggests, that one cannot separate purely legal-rational administration from the social, economic, and political obligations that converge upon the manager of the sala.

Consider the so-called personnel function in administration. The sala official is under tremendous pressure to appoint friends and relatives to government positions. The official has social obligations to family and friends; they need security from unemployment; and the official needs loyal employees in order to gain more power. Of course, there are rules requiring open, competitive examinations as a basis for hiring and promotion, but members of rival groups are simply forbidden to take the examinations or complete the training necessary to pass them. Status and personal friendship are the real tests used to screen prospective recruits. Promotion is based primarily upon loyalty. It is not at all uncommon to find a bureau set up to be run by forty employees bursting with as many as three hundred, all members of the same family, tribe, or clect. The lack of real work and the preoccupation with personal power encourage the employees to devote an extraordinary amount of time to fighting over tenure, pensions, holidays, leave time, uniforms, and the other symbols of job security.

The financial and budgetary functions are central to Western administration, where they are regulated by policies governing taxes, budgets, and expenditure control. Developing governments suffer initially from a small tax base, a problem that is accentuated by the tendency of the powerful to avoid taxes and the necessity to spend large amounts of the public purse on salaries and fringe benefits. Again, form and reality clash—on paper the salaries of most officials are abysmally low; in fact, these are supplemented with access to low-cost housing, government automobiles, and special canteens. The most sacred of sacred cows in Western personnel administration—equal pay for equal work—is monstrously difficult to achieve in prismatic societies. The income supplements are rarely fixed in law, which intensifies the personal insecurity of the bureaucrats who possess the privileges. The attractiveness of the privileges creates pressures to enlarge the parasitical class of bureaucrats. All of this tends to inflame the problem of negative development: more jobs but less economic security.

The budget, on paper at least, consists of formal allocations from the central treasury. The competition for these budgetary allocations is intense. The outcome depends considerably upon the loyalty of the sala in the eyes of the ruling elite. To avoid competition, the sala officials attempt to build up sources of autonomous revenue that they alone control—fees, earmarked taxes, "donations," and foreign support. Program coordination through expenditure control is made difficult by the general absence of program planning and the simple fact that the items in the appropriation act rarely reflect what the sala official is really spending. The tendency to overstaff, the competition for formal appropriations, and the existence of autonomous funds and special employee privileges all tend to discourage the construction of rational budget plans.

The preoccupation with power—and the fact that the sala official will engage in more than administrative functions—creates those things which appear to Western observers to be "problems of administration." Yet, from the point of view of the sala official, are these "problems," or are they the necessities of political and administrative survival? What seems to be a problem to a Western observer may be perceived as the natural state of affairs by an official in the transitional state. Consider the so-called problem of hiring one's relatives. Says Riggs:

> In a traditional setting, say a tribal society, where all elite positions depend on family positions, nepotism cannot exist. It is the incompatibility between an administrative and a conflicting family code which creates the problem of nepotism.[8]

It all depends upon one's perspective. In the sala, where administrative functions are not fully differentiated, it is not yet possible to talk about an administrative code that is separate from the social code.

The total impact of prismatic administration defeats the essential aim of development: the idea that somehow, through proper administration, it may be possible to create the desired social and economic change. As the complex, paradoxical forces of transition converge upon the institutions of the prismatic society, the chances for planned, administered change slide away. Riggs says that "actual outcomes of intentional change are likely to be the opposite of what is intended . . . the agents of change [in prismatic societies] are typically surprised by the bitter fruits of their well-intended efforts."[9]

During the early sixties, when Riggs formulated his theory, the trauma of transition was most pronounced in the developing nations. There was a widespread feeling at that time that Western nations stood at the endpoint of the modernization scale—that Western nations were capable of administering solutions to almost any problem, from a flight to the moon to the economic reconstruction of Europe, and that prismatic characteristics such as formalism and the unusual preoccupation with gaining power never occurred to any serious degree in Western institutions.

Although the prismatic theory is based on the experience of the developing nations, particularly those in Asia, Riggs warns that any society risks prismatic breakdowns when it tries to mix the old and the new in a period of rapid change. It does not matter whether the transition is between the oxcart and the automobile or between the automobile and whatever its successor might be. What matters is the capacity of the society in transition to achieve a higher level of diffraction. This is the essence of developmental change. Because they are already more differentiated, the more developed societies must create more elaborate methods of integration in order to achieve new levels of diffraction. If they fail, then the so-called developed societies, like the developing ones, will slip into their own prismatic trap.

THEORY BUILDING IN COMPARATIVE ADMINISTRATION

Through his theory of prismatic society, Riggs suggests many of the variables that affect the course of administrative development in different societies. Although this theory dominates the study of comparative administration (and this chapter), it is only one of many theories used to explain the difficulties of administrative development in the Third World. Indeed, one might suggest that the popularity of the Riggs approach set off an avalanche of theory building at the expense of more practical concerns.

Most of the theory building in public administration was done under the auspices of the Comparative Administration Group (CAG), a branch of the American Society for Public Administration which met frequently during the 1960s to read papers and discuss common concerns. In general, the papers dealt with the context of development administration, usually at a fairly high level of abstraction, and were based upon personal observation rather than empirical research. In the summer of 1965 CAG held a series of seminars devoted to problems of space and time in comparative administration. The papers on time, edited by Dwight Waldo and published as the *Temporal Dimensions of Development Administration*, are the most interesting and reflect the concerns of the group.

Everyone agreed that different perspectives on time affected the success or failure of development programs. At the simplest level, the different perspectives are the difference between factory time and rural time. Factory time, or obedience to the clock, is essential to the high degree of synchronization and the detailed long-range planning that underlies modern administration. One author asserts that the highly coordinated factory "can do without coal, iron, and steam easier than it can do without the clock."[10] Frederick Taylor launched scientific management with time-and-motion studies; in the 1920s the Soviet Union formed a league devoted to the wearing of watches in order to promote industrialization.

It was not always so. Even in the United States, throughout most of the nineteenth century, different towns kept their own systems of time based on the zenith of the sun over the village square. The modern system of standard time zones was forced on a reluctant population by the railroads. Rural time, in most parts of the world, is characterized by short-term attitudes toward work, savings, and investment and long-term fatalism regarding the possibilities for substantial change. Development projects often fail because they attempt to impose an alien factory time system upon local administrators whose lives are rooted in rural time. One author, Frank Sherwood, even presented empirical evidence demonstrating the different attitudes of Western and non-Western administrators toward synchronization, scheduling, sequencing, and the clock.

Time creates different perspectives toward administration; so does the type of political system operating in the country. Since the Comparative Administration Group was dominated by political scientists, it was only natural that some of its members should try to associate different styles of public administration with different styles of government. One of the most widely quoted regime-classification schemes was prepared by Ferrel Heady, who offered a large number of classifications accompanied by a large dose of data. For the purposes of summary, Heady's scheme can be characterized this way: public administration will be substantially different under classic bureaucratic systems, pluralistic systems, modernizing governments, and communist-totalitarian regimes.

Classic bureaucratic systems are found mainly in states once ruled by a monarch or an aristocracy and in states in which the bureaucrats—generals, perhaps—have seized power. The bureaucracy is a closed system, open only to people with special qualifications, and the techniques of bureaucratic management are used to promote continuity and stability in administration. In pluralistic systems, such as the United States, public administration is conditioned by the political process into which the bureaucrat must venture to build political support. Administrators use a mixture of political and formal-bureaucratic strategies, depending upon the task involved. Power is no less important for bureaucratic elites in the modernizing state but, because of the relative absence of nonbureaucratic participants and the lack of resources, power is sought through the methods associated with Riggs's theory of prismatic society. Finally, public administration is different in communist-totalitarian systems, which are characterized by the interlocking hierarchies of party and bureaucracy, strict limits on bureaucratic discretion, and an emphasis upon economic approaches to administrative planning.

Many of the theorists in the comparative field have sought to find the key to development. In a study of Italy, Mexico, Germany, the United States, and Great Britain, political scientists Gabriel Almond

326

and James Coleman lit upon the willingness of people to become involved in politics to achieve their demands—the joining syndrome or, as Almond and Coleman called it, the civic culture. Economists have suggested that the entrepreneurial spirit is the crucial factor, lifting countries such as Japan out of feudalism while other nations, such as Indochina, have lagged behind. In an impressive cross-cultural study, psychologist David McClelland discovered that the germ of entrepreneurial spirit began in mastery training: the child-rearing practices, especially the folk tales, by which parents give children their values. And it was probably inevitable that someone would do research on the radio as the key to development. Radio listening, movie going, and now television watching create a sense of psychic empathy, a world view that social scientist Daniel Lerner says gives villagers the ability to see beyond the life in which they are trapped and demand the rudiments of modern living—bicycles, brassieres, and more radios. Such demands, says Lerner, are the source of revolutionary political and social change.

Temporal, political, social, economic, and psychological factors such as these have an enormous impact upon the choice of administrative strategies and the chances for executing them. Smart public administrators pay attention to them when attempting to manage programs in a society enduring rapid change. However, a mere list of such factors, by itself, does not create an ecological model of administration.

> The mere enumeration of environmental conditions by no means constitutes an ecological approach. What must be demonstrated are the connections between particular environmental variables and administrative behavior . . . Without identifying relevant variables and showing how they are linked, it is impossible to demonstrate ecological relationships.[11]

Comparative public administration, in its effort to show why so many administrative strategies in developing nations failed, concentrated on the sort of theory building that avoided such practical concerns. There were some bits and pieces lying around, but as of the mid-seventies, public administration had not produced a widely accepted model that met the criteria set forth by Fred Riggs, quoted above.

THE IMPACT OF LOCAL CONDITIONS UPON ADMINISTRATIVE SUCCESS

The study of comparative public administration began with a simple effort to transfer modern administrative techniques into emerging political systems. The first techniques were drawn from the model of institutional power then dominating the Western world, a model full of administrative principles, oriented toward administrative stability, and designed to provide a greater measure of efficiency and economy in the provision of public services.

After a quarter century of experience, what have the experts learned? William Siffin, a scholar who has watched the growth of comparative public administration, cites three important lessons. First, the experts learned that exported techniques could produce unintended results. The worst cases occurred when Western experts introduced methods that did not work well at home, such as program budgeting and rapid computerization. Second, the experts learned that their administrative advice "better served the basic *maintenance* needs of the recipients than their *developmental* needs."[12] In other words, Western methods of administration helped to preserve the status quo. Since the experts were, after all, exporting the basic techniques of bureaucratic management, it should come as no surprise that elites in developing countries would use bureaucratic controls to solidify their base of power. Siffin's third lesson is the most intriguing. Some things, he says, actually worked.

> If we have learned that the key to public administration for development is not the well-developed administrative technologies of the West, they are not without their uses. It is possible to adopt a variety of administrative technologies with reasonable prospects of success.[13]

What is needed, clearly, is more knowledge about what works or does not work under what conditions. This is where the study of comparative public administration leads.

What would a model of administrative contingencies look like? One part of the answer might be found in the study by Naomi Caiden and Aaron Wildavsky titled *Planning and Budgeting in Poor Countries.* Caiden, Wildavsky, and their assistants spent five years surveying documents from eighty nations and conducting in-depth interviews in twelve. Wildavsky, the senior scholar, got the choice assignments —Ceylon and Nepal—while the others went to Ghana, Malaysia, and other places. All of them tried to look at the world of administration as the executive in the poor country has to. They accepted conditions as they existed, which included:

- Economic poverty—the per capita gross national product in these countries was less than $800 per year. The countries lacked redundancy, which is to say that they had no reserves to pay for mistakes. Unlike the rich nations, the poor nations could not afford to be wrong.
- Political instability—neither the regime in power nor the office of any executive was secure. Officials had to pay for whatever security they could find by accumulating power.
- Financial uncertainty—"unable to collect taxes in sufficient amounts, and lacking control over a significant proportion of the resources they do collect, poor governments work in a perpetual aura of financial crises."[14]

How can a nation facing these conditions write plans and make budgets? From the point of view of the financial minister, the key to the budget process is this: stay ahead of the unexpected. Financial ministers adopt strategies designed to maintain enough cash on hand

Having learned that there is no such thing as a universally correct principle of administration, public administrators have begun to search for a model of administrative contingencies that will allow them to fit the method to the situation at hand. Here residents of the Sierra Leone village of Daru use simple administrative methods to lay a drainage pipe to divert a stream so they can build a road out of their village. COURTESY OF ACTION/PEACE CORPS.

to run the government on a day-to-day basis. They make conservative revenue estimates, continually revise their expenditure priorities, and insist that department officials secure permission for every new financial transaction as if they were seeking approval for their budget. "The entire budget is treated as if each item were supplemental, subject to renegotiation at the last minute."[15] The financial minister can do several things to delay expenditures: cut funds that have been authorized, defer paying bills, pay bills with vouchers instead of money, and require an inordinate amount of paper work before transacting any business.

The agency chiefs, in turn, adopt a whole series of strategies designed to keep the money flowing. Most of these strategies are played outside of the budget review process because everyone knows that the estimates and authorizations are subject to renegotiation. The agency chiefs set up their own sources of revenue through fees or earmarked taxes. They solicit funds directly from foreign sources. They withhold information on unexpended balances and try to transfer funds between categories—anything to avoid the underspending that might let the financial minister claw the money back. Ironically, underspending—idle money in the midst of poverty—is a chronic problem in developing nations, especially in capital-development programs where the money actually has to be spent to build something rather than be soaked up by salaries.

What sort of budgetary reform is best suited to the needs of developing nations? Caiden and Wildavsky advocate a strategy which they call continuous budgeting: "ad hoc decisions on resource allocations against a background of what is known about revenue and expenditure at the time."[16] It is the most realistic budgetary decision-making strategy for a country that is poor, unstable, and financially uncertain. It is far more realistic than the complicated annual budget review cycle and the long-range planning processes used in Western nations.

The authors save their best shots for long-range planning. "If we were asked to design a mechanism to maximize every known disability and minimize any possible advantage of poor countries, we could hardly do better than comprehensive, multisectoral planning."[17] How can a country that lacks the resources to execute an annual budget guide itself through a comprehensive five-year plan? The failure of planning, say the authors, is not accidental. Planning is designed to fail. Planners are encouraged to adopt Western methods so that they will produce only paper and not interfere with the real budgetary decisions. It keeps them out of the way. Projects that succeed, claim the authors, succeed because they are small, because the planners work on implementation instead of macroeconomic models, because information about financing the project is manageable, and because executives have the skill to work within a framework of continuous budgeting.

The Caiden-Wildavsky study makes broad generalizations about major administrative processes in many developing countries. Other authors have contributed more specific pieces. John Montgomery, for example, has analyzed the effects of alternative organizational designs on the success of land reform. In a comparison of twenty-five cases, he demonstrated how the officials running the different programs made trade-offs between a centralized bureaucracy, which enhanced the power of the program, and a devolution of responsibility to local units, which increased the chances for improving the income and security of the peasants. Studies such as these could become the basis for a truly comprehensive model of administrative contingencies.

A decade ago, when the study of comparative administration was well underway, a skeptical budget examiner asked an American foreign aid officer, "Why is it that we should want to know more about Indonesian public administration than the Indonesians?"[18] The answer, obviously, is that administrative understanding depends upon comparison. Only by exploring the different conditions faced by different managers in different countries can administrative experts hope to catalog the variety of administrative strategies adopted to overcome those conditions. International experience is essential to the development of a model of administrative contingencies founded upon an appreciation for the effect of local conditions on the choice of administrative strategies.

Unfortunately for public administration, the budget examiner won the argument. Not only did the well of money once available for studies of development administration dry up, but expatriot administrators found that they were no longer welcome in developing nations.

Public administration was left at the end of the golden era of development administration without a satisfactory explanation of the relationship between local conditions and the strategies of successful administration. Today one can only say that the choice of strategies requires seasoned judgment, founded on a complete understanding of the different approaches to public administration, buttressed by knowledge about specific cases in which one strategy worked and another failed. The sources contributing to this knowledge are bewilderingly complex—so complex, in fact, that they threaten to tear the study of public administration into many little pieces.

FOR FURTHER READING

Many students enter the field of comparative administration through the short textbook by Ferrel Heady, *Public Administration: A Comparative Perspective* (Englewood Cliffs, N.J.: Prentice-Hall, 1966). The scholarly side of the field is dominated by books of readings. Two of the early classics produced while the field was at the height of its power are Ferrel Heady and Sybil L. Stokes, eds., *Papers in Comparative Public Administration* (Ann Arbor: University of Michigan Press, 1962) and Joseph G. La Palombara, ed., *Bureaucracy and Political Development* (Princeton, N.J.: Princeton University Press, 1963). A book edited by Nimrod Raphaeli came along four years later and helped to calm the confusion of approaches to the field: *Readings in Comparative Public Administration* (Boston: Allyn & Bacon, 1967).

Most of the important scholarly papers have been prepared under the auspices of the Comparative Administration Group. Two of the more popular recent studies are Dwight Waldo, ed., *Temporal Dimensions of Development Administration* (Durham, N.C.: Duke University Press, 1970) and Fred W. Riggs, ed., *Frontiers of Development Administration* (Durham, N.C.: Duke University Press, 1970). The single most important theory in comparative administration is Fred Riggs's prismatic model. The best short introduction to this ecological approach can be found in Fred W. Riggs, "Prismatic Society Revisited" (Morristown, N.J.: General Learning Press, 1973). The most complete statement of the theory is in Riggs's *Administration in Developing Countries: The Theory of Prismatic Society* (Boston: Houghton Mifflin Co., 1965). The search for the crucial environmental characteristics of public administration went on in all branches of the social sciences. Newcomers should at least look at the theory of entrepreneurship in David McClelland, *The Achieving Society* (Princeton, N.J.: D. Van Nostrand Co., 1961) and the structural-functional approach in Gabriel Almond and James Coleman, *The Politics of the Developing Areas* (Princeton, N.J.: Princeton University Press, 1960).

The United Nations Division of Public Administration is the largest repository of practical material on development administration. One popular publication is their *Handbook of Public Administration: Current Concepts and Practice with Special Reference to Developing Countries* (New York: The United Nations, 1961). Other useful studies are Kenneth Younger, *The Public Service in New States* (New York: Oxford University Press, 1960); Irving Swerdlow, ed., *Development Administration: Concepts and Problems* (Syracuse, N.Y.: Syracuse University Press, 1963); Kusum Nair, *Blossoms in the Dust* (New York: Frederick A. Praeger, 1961), on community development; Edward W. Weidner, *Technical Assistance in Public Administration Overseas* (Chicago: Public Administration Service, 1964); and Albert O. Hirschman, *Journeys Toward Progress* (New York: Twentieth Century Fund, 1963), a study of capital development and public enterprises. For the more "modern" approaches to development administration see D. Woods Thomas et. al., *Institution Building* (Cambridge, Mass.: Schenkman Publishing Co., 1973), or Warren F. Illchman and Norman T. Uphoff, *The Political Economy of Change* (Berkeley: University of California Press, 1969). The search for a contingency theory to match administrative methods against local conditions in developing nations is well represented by Naomi Caiden and Aaron Wildavsky, *Planning and Budgeting in Poor Countries* (New York: John Wiley & Sons, 1974). An article that ties the field together and provides a more extensive bibliography is Milton J. Esman and John D. Montgomery, "Systems Approaches to Technical Cooperation: The Role of Development Administration," *Public Administration Review* 29 (September/October 1969) pp. 507–539.

THE FUTURE

10

"Things fall apart; the centre cannot hold."[1] That line from the poem by Yeats describing the anarchy of the Second Coming characterizes the study of public administration in this decade. It could become an epitaph.

The whole point of this book has been to stress the diversity of public administration. Now diversity is both a blessing and a curse. It is a blessing because it creates a rich intellectual base and the sort of discontinuities that force scholars to discard simple theories of administration in favor of complex ones. Without the diversity of theory and practice that has accumulated over the past ninety years, public administration could not be as popular nor as relevant as it is today.

But diversity is also a curse. It overwhelms the experts, leading many to proclaim that the search for a general theory of public administration is futile. Even the more optimistic are reduced to muttering about how public administrators must learn to manage without models, how diversity is good for the soul, how reconciliation of conflicting theories is just around the corner—all of which are simply ways of saying that the experts are puzzled by the onslaught of new approaches to administration from diverse quarters. The result is a general fear that the academic side of public administration is beginning to resemble a dead planet, reflecting the glow of real disciplines around it but incapable of producing any light of its own.

The object of this chapter is to examine the sources of diversity in public administration—particularly as they are manifested in new trends in research and practice—and to see where they lead. This will be done, as much as possible, from the point of view of the future executive.

Public administration is passing through a period of transition. In many ways, the crisis of identity on the academic side is a reflection of the contradictions confronting the public executive. Public executives find their jobs buffeted by discontinuities that require opposite actions simultaneously. New styles of administrative regulation are

334

appearing alongside old styles of administrative politics. New forms of government organization, which one scholar characterized as "nobody in charge,"[2] are settling in next to the more traditional bureaucratic forms. The old articles of administrative faith are being challenged by a different set of convictions commonly known as the "new" public administration.

Future public administrators will have to straddle various discontinuities and the conflicting theories of administration that arise from them; they will have to master the battery of methods advanced by administrative experts standing on top of those theories. All of this has set off a search for new approaches to public administration, ones that can come to grips with diversity, are comfortable with change, are relevant to the conditions of postindustrial society, and can tie the discontinuities together with a single piece of twine.

These are the trends, already well established, that will shape the future of public administration. This chapter will examine each trend in turn, in order to determine how well (or how poorly) the profession of public administration has prepared itself for these changes and the role that its past can play in creating a path out of the jungle of administrative theories and techniques.

THE SHAPE OF THINGS TO COME

The job of the future public executive will be determined by the shape of the social, economic, technological, and political forces in society. Public administration is incredibly sensitive to such things. If one understands these forces, then one can foresee the shape of the public service.

Peter Drucker characterizes the modern era as an age of discontinuity. By this he means that the future will be determined not by the momentum of straight-line trends, but by the tearing apart of the economy, the society, and the polity by interrupted forces working in irregular directions. By and large, scholars have seen the future of public administration in terms of discontinuities, of *this* versus *that*. For every well-established trend shaping some part of public administration, one can find an equally powerful trend pushing the same part in another direction. The discontinuities will not be resolved. To manage them, public executives will have to draw upon contradictory approaches to administration.

What discontinuities are likely to have the greatest impact upon the future of public administration? A number of prognosticators have written about them, including Drucker. Six major conflicts regularly appear:

- The pluralistic base of organizational society versus the persistence of eighteenth-century liberal beliefs.
- The clash between advocates of executive control and advocates of representativeness over the issue of who shall control the work of the experts in the organizational state.

335

- An expansion of the role of government as the provider of goods and services versus movements for reprivatization and debureaucratization.
- The arrival of a global economy that must be managed by the national agencies that are made irrelevant by it.
- The advent of knowledge as the crucial resource in society versus a new moral order that is suspicious of rationalism.
- The need for institutional strength versus the need for institutional flexibility, both of which clash with human demands for privacy.

Many have characterized the plight of modern public administration as the condition of a preindustrial state trying to deal with post-industrial problems. Public affairs in the organizational state are guided by liberal beliefs left over from the eighteenth century: the belief in natural rights, individual dignity, the virtues of public service, the rule of law, limited government, and the supremacy of popular institutions, such as the legislature, over the administrative branch. These beliefs ran afoul of another liberal dogma: the belief in heroic materialism, the idea that a single individual with organizational skill could accomplish great deeds. The institutionalization of heroic materialism propelled the state into the era of organizational pluralism, where public affairs are entrusted to large institutions "organized for perpetuity and run by managers."[3] Organizational pluralism stands for the concentration of power in many places so that no single institution has all the power and resources it needs to accomplish its objectives. The result is an emphasis upon control, not only to coordinate the various centers of power, but also to constrain individual behavior so that the state might provide the mass distribution of freedom promoted by the eighteenth-century liberals. The state cannot allow everyone to climb into their campers and drive off to the mountains on the same day as a matter of liberty.

Despite the fact that 133,000 people die every day, including 10,000 from starvation or malnutrition, the world population will climb past 7,000,000,000 by the year 2000. "I suppose," says the author of *Slaughterhouse Five*, "they will all want dignity."[4] Seven billion people on a single planet will create severe management problems. Public executives will ask for the same power over the state that they believe business executives have over the firm. Already this desire has resulted in vast concentrations of power in offices ranging from the American presidency to the Soviet presidium, accompanied by the inevitable demands to limit public resistance to that power, as the Soviet leaders did when they created the *zeks*, the secret nation of prisoners of the Gulag Archipelago. At the same time, the advocates of liberalism vote and fight for more representation in organizational affairs. The consumer movement, environmentalism, citizen participation, and unionization of public employees are all products of the drive toward representation. Each group, the executives and the citizens, is suspicious of the bureaucracy. They pursue an ancient political question: who shall govern? Translated into twentieth-century realities, the question becomes: who shall control the bureaucrats whose work propels the modern state? It is probably the most important question before the public administration profession. The outcome, at least in Western nations, probably will be another discontinuity, a balance of power between the advocates of executive control and the citizen.

The clash between executives, citizens, and bureaucrats affects other discontinuities concerning the role of government in society. On the one hand, the public has come to expect the government to be the largest single producer of goods and services in society, from health care to armaments. Every national problem is a public problem, and every public problem is supposed to have an administrative solution. At the same time, the government is under enormous pressure to reprivatize and debureaucratize its operations, by contracting where it once constructed, by revenue sharing instead of controlling through grants-in-aid, by deregulating what it once regulated, by setting up public-choice mechanisms to replace public monopolies. Bureaucratic control is weakened by technological change, and industrial control is weakened by the growth of the new service industries. Yet in each case the old system is as strong as the new, creating a string of discontinuities that reenforce each other—public/private, bureaucratic/postbureaucratic, and industrialism/postindustrialism.

These discontinuities are exacerbated by a fourth: the increasing reliance upon national governments, which are fading as a symbol of authority, to solve problems of world economics that are essentially international in scope. Economists and business managers were the first to recognize that the transactions of multinational corporations are conducted beyond the control of the nation state. Public executives felt the hot breath of multinational economics when they tried to control inflation and solve the energy crisis. Simply put, the world is becoming a single market, or, as Drucker put it, a global shopping center. Executives may want to deal with problems of international trade as if the nations were the basic units, "but imperceptibly there has emerged a world economy in which common information generates the same economic appetites, aspirations, and demands—cutting across national boundaries and languages and largely disregarding political ideologies as well."[5] The world is a train, with a few nations riding splendidly in first class, the rest packed like cattle into cars in the rear, and the conductor has just opened the doors between the cars. At the same time, the nations running the train are splitting up over ethnic and regional animosities, becoming smaller and individually less powerful. This creates quite a challenge for national executives: how to develop institutional plans powerful enough to smooth out the economic convulsions caused by the scarcity of goods and resources, and how to put down the spasms of violence which occur more frequently now that the have-nots have discovered just how fragile the concentration of economic power really is.

Fears that the national executives will fail have encouraged prophecies of a new apocalypse. The world will starve itself to death or breed itself to death, the sea will turn red, the air will disappear, the polar caps will melt, or, failing all these, we shall blow ourselves up with our nuclear garbage. The celebration of death has set off a wave of antirationalism like the world has not seen since the year 999. Since everyone will be dead tomorrow, there is no need to do the unglamorous work of public administration. The antirationalism takes many forms—from the revival of mysticism to the Greening of America. Even in the sciences, men and women of knowledge are bent upon demonstrating the superiority of intuitive thinking. So where is the discontinuity? It arises because all of this antirationalism has sprung from the first civilization to make knowledge—not money, not class, not land, not status, but intelligence—the crucial resource in society. The heading for this section—The Shape of Things to Come—is the title of a screenplay by H. G. Wells, who predicted that a new age of darkness would close the twentieth century but that the modern barbarians eventually would be rescued by wiser advocates of science. The new scientists would try to create a new moral order, one stressing creativity, education, and constant change.

"Change is the law of nature. We are either in the process of dying or being born," reads a radical poster. John Gardner puts the problem this way: how can a society of institutions renew itself? Gardner is sensitive to the paradoxical discontinuities in modern organizations. He describes a friend of his, a professor, sitting in his air-conditioned office, having just returned from a trip to London, Paris, and Cairo, with a microfilm of an ancient Egyptian papyrus on the side of his desk, writing an essay "on the undiluted evil of modern technology and large-scale organization."[6] This is the institutional discontinuity—the fact that complex organizations grant freedom while taking it away. The formula for organizational tyranny, Gardner says, is written in the search for institutional strength. He likens institutional growth to personal growth. A young organization, like a young person, is creative, adaptive, and willing to experiment. With age comes maturity—and rigid, absurd, conservative self-destructive behavior. Both humans and institutions face the same problem: how to maintain the flexibility of youth after they have ceased to grow. The solution, too often, is to forgo flexibility in favor of preserving the power that accumulates with age.

When the strength of personal power triumphs over flexibility, senility is not far away. If public administration chooses strength, it will become a science of control in the service of the state. Richard Goodwin, the professional pessimist, calls bureaucracy the logic of technology. Management science, he says, aims to sustain the power of dominant economic institutions, no matter what the cost to humanity.

So what does the individual do? To escape the clutches of the administrative state, individuals make greater demands for personal privacy. But enclaves of personal freedom are temporary at best, lasting only until the state decides to make another demand on the individual, destroying one's privacy like a freeway bulldozed through a neighbor's yard. Is there no solution to the discontinuity between an overorganized society and personal freedom? Gardner thinks so. He would commit society to a process of continual rebirth. In a world that worships youth and hides its dying, the idea of institutional rebirth attracts many adherents. Gardner believes that society can reach a permanent state of renewal if it embraces pluralism as a method of encouraging participation in institutional affairs, makes the promulgation of dissent a necessity rather than a crime, and channels that dissent through instruments capable of achieving consensus on critical values and choices.

The four major new trends in public administration are all products of these discontinuities. The realization that governmental executives will be called upon to control more with institutions that do less has led to the search for new styles of regulation. The discontinuities affecting institutional strength and organizational pluralism have encouraged the search for nonbureaucratic forms of organization. The existence of eighteenth-century liberal beliefs, antirationalism, and the desire for representation in a society based on pluralism, knowledge, and executive control has spawned the "new" public administration. The fact that all of these discontinuities will lead to organizational fragmentation that must be counterbalanced by precise methods of integration is at the heart of the search for a model of managerial contingencies.

In total, the ferment created by the discontinuities of public administration will support a confusion of administrative methods. No longer will administrative experts be able to offer up a single theory of management, whether it be modern or traditional, and say, "Here, take it, one size fits all." Contradictory approaches to administration will coexist within the same organization. There will be no resolution to the problems of administrative diversity in an age of discontinuities.

THE REGULATED STATE

Scarcity breeds regulation. Governments are entering a new era of scarcity in natural resources, food, land, housing, and wealth without knowing much about new methods of regulation. Mention regulation to scholars and they will hand you a book on the control of business by independent commissions. The old regulatory commissions, however, are becoming increasingly irrelevant to the needs of the modern regulated state.

Allen Schick attempts to outline the boundaries of the new regulatory style—the first of the four new research trends—in a forecast titled "Toward the Cybernetic State." To forecast the future, Schick divides up the past. He divides the era of administrative supremacy, beginning roughly in 1883, into two periods. During the first period,

An oil spill closes in on the Statue of Liberty. Crises such as this are encouraging the search for new styles of government regulation to replace the old bureaucratic practice of political alliances with private interests.
COURTESY OF EPA—DOCUMERICA, CHESTER HIGGINS.

which he calls the "administrative state," administrative agencies respected the rule of law, followed due process in administration, deferred to legislative supremacy, and promoted the ideal of a politically neutral civil service. The most important public institution in the administrative state was the independent regulatory commission. Its primary purpose was to modify the concentration of wealth and power by regulating giant corporations.

During the Great Depression, the basic mission of government changed. The civil servant as regulator was replaced by the primacy of the public servant as the agent of growth, the subsidizer of business, the producer of public goods and services. As a result, the basic rules of administration changed. Schick calls the second period the bureaucratic state.

> In the bureaucratic state, politics and administration are united by interest-group brokers who traffic between the bureaucracies and the people, and weave complex clientele-congressional-bureau relationships for the purpose of channeling public enterprises into the service of private interests. [7]

Relations between agencies and the public in the bureaucratic state are determined by the rules of interest-group pluralism. The old criteria of law, neutrality, and separation of powers take a back seat to the new demands of interest-group politics.

American government, Schick insists, is now moving away from the bureaucratic state toward the cybernetic state. The institutions of the bureaucratic state—bureaus devoted to special purposes—have become a liability because they allow the bureaucrats to substitute special interests for general results. The old pluralism, Schick suggests, will be replaced by a corps of regulators—backed by special guidelines and multifunctional missions—who will roam through the departments, putting things in order. The style of regulation will be fundamentally internal, both within the government and as the government regulates private industry. The regulators will use goal setting, rational standards, impact assessment, work measurement —everything from the old Taylorism to the new evaluation—to fine-tune government agencies and close off inefficiencies, especially economic waste. In the private sector, the government regulators will interfere in the internal management of large industries on behalf of particular public interests, much as they now issue guidelines within the food-processing industry on behalf of consumers. Finally, the regulation will be set to an automatic trigger—the cybernetic analogy—which will activate the regulation the instant that pre-ordained perimeters are crossed, triggering, for example, special government spending when unemployment rises above a specified rate.

Politics will dry up in the cybernetic state, as administrative discretion is reduced through the precision of regulatory planning. Government will become more powerful, yet the bureaucracy will shrink in size and importance as it moves out of the limited-purpose subsidy business. The elaboration of regulation will tend to blur the lines separating public and private concerns, and it will be difficult to tell the difference between a public administrator and a business manager, either by the work they do or the methods they use.

What role will the old independent regulatory commissions play in this? Ralph Nader and a bevy of public-interest groups have criticized the work of the independent regulatory commissions. The commissions, they say, have been captured by the interests the commissions were set up to regulate. The Federal Trade Commission, Nader insists, is more responsive to the interests of big business than to the public interest which the Congress established the FTC to promote. He makes the same charges against the Interstate Commerce Commission, the Food and Drug Administration, the Civil Aeronautics Board, and the Federal Communications Commission. A common pattern emerges in each case. The commissioners and their staff fail to detect violations. They do not want to establish any long-range goals or priorities. They fail to enforce rules using existing authority, relying instead upon voluntary compliance. They avoid asking for the resources and authority that might make them effective. Finally, Nader concludes, the regulators try to hide these shortcomings through misleading public relations, secrecy, and collusive deals with the firms they regulate.

All of this is a consequence of the fact that the regulatory commissions created to serve the needs of the administrative state have had to operate within the structure of the bureaucratic state where they have been transformed into political coalitions, regulator and regulatee joined together to promote bureaucratic growth.

Nader understands this. He admits that one cannot expect old-line regulators to respond to modern necessities when they are surrounded by special interests and political pressures. Like Schick, Nader recognizes that the style of regulation will not change until these conditions are altered. Nader would like to hasten the move away from the conditions of the bureaucratic state by writing new regulatory laws that protect citizen-consumer rights, by reorganizing the commissions so as to cut special interests away from the arms of government, and by applying citizen leverage as his own Raiders have done.

Without such reforms, the regulatory agencies will remain under the influence of the old political coalitions, not regulating, but serving to protect entrenched groups fighting to hold onto their share of the status quo. This is the net of criticism that Theodore Lowi throws across modern government, not just the independent regulatory commissions, but all of the agencies devoted to pluralism in the bureaucratic state. Nader and Lowi dislike pluralism. This is why:

- Pluralism creates an image of corruption. The ideology of democratic government makes people think that they can influence public policy by participating and voting. These deranged expectations become shattered illusions when people find out that big organizations control everything. The discontinuity between ideology and reality makes people think that government is "wrong," or corrupt.

- Pluralism is not just. The primacy of the law is superseded by negotiated settlements, plea bargaining, amnesty, informal agreements, and special deals for the powerful. Nothing is ever carried to a conclusion when powerful interests are involved. This demoralizes the public, just as much as if a bank robber, caught in the act, was told by the police that they would not arrest him if he agreed to stop robbing the bank.

- Pluralism weakens constitutionalism. Because everything is settled "out of court," the government forgets how to use formal democratic procedures. A little cynicism about government is good, says Lowi, but when informal fixes are raised to a virtue, people become reluctant to submit their problems to governmental adjudication under any conditions.

- Pluralism renders government impotent. Government agencies and commissions under the control of big interests cannot propose reforms that might really change anything. The government may declare war on poverty, but it does not seriously anticipate a radical redistribution of wealth and power, especially when those programs invite the participation of powerful groups. Because they are stuck on pluralism, Lowi says, *liberal governments cannot plan.* They cannot plan to do anything but maintain the status quo.

Lowi reserves his heaviest barrage for the academic community, which, he says, has generally supported the doctrine of pluralism.

> I had not anticipated the fact that those nurtured on pluralism as an ideology, those whose entire political lives had been enveloped in the governmental principles of delegation and manipulation, would find formal democracy totally unreal, alien, and even offensive.[8]

He criticizes intellectuals for propagating the myth that a system based on groups and bargaining will be self-correcting. This is as absurd, he says, as the laissez-faire belief that the free-market system is self-correcting. The pluralists, Lowi insists, ignore the problems of imperfect competition by assuming that one group will be checked by another. The actual outcome will not be pluralism, says Lowi, but an oligopsony: a public market dominated by a few big buyers. Allen Schick calls it pluralism of the blessed.

Although this sounds like radical rhetoric, there are strong strains of conservatism in it, a conservatism that would take American administration back to its nineteenth-century origins. Lowi and Nader's solutions sound a great deal like the "political state" that preceded the era of administrative growth, a period in which public officials were preoccupied with building representative political institutions such as the Congress and the political party system. Lowi dreams of a Madisonian democracy, ruled by democratically elected officials. The senior civil service, embodying the best Roman virtues of duty to state, would regulate through the rule of law and due process. When it comes to real change, a dollar's worth of regulation produces more results than one million dollars' worth of subsidies. Lowi calls his ideal state a juridical democracy. It looks a lot like the early American constitutional system with its warts removed.

Lowi would restore the rule of law. That is the heart of his solution, which, he laughs, would "excite the strongest opposition and fear if anyone ever took it seriously."[9] The rule of law is directed against leaders who, feeling the pressures to solve a chronic problem with a public program, "formulate it vaguely, delegate great discretion to the administrator, and expect him to work out the actual program in cahoots with all the contestants."[10] Lowi pines for the days of the *Schechter* rule, the legal precedent elaborated in the sick-chicken case that the Supreme Court used to overturn acts of Congress that delegated too much lawmaking power to the executive. It was never applied after 1936. Should the court exercise its right to declare broad delegations of power unconstitutional, it would produce much disorder. Lowi likes a little disorder. It forces citizens to form new groups that petition the government to write new laws which—like the civil rights legislation for the South—produce real change. An intolerance for disorder, Lowi says, breeds permanent groups, impotent in their capacity to plan change, dependent upon government action to maintain their power and coerce their members. It leads inevitably to the suppression of dissent among citizens who find that the groups no longer represent their interests.

In the bureaucracy, Lowi would restore the rule of administrative formality. To apply or interpret the law, public officials would have to use formal, legally sanctioned procedures. In the regulatory agencies, this would be done through case-by-case adjudication, a formal advocacy process leading to the issuance of a rule in which each side publicly presents its position. The rule would not be flexible, and the contestants could not bargain over the final decision.

What sort of civil service would this produce? "A truly independent and integrated administrative class—a Senior Civil Service. A profession of public administration."[11] It would be small, elite, and centralized in the sense that its loyalty would be to the law rather than to specific agencies. The civil service would not be allowed to bargain with special interests over administration. The only way that bargaining could take place would be for the aggrieved interests to appeal administrative decisions back to the Congress, where the law was made.

Lowi's juridical democracy is not a scholar's dream. In America, at least, public frustration and a sense of governmental corruption push administration closer to Lowi's picture of reformed regulation. Public officials are prosecuted for bargaining with special interests, a practice clearly within the rules of pluralism. Government is stuck with a new moral ethic as powerful as the public outrage over racial discrimination in the sixties. Congressional tenacity is ascending and lawmakers are more willing to write specific laws and draft their own budgets. Political executives responsible for results are less willing to allow back-door bargaining in the bureaucracy. All of this, as Lowi predicts, could move the government to substitute the rule of law for the deadly virtues of pluralism.

In his attempt to tear scholars away from the worship of pluralism that began thirty years ago, with Appleby's insistence that politics was part of administration, Lowi assaults the mainstream of American public administration. By removing administrative discretion and discrediting pluralism, Lowi moves the public service back toward the old politics/administration dichotomy. This is the most serious aspect of Lowi's proposals. The revival of the politics/ administration dichotomy would wipe away thirty years of progress, of trying to free bureaucracy from the grasp of technicians. Appleby knew that a bureaucracy that had to respond to organized interests would be more democratic than a bureaucracy that did not, because a corps of unchecked technicians would very quickly challenge the oversight powers of the amateurs in the legislature. Bureaucratic power in the raw is far superior to the political power possessed by elected officials in the modern state.

There is a very real danger that Lowi's model will turn out to be counterintuitive, that it will produce unexpected results. By separating interest groups from the bureaucracy, Lowi may in fact produce a more powerful bureaucracy. By sending the interests back to Congress, he may produce a more conservative government, more beholden to interests. There is not much evidence to suggest that government in America during periods of congressional supremacy has been progressive, just, uncorrupt, and constitutional. Legislators are more vulnerable to special interests, more lacking in information, more conservative as a whole, especially in state governments. When the Federal Trade Commission dared to crimp America's smoking habit, it was the Congress, responding to tobacco interests, that crimped the FTC. Congress narrowed their discretion, just as Lowi suggested it do.

Finally, Lowi's proposal damages efforts to decentralize government through citizen participation. By encasing administrative power in a centralized civil service, Lowi removes the source of administrative discretion that is necessary to make client-centered organizations work. Client-centered organizations, many experts believe, will be the new wave of governmental organization in the postbureaucratic era.

These rebuttals do not lessen the power of Lowi's predictions. Lowi sees a piece of the future: authoritarian governments regulating growth and resources through the rule of law. It is probably true that the coalitions established to advance the purposes of the bureaucratic state will not be of much use in regulating society in the cybernetic state. Nevertheless, these new styles of regulation will not dominate public administration but will coexist alongside other forms of government organization, traditional and modern.

POSTBUREAUCRATIC FORMS OF ORGANIZATION

If Sweden gave a Nobel Prize for public administration, the first one would go to the scholar who discovered the structural principles underlying the postbureaucratic form of organization. Not since Max Weber went looking for the characteristics of bureaucracy has there been such a search. Weber found a form of organization well suited to the needs of a growing nation with stable objectives. Now that governments are embroiled in no-growth change and discontinuities, they need a theory of structure that discards bureaucracy in favor of more flexible forms of organization.

Warren Bennis contributed the first theory in this, the second major research trend. Bennis painted a picture of a nonhierarchical organization, temporary in its arrangements, governed by ability rather than by authority, with democratic methods of supervision. His model closely fit the needs of modern organizations with a specific task to perform in a rapidly changing environment. It worked, and was adopted by industries and governments. It put men on the moon. Fortunately for the theory, there were no clients on the moon. Bennis's theory does not work too well where an amorphous clientele confronts a fragmented, service-oriented institution, such as a university.

In the mid-sixties, Bennis forecast "that in the next 25 to 50 years we would participate in the end of bureaucracy as we know it and in the rise of new social systems better suited to the 20th century."[12] Bennis's fame spread with the popularity of his prediction. He was offered and accepted the presidency of the University of Cincinnati, where he instituted his antihierarchical theories. They did not work. A funny thing, he said, happened on the way to the future. "At Cincinnati we have not only a faculty senate and a student senate but sixty-nine other committees that are involved, in one way or another, in university goverance. . . . All this is supposed to add up to 'participatory democracy' but adds up, instead, to a cave of winds where the most that can usually be agreed upon is to do nothing."[13] Bennis suspected that he "had become the victim of a vast, amorphous, unwitting, unconscious conspiracy to prevent me from doing anything whatever to change the university's status quo."[14] A leader, he said, must create goals and proceed toward them without being crippled by bureaucratic machinery. He quoted Machiavelli and Neustadt, but denied that he wanted to be a man on horseback. "All I want," he said, "is to get one foot in the stirrup."[15] Not since Plato escaped from the tyrant of Syracuse who wanted to murder the man who went to educate him has there been such a glorious failure by a scholar to institute his own theories into the real world.

Clearly, what was needed was a new version of the postbureaucratic theory appropriate to the client-centered organization. Orion White, a brilliant young scholar in public administration, offered one. He developed his theory while studying a church-related social service agency serving a low-income area in San Antonio, Texas. The agency ran a clinic, a kindergarten, a day-care center, a delinquency-control program, a Neighborhood Youth Corp, and a VISTA program. It helped to build up neighborhood organizations and provide home services. A staff of thirty-two served about twelve hundred families through three neighborhood centers. The funds to operate the agency came from the church, the United Fund, and the U.S. government. White says that the agency provides "a concrete example of what a counter-bureaucratic organization would look like and what problems might be encountered in attempting to implement such a model in practice."[16]

White characterizes the agency as a dialectical organization. The dialectic, historians will remember, was the term Hegel used to characterize the tensions in society that led to change. The thesis in the dialectical organization is the bureaucratic form. The antithesis is the pressure toward debureaucratization. In the particular case of the San Antonio social service agency, the antithesis was the organization's attempt to reform itself around the needs of its clients. When the clients demanded too much, or the agency ran out of money, the forces favoring bureaucratization would reappear. Unlike Hegel's dialectic, which resulted in the creation of a synthesis, the dialectical organization never resolved its contradictioms. Disaccord became an end in itself. To White, utopia is an organization in which the dialectic provides an endless source of tension which the organization uses to continually renew itself.

A bureaucracy, in its purely ideal form, treats clients as if they were the last layer in the organizational hierarchy. It boxes clients into specialized categories and forces the clients to adjust to conditions as they exist. Because the bureaucracy suffers from scarce resources and the clients ask for too much, the bureaucrats treat the clients impersonally. If the client demands special treatment, or does not conform to the organization's definition of proper behavior, the client is not treated at all.

The San Antonio social service agency, White says, tried to reverse these patterns. Of course, it could not approximate these ideals any more than traditional organizations could be perfectly bureaucratic.

- Instead of client-as-subordinate, the agency treated clients as peers. Clients evaluated the staff.
- Instead of dealing with the problems of the clients segmentally, the staff treated them as whole persons.
- Instead of helping clients adjust to TV and *Time* magazine, the agency helped the clients to get organized to change the conditions they disliked.
- Instead of looking for clients with simple problems who would make the organization look good, the agency rewarded those employees who worked on supposedly hopeless cases.
- Instead of a well-structured homogeneous organization, the agency left roles fluid and insisted upon hiring a heterogeneous staff of both straight and freaky people.
- Instead of an Apollonian bureaucracy, trying to stretch out its life through the virtues of moderation, the agency tried to become a Dionysian organization, periodically burning itself out to attain its immediate goals.
- Instead of encouraging people to treat each other instrumentally in the competition for scarce resources, the agency stressed collaboration as a route to personal growth.

The organization was never able to solve the problem of scarce resources. The problem got worse once the agency started to receive funds from the War on Poverty, since this created pressures to set up programs that did one thing well—even though they put clients into categories—because programs that did one thing well survived the competition for federal funds. In addition, there was the normal tendency to protect the agency by rejecting demands from clients for money or staff that the agency did not have, even though that meant the staff began to dote on the need for efficiency.

Scarce resources are a primary cause of bureaucratization in public agencies. Most old-line bureaucracies resolve the problem of scarce resources by erecting boundaries. The whole idea of "the organization" implies boundaries. The bureaucracy creates a them-versus-us boundary between itself and its clients, primarily to present a unified front against excessive client demands. Boundaries are also created within the formal organization as one unit bargains against another over scarce resources. Boundary delineations are purely perceptual, based on the images inculcated by the organizational ideology. There is no *real* boundary between clients and employees who work together, just as one cannot see geographic boundary lines on the earth viewed from space. Boundaries are illusions of the mind.

The San Antonio agency took a radical approach to the problem of boundaries. It rejected the classic bureaucratic image of an artificial solid line around the organizational pyramid and instead saw boundaries encircling clients and staff. Boundaries were not used to separate people protecting scarce resources, but to bring together groups of people with problems to solve. The new definition of organizational boundaries created the need for a new ethic of organizational behavior which stressed adaptation, confrontation, and bargaining, or what White likes to call the politics of love.

Some people mistake this for anarchy. In fact, anarchy in its real-life forms, from the French Revolution to the Symbionese Liberation Army, emphasizes hierarchy and competition, often inside the organization and always outside of it. Like bureaucracy, it is just another form of organizational machismo. One group of citizens, designated superior because of their talent, office, wealth, or good intentions, is allowed to dominate and repress others. This should not be surprising. All organizational systems, especially in the Western world, begin with the assumption of hierarchy. From the barnyard to the White House, from the feudal manor to the corporation, the first principle of administration has always been hierarchy.

No real "organizational revolution" will take place until an assault is made on the principle of hierarchy. That is the thesis advanced by Frederick Thayer, a career public executive turned scholar. The problem, says Thayer, is that people assume that organization *means* hierarchy, and that the only alternative is the wildest form of anarchy imaginable. The future, he says, will be full of technology; it will be structured. But it does not need to be hierarchical.

Thayer insists that the basic tenets of democracy and economics in the West condition persons to think in terms of hierarchy. He traces constitutional democracy back to Thomas Hobbes, the English philosopher born during the reign of the Tudors. Hobbes believed that people were no damned good and wanted the state to control their bad impulses. All proposals that would reform administration by "democratizing" retain this assumption and thus seek to maintain some form of hierarchy. Thayer criticizes Lowi's juridical democracy for perpetuating a hierarchy of rulers and ruled. He criticizes the proposals for participatory democracy aimed at decentralizing decisions to neighborhood confederations. And he criticizes the public-choice model, where citizens would vote on issues at home over the telephone, or purchase services from competing bureaus. All these approaches to reforming the system, says Thayer, "would increase alienation by encouraging tyrannical social movements . . . all of these theories of government offer us organized pyramids of power, even if one of them is inverted."[17]

THE CHANGING SHAPE OF ORGANIZATIONS

In 1911 Max Weber set down the characteristics of the ideal-type bureaucracy. Fifty-five years later other organizational theorists began searching for the characteristics of the ideal postbureaucratic form of organization.

Weber's Bureaucracy	Postbureaucratic Organizations
1. Fixed Authority and Official Jurisdictions	1. Authority flows to the persons with the ability to solve the problem.
2. Written, Formal Rules	2. A dialectical organization which adapts itself to the situation at hand.
3. Impersonality	3. The client as peer.
4. A Hierarchy of Offices	4. A flat organization: a structured nonhierarchy with nobody in charge.
5. Specialization	5. Team problem solving and collective decisions.
6. Career Service	6. Professional mobility.
7. Permanence	7. A temporary organization with a Dionysian ideology.
8. Secrecy	8. Open communications.

The rule of competition in business enterprise serves the same purpose: it legitimizes the rule of one group of people by another. It excuses organizations that build pyramids, boss workers, and screw consumers. Competition is legalized banditry by organizations. "Stripped of pretense, a theory of economic competition is the equivalent of a political theory of anarchy."[18] Conventional wisdom about economics and politics, Thayer concludes, has no place in the organizational changes lying ahead.

Thayer believes that organizational hierarchy can be made to wither away, disappearing under pressures to devolve decisions; redesign the assembly line; involve clients in administration; and plan open systems that cut across organization boundaries. In its place he sees a process of *collective will,* where a collage of groups, representing the various elements involved in the solution to a problem, would interlock to map out the solution. In a way, it is like turning the organization pyramid on its side. Thayer finds evidence in the reduced power of individual executives to make binding decisions on others that his theory of *structured nonhierarchy* has already caught on.

The old system of hierarchy, Thayer suggests, could be substantially weakened if the symbols of hierarchy, such as "promotions" and salary differentials, were abolished. In the nonhierarchical world, says Thayer, "there is no logical argument for any salary differential between the member of a neighborhood block council and the individual designated President of the United States."[19] The result could be, as Orion White describes it, "a social, hyper, pluralism of bewildering diversity."[20]

What do you get when you add up the predictions of Bennis and White and Thayer? A lot of contradictions; but as White observes, this is the sort of diversity that gives energy to the renewal process. All three, however, do agree on one thing—that governments need an alternative to Max Weber's model of the efficient public institution. The chart on page 349 contains a few tentative propositions about the shape of organizations in the future, rescued from the continuing search for the ideal postbureaucratic form of organization. The new propositions are contrasted against the old principles of bureaucracy from which this book began.

All of the talk about postbureaucratic organizations is on the leading edge of administrative research. Yet these are not utopian forecasts; they are trends extrapolated from real events. Because they have already happened, they have already had a profound impact upon the way in which scholars and experts view the profession, causing many persons to reassess the basic tenets of public administration.

THE NEW PUBLIC ADMINISTRATION

In the late sixties, younger scholars and practitioners challenged the established wisdom of public administration, a fairly rare occurrence in any scientific discipline. Their challenge—which was offered at the same time that the war in Vietnam was bringing a spirit of resistance to the college campus—became known as the "New" Public Administration, the third major new trend in public administration. Its adherents wanted to recast the mold of public administration, making its practice and scholarship more relevant to the discontinuities they observed around them. Ironically, these young experts on administration did not organize themselves, so that the New PA remained more of a subtle mood than an actual movement to reform the profession.

John Rehfuss characterized the New PAers as "humanistic, dubious about technology, anti-rationalist, reformist, and generally doubtful of the ability of present organizations to adapt to a fast-changing society."[21] Cary Hershey characterized the practitioners as humanistic, proactive, independent, unalienated, and anxious to reform their bureaucracies from the inside. George Frederickson said they were simply trying to put political theory back into public administration.

Everyone agreed that the ignition point of the New PA was the Minnowbrook conference. Dwight Waldo, a member of the establishment who foresaw the coalescing movement, invited fifty young administrative professors and practitioners to a conference on the future of the profession. The participants met in 1968 at the Minnowbrook conference center in the Adirondack Mountains in upstate New York. The results of the conference were published in an anthology assembled by one of the participants, Frank Marini. These are the themes that emerged, amplified by related writings and events.

Phenomenology

Perhaps the most striking feature of the New PA is its bias against positivism. When a modern scientist speaks out against positivism, she or he is assaulting the whole foundation of scientific understanding. It is as heretical an act in the modern world as Galileo's suggestion that one could fathom the universe by looking at it through a spyglass was to the medieval mind. Faith in positivism is the reason modern scientists trust the results of their work. Emerging from the European scientific revolution, positivism asserted that laws of nature existed and could be discovered through empirical observation. It sought to dissect phenomena (which it accepted as objective facts), reduce them to their apparent similarities at the lowest common unit of analysis, and measure them. It assumed that the mind was an empty receptacle that could distinguish values from facts.

Did you ever read empirical social science research? asked the New PAers. It's awful. It's irrelevant, dull, narrow, and barren. It

In 1968 a group of young public administrators met at the Minnowbrook conference center, pictured here. Their plea for a more humane, proactive public administration challenged the old ideals of scientific, value-neutral scholarship and was widely received as a call for a "new" public administration. COURTESY OF SYRACUSE UNIVERSITY. **351**

raises common sense to a science by verifying it. It is arrogant, because it assumes that social scientists' superior methods of inquiry give them a better view of reality. It is dangerous, because scientists are instructed not to consider the consequences of their findings upon the human condition. It is stupid, because it assumes that empirical theories of the world are "value free."

So the New PAers turned to phenomenology. Phenomenology began as an attempt among German philosophers to rescue philosophy from the empiricism of Hegel, Comte, and Kant. Often called the science of perceptions, it sees the mind as an intervening force between phenomena and understanding. The mind interprets data. Most concepts in administrative theory, such as organization, group, function, and specialization, are interpretations of the world created by the perceptual screen of the mind. To the phenomenologist, an "organization" cannot exist independently of the image of it formed in the mind. To treat the organization as if it were objectively real is to ignore the most important feature of the concept, namely, its subjective origin.

The phenomenologist analyzes such concepts "through a rigorous analysis of the structure of consciousness."[22] Rejecting the positivist notion that facts exist, he (or she) holds that only ideas, centered in the mind, have certainty. Nothing is out there except your ideas about what is out there. The phenomenologist refuses to separate values from what are perceived to be facts and deals with phenomena in their essential wholeness rather than dissecting them. He tries to combine different views of reality. Any perception of reality, including works of fiction, becomes relevant when it is authentic. A skilled novelist can create an authentic narration showing the reader a perception of reality that is as powerful as a social scientist's table of statistics. Each is a credible perception of reality in its own way.

Phenomenology has a chance to supplant empirical social science in public administration because it is compatible with the world view held by young students. Wesley Bjur has explained the rise of phenomenology in light of the generation gap. Young students, weaned in the McLuhan era of the electronic image, seek explanations of the world that are holistic, make allowance for alternative perceptions of reality, and attach values to the pictures of events. This pretty well rules out the old scientific method, which was better suited to an era when experts dissected events through the linear logic of the printed word. Young people are as uncomfortable with the best examples of "scientific" research as they are with a world without television.

The Proactive Administrator

Phenomenology is often associated with existentialism, since both assert that so-called fundamental laws are only creations of one's own mind. The universe is disordered, says the existentialist; life is an absurd tragedy and God is not an active intervenor in public affairs. To the existentialist, appreciation of one's ultimate responsibility for one's own fate constitutes the highest form of knowledge. This awareness forces people to stop relying upon superior authority for guidance—the church, the state, or the bureau. Every person is absolutely responsible for his or her own actions, from the Nazi bureaucrats who ran the Jewish concentration camps to the Allied pilots who bombed Dresden. No one can morally claim that they were just following orders.

The New PA uses phenomenology and existentialism to create a bridge to a postbureaucratic society in which the administrator is expected to be proactive and the organization is restructured to allow it. Proactive administrators are expected to take risks on behalf of their clients or their moral values, to shift agency resources to help the powerless, and to fight against orders that are unjust. Executives may convert whole agencies to the proactive style, as Roosevelt did with the Securities and Exchange Commission in the thirties and Kennedy and Johnson did with the civil rights division of the Justice Department in the sixties. In those agencies, administrators were expected to invent creative strategies and fight for radical goals. In time, of course, the White House moved on to other priorities, the rules of routine overpowered the creative urge, and the proactive agency became a prisoner of the bureaucracy or the interests it sought to regulate. That is why many suggest that every proactive agency should be abolished after ten years.

Social Equity

A bureaucratic state can never achieve the ideal of bureaucratic equity, where everyone is treated equally before the law. As a society becomes more bureaucratic, problems of equity will become more acute. This is how it happens. Bureaucratic development creates progress, which in turn creates a more visible gap between the haves and the have-nots, even though the have-nots may be better off in absolute terms. The have-nots demand change, become militant, often violent, which leads to repression. The only way that the state can reduce inequities at this point is by forcing the haves to share their privileges, which leads to more coercion and a heightened sense of discrimination. Public administration, if it plays its role as servant of the state, becomes the instrument of repression.

For many years the profession of public administration has tried to maintain a position of value neutrality, not taking sides on political or social issues and concentrating on making governmental administration efficient, in the belief that efficiency would be better for everyone. The New PAers argue that value neutrality is neither possible nor desirable in public administration. It is not possible because public services provided by administrators always vary in their impact, a fact that all the talk about efficiency in administration cannot disguise. In general, the better off a citizen is, the better the services that this person receives: in education, in police protection, in recreation and a variety of other public services that presumably are provided without regard to the status of the recipient. And what should the public servant do about this situation? The servant, says George Frederickson, "is morally obliged to counter this tendency. Equity in the delivery of services, so far as it is calculable, should be one of the standards by which the 'goodness' of a public service is judged. Variations from equity should always be in the direction of providing more and better services to those in lower social, economic, and political circumstances."[23] The alternative is an administrative state that discriminates against the poor and then rebuffs them for complaining about it.

Concern for Clients

Problems of social equity in the delivery of services are exacerbated by plain old poor performance. The more modern public administration becomes, the less it seems able to diagnose or cure the problems that hit the citizen in the neighborhood. "Public administration is the doing part of government," said one critic, "and we seem not to be doing very well."[24]

If administrators are going to deliver poor services, it might as well be services that the citizens can control. Even Max Weber, the father of bureaucratic theory, expressed his admiration for a set of incompetent and corrupt officials whom "the people could oust and despise rather than a caste of expert officials who would despise [the people] and be unremovable."[25]

To reorient administration around the citizen, the New PAers backed a number of proposals. They allied themselves with the reformers who were calling for greater decentralization and citizen participation in government through neighborhood councils, rent strikes, citizen review boards, regional advisory commissions, little city halls, and community development corporations. Some suggested structural reforms. Larry Kirkhart, for example, drew up a plan for clients to be hired into organizations where they would share decision-making authority with professionals. Others proposed methods to allow clients to formally evaluate the work of the agency—and make those evaluations binding. Michael Harmon wanted to use knowledge from the behavioral sciences to humanize the client-administrator relationship, creating a climate in which clients, professionals, and executives could confront each other with their values. The administrator, others added, had a positive responsibility to search for hidden clientele and organize them so that they could join in the receipt of public services. In a modern, client-centered public administration, there is little room for executives who want to swallow their values in order to give an appearance of neutrality.

Human Adaptation

Overall, the New PA saw good administration more as a matter of personal growth than a problem of good management. Most of its reforms were aimed at changing behavior, not structure. One must remember that the New PA arose in the period between the burning of the cities and the shootings at Kent State. There was an overwhelming feeling that public administration would perish if it kept on emphasizing the methods of management control that it was accumulating.

The New PAers wanted to experiment with new styles of administrative leadership that would replace the old management technologies. Robert Biller, in his Minnowbrook paper, picked up a theme from the behavioral sciences and suggested that administrative development was not a matter of structure or formal procedures, but a problem involving the adaptive capacity of the organization. Administrative adaptation required confrontation in an atmosphere of trust, Biller said. Orion White worried about bureaucrats who viewed confrontation as synonymous with conflict—a result, White suggested, of trying to play a win-lose bargaining game with clients instead of using confrontation to promote organizational flexibility. Frank Marini, in summarizing the conference he had helped to organize, noted that the discussions about turbulence led to discussions about confrontation, participation, organizational devolution, personal adaptation, and openness toward clients. These were certainly not the old mechanical principles of administration.

One year later, Peter Savage assessed the impact of the New PA by observing that none of its themes would succeed until the profession committed itself to "infusing public administration with a benevolent social purpose."[26] The profession, he added, had once possessed that ethic—during the Depression and the "New Deal" which came out of it. Savage worried that too many public executives had traded in their sense of social purpose for the conservatism and repression that perpetuates the bureaucracy.

Savage's reflection on the spirit of the thirties raised the question of how "new" the New PA really was. To those who had lived through the New Deal, it did not sound new. The issues of social equity, client concern, proactive administration, and the reaction against the science of management had guided many New Deal administrators, even though they did not use those terms. The New PAers seemed to recognize this. Tom Lynch observed that the appearance of the New PA resembled the events during the New Deal that led to the founding of the American Society for Public Administration in 1939. Yet, somehow, the values and concerns that motivated the profession during the depression had been forgotten by the time the New PAers received their degrees.

Modern public administration was born out of a discontinuity. During the New Deal and the reform movement that preceded it, administrative professionals sought to reform government, *but to do so with bureaucratic methods.* Bureaucracy always smothers the reforming impulse that creates it. The New PA struggled with this discontinuity, just as the older generation had done during the New Deal. Only this time the reformers made a new commitment. They aimed to remove this birth defect by experimenting with counterbureaucratic methods and by embracing a model of diversity that emphasized a number of alternative approaches to public administration.

TOWARD A MODEL OF ADMINISTRATIVE CONTINGENCIES

The essential mission of any science, including the study of administration, is to discover the obvious, to reveal the simplicity of pattern that hides behind the chaos of parts. To most public executives confronting the effects of discontinuity, the chaos is outracing efforts to simplify it. There seem to be more people pressing their own approaches upon managers than scholars trying to reconcile the approaches.

The modern public executive, as a result, is confronted with a battery of confusing and contradictory management "theories." At various times, each of the approaches in this book has been offered as the proverbial key to the pedagogical puzzle—the principles of administration, the behavioral approach, the worship of pluralism, economic rationality and policy analysis, management science, adhocracies, and so on, through every chapter in this book. All of these approaches have been used to manage public organizations. All of them have their own underlying "theories," as any well-constituted approach must. To cure a sick bureaucracy, one must understand Weber's theory of bureaucracy. To play with management science, one must know something about cybernetics. Most of the members of the profession are so sick of seeing theories of management raised and destroyed that they shy away at the mild suggestion of a new one.

Nevertheless, the search continues. The fourth major research trend affecting public administration is the search for a model of administrative contingencies that can synthesize all of these different approaches and lead executives out of the management-theory jungle.

The search began to affect public administration two decades ago during the so-called behavioral revolution. A young political scientist named Herbert Kaufman thought it might be more fun to apply the behavioral perspective to the men who manage America's forests than to sit all summer in a New Haven library reading old books. Through his conversations with forest rangers, he began to realize that the U.S. Forest Service encountered powerful forces of fragmentation, not unlike the complex, inherently unresolvable discontinuities affecting government as a whole. The managers of the Forest Service, Kaufman concluded, were preoccupied with the need to integrate their fragmented organization, to insure that a forest ranger in Virginia carried out the same sorts of policies as a forest ranger in Oregon. Was this a key to the essential problem of administration?

> All organizations, in every culture, probably face difficulties in maintaining integration in the face of thrusts toward fragmentation. The centrifugal tendencies may well differ from place to place, and over time, and the modes of counteracting them are doubtless myriad. But if the tensions exist, their sources can be identified and the modes of resolving them described. [27]

The methods of integration used in the Forest Service might not work in another agency, or even in the Forest Service twenty years later. The diversity of methods, however, need not block administrative research on then. Kaufman suggested that scholars complete more clinical studies to add to *The Forest Ranger,* catalog the forces of fragmentation, note the strategies of integration, and match the two. From this, he said, it might be possible to begin to conquer the confusion surrounding the study of administrative methods.

As is too often the case in the administrative arts, the call for further research was ignored. The book sold well, but no one carried on the idea.

Four years later, two professors at the Harvard Business School, experts in organization development, began a study that ostensibly was unrelated to Kaufman's book. The professors, Paul Lawrence and Jay Lorsch, studied six industries in the plastic business, two container corporations, and two firms that prepared packaged foods. Lawrence and Lorsch wondered why some of the firms did quite well while others were a bust.

On the surface, there was no easy explanation. The companies were organized differently, but that did not explain success or failure. The managers used different administrative techniques, but they were all out of the same textbook. Lawrence and Lorsch could not explain the performance of the companies by comparing their internal administrative arrangements. So they looked outside, at the setting of each industry. The managers of the plastics companies operated in a complex, fast-moving market subject to the vagaries of technological change. The container corporations operated in exactly the opposite environment: no new products had been introduced for twenty years. The packaged-foods firms were caught in the vice of consumer fashions. Each group of companies had to adjust to different thrusts toward fragmentation. Lawrence and Lorsch found that the successful corporations were just as differentiated as their environment required them to be. But there was a catch. The more differentiated any company became, the more it tended to disintegrate. To check the centrifugal tendencies, these organizations had to adopt indigenous management strategies that reintegrated the organization—*without damaging the differentiation that made the organization successful in the first place.*

But which management strategies? Was it possible to say that one strategy fit one type of situation better than another? Two research scientists asked this question: an American psychologist by the name of Fred Fiedler and an English sociologist named Joan Woodward.

Fiedler was distressed by the bickering between the proponents of hard-nosed management and the advocates of human relations techniques, the controversy embodied in McGregor's Theory X and Theory Y. Each side claimed that its style was best; each displayed its own cases of successful management. It was obvious to Fiedler that both styles worked, that there was no "best way" to supervise. Fiedler decided to find out why. In one experiment he studied the work of bomber crews making practice runs over simulated targets—a highly precise, well-structured problem that depended upon the close cooperation of the pilot, who was ostensibly in charge, and the bombardiers, who perform the critical task. Each crew received a score based upon how close it came to the target. Fiedler discovered that the crews run along the lines of Theory X outperformed the Theory Y–type crews. Fielder continued the experiment with basketball teams, farm supply companies, managers in a steel mill, and ROTC cadets. In general, Fiedler's research confirms what many suspect—that task-style, hard-nosed management works best in groups with highly structured tasks, while creative groups with unstructured tasks need human-relations-type leaders. But there are exceptions, important ones, and by the time that Fiedler was finished explaining them, he had constructed a fairly complex seven-part model of leadership effectiveness.

While Fiedler created a contingency model for leadership, Joan Woodward experimented with organization design. She examined the principles of administration, such as span of control, which advises the executive to supervise between three and twelve subordinates and which critics found maddeningly vague, since there was little to indicate whether three or twelve or even sixteen was best. Woodward studied 100 British firms in order to resolve this problem. She discovered that assembly-line-type operations got along perfectly well with a span of control of one to forty-five out in the factory; while technologically complex firms—ones that had to process chemicals, for example—shaved their span of control down to about one to fifteen for first-line supervisors. By studying a large number of administrative variables and classifying the firms into three categories, Woodward was able to show that organizational design and supervision varied according to the production technology used by the firm—a fancy term for the flow of work.

Now other pieces fell into line. James Thompson had drawn together studies of private and public organizations to show how different types of organizations reacted differently to problems of uncertainty in their environment by developing different administrative systems. Thompson classified his organizational types as *long-linked* (a sewage treatment plant would be an example), *mediating* (a police department), and *intensive* (a research laboratory)—a classification scheme based on the tasks the organization performed and the technology it used. In 1961, Amatai Etzioni had claimed that he could correlate different patterns of organization with different patterns of social compliance—in essence, whether the organization used coercion, money, or normative values to control its employees. A coercive organization, Etzioni suggested, would have different goals, a different power structure, different methods of integration, communication, recruitment, and cohesion from those of a utilitarian or normative organization. Michael Crozier's study of bureaucratic behavior showed how organizations could deliberately ignore forces in their environment compelling the organization to adopt the relevant style of administration. The study of prismatic society by Fred Riggs showed what would happen when the pressures of differentiation outraced the ability of executives to integrate them.

There are serious problems with the contingency approach, problems reflected in the fact that most of the research in this area has been done inside business firms. The problems arise because most contingency theorists rely upon the concept of integration as the central administrative process. This leads to a biased view of the organization, a presumption that the most important administrative processes are those which top executives use to hold the organization together from the center. Such a bias might be all right for dictatorships and corporations, but it does not quite fit the needs of the public administrator in a pluralistic state.

Historically, of course, most government operations have been run as if they were private corporations, guided by a theory of organizational engineering, with the resulting emphasis upon control and integration. This view of public administration goes back nine thousand years, when humans first began to organize their public affairs around city settlements. The first "public administrators" had to oversee the differentiation of functions necessary to build up the city, its storehouses and fortifications—quite a radical undertaking for people emerging from the long night of nomadic life. The more difficult problem, of course, was to perfect methods of organizational integration appropriate to the tasks involved in city life. Out of such necessities rose the primary methods of public administration, couched in religious precepts, but easily recognizable as the fundamentals of administration. Ancient agencies such as these pose few problems for contingency theorists. The government agencies that cause trouble are all the others—those affected by the political turbulence of the eighteenth and nineteenth centuries, which saw the curtailment of monarchical power by the rise of constitutional government, the rule of law, the preeminence of the legislature, the extension of suffrage, and the ideal of citizen participation. It is on behalf of these concerns that the word *public* is prefixed to the word administration.

Any complete model of administrative contingencies for public administration will have to give coequal attention to both concerns: the classic problem of achieving organizational integration under the conditions of differentiation *and* the modern political problem of how to keep the solution public. The contingency theorist will have to discuss problems of political responsibility, distribution, equity, law, coercion, representation, and morality *as if they were the primary conditions governing the choice of administrative strategies.*

Advocates of the contingency approach believe that it can be used as a guide to administrative decision making. An administrator schooled in this type of situational analysis, they say, is in a better position to select the appropriate administrative strategies. A public executive following the contingency approach would work through a four-step model.

1. An examination of the agency and its environment. The contingency approach begins with the situational dimension, the assumption that there is something unique about each agency —the task to be performed, the core technology, the patterns of social compliance and, most important, the forces that tend to fragment the agency and the organizational differentiation that results.

2. An analysis of available administrative strategies. The contingency approach assumes that there is no universally correct "theory" of administration, but rather an encyclopedia of conflicting strategies that executives must master before they can effectively manage their agencies. It judges the utility of any administrative strategy by a simple standard: *under what conditions does it work?*

3. An assessment of political constraints. Any contingency approach to public administration will have to take into account factors such as the political limits on administrative discretion, the requirements for clientele participation and citizen representation, the diffusion of policy making, the limits on the use of coercion, and other constraints based on the specific political situation in which the agency operates.

4. The choice of administrative strategies. Contingency theorists assume that the basic administrative process is a matter of differentiation and integration, of trying to create an organization that is complex enough to deal with its environment and then to put it back together again without disturbing any of the parts. The big problem, of course, is how to choose the appropriate method of integration. This requires research—research that provides the executive with some clues as to the consequences of choosing one management strategy rather than another. One does not promote a contingency approach to public administration merely by listing all of the strategies.

By twisting the problem-solving method slightly, the contingency approach becomes a research model that can help experts catalog and compare different administrative strategies under different conditions. The researcher examines the internal and external environment of the agency under study, paying special attention to the forces of fragmentation, and reviews the range of management strategies available to the executives, including the methods officially sanctioned by the organization. The researcher then assesses which formal and informal strategies of administration are the most potent in achieving organizational integration as well as in promoting administrative feedback and conflict resolution. Kaufman, for example, emphasized the importance of the spirit of professionalism maintained by Forest Service executives as the primary force in promoting voluntary conformity to organizational policy. Finally, the researcher attempts to explain why that particular pattern of administration evolved, given the political situation and other factors in the environment of the agency.

The result, presumably, is a clearer understanding of the effects of different administrative strategies under different situations, in the same way that a physician comes to understand the effects of different medicines upon different diseases. It makes the administrative expert a diagnostician, an analyzer of conditions, prepared to follow a process of problem solving that leads to the appropriate strategy. Unfortunately, the contingency approach has not yet reached this level of analysis (if it had, the reader would not have to wait until a chapter on the future to learn about it). At this stage, the contingency approach offers the executive a problem-solving framework and a list of administrative methods. It is not a complete theory and will not become one until scholars have collected sufficient empirical findings to reveal why different forms of politically acceptable administrative integration take place under different conditions.

Therein lies the plight of the modern public administrator. The number of approaches to administration—and the strategies they embrace—continues to multiply faster than systematic explanations about when and where and why to use them.

THE IDENTITY CRISIS IN PUBLIC ADMINISTRATION

During the 1930s, when the American Society for Public Administration was formed, the profession was confident about its knowledge and excited about its influence. Its best scholars, men like Luther Gulick, had unparalleled access to government policy makers. The leading practitioners, men like Paul Appleby, participated in the public administration movement and made scholarly contributions to the field. Herbert Kaufman remembers that "bureaucrats in the thirties were regarded by many as heroes in the struggles for a better social order."[28] Public administration, as a field of study and as a profession, was young, vigorous, confident, and optimistic. It seemed like the golden age of public administration.

Sometime in the years after the thirties, feeblemindedness set in. At the Minnowbrook conference, Todd LaPorte chastised what he called the babble of the literature—a lot of seemingly contradictory theories that were often irrelevant to the administrator confronting the anger of change. Marini noted that relevance, the key word at

Minnowbrook, brought out "arguments quite critical of the contemporary state of the academic literature of public administration," critical of its ethical insensitivity as well as its lack of utility for the practicing executive.[29] Another young scholar put it more directly: public administration has come apart and cannot be put back together again.[30]

Back in the thirties, most of what was known about public administration would fit into the scope of the first chapter of this book. In forty years, the knowledge about public administration has simply exploded, not only among experts who identify with the profession, but outside of it as well, as disciplines from biology to mathematics have stuck their heads underneath the governmental tent to test their own approaches to administration. The proliferation of approaches, Dwight Waldo says, is the primary source of the afflicting malady.

> Public Administration is suffering from an identity crisis, having enormously expanded its periphery without retaining or creating a unifying center.[31]

In practical terms, the identity crisis manifests itself in the contradictory bits of advice advanced by people who call themselves administrative experts. For every group of people advancing one approach, you can find another group arguing plausibly for just the opposite. As an example, study the controversy over the future of bureaucracy. The New PA is openly antibureaucratic. Its advocates want to debureaucratize the government and replace the bureau with a more flexible, humane, democratic form of organization. It is a fact, well known to practicing executives, that many phases of a governmental operation cannot be run according to bureaucratic formulas, especially at the top of the organization. At the same time, there are other parts of the government where bureaucracy has a positive value: not just at low levels, where fifteen uniforms go in and fifteen uniforms come out, but at high levels as well. Never forget that it was a sense of bureaucratic responsibility to the law that prompted many officials in the Internal Revenue Service to threaten to resign when officials in the White House, which is not a bureaucracy, pressured the bureaucrats to use the tax audit to get at "political enemies." And it was bureaucratic momentum, pointed toward a fixed goal, that kept Justice Department prosecutors in the courts despite Nixon's plea that "one year of Watergate is enough."

This is just one of the controversies embroiling public administration. Every approach discussed in this book has its adherents and its critics. Those who treat public administration as a scientific problem are opposed by those who see administrative improvement as primarily a matter of human behavior. There are the pluralists who want to preserve the democratic state by exposing administrators to the political process, and there are the reformers who want to purify administration by taking the bureaucrat out of interest-group politics. The analysts, who want to make administration rational through economic models and evaluation, are opposed by the incremen-

362

talists, who want a more realistic model of decision making. Some want to balance all of these approaches through the contingency approach to administration; others feel that the contingency approach holds out a hollow promise.

It is only natural that people who disagree on approach and method should also disagree on the fundamental issues of administration. One year after the Minnowbrook Conference, Dwight Waldo brought the New PA together again at the convention of the American Political Science Association. Waldo discussed what he perceived to be the major administrative issues underlying the controversies over approach and method. These were Waldo's concerns, written down in the book *Public Administration in a Time of Turbulence:*

- The advocates of states' rights and "power to the people" oppose those who know that centralization is necessary to promote national priorities and administrative reform.

- The advocates of greater citizen participation in administration, including citizens and employees, confront the fact that "ultimately a democratic country must limit participation because it is committed to democracy."[32]

- Economists, management scientists, radicals, and constitutional theorists are reviving the politics/administration dichotomy, stupifying members of the old guard who thought they had driven this devil out of the profession thirty years ago.

- The gospel of efficiency still haunts a profession that does not want to make it the central value of administration but refuses to embrace any substitute criterion that smacks of inefficiency.

- The Dionysians assault organizational life for creating "a monstrous world of chrome and plastic" from inside a profession

In thirty years, public administration has grown from a field of study dominated by a single approach to an emerging profession based upon multiple sources of knowledge. As a young professor, Dwight Waldo helped to discredit the single approach with his attacks upon the criterion of efficiency. Since then, Waldo has done more than any other scholar to shape the development of public administration, explaining the "identity crisis" created by the proliferation of approaches and showing scholars how to deal with it. Waldo is currently a professor of public administration at Syracuse University. COURTESY OF THE MAXWELL SCHOOL, SYRACUSE UNIVERSITY.

363

built on the Apollonian virtues of moderation, logic, and rationality.[33]

- The knowledge that organizational societies are intrinsically more progressive than primitive civilizations runs aground on the belief that organizations are monsters enslaving the human race.

Modern executives, for whom ambiguity is a virtue and discontinuity a way of life, seem prepared to live with these controversies. On the academic side of public administration, however, such diversity is a threat because of the traditional requirement that any respectable field of inquiry be able to agree upon a fundamental theory that shapes its approach to the phenomenon it studies. It is this search for a single dominant theory of public administration that lies at the heart of the identity crisis.

Vincent Ostrom states the problem very well. The search for a dominant theory, Ostrom explains, began when Woodrow Wilson asked American scholars to forget their "paper pictures" of good government and study how administration really worked. By telling scholars to study France and Prussia, Wilson established four guiding assumptions. First, the science of administration would be based on a single organizational prototype universally applicable to all political regimes; second, any good science of administration would have to divorce itself from the field of politics; third, the guiding value of the science of administration would be efficiency; and fourth, efficient public administration would require a single dominant center of governmental power.

Public administration never really wanted to accept the Wilson paradigm. The strongest attack came from Herbert Simon, who demonstrated that the basic principles of administration, being overly imprecise, would produce *inefficiency*. In doing so, Simon accidently perpetuated the system he was trying to destroy. He attacked the orthodox movement, but he did so with the assumptions that bolstered it: the search for a universal model of administration which would promote efficiency. Having torn down the principles of administration, Simon failed to erect any alternative model in their place. (He suggested that scholars study administrative decisions, but it never caught on.) As Simon criticized, Weber's theories were translated into English. Having been challenged, the study of public administration went skidding back into the familiar Wilson-Weberian paradigm. Although few were really devoted to the search for administrative universals, it remained the mainstream of academic public administration.

The rejected alternative, Ostrom asserts, is the theory of democratic administration. Its roots are in the concepts of self-government established at the time of the American founding. Ostrom lists nine characteristics of democratic administration, which boil down to the idea that the public administrator is in business to serve the persons who consume public goods and services and to enhance "the welfare

CHAPTER 10: THE FUTURE

of discreet human beings."[34] Ostrom argues that Madison and Hamilton stress this theory of popular administration in the *Federalist Papers,* that both were in favor of a divided system of administration for the states and federal government as a whole. Ironically, Weber also outlined such a theory of democratic administration, based on the egalitarian assumption that everyone was qualified to participate in matters of public choice and on the idea that the power of command be minimized. Both Weber and the earlier traveler, De Tocqueville, admired the actual structure of democratic administration in America and thought that it provided a practical alternative to the bureaucratic despotism sweeping across the world.

It was these "paper pictures" that Wilson urged his ethnocentric American colleagues to forget. Although public administrators disliked the emphasis upon efficiency and rationality in the bureaucratic model, they disliked even more the extreme fragmentation of administrative authority which was the consequence of allowing the spoils system to corrupt the popular model. A compromise of sorts between the bureaucratic and democratic models was struck when Paul Appleby suggested that organized clientele become the source of bureaucratic power in a democracy. That solution remained unacceptable to both the rationalists and the classical democrats, and it rarely worked outside of the United States.

The theory of democratic administration, Ostrom says, was resurrected in the 1960s by a group of scholars well removed from the mainstream of American public administration: the public-choice economists. These scholars viewed the citizen as the ultimate source of administrative power, not because of a specific commitment to democratic theory, but because they saw the citizen as a rational consumer of public goods and services. The institutional rules and arrangements associated with the bureaucratic model of administration, from their point of view, interfered with the power of citizens to express their preferences because these institutions limited public choice. Control by a single center of power, says Ostrom, will "reduce the capability of a large administrative system to respond to diverse preferences among citizens for many different public goods and services and cope with diverse environmental conditions."[35] To respond to the preferences of the public and to avoid the institutional weaknesses created by a dominant bureaucratic form, the government must divide administrative power and offer it to the citizen in many different forms.

A variety of organizational arrangements will be required to provide different goods and services. That is the essence of the theory of public choice. It is not possible, for example, to talk about centralization *versus* decentralization. In a complex democratic state, "elements of centralization and decentralization must exist simultaneously among several jurisdictions with concurrent authority."[36] The same observation applies to all the other discontinuities mentioned above. If public administration does not learn to use these contradictions, it will cease to be useful.

365

The job of the public administrator, says Ostrom, is to anticipate the consequences of various institutional arrangements so that weaknesses in form are minimized and the preferences of citizens are maximized. The job of the public administration scholar is to create a theory with concepts to explain this. Regardless of what one thinks of the organizational arrangements favored by the public-choice economists (which have their particular weaknesses), Ostrom has thrown out a real challenge. Create a democratic theory of administration, he says, that accentuates diversity.

An emphasis upon diversity, Waldo says, would do much to relieve the current identity crisis over the place of public administration in the spectrum of knowledge. Public administration, he suggests, should think of itself as roughly analogous to the medical profession. Medicine is guided by no single theory; rather it draws upon a number of different medical sciences to treat the multiple ills of the human patient. Schools of medicine are in business to train practitioners to use different academic disciplines. Public administration, Waldo says, should see itself in an equivalent posture: assembling knowledge from different disciplines to prepare practitioners for careers in the public service. He tells his colleagues to quit worrying about their place among the disciplines and "seek what we need wherever it may be located."[37]

THE FUTURE PUBLIC ADMINISTRATOR

The future public administrator will need to possess a set of skills as diverse as the discontinuities that affect government as a whole. This book has been a treatise on diversity, presenting the full range of approaches to public administration. Each of the chapters represents one of the major approaches; each of the approaches creates a different role for the public administrator. To be effective, the future public administrator will have to be able to play all of the roles, to be all of these things:

1. An Organizer, who can use a knowledge of the principles and functions of administration to structure the formal organization.
2. A Leader, who understands the behavioral basis of administration.
3. A Pathologist, who knows how to diagnose the ills of bureaucracy and cure them.
4. A Politician, who knows how to build political support for his or her program and get along with competing interests.
5. A Policy Analyst, who knows how to calculate the effects and costs of public policy.
6. An Expediter, who knows the advantages of power and how to use it.
7. A Scientist, who knows how to use scientific decision making to manage change.

8. A Change Agent, who knows how to use Organization Development to maximize human resources in the agency.

9. An Internationalist, who appreciates the impact of local conditions upon administration.

10. A Reformer, who can predict future discontinuities and prepare the organization for them.

These roles are supported by the accumulation of knowledge through the study of public administration, a field of inquiry which, since its beginnings in the 1880s, has progressed from the simple to the complex. The study of administration began, simultaneously, in mines and bureaus, cities and factories. American public administration was born on the streets of New York and Chicago, where public-minded citizens met to reform the big-city machines. Some borrowed scientific management from business; some studied the peculiar administrative needs of the public service. Together they produced a powerful model of administrative orthodoxy based on efficiency and reform.

While the old guard of public administration was advising presidents, a new generation of public administrators learned about the mechanics of government at lower levels. The trauma of the war—seeing administration close up—sent these scholars back to the campuses determined to shake public administration out of its orthodox beliefs. They demanded that public administration pay more attention to administrative behavior and to the dysfunctions of bureaucracy. They demanded an end to the separation of politics and administration. A large number of social scientists began to write about public administration in special policy areas—agriculture, science, regulation, war agencies, natural resources, and city government—in books and case studies about particular administrative decisions.

Despite all this realism, public administration was poorly prepared for the explosion of governmental programs in the sixties. Public executives asked: how do we organize for results? how do we manage technology? how do we handle demands for participation? how should we administer overseas programs? Public administration, with its value-free, scientific, descriptive studies, simply did not have all the answers. This set off a scramble for solutions. Political scientists and economists contributed the policy approach, while pragmatists cataloged the lessons of practical executive control. Systems analysts reintroduced management science into the public service. Social psychologists salvaged what they could out of the human relations movement to create a planned change strategy called organization development. Public administrators struggled to match modern administrative methods with the local conditions in developing countries. And younger scholars agitated for new values, new forms of organization, a new sensitivity to the discontinuities of change in modern governments.

Each major approach tended to develop its own underlying theory, its own values, its own view of the organization, its own image of the job of the executive, its own management strategies. Each approach tended to acquire advocates who saw their strategies as the administrative panacea: the PPB missionaries, the people who believed that fluid organizations were the salvation of modern government, and on and on.

There are no universals in public administration. The future public administrator will need all of these approaches to manage the modern public agency. Public administration, after all, is essentially circular. Each approach possesses its own particular deficiencies, which push the executive toward another approach. Cut into the circle at the principles of administration, and the administrator sees a bureaucracy. The bureaucracy becomes rigid. Rigidity can be cured by exposing the bureaucracy to the political process, but political bureaucracies tend to excite factions that want special access to administrative policy making. That creates subgovernments. To get results, executives centralize power through a planning-and-control system. Their management science approach leads to program management and other flexible forms of organization, which create a role for the behavioralists who want to reform institutions through organization development. The reform of government leads to demands for a cybernetic state in which administrative discretion is replaced by the rule of law, which in turn leads back to legal debates about separating politics and administration, whence the original principles came. Even political revolutionaries come back to the principles of administration. The circle is joined. This is only one of many possible scenarios. In a complex organization, many circles of administration are being played out simultaneously.

The profession of public administration is now poised on the edge of transition. It has accumulated an amazing storehouse of knowledge over the past ninety years, a storehouse that makes public administration rich but a bit unstable. Public administration as a field of study resembles Collyer's mansion, a mid-Victorian brownstone on Fifth Avenue in New York owned by a pair of rich eccentrics named Langley and Homer Collyer. These two brothers never threw anything out. After their death in 1947, the police took 120 tons of accumulated possessions out of the house, including 14 grand pianos, 5,000 books, and a thirty-year collection of old newspapers. This example of indiscriminate accumulation spawned the term *Collyerism* and a generation of Irish mothers who admonished their children to clean up their rooms so that they would not look like Collyer's mansion.

Public administration suffers from Collyer's dilemma—how to straighten up the house without throwing out something that might prove valuable. No one technique, no one theory, no one approach to public administration is really dispensable. Public administration needs all of its approaches; it is most unwise to throw out a strategy or theory just because it is old or controversial. At the same time, public administration needs some sense of order to its affairs, a guid-

Here is one artist's vision of the totally administered state—a space colony fixed in orbit in the vicinity of the moon. The city lights are reflected in the mirrors that direct sunlight into the interior, regulating the day and night and the growing seasons. Public administrators of the future, on earth as well as in space, will need to master knowledge and techniques from a number of academic disciplines. COURTESY OF NASA.

ing theory. Diversity without a guiding theory creates an intellectual madhouse that forces scholars to flee to more solid disciplines. Unfortunately, all the single-purpose theories that have served public administration in the past are too narrow to solve this problem; yet if public administration abandons its search for a guiding theory, it will damage its potential as a major field of study.

Diversity killed old Langley Collyer. He died in a tunnel maze that he had built out of old newspapers. Crawling through the maze of newsprint, he accidently touched off a booby trap he had set to discourage burglars. The tunnel collapsed and sealed Langley off from Homer, who had been blind for fifteen years. They both starved to death. Their home was cleaned up and their possessions sold at an open auction supervised by the office of the New York City Public Administrator.

FOR FURTHER READING

A number of authors view the future in terms of the ferment created by discontinuous trends working against each other. Peter Drucker takes a global view in *The Age of Discontinuity: Guidelines to our Changing Society* (New York: Harper & Row, 1968). John W. Gardner examines the potential for conflict between the individual and the organized society in *Self-Renewal* (New York: Harper & Row, 1964), while Dwight Waldo explains how these discontinuities create antinomies within public administration in "Developments in Public Administration," *The Annals of the American Academy* 404 (November 1972), pp. 217–245. There are four new trends in research and practice emerging from this ferment. Theodore J. Lowi offers a comprehensive indictment of pluralism and planning in *The End of Liberalism* (New York: W. W. Norton & Co., 1969) and outlines his solution for a regulated state. A germinal work in the search for the postbureaucratic public organization is Orion F. White, "The Dialectical Organization: An Alternative to Bureaucracy," *Public Administration Review* 29 (January/February 1969), pp. 32–42. H. George Frederickson sums up the mood of the New PA in Chapter 11 of Frank Marini, ed., *Toward a New Public Administration: The Minnowbrook Perspective* (Scranton, Pa.: Chandler Publishing Co., 1971). Fred Luthans summarizes the various contributions to the contingency approach, albeit from a business manager's point of view, in *Introduction to Management: A Contingency Approach* (New York: McGraw-Hill Book Co., 1976).

Vincent Ostrom argues the case for diversity in administration in *The Intellectual Crisis in American Public Administration* (University: University of Alabama Press, 1973). The source of that diversity is laid out in Frederick C. Mosher, ed., *American Public Administration* (University: University of Alabama Press, 1975), a comprehensive history of the study of public administration in the United States. As the publication of Mosher's anthology suggests, public administration is caught up in a reexamination of the scholarly side of the profession.

Dwight Waldo has been the guardian of that academic development for thirty years. Key works of his are Dwight Waldo, *The Administrative State* (New York: Ronald Press, 1948); "Public Administration," *International Encyclopedia of the Social Sciences*, vol. 13 (New York: Macmillan Co. and The Free Press, 1968); and *Public Administration in a Time of Turbulence* (Scranton, Pa.: Chandler Publishing Co., 1971).

NOTES

PREFACE

1. A few years ago I sought to locate the sources of our knowledge by identifying the most important books being used by teachers of public administration. That survey led to the publication of a bibliography on public administration. This textbook is based on the sources identified in that bibliography, as well as on other books and materials of special importance. Howard E. McCurdy, *Public Administration: A Bibliography* (Washington, D.C.: College of Public Affairs, The American University, 1972).

2. Dwight Waldo, *The Novelist on Organization & Administration* (Berkeley: Institute of Governmental Studies, University of California, 1968), or Howard McCurdy, "Fiction, Phenomenology, and Public Administration, *Public Administration Review* 33 (January/February 1973), pp. 52–60.

CHAPTER 1

1. A survey of Henri Fayol's work can be found in the introduction to his book *General and Industrial Management* (New York: Pitman Publishing Corporation, 1949).

2. Henri Fayol, "The Administrative Theory in the State," in *Papers on the Science of Administration*, ed. Luther Gulick and L. Urwick (New York: Augustus M. Kelley Publishers, 1937), p. 101.

3. Fayol, *General and Industrial Management*, p. 21.

4. Luther Gulick, "Notes on the Theory of Organization," in *Papers*, ed. Gulick and Urwick, p. 9.

5. Fayol, *General and Industrial Management*, p. 21.

6. Ibid., p. 21.

7. Gulick, "Notes," p. 3.

8. Frederick Taylor, *Principles of Scientific Management* (New York: W. W. Norton & Co., 1911), pp. 44–46.

9. Frederick Taylor, "Testimony before the Special House Committee," in *Scientific Management*, Taylor (New York: Harper & Bros., 1947), p. 46.

10. Theodore Roosevelt, *Theodore Roosevelt: An Autobiography* (New York: The Macmillan Co., 1913), in the order of the quotations, pp. 229, 237, 239, and 231–32.

11. Che Guevara, "La Guerra de Guerrillas," *Army* 11 (March 1961), p. 23.

12. Woodrow Wilson, "The Study of Administration," *Political Science Quarterly*, June 1887, reprinted in 56 (December 1941), p. 484.

13. Ibid., p. 504.

14. Ibid., p. 483.

15. Robert Caro, *The Power Broker: Robert Moses and the Fall of New York* (New York: Alfred A. Knopf, 1974), p. 96.

16. Ibid., p. 97.

17. Leonard D. White, *Introduction to the Study of Public Administration*, 2d ed., (New York: Harper & Brothers, 1935), pp. vii–viii.

18. Peter Drucker, *Managing for Results* (New York: Harper & Row, 1964), p. 5.

19. Ibid., p. 8.

20. Ibid., p. 200.

21. Stephen J. Carroll and Henry L. Tosi, *Management by Objectives* (New York: The Macmillan Co., 1973), p. 2.

22. F. J. Roethlisberger and William F. Dickson, *Management and the Worker* (Cambridge, Mass.: Harvard University Press, 1939), p. 17.

23. Elton Mayo, *The Social Problems of an Industrial Civilization* (New York: The Viking Press, 1945), p. 65.

24. Quoted from Elton Mayo, *Social Problems*, p. 74.

25. Ibid., p. 116.

26. Luther Gulick, "Science, Values, and Public Administration," in *Papers*, ed. Gulick and Urwick, p. 195.

27. Comments taken from Herbert Simon, *Administrative Behavior* (New York: The Macmillan Co., 1947), p. 20; and Simon, "The Proverbs of Administration," *Public Administration Review* 6 (Winter 1946), p. 53.

28. Simon, *Administrative Behavior*, p. 44.

29. Gulick, "Science, Values, and Public Administration," pp. 192–93.

30. Dwight Waldo, *The Administrative State* (New York: Ronald Press, 1948), p. 195.

31. Ibid., p. 202.

32. Ibid., pp. 202–203.

33. Henry Lansberger, *Hawthorne Revisited* (Ithaca, N.Y.: Cornell University Press, 1958), p. 38.

34. Ibid., p. 32.

CHAPTER 2

1. Jean-Francois Steiner, *Treblinka* (New York: Signet Books, 1966), pp. 172, 175.

2. Ibid., p. 271.

3. Chester I. Barnard, *The Functions of the Executive* (Cambridge, Mass.: Harvard University Press, 1938), p. 73.

4. F. J. Roethlisberger, "Chester I. Barnard," *International Encyclopedia of the Social Sciences*, vol. 2 (New York: The Macmillan Co. and The Free Press, 1968), p. 12.

5. Dennis Smith, *Report from Engine Co. 82* (New York: Pocket Books, 1972), p. 28.

6. Herbert Simon, *Administrative Behavior* (New York: The Macmillan Co., 1947), p. 79.

7. James G. March and Herbert A. Simon, *Organizations* (New York: John Wiley & Sons, 1958), p. 169.

8. Alexander Leighton, *The Governing of Men* (Princeton, N.J.: Princeton University Press, 1945), p. 364.

9. Victor A. Thompson, *Modern Organization* (New York: Alfred A. Knopf, 1961), p. 138.

10. Theodore Sorenson, *Decision-Making in the White House* (New York: Columbia University Press, 1963), p. 84.

11. Melville Dalton, *Men Who Manage* (New York: John Wiley & Sons, 1959), p. 3.

12. John Steinbeck, *In Dubious Battle* (New York: Bantam Books, 1936), p. 230.

13. Quoted from March and Simon, *Organizations*, p. 84.

14. Philip Selznick, *Leadership in Administration* (New York: Row, Peterson, 1957), p. 63.

CHAPTER 3

1. Dwight Waldo, ed., *Public Administration in a Time of Turbulence* (Scranton, Pa.: Chandler Publishing Co., 1971), p. 282.

2. H. H. Gerth and C. Wright Mills, *From Max Weber* (New York: Oxford University Press, 1946), p. 11.

3. Ibid., p. 198.

4. Ibid., p. 197.

5. Ibid., p. 199.

6. Ibid., p. 199.

7. Ibid., p. 228.

8. Ibid., p. 214.

9. Peter M. Blau, *Bureaucracy in Modern Society*, 1st ed. (New York: Random House, 1956), pp. 61–66.

10. Franz Kafka, "The Metamorphosis," from *In the Penal Colony* (New York: Schocken Books, 1948), p. 67.

11. Ibid., pp. 75, 77.

12. Ibid., p. 78.

13. Robert Presthus, *The Organizational Society* (New York: Alfred A. Knopf, 1962), p. 257.

14. Ibid., p. 258.

15. Ken Kesey, *One Flew over the Cuckoo's Nest* (New York: Viking Press, 1962), p. 28.

16. Ibid., p. 69.

17. This definition is generally attributed to Michel Crozier, *The Bureaucratic Phenomenon* (Chicago: University of Chicago Press, 1964), p. 187.

18. Victor A. Thompson, *Modern Organization* (New York: Alfred A. Knopf, 1961), p. 6.

19. Ibid., p. 164.

20. Lawrence J. Peter and Raymond Hull, *The Peter Principle* (New York: Bantam Books, 1969), p. 8.

21. Thompson, *Modern Organization*, p. 167.

22. Ibid., p. 170.

23. Crozier, *Bureaucratic Phenomenon*, p. 86.

24. Ibid., p. 139.

25. Ibid., p. 101.

26. Ibid., p. 107.

27. Ibid., p. 193.

28. Ibid., p. 139.

29. Ibid., p. 198.

30. Ibid., p. 196.

31. Anthony Downs, *Inside Bureaucracy* (Chicago: University of Chicago Press, 1965), p. 37.

32. Ibid., p. 39.

33. Ibid., p. 40.

34. Ibid., p. 2.

35. Ibid., p. 36.

36. C. Wright Mills, *White Collar* (New York: Oxford University Press, 1951), p. 95.

37. Ludwig Von Mises, *Bureaucracy* (New Haven, Conn.: Yale University Press, 1944), p. 19.

38. Downs, *Inside Bureaucracy*, p. 280.

CHAPTER 4

1. The logic of this point can be found in Paul H. Appleby's book *Big Democracy* (New York: Alfred A. Knopf, 1945), which begins with the argument that government in general and administration in particular are "different." The quote by Wallace Sayre is part of the oral tradition of public administration, carried on by his students and colleagues.

2. Paul H. Appleby, *Policy and Administration* (University: University of Alabama Press, 1949), p. 5.

3. Appleby, *Big Democracy*, p. 7.

4. Appleby, *Policy and Administration*, p. 170.

5. A. Lee Fritschler, *Smoking and Politics* (Englewood Cliffs, N.J.: Prentice-Hall, 1975), p. 170.

6. Ibid., p. 8.

7. Francis E. Rourke, *Bureaucracy, Politics, and Public Policy* (Boston: Little, Brown & Co., 1969), p. 11.

8. Marver H. Bernstein, *The Job of the Federal Executive* (Washing-

ton, D.C.: The Brookings Institution, 1958), p. 33.

9. Harold Seidman, *Politics, Position & Power* (New York: Oxford University Press, 1975), p. 38.

10. Ibid., p. 40.

11. Phillip O. Foss, *Politics and Grass: The Administration of Grazing on the Public Domain* (Seattle: University of Washington Press, 1961), pp. 199–200.

12. Philip Selznick, *TVA and the Grass Roots* (New York: Harper & Row, 1949), p. 265.

13. Morris Janowitz, *The Professional Soldier* (New York: The Free Press, 1960), p. 6.

14. Quoted from Frederick C. Mosher, *Democracy and the Public Service* (New York: Oxford University Press, 1968), p. 141.

15. Herbert Kaufman, *The Forest Ranger* (Baltimore: Johns Hopkins Press, 1960), p. 83.

16. Ibid., p. 198.

17. Morton Grodzins, "Centralization and Decentralization in the American Federal System," in *A Nation of States*, ed. Robert A. Goldwin (Chicago: Rand McNally & Co., 1961), p. 4.

18. Ibid., p. 22.

19. Ibid., p. 7.

20. Terry Sanford, *Storm over the States* (New York: McGraw-Hill Book Co., 1967), p. 80.

21. U.S. Department of Commerce, *Survey of Current Business*, vol. 54, no. 7 (Washington, D.C.: Government Printing Office, 1974), p. 32.

22. Jean J. Couturier, "Chaos or Creativity in Public Labor-Management Relations," *Managing Government Labor Rela-*tions, ed. Chester Newland (Washington, D.C.: Manpower Press, 1972).

23. Felix A. Nigro, *Modern Public Administration*, 2d. ed. (New York: Harper & Row, 1970), p. 337.

24. Saul Alinsky, *Reveille for Radicals* (Chicago: University of Chicago Press, 1946), p. 3.

25. Leonard D. White, *The Republican Era* (New York: The Macmillan Co., 1958), p. 393.

26. Herbert Kaufman, "Administrative Decentralization and Political Power," *Public Administration Review* 29 (Jan./Feb. 1969), p. 11.

27. Emmette S. Redford, *Democracy in the Administrative State* (New York: Oxford University Press, 1969), p. 196.

28. Douglas Cater, *Power in Washington* (New York: Vintage Books, 1965), p. 42.

CHAPTER 5

1. Harold Seidman, *Politics, Position & Power* (New York: Oxford University Press, 1975), p. 12.

2. Richard M. Nixon, "State of the Union Address," *Weekly Compilation of Presidential Documents*, vol. 7 (Washington, D.C.: Government Printing Office, 1971), p. 93.

3. "Executive Reorganization," *Congressional Quarterly*, vol. 29 (Washington, D.C.: CQ Weekly Reports, 1971), p. 1212.

4. Lyndon B. Johnson, "News Conference," *Weekly Compilation of Presidential Documents*, vol. 1 (Washington, D.C.: Government Printing Office, 1965), p. 143.

375

5. Charles L. Schultze, *The Politics and Economics of Public Spending* (Washington, D.C.: The Brookings Institution, 1965), p. 23.

6. Ibid., p. 31.

7. Ibid., p. 31.

8. Charles J. Hitch and Roland N. McKean, *The Economics of Defense in the Nuclear Age* (Cambridge, Mass.: Harvard University Press, 1960), p. 120.

9. Ibid., p. 120.

10. Stephen Enke, ed., *Defense Management* (Englewood Cliffs, N.J.: Prentice-Hall, 1967), p. 111.

11. Mancur Olson, *The Logic of Collective Action* (New York: Schocken Books, 1965), p. 1.

12. Ibid., p. 2.

13. Quoted from Lee Rainwater and William Yancey, *The Moynihan Report and the Politics of Controversy* (Cambridge, Mass.: The MIT Press, 1967), p. 24.

14. Karl Deutsch, *The Nerves of Government* (New York: The Free Press, 1963), p. ix.

15. Thomas R. Dye, *Politics, Economics and the Public* (Chicago: Rand McNally & Co., 1966), p. 7.

16. James Q. Wilson, ed., *City Politics and Public Policy* (New York: John Wiley & Sons, 1968), p. 7.

17. Joseph S. Wholey et. al., *Federal Evaluation Policy* (Washington, D.C.: The Urban Institute, 1970), p. 19.

18. Ibid., p. 55.

19. Alice M. Rivlin, *Systematic Thinking for Social Action* (Washington, D.C.: The Brookings Institution, 1971), p. 142.

20. Yehezkel Dror, *Ventures in Policy Sciences* (New York: American Elsevier, 1971), p. 17.

21. This is taken from the example used by Charles E. Lindblom in "The Science of 'Muddling Through'," *Public Administration Review* 19 (Spring 1959), pp. 79–88.

22. Ibid., p. 80.

23. Yehezkel Dror, *Public Policymaking Reexamined* (San Francisco: Chandler Publishing Co., 1968), pp. 144–45.

24. Daniel P. Moynihan, *Maximum Feasible Misunderstanding* (New York: The Free Press, 1979), p. 179.

25. Charles E. Lindblom, *The Intelligence of Democracy* (New York: The Free Press, 1965), p. 3.

CHAPTER 6

1. Niccolò Machiavelli, *The Prince and the Discourses* (New York: Modern Library, 1950), Chapter 21.

2. Ibid., Chap. 18.

3. Ibid., Chap. 17.

4. Ibid., Chap. 17.

5. Ibid., Chap. 22.

6. Ibid., Chap. 23.

7. Richard Neustadt, *Presidential Power* (New York: John Wiley & Sons, 1960), p. 148.

8. Ibid., p. 46.

9. Ibid., pp. 58, 63, 64, and 64, respectively.

10. Ibid., p. 87.

11. Quoted from W. Henry Lambright, *Shooting Down the Nuclear Plane*, Inter-University Case Program #104 (Indianapolis: Bobbs-Merrill Co., 1967), p. 8.

12. Ibid., p. 9.

13. Ibid., p. 12.

14. Aaron Wildavsky, *The Politics of the Budgetary Process*, 2d ed. (Boston: Little, Brown & Co., 1974), p. 15.

NOTES

15. Ibid., p. 11.

16. Ibid., p. 166.

17. Ibid., pp. 74–75.

18. Ibid., p. 78.

19. Quoted from Wildavsky, *Politics of the Budgetary Process*, pp. 96–97.

20. Ibid., p. 91.

21. David Novick, ed., *Program Budgeting* (Cambridge, Mass.: Harvard University Press, 1965), p. vi.

22. Allen Schick, "Systems Politics and Systems Budgeting," *Public Administration Review* 29 (March/April 1969), p. 150.

23. Wildavsky, *Politics of the Budgetary Process*, p. 201.

24. Ibid., p. 200.

25. Allen Schick, "A Death in the Bureaucracy: the Demise of Federal PPB," *Public Administration Review* 33 (March/April 1973), p. 146.

26. Charles L. Schultze, *The Politics and Economics of Public Spending* (Washington, D.C.: The Brookings Institution, 1965), p. 75.

27. Ibid., p. 101.

28. Ibid., p. 102.

29. Harold L. Wilensky, *Organizational Intelligence* (New York: Basic Books, 1968), p. 48.

30. Ibid., p. 174.

31. Quoted from Louis W. Koenig, *The Invisible Presidency* (New York: Rinehart, 1960), p. 308.

32. Edward Schreiber, "Nepotism Charge Raises Daley's Ire," *Chicago Tribune*, July 22, 1971, pp. 1, 5.

33. Robert F. Kennedy, *Thirteen Days* (New York: W. W. Norton & Co., 1969), p. 46.

34. Robert Caro, *The Power Broker* (New York: Alfred A. Knopf, 1974), p. 218.

35. Quoted from an essay written by Henry Kissinger in the spring of 1968 for the Securities Studies project of the University of California. This excerpt appeared in an article by Don Oberdorfer, "Putting It Together," *Washington Post*, January 30, 1972, p. D1, D4.

36. Joseph F. Clerk, "The Art of the Memorandum," *Washington Monthly* 1 (March 1969), p. 58.

37. Quoted from Neustadt, *Presidential Power*, p. 9.

38. Quoted from Charles Peters and Taylor Branch, eds., *Blowing the Whistle* (New York: Praeger Publishers, 1972), p. 162.

39. Ralph Nader, Peter Petkas, and Kate Blackwell, eds., *Whistle Blowing* (New York: Bantam Books, 1972), p. 193.

40. Dwight Waldo, "Developments in Public Administration," *The Annals of the American Academy of Political and Social Science* 404 (November 1972), p. 224.

CHAPTER 7

1. Norbert Wiener, *Cybernetics*, 2d ed. (Cambridge, Mass.: The MIT Press, 1961), p. 11.

2. Michael Crichton, *The Terminal Man* (New York: Bantam Books, 1973), p. 89.

3. Robert N. Anthony, *Planning and Control Systems* (Boston: Harvard Business School, 1965), p. 16.

4. Ibid., p. 17.

5. Ibid., p. 18.

6. Ibid., p. 34.

7. Russell L. Ackoff, "Management Misinformation Systems," in *Computers and Management*, Donald H. Sanders,

2d ed. (New York: McGraw-Hill Book Co., 1974), p. 36.

8. David W. Miller and Martin Starr, *Executive Decisions and Operations Research* (Englewood Cliffs, N.J.: Prentice-Hall, 1960), p. 104.

9. Alvin W. Drake et al., *Analysis of Public Systems* (Cambridge, Mass.: The MIT Press, 1972), p. ix.

10. Eliot D. Chapple and Leonard R. Sayles, *The Measurement of Management* (New York: The Macmillan Co., 1961), p. 34.

11. Harvey M. Sapolsky, *The Polaris System Development* (Cambridge, Mass.: Harvard University Press, 1972), p. 111.

12. Ibid., p. 120.

13. U.S. National Aeronautics and Space Administration, Lyndon B. Johnson Space Center, "Organization Chart," April 27, 1973.

14. Herbert A. Simon, *The Shape of Automation for Men and Management* (New York: Harper & Row, 1965), p. vii.

15. Ibid., p. 81.

16. Chris Argyris, "Some Limits of Rational Man Organizational Theory," *Public Administration Review* 33 (May/June 1973), p. 255.

17. Herbert A. Simon, "Organizational Man: Rational or Self-Actualizing?" *Public Administration Review* 33 (July/August 1973), pp. 349–52.

18. Chris Argyris, "Organizational Man: Rational *and* Self-Actualizing," *Public Administration Review* 33 (July/August 1973), pp. 355–56.

19. Ibid., p. 356.

20. Simon, "Organizational Man," p. 350.

21. Argyris, "Rational Man Or-

ganizational Theory," pp. 263, 266.

22. Simon, "Organizational Man," p. 351.

23. Argyris, "Organizational Man," pp. 354, 356.

24. William W. Cooper, H. J. Leavitt, and M. W. Shelly, eds., *New Perspectives in Organizational Research* (New York: John Wiley & Sons, 1964).

CHAPTER 8

1. Kenneth E. Boulding, *The Organizational Revolution* (New York: Harper, 1953), p. 3.

2. Warren Bennis, *Organization Development* (Reading, Mass.: Addison-Wesley Publishing Co., 1969), p. 2.

3. William H. Whyte, *The Organization Man* (New York: Anchor Press/Doubleday, 1957), p. 3.

4. Alvin Toffler, *Future Shock* (New York: Bantam Books, 1970), p. 141.

5. Warren Bennis and Philip E. Slater, *The Temporary Society* (New York: Harper & Row, 1968), p. 4.

6. Larry Kirkhart and Orion F. White, Jr., "The Future of Organization Development," *Public Administration Review* 34 (March/April 1974), p. 139.

7. Chris Argyris, *Personality and Organization* (New York: Harper & Brothers, 1957), p. 233.

8. Douglas McGregor, *The Human Side of Enterprise* (New York: McGraw-Hill Book Co., 1967), pp. 33–34.

9. Ibid., pp. 47–48.

10. Ibid., p. 48.

11. A quotation attributed to Ray Schoenke of the Washington Redskins football team by Tex Maule, "When You're As Old

As a Lot of Us, You Learn the Shortcuts," *Sports Illustrated,* January 8, 1973, p. 18.

12. Rowland Egger, "A Fable for Wise Men," *Public Administration Review* 4 (Autumn 1944), p. 371.

13. John Hersey, *A Bell for Adano* (New York: Bantam Books, 1944), pp. 41–42.

14. Ibid., p. 49.

15. Carl Rogers, *On Becoming a Person* (Boston: Houghton Mifflin Co., 1961), p. 276.

16. Leland P. Bradford, Jack R. Gibb, and Kenneth D. Beene, eds., *T-Group Theory and Laboratory Method* (New York: John Wiley & Sons, 1964), p. 151.

17. Edward E. Klein and Boris M. Astrachan, "Learning in Groups: A Comparison of Study Groups and T Groups," *The Journal of Applied Behavioral Science,* vol. 7, no. 6 (1971), p. 672.

18. Ibid., p. 672.

19. "Keelhauling the United States Navy," *Time,* November 27, 1972, p. 20.

20. N.B.C. News, "The Man Who Changed the Navy," February 5, 1974, p. 1 of mimeographed script.

21. "Humanizing the U.S. Navy," *Time,* December 21, 1970, p. 22.

22. Wendell L. French and Cecil H. Bell, *Organization Development* (Englewood Cliffs, N.J.: Prentice-Hall, 1973), p. 113.

23. Edgar H. Schein, *Process Consultation* (Reading, Mass.: Addison-Wesley Publishing Co., 1969), p. 7.

24. Robert Townsend, *Up the Organization* (New York: Alfred A. Knopf, 1970), p. 11.

25. Chris Argyris, *Integrating the Individual and the Organization* (New York: John Wiley & Sons, 1964), p. 150.

26. Edgar H. Schein, *Organizational Psychology* (Englewood Cliffs, N.J.: Prentice-Hall, 1965), pp. 120–124.

27. Quoted from Schein, *Organizational Psychology,* p. 118.

28. Chris Argyris, *Some Causes of Organizational Ineffectiveness within the Department of State.* (Washington, D.C.: Center for International Systems Research, Department of State, 1967), pp. 1, 2.

29. Robert R. Golembiewski, "Organization Development in Public Agencies," *Public Administration Review* 29 (July/August 1969), p. 373.

CHAPTER 9

1. J. Donald Kingsley, "Bureaucracy and Political Development, with Particular Reference to Nigeria," in *Bureaucracy and Political Development,* ed. Joseph G. La Palombara (Princeton, N.J.: Princeton University Press, 1963), p. 303.

2. Tom Wolfe, *Radical Chic and Maumauing the Flak Catchers* (New York: Farrar, Straus, and Giroux, 1970), pp. 117–18.

3. United Nations, Department of Economic and Social Affairs, *A Handbook of Public Administration* (New York: The United Nations, 1961), p. 70.

4. George Orwell, "Shooting an Elephant," in *The Orwell Reader* (New York: Harcourt, Brace & Co., 1956), p. 4.

5. Ibid., pp. 6–7.

6. United Nations, Department of Economic and Social Affairs, *Interregional Seminar on Major Administrative Reforms in Developing Countries* (New York:

The United Nations, 1973), p. 13.

7. Fred W. Riggs, *Administration in Developing Countries* (Boston: Houghton Mifflin Co., 1963), p. 263.

8. Fred W. Riggs, *The Ecology of Public Administration* (New York: Asia Publishing House, 1961), p. 137.

9. Fred W. Riggs, *Prismatic Society Revisited* (Morristown, N.J.: General Learning Press, 1973), p. 41.

10. Quoted from Warren F. Ilchman, "New Time in Old Clocks," in *Temporal Dimensions of Development Administration*, ed. Dwight Waldo, (Durham, N.C.: Duke University Press, 1970), p. 152.

11. Riggs, *Administration in Developing Countries*, p. 427.

12. William J. Siffin, *Two Decades of Public Administration in Developing Countries* (Bloomington, Ind.: International Development Research Center, 1974), p. 13. A similar statement can be found in an article of the same title in the *Public Administration Review* 36 (January/February 1976), pp. 61–71.

13. Ibid., p. 14.

14. Naomi Caiden and Aaron Wildavsky, *Planning and Budgeting in Poor Countries* (New York: John Wiley & Sons, 1974), p. 302.

15. Ibid., p. 72.

16. Ibid., p. 316.

17. Ibid., p. 273.

18. The question, slightly amended, was asked of Garth N. Jones, who pondered his reply in the "Failure of Technical Assistance in Public Administration Abroad," *Journal of Comparative Administration* 2

(May 1970), p. 38. I have allowed myself some poetic license with the question.

CHAPTER 10

1. William Butler Yeats, *The Collected Poems of W. B. Yeats* (New York: The Macmillan Co., 1951), p. 184.

2. The scholar is Harlan Cleveland. The book is *The Future Executive* (New York: Harper & Row, 1972). The term is one that he uses in speeches about the book.

3. Peter Drucker, *The Age of Discontinuity* (New York: Harper & Row, 1968), p. x.

4. Kurt Vonnegut, *Slaughterhouse Five* (New York: Delta Books, 1969), p. 184.

5. Drucker, *Age of Discontinuity*, p. x.

6. John W. Gardner, *Self-Renewal* (New York: Harper & Row, 1964), p. 62.

7. Allen Schick, "Toward the Cybernetic State," in *Public Administration in a Time of Turbulence*, ed. Dwight Waldo (Scranton, Pa.: Chandler Publishing Co., 1971), p. 219.

8. Theodore J. Lowi, *The Politics of Disorder* (New York: Basic Books, 1971), p. xviii.

9. Theodore J. Lowi, *The End of Liberalism* (New York: W. W. Norton & Co., 1969), p. 297.

10. Lowi, *Politics of Disorder*, p. 59.

11. Lowi, *End of Liberalism*, p. 304.

12. Warren Bennis, "Post-Bureaucratic Leadership," *Transaction* 6 (July/August 1969), p. 44.

13. Warren Bennis, "The University Leader," *Saturday Review of Education* 55 (January, 1973), p. 44.

14. Ibid., p. 43.

15. Ibid., p. 50.

16. Orion White, "The Dialectical Organization: An Alternative to Bureaucracy," *Public Administration Review* 29 (January/February 1969), p. 35.

17. Frederick C. Thayer, *An End to Hierarchy! An End to Competition!* (New York: New Viewpoints, 1973), p. 74.

18. Ibid., p. 83.

19. Ibid., p. 181.

20. Orion White, "Organization and Administration for New Technological and Social Imperatives," in *Time of Turbulence*, ed. Waldo, p. 165.

21. John Rehfuss, *Public Administration as Political Process* (New York: Charles Scribner's Sons, 1973), p. 224.

22. Larry Kirkhart, "Toward a Theory of Public Administration," in *Toward a New Public Administration*, ed. Frank Marini (Scranton, Pa.: Chandler Publishing Co., 1971), p. 134.

23. H. George Frederickson, "Creating Tomorrow's Public Administration," *Public Management* 53 (November 1971), p. 3.

24. H. George Frederickson, "Curriculum Essays on Citizens, Politics, and Administration in Urban Neighborhoods: Introduction," *Public Administration Review* 32 (October 1972), p. 567.

25. H. H. Gerth and C. Wright Mills, *From Max Weber: Essays in Sociology* (New York: Oxford University Press, 1946), p. 18.

26. Peter Savage, "Contemporary Public Administration," in *Time of Turbulence*, ed. Waldo, p. 56.

27. Herbert Kaufman, *The Forest Ranger* (Baltimore: Johns Hopkins Press, 1960), p. 240.

28. Herbert Kaufman, "Administrative Decentralization and Political Power," *Public Administration Review* 29 (January/February 1969), p. 3. Reprinted in *Time of Turbulence*, ed. Waldo, p. 1.

29. Marini, *New Public Administration*, p. 349.

30. Allen Schick, "The Trauma of Politics," in *American Public Administration*, ed. Frederick C. Mosher (University: University of Alabama Press, 1975), p. 157.

31. Dwight Waldo, "Education for Public Administration in the Seventies," in *American Public Administration*, ed. Mosher, p. 185.

32. Waldo, *Time of Turbulence*, p. 262.

33. Ibid., p. 272.

34. Vincent Ostrom, *The Intellectual Crises in American Public Administration* (University: University of Alabama Press, 1973), p. 131.

35. Ibid., p. 112.

36. Ibid., p. 73.

37. Waldo, "Education for Public Administration," p. 224.

CHAPTER 1: ORGANIZATION

AITKEN, Hugh G. J. *Taylorism at Watertown Arsenal.* Cambridge, Mass.: Harvard University Press, 1960.

BANOVETZ, James M. *Managing the Modern City.* Washington, D.C.: International City Management Association, 1971.

BLUMBERG, Paul. *Industrial Democracy: The Sociology of Participation.* New York: Schocken Books, 1969.

BURKHEAD, Jesse. *Government Budgeting.* New York: John Wiley & Sons, 1956.

CARROLL, Stephen J., and Tosi, Henry L. *Management by Objectives.* New York: The Macmillan Co., 1973.

COBB, Humphrey. *Paths of Glory.* New York: Popular Library, 1935.

DALE, Ernest. *Management: Theory and Practice.* New York: McGraw-Hill Book Co., 1969.

———. *Planning and Developing the Company Organization Structure.* New York: American Management Association, 1952.

DALE, Ernest, and Urwick, L. *Staff in Organization.* New York: McGraw-Hill Book Co., 1960.

DAVIS, Kenneth C. *Administrative Law and Government.* St. Paul, Minn.: West Publishing Co., 1975.

DRUCKER, Peter. *The Concept of the Corporation.* Boston: Beacon Press, 1960.

———. *Management.* New York: Harper & Row, 1973.

———. *Managing for Results.* New York: Harper & Row, 1964.

———. *The Practice of Management.* New York: Harper & Row, 1954.

EMMERICH, Herbert. *Federal Organization and Administrative Manage-* *ment.* University: University of Alabama Press, 1971.

FAYOL, Henri. *General and Industrial Management.* New York: Pitman Publishing Corporation, 1949.

FESLER, James W. *Area and Administration.* University: University of Alabama Press, 1949.

FOLLETT, Mary Parker. *Dynamic Administration: The Collected Papers of Mary Parker Follett.* Edited by Henry C. Metcalf and L. Urwick. New York: Harper & Brothers, 1940.

GELLHORN, Walter, and Byse, Clark. *Administrative Law: Cases and Comments.* Mineola, N.Y.: Foundation Press, 1973.

GULICK, Luther and Urwick, L., eds. *Papers on the Science of Administration.* New York: Augustus M. Kelley Publishers, 1937.

HEYEL, Carl, ed. *The Encyclopedia of Management.* 2d ed. New York: Van Nostrand Reinhold Co., 1973.

JUN, John S., ed. "Management by Objectives in the Public Sector." *Police Administration Review* 36 (January/February 1976), pp. 1–45.

KAKAR, Sudhir. *Frederick Taylor: A Study in Personality and Innovation.* Cambridge, Mass.: The MIT Press, 1970.

KOONTZ, Harold, and O'Donnell, Cyril. *Principles of Management.* 5th ed. New York: McGraw-Hill Book Co., 1972.

KRANZ, Harry. *The Participatory Bureaucracy.* Lexington, Mass.: Lexington Books, 1976.

LANSBERGER, Henry. *Hawthorne Revisited.* Ithaca, N.Y.: Cornell University Press, 1958.

LEE, Robert D., and Johnson, Ronald W. *Public Budgeting Systems.* Baltimore: University Park Press, 1973.

MARX, Fritz Morstein, ed. *Elements of Public Administration.* 1st ed. Englewood Cliffs, N.J.: Prentice-Hall, 1946.

MAYO, Elton. *The Human Problems of an Industrial Civilization.* New York: The Viking Press, 1933.

————. *The Social Problems of an Industrial Civilization.* New York: The Viking Press, 1945.

MELLEN, Jean. *Filmguide to the Battle of Algiers.* Bloomington: Indiana University Press Filmguide Series, 1973.

NEWLAND, Chester A., ed. "Public Policy Forum: Management by Objectives in the Federal Government." *The Bureaucrat* 2 (Winter 1974), pp. 351–426.

NEWMAN, William H. *Administrative Action.* 2d ed. Englewood Cliffs, N.J.: Prentice-Hall, 1963.

NEWMAN, William H.: Summer, Charles E.; and Warren, E. Kirby. *The Process of Management.* 2d ed. Englewood Cliffs, N.J.: Prentice-Hall, 1967.

NIGRO, Felix A., and Lloyd G. *The New Public Personnel Administration,* Itasca, Ill.: F. E. Peacock Publishers, 1976.

PFIFFNER, John M., and Sherwood, Frank P. *Administrative Organization.* Englewood Cliffs, N.J.: Prentice-Hall, 1960.

ROETHLISBERGER, F. J., and Dickson, William J. *Management and the Worker.* Cambridge, Mass.: Harvard University Press, 1939.

ROOSEVELT, Theodore. *Theodore Roosevelt: An Autobiography.* New York: The Macmillan Co., 1913.

SECKLER-HUDSON, Catheryn. *Organization and Management.* Washington, D.C.: The American University Press, 1955.

SIMON, Herbert A. "The Proverbs of Administration," *Public Administration Review* 6(Winter 1946), pp. 53–67.

SMITHIES, Arthur. *The Budgetary Process in the United States.* New York: McGraw-Hill Book Co., 1955.

STAHL, O. Glenn. *Public Personnel Administration.* 6th ed. New York: Harper & Row, 1971.

TAYLOR, Frederick W. *Principles of Scientific Management.* New York: W. W. Norton & Co., 1911.

————. *Scientific Management.* New York: Harper & Brothers, 1947.

URWICK, Lyndall. *The Elements of Administration.* New York: Harper & Brothers, 1947.

VAN RIPER, Paul. *History of the United States Civil Service.* New York: Row, Peterson, 1958.

WALDO, Dwight. *The Administrative State.* New York: Ronald Press, 1948.

WALLACE, Schuyler. *Federal Departmentalization.* New York: Columbia University Press, 1941.

WHITE, Leonard D. *Introduction to the Study of Public Administration.* 1st ed. New York: Harper & Brothers, 1926.

WILSON, Woodrow. "The Study of Administration." *Political Science Quarterly,* June 1887, reprinted in 56 (December 1941), pp. 481–506.

WREN, Daniel A. *The Evolution of Management Thought.* New York: The Ronald Press Co., 1972.

ZOLA, Émile. *Germinal.* New York: Penguin Books, 1885.

CHAPTER 2: HUMAN BEHAVIOR IN ORGANIZATIONS

BARNARD, Chester I. *The Functions of the Executive.* Cambridge, Mass.: Harvard University Press, 1938.

BASS, Bernard M. *Leadership, Psychology and Organizational Behavior.* New York: Harper & Brothers, 1960.

————. *Organizational Psychology.* Boston: Allyn & Bacon, 1965.

BENDIX, Reinhard. *Work and Authority in Industry.* New York: Chapman & Hall, 1956.

BENDIX, Reinhard, and Lipset, Seymour M., eds. *Class, Status and Power: A Reader in Social Stratification.* New York: The Free Press, 1953.

BERELSON, Bernard, and Steiner, Garry A. *Human Behavior: An Inventory of Scientific Findings.* New York: Harcourt, Brace & World, 1964.

BLACK, Max. *The Social Theories of Talcott Parsons.* Englewood Cliffs, N.J.: Prentice-Hall, 1962.

BOULDING, Kenneth E. *The Image.* Ann Arbor: University of Michigan Press, 1956.

BOULLE, Pierre. *Bridge over the River Kwai.* New York: Vanguard Press, 1954.

BRINTON, Crane. *The Anatomy of Revolution.* Rev. ed. New York: Vintage Random House, 1957.

CAMUS, Albert. *The Plague.* New York: The Modern Library, 1948.

CARTWRIGHT, Dorwin. *Studies in Social Power.* Ann Arbor: University of Michigan Press, 1959.

CARTWRIGHT, Dorwin, and Zander, Alvin, eds. *Group Dynamics Research and Theory.* New York: Harper & Row, 1968.

COSER, Lewis A. *The Functions of Social Conflict.* New York: The Free Press, 1956.

COSTELLO, Timothy W., and Zalkind, Sheldon S. *Psychology in Administration.* Englewood Cliffs, N.J.: Prentice-Hall, 1963.

CYERT, Richard M., and March, James G. *A Behavioral Theory of the Firm.* Englewood Cliffs, N.J.: Prentice-Hall, 1963.

DALTON, Melville. *Men Who Manage.* New York: John Wiley & Sons, 1959.

DUBIN, Robert, ed. *Human Relations in Administration.* 2d ed. Englewood Cliffs, N.J.: Prentice-Hall, 1961.

ETZIONI, Amitai. *Modern Organizations.* Englewood Cliffs, N.J.: Prentice-Hall, 1964.

FESTINGER, Leon. *A Theory of Cognitive Dissonance.* Stanford, Calif.: Stanford University Press, 1957.

GAWTHROP, Louis C., *Bureaucratic Behavior in the Executive Branch.* New York: The Free Press, 1969.

GORE, William J. *Administrative Decision-Making: A Heuristic Model.* New York: John Wiley & Sons, 1965.

GROSS, Bertram M. *The Managing of Organizations: The Administrative Struggle.* 2 vols. New York: The Free Press, 1964.

HAIRE, Mason, ed. *Modern Organization Theory.* New York: John Wiley & Sons, 1959.

HALL, Richard H. *Organizations.* Englewood Cliffs, N.J.: Prentice-Hall, 1972.

HOMANS, George C. *The Human Group.* New York: Harcourt, Brace & Co., 1950.

KAHN, Robert L. et al. *Organizational Stress: Studies in Role Conflict and Ambiguity.* New York: John Wiley & Sons, 1965.

KATZ, Daniel, and Kahn, Robert L. *The Social Psychology of Organizations.* New York: John Wiley & Sons, 1966.

LEAVITT, Harold J. *Managerial Psychology.* Chicago: University of Chicago Press, 1964.

———, ed. *The Social Science of Organizations.* Englewood Cliffs, N.J.: Prentice-Hall, 1963.

LEAVITT, Harold J., and Pondy, Louis R., eds. *Readings in Managerial Psychology.* Chicago: University of Chicago Press, 1965.

LEIGHTON, Alexander. *The Governing of Men.* Princeton, N.J.: Princeton University Press, 1945.

LUCE, R. Duncan, and Raiffa, Howard. *Games and Decisions.* New York: John Wiley & Sons, 1957.

LYDEN, Fremont L.; Shipman, George A.; and Kroll, Morton, eds. *Policies, Decisions, and Organization.* New York: Appleton-Century-Crofts, 1969.

MARCH, James G., ed. *Handbook of Organizations.* Chicago: Rand McNally & Co., 1965.

MARCH, James G., and Simon, Herbert A. *Organizations.* New York: John Wiley & Sons, 1958.

PARSONS, Talcott. *The Social System.* New York: The Free Press, 1951.

——. *Structure and Process in Modern Societies.* New York: The Free Press, 1960.

RUBENSTEIN, Albert H., and Haberstroh, Chadwick J., eds. *Some Theories of Organization.* Rev. ed. Homewood, Ill.: Dorsey Irwin Press, 1966.

SAYLES, Leonard R. *Behavior of Industrial Work Groups.* New York: John Wiley & Sons, 1958.

SAYLES, Leonard R., and Strauss, George. *Human Behavior in Organizations.* Englewood Cliffs, N.J.: Prentice-Hall, 1966.

SELZNICK, Philip. *Leadership in Administration.* New York: Row, Peterson, 1957.

SIMMEL, George. *Conflict and the Web of Group Affiliations.* Translated by Karl H. Wolff and Reinhard Bendix. New York: The Free Press, 1955.

SIMON, Herbert A. *Administrative Behavior.* New York: The Macmillan Co., 1947.

——. *Models of Man.* New York: John Wiley & Sons, 1957.

SMITH, Dennis. *Report from Engine Co. 82.* New York: Pocket Books, 1972.

SORENSEN, Theodore. *Decision-Making in the White House.* New York: Columbia University Press, 1963.

STEINBECK, John. *In Dubious Battle.* New York: Bantam Books, 1936.

STEINER, Jean-Francois. *Treblinka.* New York: Signet Books, 1966.

THOMPSON, James D. *Organizations in Action.* New York: McGraw-Hill Book Co., 1967.

VITELES, Morris S. *Motivation and Morale in Industry.* New York: W. W. Norton & Co., 1953.

WEBER, Max. *The Theory of Social and Economic Organization.* Translated by A. M. Henderson and Talcott Parsons. New York: Oxford University Press, 1947.

WHYTE, William F. *Money and Motivation.* New York: Harper & Brothers, 1955.

CHAPTER 3: PROBLEMS OF BUREAUCRACY

ALTSHULER, Alan A. *The Politics of the Federal Bureaucracy.* New York: Dodd, Mead & Co., 1968.

BENDIX, Reinhard. *Max Weber: An Intellectual Portrait.* Garden City: Doubleday & Co., 1960.

BLAU, Peter. *The Dynamics of Bureaucracy.* Chicago: University of Chicago Press, 1964.

BLAU, Peter M., and Meyer, Marshall W. *Bureaucracy in Modern Society.* New York: Random House, 1971.

BLAU, Peter, and Scott, W. Richard. *Formal Organizations: A Comparative Approach.* San Francisco: Chandler Publishing Co., 1962.

BURNHAM, James. *The Managerial Revolution.* New York: John Day Co., 1942.

CAMUS, Albert. *The Stranger.* New York: Vintage Books, 1942.

CROZIER, Michel. *The Bureaucratic Phenomenon.* Chicago: University of Chicago Press, 1964.

——. *The Stalled Society.* New York: Viking Press, 1973.

DOWNS, Anthony. *Inside Bureaucracy.* Boston: Little, Brown & Co., 1967.

GALBRAITH, John Kenneth. *The New Industrial State*. Boston: Houghton Mifflin Co., 1967.

GLADDEN, E. N. *A History of Public Administration*. 2 vols. London: Frank Cass, 1972.

GOULDNER, Alvin. *Patterns of Industrial Bureaucracy*. New York: The Free Press, 1954.

————. "Red Tape As a Social Problem." In *Reader in Bureaucracy*, ed. Robert K. Merton et al. New York: The Free Press, 1952.

HELLER, Joseph. *Catch-22*. New York: Dell Publishing Co., 1961.

HOFMEYR, J. H. "Civil Service in Ancient Times." *Public Administration* 5 (January 1927), pp. 76–93.

HYNEMAN, Charles. *Bureaucracy in a Democracy*. New York: Harper & Brothers, 1950.

KAFKA, Franz. "The Metamorphosis." *In the Penal Colony*. New York: Schocken Books, 1948.

KAUFMAN, Herbert. *The Limits of Organizational Change*. University: University of Alabama Press, 1971.

KESEY, Ken. *One Flew over the Cuckoo's Nest*. New York: Viking Press, 1962.

KHARASCH, Robert N. *The Institutional Imperative: How to Understand the United States Government and Other Bulky Objects*. New York: Charterhouse Books, 1973.

MERTON, Robert K. "Bureaucratic Structure and Personality." *Social Forces* 17 (1940), pp. 560–68.

————. *Social Theory and Social Structure*. Rev. ed. New York: The Free Press, 1957.

MERTON, Robert K. et al., eds. *Reader in Bureaucracy*. New York: The Free Press, 1954.

MICHELS, Robert K. *Political Parties*. Translated by Eden and Cedar Paul. New York: The Free Press, 1959.

MILLS, C. Wright. *The Power Elite*. New York: Oxford University Press, 1956.

————. *White Collar*. New York: Oxford University Press, 1951.

MOONEY, James D. *The Principles of Organization*. Rev. ed. New York: Harper & Row, 1947.

MOUZELIS, Nicos P. *Organization and Bureaucracy*. Chicago: Aldine Publishing Co., 1968.

ORWELL, George. *Homage to Catalonia*. Boston: Beacon Press, 1952.

————. *Nineteen-Eighty-Four*. New York: Harcourt, Brace & World, 1949.

PARKINSON, C. Northcote. *Parkinson's Law and Other Studies in Administration*. Boston: Houghton Mifflin Co., 1957.

PERROW, Charles. *Complex Organizations*. Glenview, Ill.: Scott, Foresman & Co., 1972.

PETER, Lawrence J., and Hull, Raymond. *The Peter Principle*. New York: Bantam Books, 1969.

PRESTHUS, Robert. *The Organizational Society*. New York: Alfred A. Knopf, 1962.

THOMPSON, Victor A. *Bureaucracy and Innovation*. University: University of Alabama Press, 1969.

————. *Modern Organization*. New York: Alfred A. Knopf, 1961.

TOUT, Thomas F. *Chapters in the Administrative History of Medieval England*. 6 vols. Manchester, Eng.: The University Press, 1920.

TULLOCK, Gordon. *The Politics of Bureaucracy*. Washington, D.C.: Public Affairs Press, 1965.

VON MISES, Ludwig. *Bureaucracy*. New Haven, Conn.: Yale University Press, 1944.

WALDO, Dwight. "Development of Theory of Democratic Administration" (article, comments, reply).

American Political Science Review 46 (March & June 1952), pp. 81–103 and 494–503, respectively.

WEBER, Max. From Max Weber: Essays in Sociology. Translated, edited, and with an introduction by H. H. Gerth and C. Wright Mills. New York: Oxford University Press, 1946.

———. The Protestant Ethic and the Spirit of Capitalism, 1904–5. Translated by Talcott Parsons. New York: Charles Scribner's Sons, 1958.

WOLL, Peter. American Bureaucracy. New York: W. W. Norton & Co., 1963.

CHAPTER 4: THE POLITICS OF ADMINISTRATION

ALINSKY, Saul. Reveille for Radicals. Chicago: University of Chicago Press, 1946.

ALTSHULER, Alan. Community Control: The Black Demand for Participation in Large American Cities. New York: Pegasus Books, 1970.

APPLEBY, Paul H. Big Democracy. New York: Alfred A. Knopf, Inc., 1945.

———. Policy and Administration. University: University of Alabama Press, 1949.

BAILEY, Stephen K., and Mosher, Edith K. ESEA: The Office of Education Administers a Law. Syracuse, N.Y.: Syracuse University Press, 1968.

BERNSTEIN, Marver H. The Job of the Federal Executive. Washington, D.C.: The Brookings Institution, 1958.

CALDWELL, Lynton K. The Administrative Theories of Hamilton and Jefferson. Chicago: University of Chicago Press, 1944.

CATER, Douglas. Power in Washington. New York: Vintage Books, 1965.

COUTURIER, Jean J. "Chaos or Creativity in Public Labor-Management Relations." In Managing Government Labor Relations, ed. Chester Newland. Washington, D.C.: Manpower Press, 1972.

DANHOF, Clarence H. Government Contracting and Technological Change. Washington, D.C.: The Brookings Institution, 1968.

EASTON, David. The Political System. New York: Alfred A. Knopf, 1953.

ELAZAR, Daniel J. American Federalism: A View from the States. New York: Thomas Y. Crowell, 1966.

———. The Politics of American Federalism. Lexington, Mass.: D.C. Heath & Co., 1969.

ELAZAR, Daniel J. et al., eds. Cooperation and Conflict: Readings in American Federalism. Lexington, Mass.: D.C. Heath & Co., 1969.

FANTINI, Mario, and Gittell, Marilyn. Decentralization: Achieving Reform. New York: Praeger Publishers, 1973.

FENNO, Richard. The Power of the Purse. Boston: Little, Brown & Co., 1966.

FOSS, Phillip O. Politics and Grass: The Administration of Grazing on the Public Domain. Seattle: University of Washington Press, 1961.

FREDERICKSON, George, Neighborhood Control in the 1970's. New York: Chandler Publishing Co., 1973.

FREEMAN, J. Leiper. The Political Process: Executive Bureau–Legislative Committee Relations. New York: Random House, 1965.

FRITSCHLER, A. Lee. Smoking and Politics: Policymaking and the Federal Bureaucracy. 2d ed. Englewood Cliffs, N.J.: Prentice-Hall, 1975.

GOLDWIN, Robert, ed. A Nation of States. Chicago: Rand McNally & Co., 1961.

GRODZINS, Morton. The American System. Chicago: Rand McNally & Co., 1966.

387

HARRIS, Joseph P. *Congressional Control of Administration.* Washington, D.C.: The Brookings Institution, 1964.

JANOWITZ, Morris. *The Professional Soldier.* New York: The Free Press, 1960.

KAUFMAN, Herbert. "Administrative Decentralization and Political Power." *Public Administration Review* 29 (January/February 1969), pp. 3–15.

———. *The Forest Ranger.* Baltimore: Johns Hopkins Press, 1960.

KAUFMAN, Richard F. *The War Profiteers.* New York: Doubleday & Co., 1972.

LEVINE, Naomi. *Ocean Hill–Brownsville: A Case History of Schools in Crisis.* New York: Popular Library, 1969.

LOWI, Theodore J. *The Politics of Disorder.* New York: Basic Books, 1971.

MAASS, Arthur. *Muddy Waters.* Cambridge, Mass.: Harvard University Press, 1951.

MADISON, James. "The Federalist Papers: Number 10." Chicago: Encyclopedia Britannica, 1787.

MARTIN, Roscoe. *The Cities and the Federal System.* New York: Atherton Press. 1965.

———. *Public Administration and Democracy.* Syracuse, N.Y.: Syracuse University Press, 1965.

MOSHER, Frederick C. *Democracy and the Public Service.* New York: Oxford University Press, 1968.

NIGRO, Felix A., ed. "Symposium on Collective Bargaining in the Public Service," *Public Administration Review* 32 (March/April 1972), pp. 97–126.

NORDLINGER, Eric A. *Decentralizing the City: A Study of Boston's Little City Halls.* Cambridge, Mass.: The MIT Press, 1972.

REDFORD, Emmette S. *Democracy in the Administrative State.* New York: Oxford University Press, 1969.

RICE, Berkeley. *The C-5A Scandal: An Inside Story of the Military–Industrial Complex.* Boston: Houghton Mifflin Co., 1971.

ROURKE, Francis E. *Bureaucracy, Politics, and Public Policy.* Boston: Little, Brown & Co., 1969.

SANFORD, Terry. *Storm over the States.* New York: McGraw-Hill Book Co., 1967.

SAYRE, Wallace, and Kaufman, Herbert. *Governing New York City.* New York: Russell Sage Foundation, 1960.

SCHUBERT, Glendon A. *The Public Interest.* New York: Free Press, 1960.

SEIDMAN, Harold. *Politics, Position & Power: The Dynamics of Federal Organization.* 2d ed. New York: Oxford University Press, 1975.

SELZNICK, Philip. *TVA and the Grass Roots.* New York: Harper & Row, 1949.

STEIN, Harold. *Public Administration and Policy Development: A Casebook.* New York: Harcourt, Brace & Co., 1952.

STENBERG, Carl W. "Citizens and the Administrative State." *Public Administration Review* 32 (May/June 1972), pp. 190–98.

SUNDQUIST, James L. *Making Federalism Work.* Washington, D.C.: The Brookings Institution, 1969.

TRUMAN, David. *The Governmental Process.* New York: Alfred A. Knopf, 1951.

WARNER, W. Lloyd et. al. *The American Federal Executive.* New Haven, Conn.: Yale University Press, 1963.

WEIDENBAUM, Murray L. "Arms and the American Economy: A Domestic Convergence Hypothesis." *American Economic Association: Papers and Proceedings* 58 (May 1968), pp. 428–37.

WHITE, Leonard D. *The Federalists, The Jeffersonians, The Jacksonians,* and *The Republican Era.* New York: The Macmillan Co., 1948, 1951, 1954, 1958.

WILDAVSKY, Aaron. *The Politics of the Budgetary Process.* 2d ed. Boston: Little, Brown & Co., 1974.

ZAGORIA, Sam. *Public Workers and Public Unions.* Englewood Cliffs, N.J.: Prentice-Hall, 1972.

CHAPTER 5: POLICY ANALYSIS

ART, Robert J. *The TFX Decision.* Boston: Little, Brown & Co., 1968.

BATOR, Francis. *The Question of Government Spending.* New York: Harper & Row, 1960.

BAUER, Raymond A., and Gergen, Kenneth J., eds. *The Study of Policy Formulation.* New York: The Free Press, 1968.

BAUER, Raymond; de Sola Pool, Ithiel; and Dexter, Lewis. *American Business and Public Policy: The Politics of Foreign Trade.* New York: Atherton Press, 1963.

BISH, Robert L. *The Public Economy of Metropolitan Areas.* Chicago: Markham Publishing Co., 1971.

BONAFEDE, Dom. "White House Report: Bureaucracy, Congress, Interests See Threat in Nixon Reorganization Plan." *National Journal* 3 (May 8, 1971), pp. 977–86.

BRAYBROOKE, David, and Lindblom, Charles E. *A Strategy of Decision: Policy Evaluation As a Social Process.* New York: The Free Press, 1963.

COLEMAN, James S. *Equality of Educational Opportunity.* Washington, D.C.: U.S. Department of Health, Education, and Welfare, 1966.

DAHL, Robert A., and Lindblom, Charles E. *Politics, Economics and Welfare.* New York: Harper & Brothers, 1953.

DEUTSCH, Karl. *The Nerves of Government.* New York: The Free Press, 1963.

DORFMAN, Robert, ed. *Measuring Benefits of Government Investments.* Washington, D.C.: The Brookings Institution, 1965.

DOWNS, Anthony. *An Economic Theory of Democracy.* New York: Harper & Brothers, 1957.

DROR, Yehezkel. *Design for Policy Sciences.* New York: American Elsevier, 1971.

―――. *Public Policymaking Reexamined.* San Francisco: Chandler Publishing Co., 1968.

―――. *Ventures in Policy Sciences.* New York: American Elsevier, 1971.

DYE, Thomas R. *Politics, Economics and the Public: Policy Outcomes in the American States.* Chicago: Rand McNally & Co., 1966.

―――. *Understanding Public Policy.* Englewood Cliffs, N.J.: Prentice-Hall, 1972.

ENKE, Stephen, ed. *Defense Management.* Englewood Cliffs, N.J.: Prentice-Hall, 1967.

FREEMAN, Howard E., and Sherwood, Clarence C. *Social Research and Social Policy.* Englewood Cliffs, N.J.: Prentice-Hall, 1970.

FRIEDMAN, Milton. "The Role of Government in Education." In *Educational Vouchers,* edited by George R. La Noue. New York: Teachers College Press, 1972.

GOLEMBIEWSKI, Robert T., ed. *Public Budgeting and Finance.* Itasca, Ill.: F. E. Peacock Publishers, 1968.

HATRY, Harry P.; Winnie, Richard E.; and Fisk, Donald M. *Practical Program Evaluation for State and Local Government Officials.* Washington, D.C.: The Urban Institute, 1973.

HATRY, Harry P. et. al. *Program Analysis for State and Local Governments.* Washington, D.C.: The Urban Institute, 1976.

389

HITCH, Charles J., *Decision-Making for Defense.* Berkeley: University of California Press, 1965.

HITCH, Charles J., and McKean, Roland N. *The Economics of Defense in the Nuclear Age.* Cambridge, Mass.: Harvard University Press, 1960.

HOFFERBERT, Richard I. *The Study of Public Policy.* Indianapolis: Bobbs-Merrill Co., 1974.

LINDBLOM, Charles E. *The Intelligence of Democracy: Decision Making through Mutual Adjustment.* New York: The Free Press, 1965.

———. *The Policy-Making Process.* Englewood Cliffs, N.J.: Prentice-Hall, 1968.

———. "The Science of 'Muddling Through'." *Public Administration Review* 19 (Spring 1959), pp. 79–88.

LOWI, Theodore J. "American Business, Public Policy, Case-Studies, and Political Theory." *World Politics* 16 (July 1964), pp. 677–715.

———. "Four Systems of Policy, Politics, and Choice." *Public Administration Review* 32 (July/August 1972), pp. 298–310.

LYDEN, Fremont J. and Miller, Ernest G., eds. *Planning-Programming-Budgeting.* Chicago: Markham Publishing Co., 1968.

MCKEAN, Roland N. *Efficiency in Government through Systems Analysis.* New York: John Wiley & Sons, 1958.

MORGAN, James N. et. al. *Five Thousand American Families: Patterns of Economic Progress.* 2 vols. Ann Arbor: University of Michigan, Institute for Social Research, 1974.

MOSHER, Frederick C., ed. *Governmental Reorganizations: Cases and Commentary.* Indianapolis: Bobbs-Merrill Co., 1967.

MOYNIHAN, Daniel P. *Maximum Feasible Misunderstanding.* New York: The Free Press, 1969.

NATHAN, Richard P. *The Plot That Failed: Nixon and the Administrative Presidency.* New York: John Wiley & Sons, 1975.

NEWLAND, Chester A., ed. "Productivity in Government: A Symposium." *Public Administration Review* 32 (November/December 1972), pp. 739–850.

NORTH, Douglass C., and Miller, Roger L. *The Economics of Public Issues.* 3d. ed. New York: Harper & Row, 1976.

NOVICK, David, ed. *Program Budgeting.* Cambridge, Mass.: Harvard University Press, 1965.

OLSON, Mancur. *The Logic of Collective Action: Public Goods and the Theory of Groups.* New York: Schocken Books, 1965.

OSTROM, Elinor et. al. *Community Organization and the Provision of Police Services.* Beverly Hills, Calif.: Sage Publishers, 1973.

RAINWATER, Lee, and Yancey, William. *The Moynihan Report and the Politics of Controversy.* Cambridge, Mass.: The MIT Press, 1967.

RIVLIN, Alice M. *Systematic Thinking for Social Action.* Washington, D.C.: The Brookings Institution, 1971.

SCHULTZE, Charles L. *The Politics and Economics of Public Spending.* Washington, D.C.: The Brookings Institution, 1965.

SHARKANSKY, Ira, ed. *Policy Analysis in Political Science.* Chicago: Markham Publishing Co., 1970.

STEINER, Gilbert Y. *Social Insecurity: The Politics of Welfare.* Chicago: Rand McNally & Co., 1966.

SUNDQUIST, James L. *Politics and Policy: The Eisenhower, Kennedy and Johnson Years.* Washington, D.C.: The Brookings Institution, 1968.

U.S. Executive Office of the President. *Papers Relating to the President's Departmental Reorganization Program.* Washington, D.C.: Government Printing Office, 1972.

U.S. President's Committee on Administrative Management (Brownlow Committee). *Report of the Committee*. Washington, D.C.: Government Printing Office, 1937.

WEISS, Carol H. *Evaluation Research*. Englewood Cliffs, N.J.: Prentice-Hall, 1972.

WHOLEY, Joseph S. et. al. *Federal Evaluation Policy*. Washington, D.C.: The Urban Institute, 1970.

WILSON, James Q., ed. *City Politics and Public Policy*. New York: John Wiley & Sons, 1968.

————. *Varieties of Police Behavior*. Cambridge, Mass.: Harvard University Press, 1968.

CHAPTER 6: EXECUTIVE POWER

APPLEBY, Paul. *Morality and Administration in Democratic Government*. Baton Rouge: Louisiana State University Press, 1952.

BAILEY, Stephen. *Congress Makes a Law*. New York: Columbia University Press, 1950.

BANFIELD, Edward C. *Political Influence*. New York: The Free Press of Glencoe, 1961.

BOCK, Edwin A. *State and Local Government: A Casebook*. University: University of Alabama Press, 1963.

BURNS, James M. *Roosevelt: The Lion and the Fox*. New York: Harcourt, Brace & World, 1956.

CARO, Robert A. *The Power Broker: Robert Moses and the Fall of New York*. New York: Alfred A. Knopf, 1974.

CLERK, Joseph F. "The Art of the Memorandum." *Washington Monthly* 1 (March 1969), pp. 58–62.

COLLINS, Larry, and Lapierre, Dominique. *Is Paris Burning?* New York: Simon & Schuster, 1965.

CRONIN, Thomas E., and Greenberg, Sanford D., eds. *The Presiden-tial Advisory System*. New York: Harper & Row, 1969.

DAHL, Robert A. *Who Governs?* New Haven, Conn.: Yale University Press, 1961.

DALEY, Robert. *Target Blue: An Insider's View of the N.Y.P.D.* New York: Dell Publishing Co., 1973.

EVANS, Rowland, and Novak, Robert. *Lyndon B. Johnson: The Exercise of Power*. New York: New American Library, 1966.

FISHER, Louis. *Presidential Spending Power*. Princeton, N.J.: Princeton University Press, 1975.

FLASH, Edward S., Jr. *Economic Advice and Presidential Leadership*. New York: Columbia University Press, 1965.

FREDERICKSON, H. George, ed. "Social Equity and Public Administration." *Public Administration Review* 34 (January/February 1974), pp. 1–51.

HELLER, Walter W. *New Dimensions of Political Economy*. New York: W. W. Norton & Co., 1967.

JANIS, Irving J. *Victims of Groupthink*. Boston: Houghton Mifflin Co., 1972.

JOHNSON, Richard Tanner. *Managing the White House: An Intimate Study of the Presidency*. New York: Harper & Row, 1974.

KENNEDY, Robert F. *Thirteen Days*. New York: W. W. Norton & Co., 1969.

KOENIG, Louis W. *The Invisible Presidency*. New York: Rinehart, 1960.

LAMBRIGHT, W. Henry. *Shooting Down the Nuclear Plane*. Inter-University Case Program #104. Indianapolis: Bobbs-Merrill Co., 1967.

LASSWELL, Harold D. *Politics: Who Gets What, When, How*. Cleveland: Meridian Books, 1936.

MAAS, Peter. *Serpico*. New York: Viking Press, 1973.

MCCONNELL, Grant. *The Steel Seizure of 1952.* Inter-University Case Program #52. Indianapolis: Bobbs-Merrill Co., 1960.

MACHIAVELLI, Niccolò. *The Prince and the Discourses.* New York: Modern Library, 1950.

MCNALLY, Raymond T., and Florescu, Radu. *In Search of Dracula.* New York: Warner Books, 1972.

NADER, Ralph et. al. *Whistle Blowing.* New York: Bantam Books, 1972.

NEUSTADT, Richard. *Presidential Power,* New York: John Wiley & Sons, 1960.

PETERS, Charles, and Branch, Taylor, eds. *Blowing the Whistle.* New York: Praeger Publishers, 1972.

PETERS, Charles, and Rothchild, John. *Inside the System.* New York: Praeger Publishers, 1973.

SCHATTSCHNEIDER, E. E. *The Semi-Sovereign People.* New York: Holt, Rinehart & Winston, 1960.

SCHICK, Allen. "A Death in the Bureaucracy: The Demise of Federal PPB." *Public Administration Review* 33 (March/April 1973), pp. 146–56.

SCHULTZE, Charles L. *The Politics and Economics of Public Spending.* Washington, D.C.: The Brookings Institution, 1965.

SHARKANSKY, Ira. *The Politics of Taxing and Spending.* Indianapolis: Bobbs-Merrill Co., 1969.

SHERMAN, Harvey. *It All Depends: A Pragmatic Approach to Organization.* University: University of Alabama Press, 1966.

SHERWOOD, Robert E. *Roosevelt and Hopkins.* New York: Harper & Row, 1950.

STEIN, Harold, ed. *American Civil-Military Decisions: A Book of Case Studies.* University: University of Alabama Press, 1963.

WARREN, Robert Penn. *All the King's Men.* New York: Modern Library, 1953.

WILDAVSKY, Aaron. *Budgeting: A Comparative Theory of Budgetary Process.* Boston: Little, Brown & Co., 1975.

————. "The Political Economy of Efficiency." *Public Administration Review* 26 (December 1966), pp. 292–310.

————. *The Politics of the Budgetary Process.* 2d ed. Boston: Little, Brown & Co., 1974.

————. "Rescuing Policy Analysis from PPBS." *Public Administration Review* 29 (March/April 1969), pp. 189–202.

WILENSKY, Harold L. *Organizational Intelligence: Knowledge and Policy in Government and Industry.* New York: Basic Books, 1968.

WILLIAMS, T. Harry. *Huey Long.* New York: Alfred A. Knopf, 1969.

WOHLSTETTER, Roberta. *Pearl Harbor: Warning and Decision.* Stanford, Calif.: Stanford University Press, 1962.

CHAPTER 7: MANAGEMENT SCIENCE

ACKOFF, Russell L. "Management Misinformation Systems." *Management Science* (Application Series) 14 (December 1967), pp. B-147–56.

ANTHONY, Robert N. *Planning and Control Systems.* Boston: Harvard Business School, 1965.

ARGYRIS, Chris. "Some Limits of Rational Man Organization Theory," and "Organizational Man" with Herbert Simon. *Public Administration Review* 33 (May/June and July/August 1973), pp. 253–67, and 346–57.

BARKAN, Joel D., and Bruno, James E. "Operations Research in Planning Political Campaign Strategies." *Operations Research* 20 (September/October 1972), pp. 925–41.

BEER, Stafford. *Cybernetics and Management*. New York: John Wiley & Sons, 1959.

BURDICK, Eugene. *The Four-Eighty*. New York: McGraw-Hill Book Co., 1964.

CARZO, Rocco, and Yanouzas, John N. *Formal Organization: A Systems Approach*. Homewood, Ill.: Irwin & Dorsey Press, 1967.

CHAPPLE, Eliot D., and Sayles, Leonard R. *The Measurement of Management*. New York: The Macmillan Co., 1961.

CHURCHMAN, C. West. *The Systems Approach*. New York: Delta Books, 1968.

CHURCHMAN, C. West; Ackoff, Russell; and Arnoff, E. Leonard. *Introduction to Operations Research*. New York: John Wiley & Sons, 1957.

CLARKE, Arthur C. *2001: A Space Odyssey*. New York: The New American Library, 1968.

CLELAND, David, and King, William R. *Systems Analysis and Project Management*. New York: McGraw-Hill Book Co., 1968.

COOPER, William W.; Leavitt, H. J.; and Shelly, M. W., eds. *New Perspectives in Organizational Research*. New York: John Wiley & Sons, 1964.

CRICHTON, Michael. *The Terminal Man*. New York: Bantam Books, 1973.

CROWTHER, J. G., and Whittington, R. *Science at War*. New York: Philosophical Library, 1948.

DANIKEN, Erich von. *Chariots of the Gods?* New York: Putnam, 1969.

DRAKE, Alvin W.; Keeney, Ralph L.; and Morse, Philip M., eds. *Analysis of Public Systems*. Cambridge, Mass.: The MIT Press, 1972.

FERKISS, Victor C. *Technological Man*. New York: George Braziller, 1969.

FORRESTER, Jay W. *World Dynamics*. Cambridge, Mass.: Wright-Allen Press, 1971.

HATTERY, Lowell H., and Bush, George P., eds. *Electronics in Management*. Washington, D.C.: The University Press of Washington, D.C., 1956.

KAST, Fremont E., and Rosenzweig, James E., eds. *Science and Technology and Management*. New York: McGraw-Hill Book Co., 1963.

KELLY, Joseph F. *Computerized Management Information Systems*. New York: The Macmillan Co., 1970.

MEADOWS, Donella et. al., *The Limits to Growth*. New York: Universe Books, 1972.

MEIER, Robert C.; Newell, William T.; and Pazer, Harold L. *Simulation in Business and Economics*. Englewood Cliffs, N.J.: Prentice-Hall, 1969.

MILLER, David W., and Starr, Martin. *Executive Decisions and Operations Research*. Englewood Cliffs, N.J.: Prentice-Hall, 1960.

PELZ, Donald C., and Andrews, Frank M. *Scientists in Organizations*. New York: John Wiley & Sons, 1966.

PRICE, Don D. *Government and Science*. New York: New York University Press, 1954.

QUINN, James. "Technology Forecasting." *Harvard Business Review* 45 (March/April 1967), pp. 89–106.

ROMAN, Daniel D. *Research and Development Management*. New York: Appleton-Century-Crofts, 1968.

SANDERS, Donald H. *Computers and Management*, 2d ed. New York: McGraw-Hill Book Co., 1974.

SAPOLSKY, Harvey M. *The Polaris System Development*. Cambridge, Mass.: Harvard University Press, 1972.

SAYLES, Leonard R., and Chandler, Margaret K. *Managing Large Systems.* New York: Harper & Row, 1971.

SIMON, Herbert A. *The Sciences of the Artificial.* Cambridge, Mass.: Harvard University Press, 1969.

————. *The Shape of Automation for Men and Management.* New York: Harper & Row, 1965.

STARR, Martin K. *Management: A Modern Approach.* New York: Harcourt Brace Jovanovich, 1971.

WAGNER, Harvey M. *Principles of Management Science.* Englewood Cliffs, N.J.: Prentice-Hall, 1970.

WATSON, James D. *The Double Helix.* New York: Atheneum, 1968.

WEBB, James. *Space Age Management.* New York: McGraw-Hill Book Co., 1969.

WIENER, Norbert. *Cybernetics.* 2d ed. Cambridge, Mass.; The MIT Press, 1961.

————. *The Human Use of Human Beings.* Boston: Houghton Mifflin Co., 1956.

WITHINGTON, Frederic C. *The Real Computer.* Reading, Mass.: Addison-Wesley Publishing Co., 1969.

CHAPTER 8: ORGANIZATION DEVELOPMENT

ARGYRIS, Chris. *Integrating the Individual and the Organization.* New York: John Wiley & Sons, 1964.

————. *Personality and Organization.* New York: Harper & Row, 1957.

————. *Some Causes of Organizational Ineffectiveness within the Department of State.* Washington, D.C.: Center for International Systems Research, Department of State, 1967.

————. *Understanding Organizational Behavior.* Homewood, Ill.: Dorsey Press, 1960.

BECKHARD, Richard. *Organization Development: Strategies and Models.* Reading, Mass.: Addison-Wesley Publishing Co., 1969.

BENNIS, Warren. *Changing Organizations.* New York: McGraw-Hill Book Co., 1966.

————. *Organization Development: Its Nature, Origins, and Prospects.* Reading, Mass.: Addison-Wesley Publishing Co., 1969.

BENNIS, Warren, and Slater, Philip E. *The Temporary Society.* New York: Harper & Row, 1968.

BLAKE, Robert R., and Mouton, Jane S. *Building a Dynamic Corporation through Grid Organization Development.* Reading, Mass.: Addison-Wesley Publishing Co., 1969.

————. *Corporate Excellence through Grid Organization Development.* Houston: Gulf Publishing Co., 1968.

BOULDING, Kenneth E. *The Organizational Revolution.* New York: Harper, 1953.

BRADFORD, Leland P.; Gibb, Jack R.; and Benne, Kenneth D., eds. *T-Group Theory and Laboratory Method.* New York: John Wiley & Sons, 1964.

BURGESS, Anthony. *A Clockwork Orange.* New York: W. W. Norton & Co., 1962.

BURNS, Tom, and Stalker, G. M. *The Management of Innovation.* London: Tavistock Publications, 1961.

FRENCH, Wendell L., and Bell, Cecil H. *Organization Development: Behavioral Science Interventions for Organization Improvement.* Englewood Cliffs, N.J.: Prentice-Hall, 1973.

FROMM, Erich. *Escape from Freedom.* New York: Holt, Rinehart & Winston, 1941.

GIBSON, Frank K., and Teasley, Clyde E. "The Humanistic Model of Organizational Motivation." *Public Administration Review* 33 (January/February 1973), pp. 89–96.

GOLEMBIEWSKI, Robert T. "Organization Development in Public

Agencies: Perspectives on Theory and Practice." *Public Administration Review* 29 (July/August 1969), pp. 367–77.

GUEST, Robert H. *Organizational Changes: The Effect of Successful Leadership.* New York: Richard D. Irwin, Inc., 1962.

HAMPTON, David R.; Summer, Charles E.; and Webber, Ross A. *Organizational Behavior and the Practice of Management.* Chicago: Scott, Foresman & Co., 1968.

HERSEY, John. *A Bell for Adano.* New York: Bantam Books, 1944.

HERZBERG, Frederick; Mausner, Bernard; and Snyderman, Barbara. *The Motivation to Work.* 2d ed. New York: John Wiley & Sons, 1959.

HUXLEY, Aldous L. *Brave New World.* New York: Harper & Row, 1946.

JAQUES, Elliott. *The Changing Culture of a Factory.* New York: The Dryden Press, 1952.

KIRKHART, Larry, and Gardner, Neely. "Symposium: Organization Development." *Public Administration Review* 34 (March/April 1974), pp. 97–140.

KLEIN, Edward B. and Boris M. Astrachan. "Learning in Groups: A Comparison of Study Groups and T Groups." *The Journal of Applied Behavioral Science,* vol. 7, no. 6 (1971), pp. 659–83.

LIKERT, Rensis. *New Patterns of Management.* New York: McGraw-Hill Book Co., 1961.

LIPPITT, Ronald; Watson, Jeanne; and Westley, Bruce. *The Dynamics of Planned Change.* New York: Harcourt Brace Jovanovich, 1958.

MCGREGOR, Douglas. *The Human Side of Enterprise.* New York: McGraw-Hill Book Co., 1967.

———. *The Professional Manager.* New York: McGraw-Hill Book Co., 1967.

MANSO, Peter, ed. *Running against the Machine: The Breslin-Mailer Campaign.* New York: Doubleday & Co., 1969.

MARROW, Alfred J. *The Practical Theorist: The Life and Work of Kurt Lewin.* New York: Basic Books, 1969.

MASLOW, Abraham H. *Eupsychian Management.* Homewood, Ill.: Irwin & Dorsey Press, 1965.

———. *Motivation and Personality.* New York: Harper & Row, 1954.

RIESMAN, David with Nathan Glazer and Reuel Denney. *The Lonely Crowd.* New Haven, Conn.: Yale University Press, 1950.

RIOCH, Margaret J. "The Work of Wilfred Bion on Groups." *Psychiatry* 33 (February 1970), pp. 56–66.

ROGERS, Carl. *On Becoming a Person.* Boston: Houghton Mifflin Co., 1961.

RUSH, Harold M. F. *Behavioral Science: Concepts and Management Application.* New York: National Industrial Conference Board, 1969.

SCHEIN, Edgar H. *Organizational Psychology.* Englewood Cliffs, N.J.: Prentice-Hall, 1965.

———. *Process Consultation: Its Role in Organization Development.* Reading, Mass.: Addison-Wesley Publishing Co., 1969.

SCHEIN, Edgar H. and Bennis, Warren G. *Personal and Organizational Change through Group Methods.* New York: John Wiley & Sons, 1965.

SHETHAR, Allen, and Stovall, Jim. "A Look at the Human Side." *All Hands* 682 (November 1973), pp. 2–9.

SKINNER, B. F. *Beyond Freedom and Dignity.* New York: Alfred A. Knopf, 1971.

TANNENBAUM, Robert et. al. *Leadership and Organization.* New York: McGraw-Hill Book Co., 1961.

TOFFLER, Alvin. *Future Shock.* New York: Bantam Books, 1970.

395

TOWNSEND, Robert. *Up the Organization*. New York: Alfred A. Knopf, 1970.

VROOM, Victor H. *Work and Motivation*. New York: John Wiley & Sons, 1964.

WHYTE, William H. *The Organization Man*. New York: Anchor Press/Doubleday, 1957.

CHAPTER 9: COMPARATIVE PUBLIC ADMINISTRATION

ABRAMSON, Robert. *United Nations Development Programme/East Africa Community Administrative Improvement and Training Project (RAF/68/109): A Revised Concept of Organization Development*. Arusha, Tanzania: East African Community Management Institute, 1973.

ADU, A. L. *The Civil Service in New African States*. New York: Frederick A. Praeger, 1965.

ALDERFER, Harold F. *Local Government in Developing Countries*. New York: McGraw-Hill Book Co., 1970.

ALMOND, Gabriel A. and Verba, Sidney. *The Civic Culture*. Princeton, N.J.: Princeton University Press, 1963.

ALMOND, Gabriel, and Coleman, James. *The Politics of Developing Areas*. Princeton, N.J.: Princeton University Press, 1960.

BLASE, Melvin G. *Institution Building: A Source Book*. Beverly Hills, Calif.: Sage Publications, 1973.

BRAIBANTI, Ralph, ed. *Political and Administrative Development*. Durham, N.C.: Duke University Press, 1969.

BRAIBANTI, Ralph, and Spengler, Joseph J. *Administration and Economic Development in India*. Durham, N.C.: Duke University Press, 1963.

CAIDEN, Naomi, and Wildavsky, Aaron. *Planning and Budgeting in Poor Countries*. New York: John Wiley & Sons, 1974.

DALAND, Robert T. *Brazilian Planning: Development Politics and Administration*. Chapel Hill: The University of North Carolina Press, 1967.

DANG, Nghiem. *Vietnam: Politics and Public Administration*. Honolulu: East-West Center Press, 1966.

EISENSTADT, Samuel N. *Modernization: Protest and Change*. Englewood Cliffs, N.J.: Prentice-Hall, 1966.

ESMAN, Milton J. *The Institution Building Concepts—An Interim Appraisal*. Pittsburgh: Graduate School of Public and International Affairs, University of Pittsburgh, 1967.

ESMAN, Milton J., and Montgomery, John D. "Systems Approaches to Technical Cooperation: The Role of Development Administration." *Public Administration Review* 29 (September/October 1969), pp. 507–39.

GOODNOW, Henry Frank. *The Civil Service of Pakistan*. New Haven and London: Yale University Press, 1964.

HAGAN, Everett. *On the Theory of Social Change*. Homewood, Ill.: Dorsey Press, 1962.

HALL, Edward T. *The Silent Language*. Greenwich, Conn.: Fawcett Premier Books, 1959.

HEADY, Ferrel. *Public Administration: A Comparative Perspective*. Englewood Cliffs, N.J.: Prentice-Hall, 1966.

HEADY, Ferrel, and Stokes, Sybil L., eds. *Papers in Comparative Public Administration*. Ann Arbor: University of Michigan Press, 1962.

HEAPHEY, James, ed. *Spatial Dimensions of Development Administration*. Durham, N.C.: Duke University Press, 1971.

HIRSCHMAN, Albert O. *Development Projects Observed*. Washington, D.C.: The Brookings Institution, 1967.

BIBLIOGRAPHY

————. *Journeys toward Progress.* New York: Twentieth Century Fund, 1963.

HONEY, J. C. *Toward Strategies for Public Administration Development in Latin America.* Syracuse, N.Y.: Syracuse University Press, 1968.

ILCHMAN, Warren F. and Uphoff, Norman T. *The Political Economy of Change.* Berkeley: University of California Press, 1969.

KHERA, S. S. *District Administration in India.* London: Asia Publishing House, 1964.

KRIESBERG, Martin. *Public Administration in Developing Countries.* Washington, D.C.: The Brookings Institution, 1965.

LA PALOMBARA, Joseph G., ed. *Bureaucracy and Political Development.* Princeton, N.J.: Princeton University Press, 1963.

LERNER, Daniel. *The Passing of Traditional Society.* New York: The Free Press, 1958.

MCCLELLAND, David. *The Achieving Society.* Princeton, N.J.: D. Van Nostrand Co., 1961.

MCCORD, William. *The Springtime of Freedom.* New York: Oxford University Press, 1965.

MEYER, Paul. *Administration Organization: A Comparative Study of the Organization of Public Administration.* London: Stevens & Sons, 1957.

MONTGOMERY, John D. "The Allocation of Authority in Land Reform Programs." In *The Political Economy of Change* edited by Warren Ilchman and Norman Uphoff. Berkeley: University of California Press, 1969, pp. 449–62.

MONTGOMERY, John D. and Siffin, William J. *Approaches to Development, Politics, Administration and Change.* New York: McGraw-Hill Book Co., 1966.

NAIR, Kusum. *Blossoms in the Dust.* New York: Frederick A. Praeger, 1961.

NARAYAN, R. K. *The Financial Expert.* New York: The Noonday Press, 1953.

ORWELL, George. "Shooting an Elephant." In *The Orwell Reader.* New York: Harcourt, Brace & Co., 1956.

PHILLIPS, Hiram S. *Guide for Development.* New York: Praeger Publishers, 1969.

PLAMENATZ, John. *On Alien Rule and Self-Government.* New York: Humanities Press, 1960.

RAPHAELI, Nimrod, ed. *Readings in Comparative Public Administration.* Boston: Allyn & Bacon, 1967.

RIGGS, Fred W. *Administration in Developing Countries: The Theory of Prismatic Society.* Boston: Houghton Mifflin Co., 1965.

————. *The Ecology of Public Administration.* New York: Asia Publishing House, 1961.

————. *Frontiers of Development Administration.* Durham, N.C.: Duke University Press, 1970.

————. *Prismatic Society Revisited.* Morristown, N.J.: General Learning Press, 1973.

————. *Thailand: The Modernization of a Bureaucratic Polity.* Honolulu: East-West Center Press, 1965.

SCOTT, James C. *Comparative Political Corruption.* Englewood Cliffs, N.J.: Prentice Hall, 1972.

SIFFIN, William J. *The Thai Bureaucracy: Institutional Development.* Honolulu: East-West Center Press, 1966.

————. "Two Decades of Public Administration in Developing Countries." *Public Administration Review* 36 (January/February 1976), pp. 61–71.

SUFRIN, Sidney C. *Technical Assistance—Theory and Guidelines.* Syracuse, N.Y.: Syracuse University Press, 1966.

SWERDLOW, Irving. *Development Administration: Concepts and Problems.* Syracuse, N.Y.: Syracuse University Press, 1963.

TEXTOR, Robert B., ed. *Cultural Frontiers of the Peace Corps.* Cambridge, Mass.: The MIT Press, 1966.

THOMAS, D. Woods et. al. *Institution Building.* Cambridge, Mass.: Schenkman Publishing Co., 1973.

UNITED NATIONS, Department of Economic and Social Affairs. *A Handbook of Public Administration: Current Concepts and Practice with Special Reference to Developing Countries.* New York: The United Nations, 1961.

————. *Interregional Seminar on Major Administrative Reforms in Developing Countries.* New York: The United Nations, 1973.

————. *Public Administration in the Second United Nations Development Decade.* New York: The United Nations, 1971.

————. *Report of the Interregional Seminar on the Use of Modern Management Techniques in the Public Administration of Developing Countries.* New York: The United Nations, 1971.

WALDO, Dwight, ed. *Temporal Dimensions of Development Administration.* Durham, N.C.: Duke University Press, 1970.

WATERSON, Albert. *Planning in Pakistan.* Baltimore: Johns Hopkins Press, 1963.

WEIDNER, Edward. *Technical Assistance in Public Administration Overseas: The Case for Development Administration.* Chicago: Public Administration Service, 1964.

WICKWAR, W. Hardy. *Modernization of Administration in Near East.* London: Constable & Co., 1963.

WOLFE, Tom. *Radical Chic and Maumauing the Flak Catchers.* New York: Farrar, Straus & Giroux, 1970.

WRAITH, Ronald. *Local Government in West Africa.* New York: Frederick A. Praeger, 1964.

YOUNGER, Kenneth. *The Public Service in New States.* London: Oxford University Press, 1960.

CHAPTER 10: THE FUTURE

BELL, Daniel. *The Coming of Post-Industrial Society.* New York: Basic Books, 1973.

BENNIS, Warren. "Post-Bureaucratic Leadership." *Transaction* 6 (July/August 1969), pp. 44–51.

————. *The Unconscious Conspiracy: Why Leaders Can't Lead.* New York: AMACOM, 1976.

BILLER, Robert. "Adaptation Capacity and Organizational Development." In *Toward a New Public Administration,* edited by Frank Marini. Scranton, Pa.: Chandler Publishing Co., 1971, pp. 93–121.

BJUR, Wesley. "The Generation Gap and the Public Administrator." Los Angeles: School of Public Administration, University of Southern California, 1971.

CLARK, Kenneth. "Heroic Materialism." In *Civilisation.* New York: Harper & Row, 1969, pp. 321–47.

CLEVELAND, Harlan. *The Future Executive.* New York: Harper & Row, 1972.

COX, Edward et. al. *The Nader Report on the Federal Trade Commission.* New York: R. W. Baron, 1969.

CUSHMAN, Robert E. *The Independent Regulatory Commissions.* New York: Oxford University Press, 1941.

DRUCKER, Peter. *The Age of Discontinuity: Guidelines to Our Changing Society.* New York: Harper & Row, 1968.

ETZIONI, Amitai. *A Comparative Analysis of Complex Organizations.* New York: The Free Press, 1961.

FIEDLER, Fred E. *A Theory of Leadership Effectiveness.* New York: McGraw-Hill Book Co., 1967.

FREDERICKSON, H. George. "Creating Tomorrow's Public Administration." *Public Management* 53 (November 1971), pp. 2–4.

————, ed. "Curriculum Essays on Citizens, Politics, and Administration in Urban Neighborhoods." *Public Administration Review* 32 (October 1972).

————. "Toward a New Public Administration." In *Toward a New Public Administration,* edited by Frank Marini. Scranton, Pa.: Chandler Publishing Co., 1971, pp. 309–31.

GARDNER, John W. *Self-Renewal: The Individual and the Innovative Society.* New York: Harper & Row, 1964.

GOODWIN, Richard. *The American Condition.* New York: Doubleday & Co., 1974.

HARMON, Michael. "Normative Theory and Public Administration." In *Toward a New Public Administration,* edited by Frank Marini. Scranton, Pa.: Chandler Publishing Co., 1971, pp. 172–85.

HEILBRONER, Robert L. *An Inquiry into the Human Prospect.* New York: W. W. Norton & Co., 1974.

HERSHEY, Cary. *Protest in the Public Service.* Lexington, Mass.: Lexington Books, 1973.

KAUFMAN, Herbert. *The Forest Ranger: A Study in Administrative Behavior.* Baltimore: Johns Hopkins Press, 1960.

KIRKHART, Larry. "Toward a Theory of Public Administration," with a comment by Frank McGee. In *Toward a New Public Administration,* edited by Frank Marini. Scranton, Pa.: Chandler Publishing Co., 1971.

LA PORTE, Todd R. "The Recovery of Relevance in the Study of Public Organizations." In *Toward a New Public Administration,* edited by Frank Marini. Scranton, Pa.: Chandler Publishing Co., 1971.

LAWRENCE, Paul R. and Lorsch, Jay W. *Organization and Environment: Managing Differentiation and Integration.* Homewood, Ill.: Richard Irwin, 1969.

LOWI, Theodore. *The End of Liberalism.* New York: W. W. Norton & Co., 1969.

LUIJPEN, William A., and Koren, Henry J. *A First Introduction to Existential Phenomenology.* Pittsburgh: Duquesne University Press, 1969.

LUTHANS, Fred. *Introduction to Management: A Contingency Approach.* New York: McGraw-Hill Book Co., 1976.

MCLUHAN, Herbert M., and Fiore, Quentin. *The Medium is the Massage.* New York: Random House, 1967.

MARINI, Frank, ed. *Toward a New Public Administration: The Minnowbrook Perspective.* Scranton, Pa.: Chandler Publishing Co., 1971.

NEWSTROM, John W. et. al., eds. *A Contingency Approach to Management.* New York: McGraw-Hill Book Co., 1975.

OSTROM, Vincent. *The Intellectual Crisis in American Public Administration.* University: University of Alabama Press, 1973.

SAVAGE, Peter. "Contemporary Public Administration: The Changing Environment and Agenda." In *Public Administration in a Time of Turbulence,* edited by Dwight Waldo. Scranton, Pa.: Chandler Publishing Co., 1971, pp. 43–58.

SCHICK, Allen. "Toward the Cybernetic State." In *Public Administration in a Time of Turbulence,* edited by Dwight Waldo. Scranton, Pa.: Chandler Publishing Co., 1971.

————. "The Trauma of Politics." In *American Public Administration,* edited by Frederick C. Mosher. University: University of Alabama Press, 1975.

SEGAL, Morley. "Organization and Environment: A Typology of Adaptability and Structure." *Public Administration Review* 34 (May/June 1974), pp. 212–20.

SOLZHENITSYN, Aleksandr I. *The Gulag Archipelago*. New York: Harper & Row, 1973.

THAYER, Frederick C. *An End to Hierarchy! An End to Competition!* New York: New Viewpoints, 1973.

THOMPSON, James D. *Organizations in Action*. New York: McGraw-Hill Book Co., 1967.

THOMPSON, James D. et. al., eds. *Comparative Studies in Administration*. Pittsburgh: University of Pittsburgh Press, 1959.

VONNEGUT, Kurt. *Slaughterhouse Five*. New York: Delta Books, 1969.

WALDO, Dwight. *The Administrative State*. New York: Ronald Press, 1948.

———. "Developments in Public Administration." *The Annals of the American Academy* 404 (November 1972), pp. 217–45.

———. "Education for Public Administration in the Seventies." In *American Public Administration*, edited by Frederick C. Mosher. University: University of Alabama Press, 1975.

———. "Public Administration." *International Encyclopedia of the Social Sciences*, vol. 13. New York: Macmillan & The Free Press, 1968.

———, ed. *Public Administration in a Time of Turbulence*. Scranton, Pa.: Chandler Publishing Co., 1971.

WHITE, Orion. "The Dialectical Organization: An Alternative to Bureaucracy." *Public Administration Review* 29 (January/February 1969), pp. 32–42.

———. "Organization and Administration for New Technological and Social Imperatives." In *Public Administration in a Time of Turbulence*, edited by Dwight Waldo. Scranton, Pa.: Chandler Publishing Co., 1971.

This glossary catalogs the concepts and techniques that professional public administrators frequently apply to practical administrative problems. The number following each definition refers to the chapter in which the term is discussed.

accounting: the process of classifying, measuring, and interpreting financial transactions. *Cash accounting* is the recording of transactions at the time the payment is actually made; *accrual accounting* means that revenues are recorded when they are earned and expenses are recorded as they are incurred. (1)

action research: one of the basic behavioral techniques upon which organization development is founded; the process of collecting data, feeding it back into the system under study, making changes in the system based on the data, and evaluating the results. (8)

adhocracy: a postbureaucratic form of organization designed to be flexible and responsive to change. It is characterized by the relative absence of hierarchy, by temporary patterns of organization, by a distribution of responsibility based upon ability rather than upon formal authority, and by styles of supervision that can be characterized as democratic and participatory. (8)

administrative discretion: a general principle of administration encompassing a number of points in administrative law; the requirement that the actions of any public official be based upon a specific, legal grant of authority which establishes strict limits on official action. (1)

administrative due process: a term encompassing a number of points in administrative law which require that the administrative procedures of government agencies and regulatory commissions, as they affect private parties, be based upon written guidelines that safeguard individual rights and protect against the arbitrary or inequitable exercise of bureaucratic power. (1)

administrative law: formal constraints upon the activities of public agencies, including their adjudication, rule-making, investigating, prosecuting, negotiating, contracting, or granting activities, as these affect the rights of private parties; especially those constraints created as a result of the judicial review of the powers and procedures of administrative agencies. (1)

advocacy, administrative: the recognition that public administration is a highly political process involving severe differences of judgment in which the most feasible course of action is likely to emerge from the competition produced when each group pleads for the cause which it represents, whether that cause be more funds to carry out agency policies, the survival of a program, a particular piece of advice, or the desire for a more efficient system of administrative decision making. (6)

affirmative action: the requirement that public administrators present personnel selection and promotion plans designed to increase employment opportunities for groups that are substantially underrepresented at various levels of the public service and whose position would not be significantly improved by enforcing the standards of "equal opportunity" employment because of a past history of discrimination, poor education, or social impoverishment. (1)

allotment: the system by which departments control spending by lower units; a legal authorization to incur expenditures for a given amount of money for a specific purpose made on a monthly or quarterly basis. (1)

arbitration: a technique often used to settle disputes in collective bargaining, especially after direct negotiations, fact finding, and mediation have failed. The parties in dispute allow an impartial arbitrator to hear evidence and arguments presented by the parties and then render a decision, called an *award*; by prior agreement, the arbitrator's decision may be either binding or nonbinding on the parties involved. (4)

audit: the final phase of the budgetary process; a review of the operations of the agency, especially its financial transactions, to determine

401

whether the agency has spent the money in accordance with the law, in the most efficient manner, and with desired results. (1)

the base: the point from which most budgetary calculations begin, generally that appropriation which the agency received in the previous fiscal year, with the expectation that spending in each agency will approximate the existing level of expenditures. (6)

block grants: federal grants-in-aid to state and local governments for broadly defined purposes, such as health or job training, which are designed to allow top state and local executives more discretion in deciding how to spend the money than is afforded under the narrow, categorical grant-in-aid. (5)

bureaucracy: an organization that possesses special structural characteristics designed to promote efficiency in pursuit of established goals; an organization that cannot correct its behavior by listening to its errors. (3)

bureaucratic risk taking: an extraordinary action, generally resisted by the persons in charge, taken by a public servant who commits the government to a profitable course of action, blocks the execution of an illegal or immoral order, or exposes corruption, deceit, or an unlawful act taking place within the bureaucracy. (6)

camel's nose: one of the principal strategies bureaucrats use to obtain funding for a new program. They begin with an appropriation request which appears insignificant but which then becomes part of the agency's base and must be funded at a much higher level in order to complete the program. (6)

capital budgeting: the separation of expenditures that produce long-term benefits, especially those involving the construction of public facilities, from the annual operating costs of government; the process for reviewing expenditure decisions for capital projects and deciding on the methods for financing them, usually through the sale of bonds. (1)

citizen participation: the involvement of citizens in a wide range of administrative policy-making activities, including the determination of levels of service, budget priorities, and the acceptability of physical construction projects, in order to orient government programs toward community needs, build public support, and encourage a sense of cohesiveness within neighborhoods. (4)

collective bargaining: the process by which an agent chosen by public employees negotiates a formal labor agreement or settles day-to-day labor disputes on behalf of the employees in the areas of wages, benefits, working conditions, and administrative policy with parties representing the top politically elected or appointed executives. (4)

community control: an extreme form of citizen participation in which democratically selected representatives of a neighborhood-sized governmental jurisdiction are given administrative and financial control over local programs such as education, land use, and police protection. Community control is generally distinguished from *administrative decentralization*, which is the practice of delegating bureaucratic authority to officials in the field who are told to involve more citizens in public affairs and improve community relations without relinquishing control over the centrally directed program. (4)

community development: an approach to the administration of social and economic development programs in which government officials are dispatched to the field to act as catalysts at the local level, encouraging local residents to form groups, define their own needs, and develop self-help projects. The government provides technical and material assistance and helps the community establish institutions, such as farm cooperatives, to carry on the development programs after the officials have left. (9)

computerization and automation: the use of electronic data-processing equipment in place of conventional administrative methods for functions such as process control, billing, payroll administration, payment of benefits, and record keeping; a mechanized, self-adjusting system of organizational planning or control that can operate without significant human intervention. (7)

GLOSSARY: 101 ADMINISTRATIVE METHODS AND STRATEGIES

conflict, functions of: the view that conflict is healthy for the organization when it is used to unify the organization; to shape the beliefs, goals, and identity of the organization; to act as a safety valve to bring disputes and struggles for power out into the open; and to force the creation of coalitions leading to the resolution of disputes. (2)

contingency approach: the use of different administrative strategies under different conditions; the study of the relationship between factors such as the task an agency performs or the technology it uses and the style of supervision, type of organizational design, and other administrative strategies that will work best given those factors. (10)

continuous budgeting: an approach to financial management advocated for poor, unstable countries in which budgetary and financial decisions are made on an ad hoc rather than a long-range basis according to the current level of revenues and expenditures. (9)

contracting: the legal process by which the government enters into relationships with firms in the private sector that administer public programs or provide the government with goods or services. The contract may provide that the government reimburse the firm for the costs it incurs or that the government pay a fixed price for the product; both types of contracts may contain incentive provisions that reward the contractor for meeting deadlines and staying within cost estimates. (4)

co-optation: alliance building between an administrative agency and a clientele group in which the clientele group is allowed to influence agency policy making, in return for which the clientele group tacitly agrees to support the general mission of the agency, provide it with political support, and defend the agency against assaults on its powers, programs, or budget. (4)

cost-benefit analysis: a systematic attempt to treat governmental decisions as economic problems and to allocate scarce resources efficiently by quantifying and comparing the benefits and costs, both tangible and intangible, of various alternative methods of achieving specific governmental objectives; also used

to evaluate whether a specific program will provide a favorable return on the investment of public resources. (5)

critical path method: a type of network analysis, similar to PERT, which monitors progress during critical phases in the development of a specific project by charting the longest continual path of events—called the critical path—that must be performed in sequence in order to complete the project. (7)

dialectical organization: a postbureaucratic form of organization designed to be responsive to clientele needs; *dialectical* refers to the permanent state of tension between the tendency toward bureaucratization and the tendency toward responsiveness to clients, a tension the organization uses to continually renew itself. (10)

division of work: one of the fundamental principles upon which the science of administration is based; increased specialization in the organization of work in order to narrow the range of tasks for which each person is responsible, which in turn increases the need for administrative planning and coordination and raises the productivity of the organization as a whole. (1)

ecology of public administration: the view that the social, economic, and political conditions surrounding any administrative system will determine how it operates in practice; moreover, that the model of bureaucratic efficiency developed by industrialized nations, if introduced into a developing country with a different social, economic, and political heritage, will produce an administrative system that may be bureaucratic in form or structure but not in the actual functions it performs. (9)

efficiency: the promotion of administrative methods that will produce the largest store of results for a given objective at the least cost; the reduction of material and personnel costs while maximizing precision, speed, and simplicity in administration. According to the traditional view, efficiency is the primary aim of the administrative sciences. (1)

evaluation: the use of research techniques to measure the past performance of a specific

403

program—in particular, the program's impact on the conditions it seeks to modify—for the purpose of changing the operation of the program so as to improve its effectiveness at achieving its objectives. (5)

executive budget: the process by which agency requests for appropriations are prepared and submitted to a budget bureau under the chief executive for review, alteration, and consolidation into a single budget document that can be compared to expected revenues and executive priorities before submission to the legislature; also refers to the methods for controlling departmental spending after the legal appropriations have been made. (1)

federal executive service: the proposal for a top-level corps of professional administrators who would be responsive to professional administrative standards and executive priorities rather than special bureaucratic interests. Members of the FES would be certified by the Civil Service Commission, would serve under renewable multiyear contracts, and at the end of the contract period could be rotated into an agency in which they had not previously worked. (5)

groupthink: an emphasis upon group cohesiveness and individual concurrence with group beliefs in decision making and intelligence gathering (as opposed to advocacy and competition) which results in a deterioration of the group's ability to test reality, weigh risks, make critical decisions, and exercise moral judgment. (6)

homogeneity, principle of: also known as unity of direction; the principle of administration that advises the executive to group the major functions of an organization together according to their purpose, the process used, the persons served, or the places where it takes place, with each constituted as a single unit under the direction of a single administrator guided by a single plan of action. (1)

human relations: an early approach to administration that grew out of the Hawthorne experiments conducted during the 1920s. Human relations advocates held that productivity could be increased by working through informal groups, adopting a participatory style of supervision, and motivating workers through social rewards and sanctions rather than by following the principles of scientific management. (1)

incrementalism: an approach to decision making in government in which executives begin with the current situation, consider a limited number of changes in that situation based upon a restricted range of alternatives, and test those changes by instituting them one at a time; a normative theory of government that views policy making as a process of bargaining and competition involving the participation of different persons with conflicting points of view. (5)

institution building: an approach to technical assistance in developing countries that promotes developmental change by identifying a particular organization possessing technical capability, managerial skill, and an internal commitment to change and then forging linkages between this organization and the groups in its environment that provide the organization with resources, support, and outlets for its products or services. (9)

intelligence function: the use of techniques that encourage organizational advocacy and competitiveness in the gathering, interpreting, and communicating of information in order to give executives accurate and up-to-date information for use in decision making and administration. (6)

intergovernmental relations: the fiscal and administrative processes by which higher units of government share revenues and other resources with lower units of government, generally accompanied by special conditions that the lower units must satisfy as prerequisites to receiving the assistance. (4)

job enrichment: a behavioral technique that uses work itself to improve the motivation of employees by providing them with more responsibility, more autonomy, and a more natural unit of work (in contrast to the specialization of the assembly line), thus making their jobs more challenging and increasing the employees' sense of accomplishment. (8)

juridical democracy: the restoration of the rule of law and the requirements of administrative formality in which a corps of professional administrators would implement detailed legislative policies through formal administrative procedures instead of receiving broad delegations of power and developing governmental policy themselves in conjunction with special interest groups. (10)

laboratory training: one of the basic methods upon which organization development is founded; group situations under the tutelage of a professional trainer in an artificial environment free from distractions in which participants use the experiences and feelings present in the group, including feedback from other participants, to study their own behavior and their ability to work effectively in groups. (8)

line-item budget: the classification of budgetary accounts according to narrow, detailed objects of expenditure (such as motor vehicles, clerical workers, or reams of paper) used within each particular agency of government generally without reference to the ultimate purpose or objective served by the expenditure. (1)

linking pin: a person who occupies key positions in two or more work groups within an organization, generally at different levels of the hierarchy, and serves as a channel of communication and coordination between those groups; a manager whose authority is based upon a willingness to interact with subordinates and be influenced by them and by the subordinates' sense that the manager can interact with or influence superiors. (8)

management by objectives: a process for clarifying the mission of the agency and the specific areas of responsibility within it, including the methods for planning, measuring, and evaluating the activities of employees in relation to agency goals; the process of joint target setting and periodic performance review conducted between a superior and a subordinate. (1)

management information system: a special type of information system, generally computer based, that collects data about past, present, and projected activities and transforms this data into information that managers can use to plan the future course of the organization and to make decisions about the optimal utilization of resources. (7)

management science: a general approach to business and government administration that views organizations as economic-technological systems whose management can be planned and controlled through the use of economic, engineering, mathematical, and computer-based techniques. (7)

managerial grid: a systematic, long-range OD intervention strategy that integrates laboratory training, team building, planning, and evaluation into a six-phase program designed to promote managerial and organizational change; the two-dimensional grid used during the early phases of the program to scale each supervisor's management style in terms of that individual's concern for people and production. (8)

merit system: a professional system of personnel administration, free from political interference, in which selection and progress in the service are based upon the performance, expertise, and technical qualifications of each employee, measured objectively, (often through open, competitive examinations), accompanied by the development of a position classification and salary standardization system and administered through offices of personnel administration and a central civil service commission. (1)

modeling: the identification of the fixed and variable components in a system, assigning them numerical or economic values and relating them to each other in a logical fashion so that one can derive optimal solutions to operational problems by manipulating the components of the model. (7)

morality, administrative: the use of religious, political, or social precepts to create standards by which the quality of public administration may be judged; in the main, the standards of honesty, responsiveness, efficiency, effectiveness, competence, effect on individual rights, adherence to democratic procedures, and social equity. (6)

motivation: the degree of readiness among employees to pursue designated goals; recent

405

research indicates that the highest degree of motivation is achieved by factors such as achievement, recognition, responsibility, personal growth, and work itself, after the basic needs of salary, status, job security, and working conditions are satisfied. (8)

new public administration: a general, mostly undefined movement inspired mainly by younger scholars who challenged several tenets of public administration, primarily the emphasis upon value-neutrality in administrative research and practice, and appealed to scholars and practitioners to take a more proactive role, guided not only by the search for efficiency, but by a sensitivity to the forces of change, the needs of clients, and the problems of social equity in service delivery. (10)

operations research: the application of scientific methods, including mathematical or logical analysis, to fairly well defined problems involving the operation of systems in order to provide optimal solutions given a predetermined set of objectives and a fixed range of acceptable alternatives. (7)

organization development: a major approach to administration based on the application of behavioral science theories and techniques to practical administrative problems. OD interventions are generally conducted under the guidance of a consultant who works to improve the ability of the organization and its members to solve problems and respond to rapid change primarily by developing a more collaborative work environment and improving the capacity of people to work together in groups. (8)

performance budgeting: the grouping of budget accounts into categories related to the specific services or products an agency produces (as opposed to the objects it purchases) and the development of product-cost measurements of these activities so that managers can measure the productivity or efficiency of past operations as part of the budgetary review process. (1)

PERT: program evaluation and review technique; a quantitative approach to the planning and scheduling of work, usually computer based, outlining an optimal schedule of events for a specific project. The schedule is visually presented as a PERT chart, which project managers use to monitor day-to-day activities on the project and to insure that project goals are met with the best possible use of resources given overall time and cost constraints. (7)

planning and control systems: a framework associated with the systems approach that characterizes the essential functions performed in any complex organization, namely, strategic planning, management control, and operational control. (7)

planning-programming-budgeting: an elaborate version of program budgeting which requires agency directors to identify program objectives, develop methods of measuring program output, calculate total program costs over the long run, prepare detailed multiyear program and financial plans, and analyze the costs and benefits of alternative program designs. (5)

policy analysis: the application of systematic research techniques, drawn largely from the social sciences and based on measurements of program effectiveness, quality, cost, and impact, to the formulation, execution, and evaluation of public policy in order to create a more rational or optimal administrative system. (5)

politics/administration dichotomy: the belief, growing out of the early administrative reform movement and its reaction against the spoils system, which held that political interference in administration would erode the opportunity for administrative efficiency, that the policy-making activities of government ought to be wholly separated from the administrative functions, and that administrators had to have an explicit assignment of objectives before they could begin to develop an efficient administrative system. (1)

politics of the budgetary process: the requirement that administrators act as advocates for their own programs during the appropriation process by soliciting outside support, protecting their budgetary base, and inching ahead with new programs; a budgetary system that deals with complex problems by relying upon incremental methods of decision making, information drawn from past experience rather than analysis, and satisfactory rather than optimal standards of quality. (6)

POSDCORB: the acronym representing an early attempt in professional public administration to define the administrative process by classifying the functions of top executives, namely, planning, organizing, staffing, directing, coordinating, reporting, and budgeting. (1)

position classification: one of the basic elements of a merit civil service system; the grouping together of jobs that have similar duties, responsibilities, and qualifications in order to establish common personnel policies in areas such as selection and compensation for each class and to provide a rational justification for different treatment for different types of employees. (1)

principles of administration: the core of the early attempt to create a science of administration; a certain number of conditions pertaining to the formal structure and working order of the organization which are designed to promote a high degree of efficiency and precision in administration. (1)

process consultation: a restrained consulting role used in organization development in which an outside consultant sits in on the activities of an organization and calls attention to organizational processes in order to help members of the organization better perceive, define, and act upon organizational problems by themselves. (8)

productivity improvement: programs to improve agency output or impact after the cost-effectiveness of different activities within the agency has been assessed. The idea is to produce more at the same cost or to cut costs without reducing the level of output. (5)

professionalism: the tendency for public organizations to come under the domination of a single profession that sets itself up as an elite class within the agency in order to control employment standards, administrative policy, and the methods of work; an informal strategy for creating employee conformity to agency policy by recruiting personnel from the ranks of a single profession. (4)

program budgeting: a long-range approach to budgetary decision making that relates future expenditures to the broadly defined purposes or objectives of government, thus providing top executives with information on the distribution of scarce resources between competing objectives and revealing the total program costs required to accomplish any given objective. (1)

programming: a general term that refers to a number of mathematical techniques, such as linear programming or dynamic programming, which are applied to complex problems with certain distinctive characteristics in order to calculate optimal solutions to these problems. (7)

project management: also known as program or matrix management; an application of the systems approach to the organization and administration of specific projects with specific deadlines. A manager and various teams are responsible for the overall planning and control of the different activities necessary to complete the project, especially the integration of those activities which cut across functional or departmental lines. (7)

public-choice economics: an approach to public administration based on microeconomic theory which views the citizen as a consumer of government goods and services and would attempt to maximize administrative responsiveness to citizen demand by creating a market system for governmental activities in which public agencies would compete to provide citizens with goods and services. This would replace the current system under which administrative agencies in effect act as monopolies under the influence of organized pressure groups which, the public-choice economists argue, are institutionally incapable of representing the demands of individual citizens. (5)

queuing theory: a mathematical technique used in simulation and operations research that allows an analyst to identify the optimal use of agency personnel and equipment in situations that have the characteristics of a waiting line. (7)

reorganization: changes in the administrative structure or formal procedures of government, traditionally in the areas of departmental consolidation, executive office expansion, budgetary reform, and personnel administration, generally for the purpose of promoting bureaucratic responsiveness to central executive control and, secondly, to simplify or professionalize administrative affairs. (1 & 5)

revenue sharing: the transfer of federal tax revenues to state and local governments without advance specification as to how the money must be spent and without elaborate procedures governing its use. (5)

rules, principle of: one of the principal characteristics of bureaucratic administration; the existence of formal, written procedures, generally not open to public scrutiny, which prescribe specific courses of action to be taken under specific situations and which bureaucrats must follow without regard to personal preferences or special interests. (1)

salary standardization: equal pay for equal work; the process of integrating the rates of pay into the position classification system so that similarities and differentials in pay are clearly related to the duties and responsibilities performed by broad classes of employees. (1)

satisficing: the process of decision making that characterizes most governmental action; a limited search through familiar patterns of behavior for a course of action that meets pre-established, minimum standards of performance, rather than an exhaustive review of all alternatives in search of the optimal solution to the problem at hand. (2)

scalar chain: also known as hierarchy; the direct, uninterrupted lines of authority through which all official decisions and communications must pass, established by instituting the principle of unity of command from the highest to the lowest levels of the organization. (1)

scientific management: an early approach to administration, based on the work of Frederick Taylor, that sought to raise the level of productivity in an organization by scientifically identifying the shortest and most efficient method of performing each job and by giving control of the planning of work and the selection and supervision of employees to the ad-

ministrative experts rather than the workers themselves. (1)

sensitivity training: also called T-groups; one of the most frequently used types of laboratory training in which the consultant, called a trainer, uses relatively unstructured, agenda-free group sessions to encourage group members to drop their facades, study their own behavior, and develop a style of interpersonal relations that is open, authentic, collaborative, and productive. (8)

simulation: the use of computer-based models capable of replicating a complex system, its major elements, and their relationships with one another so that analysts can study the consequences of proposed policies or estimate future conditions before actually committing the organization to a new course of action. (7)

social equity: the normative standard that makes equity, rather than efficiency, the primary criterion for judging the "goodness" of administrative policy. In accordance with this standard, public administrators must weigh the impact of their programs upon the welfare of individual human beings in order to promote a fair and equitable distribution of services, to eliminate the injurious effects of programs, and to make certain that any inequities in service are always in the direction of enhancing the power and well-being of disadvantaged groups. (6 & 10)

span of control: one of the early principles of administration which states that there is an upper limit to the number of subordinates any administrator can directly supervise, generally set at twelve, and advises administrators to eliminate any violations of this principle by reducing the number of officials reporting to them by either merging certain offices or stretching out the scalar chain. (1)

the staff principle: the principle of administration which states that the executive should be assisted by officers who are not in the line of operations but are essentially extensions of the personality of the executive and whose duties consist primarily of assisting the executive in controlling and coordinating the organization and, secondly, of offering advice. (1)

strategy of calculated competition: the practice of creating overlapping delegations of authority in which two separate units or persons with equal access to the executive are given general responsibilities for what is essentially the same job in order to promote honesty and creativity in administration and encourage the upward flow of information. (6)

subgovernments: the tendency of bureaucrats to seek political support for their programs by building informal alliances outside of the official hierarchy with groups that possess resources the bureaucrats lack, primarily with legislative committees and organized pressure groups. (4)

systematic experimentation: an advanced form of policy analysis that examines proposed and ongoing programs through controlled research experiments with test groups, control groups, common measures of performance, and checks on extraneous variables. (5)

systems analysis: a continuous process of reviewing objectives, designing alternative methods of achieving them, and weighing the effectiveness and costs of the alternatives, largely in economic terms. (7)

systems approach: a holistic approach to administration that provides a conceptual framework for visualizing the relationships between the parts that must be coordinated in order to accomplish a specific set of goals, including the components of the system; the resources, technology, and type of management the system uses; and the prominent elements in its environment. (7)

task force: a temporary work group whose members are drawn from different organizational situations and function as a team without rank or hierarchy to solve a specific problem with the expectation that the group will generate new ideas or present contrasting points of view. (6)

Tavistock: a psychoanalytic approach to laboratory training in which a consultant forces members of the study group to confront their basic assumptions and the effect these assumptions have upon the overt behavior of the members and their effectiveness as a group; an organization development institute in Great Britain which pioneered studies on the relationship between the technological structure of work and the type of social system operating within the organization. (8)

team building: an organization development strategy aimed at strengthening the effectiveness of management teams within a particular organization. The OD consultant helps team members diagnose their own problems, study their own behavior, develop effective group relationships, acquire necessary skills, and alter the organizational procedures that may be blocking effective team management. (8)

technology forecasting: the use of special techniques, such as systematic surveys of experts in a field or the assessment of future demand, to anticipate new technological developments that will change the management of an organization or the character of the environment in which it will operate. (7)

Theory X and Theory Y: two opposing assumptions about people at work that lead to opposing styles of management. Theory X assumes that most people hate work, avoid responsibility, prefer to be directed, and have to be controlled and coerced to put out a fair day's work; Theory Y assumes that people will seek responsibility, demonstrate a high degree of imagination, and exercise self-direction if they have a creative, challenging job to which they can become committed. (8)

unity of command: "one man, one master"; a fundamental principle of administration which states that an employee should receive orders from one superior only and that any violation of this principle will produce confusion and inefficiency in administration. (1)

zero-base budgeting: a procedure for forcing a review of an agency's entire budget by assuming that the minimum funding level for the agency is zero, thereby requiring agency administrators to justify all expenditures by the same standards of review that normally are applied only to new programs or increments above the base. (1)

INDEX

411

413

INDEX

415

417

Personnel administration
  affirmative action, 23
  arbitration in labor-management
    disputes, 135–136
  changing characteristics of
    employees, 269–272
  civil service commission, 22, 136
  in developing nations, 302,
    305–306, 323
  dismissal and removal, 154
  Federal Executive Service, 154,
    344
  lack of personnel in developing
    nations, 302, 305
  merit system, 18–23, 136
  offices of, 22
  organization development,
    268–294
  position classification, 22–23
  salary standardization, 22–23
  selection and promotion, 23, 215
  spoils system, 19–21, 141
  training, 305–306
  unionization of public employees,
    23, 133–136
Perspectives on time, 299, 325–326
Persuasion, 199
Peter, Lawrence J., 89
Peter Principle, 89
Pfiffner, John M., 37
Phenomenology, 351–352
Philippines, 311
Philosophy of human control, 13
Pizarro, Francisco, 252–253
Planned change in developing
  nations, 301, 324
Planning, 97–98, 161–162, 187–193,
  233, 250–252, 285–287, 300,
  309–310, 330
Planning-and-control systems,
  233–234, 254–255
Pluralism, 108, 120–121, 142–144,
  170, 179–180, 192–193, 336,
  340, 342–344, 350, 365
  effect of on organization
    development, 292
Polaris missile system, 248–250

Police departments, 182–183,
  185–186, 219–220, 241
Policy analysis, 150–194
  compatability of with politics,
    205–208
  defined, 150, 159
  model of, 174–176
Policy formulation, 174–176,
  179–181
Policy impact, 169, 176, 226–227
Policy making by administrators,
  107, 134–136, 343–344
Policy output, 161, 176
Political centralization, 150–151,
  157–158
Political constraints on
  administrators, 107, 114,
  359–360
Politically neutral competence, 141
Political regimes and administrative
  systems, 326
Political support for administrators,
  111–114, 119, 143, 203–204,
  311–312
Politics/administration dichotomy,
  19, 29, 106–108, 234, 344, 363
Politics of advice, 119, 211–213
Politics of research, 178–179
Pony express, 244
Port Authority of New York and
  New Jersey, 245–246
POSDCORB, 4
Positivism, 351–352
Postal workers' strike, 135
Postbureaucratic forms of
  organization, 270–272, 291,
  345–350
Power broker, 216
Power elite, 98–99, 179–180, 319
Power struggles in administration,
  60, 61, 92–94, 237, 322–324
Pressure groups, 109–111, 142–144,
  192
Presthus, Robert, 84–85, 104
Price, Don, 156
Principles of administration, 7–8,
  12–13, 15–18, 36, 254, 262, 298,
  311, 313–314, 358

NOTES